The Saydisc & Village Thing Discography

Anniversary celebration

The Saydisc & Village Thing Discography

Anniversary celebration

Mark Jones

 TRP The Record Press

This edition published 2010 by

The Record Press

The Record Press is an imprint of Bristol Folk Publications
www.bristol-folk.co.uk

ISBN 978-0-9563531-2-2

Layout and design by Bristol Folk Publications.
Printed and bound in the EU by Akcent Media.

Contents

Contents v

Introduction 1
    Notes on illustrations 2
    Thanks to 2
    Photographic and image credits..2

Foreword by Gef Lucena 3
    Of people and places...3

A potted history of Saydisc, Village Thing and associated labels.................7
    Saydisc Specialized Recordings Ltd...7
    The Village Thing..11
    Epilogue 15
    Section notes 15

Discographies...16
    Source acronyms used in lists 16
    Saydisc – the SD catalogue sequence 16
    Matchbox – SD series summary listing 143
    Roots..144
    Ahura Mazda...155
    The Village Thing..156
    Amon Ra 163
    Matchbox Bluesmaster 184
    Education packs...195
    Contract pressings 197
    Bornand collection of mechanical music..205

Where to buy the music..207
    Saydisc...207
    Weekend Beatnik 207

In memory of Fred Wedlock, who, amongst many other things, provided Saydisc with its first ever release and went on to record Village Thing's two best selling LPs.

I was on holiday in Egypt, planning this book and thinking about who might be willing to contribute some memories. After the excellent piece Fred had written for my first book, *Bristol Folk*, I had already broached the subject of him contributing some more of the same and he had agreed...or at least he hadn't said no. Meanwhile, back in Egypt, the last thing I had written this particular morning was "Contact Fred on return to UK" before I checked the previous day's messages. The first item in the inbox was a message with the sad news about Fred. Well, this book – and the folk circuit – is a lot less rich without Fred's input. Still, what a send–off he had at St. Mary Redcliffe – a shame he couldn't have been there to enjoy it, really.

Introduction

It's a funny thing – I thought that I was writing this book three years ago, but something completely different appeared instead. This 'something' was *Bristol Folk*, a history of my home town's folk scene in the '60s and '70s, which gained unanimously excellent reviews, making me feel that I must be doing something right. Be that as it may, this meant that I still hadn't written *The Saydisc and Village Thing Discography* – so I started work on it immediately, didn't I? Ah, well – no, I didn't.

The thing was that *Bristol Folk* wasn't the first book that I had written. There was another lurking about near–finished from a couple of years before, but abandoned because of a sad lack of publisher interest. This was a discography and potted history of the 'Famous' Charisma label, which I had wheeled around various publishers before giving it up as a bad lot (not the book, but trying to deal with publishers, most of whom didn't seem to have a clue). Hang on a second, I'd started my own publishing company to market *Bristol Folk*, hadn't I, and I'd also had a crash–course in the vagaries, usage and abusage of publishing software? Hmm, the final barriers to getting the Charisma book published were lifted. So out of the proverbial bottom drawer – an archived disk, to be more accurate – came *The Famous Charisma Discography* to be dusted off and – in light of my recent experience as writer, typist, editor, proof reader, graphic designer, publisher, marketer and distributor of *Bristol Folk* – to be ruthlessly edited: apologies to those who would actually have been interested in the chapter on comparative pricing strategies within Charisma, but it bored even me, so out it came.

The only remaining problem was that a book on Charisma didn't really fit well with my publishing company, which I'd given a remit to publish all things Bristolian, with a special focus on Bristol's musical heritage. Ok, so how about an imprint of *Bristol Folk Publications* called...oh, I don't know...erm, um...ah! How about *The Record Press*? Yes, that will do nicely – another discography, hot off *The Record Press*!

The Famous Charisma Discography came out to celebrate that company's 40th anniversary year, and here we were coming up to Saydisc's 45th and Village Thing's 40th anniversaries in 2010. Well, that decided what the second volume in the hastily–invented *Great British Record Labels* series was going to be. Also, it rather suggested a theme of celebrating various significant record company anniversaries...though, what with the success of the Charisma discography, can I really wait until 2013 to publish Virgin's 40th anniversary discography or 2014 to celebrate Harvest's 45th anniversary in similar fashion? Probably not – in fact work has already started on both.

Meanwhile, back to *The Saydisc and Village Thing Discography*, and this is what we've got:

- Listings of all known LPs, 7" records and CDs, all bar an elusive few with full track listings;
- Sleeve illustrations for the vast majority of the records listed;
- Many previously unpublished photographs from the owners' and other private collections;
- Documentation of all known cassette releases – not to mention the three 8–tracks;
- A potted history of Saydisc and Village Thing, with contributions from the owners.

Unfortunately, Saydisc's archives are incomplete with various bits and pieces having gone missing down the years. Some of the gaps have been filled either by my own research or through kind people getting in touch with details of some of the more elusive records. However, unknowns still exist, and information on these would be very welcome. Also, in a work of this sort, there are bound to be a few mistakes along the way, so if you spot any mistakes, can shed light on one or two of the unknowns or otherwise provide further information, please contact the publisher via www.bristol–folk.co.uk.

Notes on illustrations

Some of the sleeves shown in the illustration section leave a little to be desired on the quality front. Many have obviously seen better days, with imperfections–galore in evidence, from tears, severe discolouration (still visible even in black and white) to several cases of fairly obvious water damage, following years in a damp junk shop until rescued. Some images have been sourced from fairly poor original photographs and some had to be sourced from original catalogues, where there were imperfections in the original printing. However, I was faced with a fairly simple choice, which was to include every sleeve for which I had managed to source an image, or to leave many out just because of quality issues. I decided that most people would rather see a sleeve than not, whatever the image quality...and after all, some of these records are so rare that even Saydisc doesn't have copies, so even getting photos of some was something of a challenge.

Most CD illustrations are from pdf files sourced from Saydisc and for the most part these show the second sleeve design (those that show the original design have this fact highlighted). In most cases the later designs differ only slightly from the original issue in that layout or type face was altered for the second issue. So basically, if you find a copy that differs slightly from that shown, then you have an original! Where the second issue had a vastly different sleeve, both sleeves are included where possible. This way, at least you are guaranteed very good quality images of CD sleeves throughout.

Thanks to

Especial thanks to Gef and Genny Lucena and Ian Anderson for, amongst many other things, allowing access to their memories and their archives. I would also like to thank those kind people who provided records, catalogues and/or other information and memorabilia, so thanks to Alan Balfour, Angie at the Fumble website, Mike Cooper, Colin Evans, Des Henly, Kevyn Fortey–Jones, Richie Gould, Sue Kearney, Graham Kilsby, Andy Leggett, Al Read, Ian Turner (RIP), Craig Walker, Sue Wedlock.

There were many more kind people who provided me with information and memorabilia when the Saydisc and Village Thing discographies were available on the old VinylAttic website, but their names were lost in the PC upgrade from hell ("...oh, we wiped the backup by mistake as well, is that a problem?") If your name should be here, please contact the publisher via www.bristol-folk.co.uk for inclusion in subsequent editions.

Photographic and image credits

The photos of Friends Meeting House, the Jing Ying Soloists and Roy Mickleburgh on page 119 plus all photos on pages 120–121 courtesy of Gef Lucena and © the Saydisc Archive. Both photos on page 122, photos of Ian Anderson, Anderson Jones Jackson and White on Black on page 123, all images on page 124, photos of Sun Also Rises, Lackey and Sweeney and Tucker Zimmerman on page 125, plus the button badge and promotional stickers on page 126 courtesy of the fRoots archive. The photo of Frank Evans on page 123 courtesy of Colin Evans. The photo of Fred Wedlock on page 123 and the photos of Fred Wedlock and Mike Evans, Strange Fruit and Hunt and Turner on page 125 courtesy of Richie Gould. The scanned copy of Andy Leggett's idealised drawing of Clifton as a village on page 105 courtesy of Al Read, Andy Leggett's son having mislaid the original! Many of the (good quality) record and CD sleeve images were supplied by Gef Lucena or Ian Anderson, for which yet more thanks are due.

Photos of Ian Anderson and Mike Cooper recording at Frenchay by David Harrison; photo of Royal York Crescent entourage by Jo Gedrych; photo of Lackey and Sweeney by Dave Mason. Other photographers remain unknown.

Foreword by Gef Lucena

Of people and places

Much of this discography is rightly taken up with the music and the musicians, but all the complexities of planning, recording, editing, production, marketing and administration need people and I would like to acknowledge some of our key personnel over the years. Of paramount importance also are the places that we carefully chose as venues that had the appropriate acoustics for our recordings.

The Back Room Boys (well mostly girls)

In the early years I did all the recording, editing and admin until I married Genny in 1968 and moved from The Meeting House, Frenchay to The Barton, Inglestone Common and we then worked together building the company.

My brother John joined us as administrator and dispatcher for some five years from 1971 to 1976 and then our neighbour Rosemary Willcox took over the increasing volume of dispatching with Genny preparing the mail order. Genny also did the catering for recording and taking stocks round the Bristol and South Glos shops. Later Rosemary's daughter Sarah joined us on the admin side. They both came with us on the Company's move to Chipping Manor, Wotton-Under-Edge for the first couple of years of our 15 year tenancy there from 1985. Our younger daughter, Arwen then spent 13 years with us until my 'retirement' in early 2001 and the semi-dormant Company's return to Inglestone Common. Arwen singlehandedly coped with our busiest period with mail order flooding in at £1000+ per day in the pre-Christmas rush as well as packing and dispatching large orders to our UK distributors and export agents throughout the world.

Recording

It must have been sometime in 1972 that, what could have been an unfortunate double booking, turned out to our advantage. We had been booked by an amateur mediaeval music group to record them at The Meeting House, Frenchay. Another member of the group, a medical man, however had booked an amateur recordist and fellow medic to record the same event. So anaesthetist David Wilkins arrived as I was setting up with my Revox A77 tape recorder and AKG C451 microphones. He only had an earlier model Revox and cheaper mics, but he did have a much greater knowledge and interest in the technical side than me. So rather than fight about it I let him take over with my equipment and together we recorded this group – who actually were not very good and the recording came to naught. From then on though David and I worked together on all our major ventures and on into the digital era in January1983 using Sony PCM F1 processer recording digital data onto Betamax tape. The first four recordings being SAR 9, 10, 11 and 12 recorded in a solid fortnight at Finchcocks Museum in Goudhurst. Being unsure of the new digital medium we recorded all four albums in analogue at the same time which gave us some useful comparative material when faced with the analogue v digital debate raging at the time. A posse of top reviewers from Hi Fi News came to visit and we challenged them to spot the difference. One pro-analogue reviewer, who shall go unnamed, consistently but unawares preferred the digital recording, but whose parting shot was 'but I still prefer analogue'. So, dignity and preconceptions intact, he left.

Digital editing was not possible from the F1 format and David developed the Clue system of editing which was taken up by the leading professional recording equipment suppliers HHB and marketed by them until hard disc recording and editing became commonplace. David Wilkins comments: "we evolved from plain tape recording on Revox to professional Dolby A noise reduction prior to the arrival of PCM F1 and the development of CLUE, which in its turn was superseded by Digital Audio Tape (DAT). In 1988 we built a purpose designed studio extension to my house, which became the recording location of many of our projects, replacing the Frenchay Meeting House. In the studio we moved on to non-linear editing on computer, with DAT being replaced by recording straight to hard disk attached to the computer. We have always tried to remain as close to the cutting edge as was possible for a small business, as also exemplified by our early adoption of CD."

But now moving backwards in time away from the dizzy heights of digital technology to the earliest days of putting sound onto wax and shellac. Saydisc has always had a fascination for phonograph cylinders and early 78s and mention must be made of ex Temperance Seven player, John R.T. Davies. Having established the actual speed that the original 78 was recorded at (this was often 80 rpm) by means of adjusting the speed by reference to the pitch of his cornet, John would transcribe the scratchy old originals using a truncated stylus which avoided picking up the muck and scratches in the bottom of the grooves. He would record onto magnetic tape via a noise gate which cut out frequencies he knew would not have been present on recordings of that particular vintage and provenance. But then cleverly and painstakingly he would physically edit out the main clicks and scratches remaining by scraping away the oxide on the tape with a razor blade. Today the cleaning up of old recordings is done using the CEDAR noise reduction system but our re-issues long pre-dated such sophistication. NB: John only transcribed re-issues on Saydisc issues and not Matchbox Bluesmaster which were re-issued as transcribed by Johnny Parth.

Some of our recording work required working in unusual locations and church bells, in particular, posed a challenge due to where they sounded best and away from the unwanted sound intrusions of the 20th century. One early recording that I made was of the Bells of Bristol and, for St Mary Redcliffe Church, in order to avoid the roar of traffic on the roundabout next to the church and to hear the bells at their most melodious I needed to lug the very heavy mono Ferrograph recorder and other equipment up the tower, through the bell chamber, out onto the parapet, and climb into the chamber above the bells. Bells speak upwards and this was certainly the best place to record – but it was loud. When I recorded the full LP of Redcliffe Bells some years later, the Revox stereo equipment was somewhat lighter but I needed to make that climb many times in order to obtain as near perfect change ringing as possible. The ringing master, Emlyn Hancock, was a stickler for ringing perfection and I think that album (SDL 243) is still considered to be one of the finest examples of English change ringing.

We have been very fortunate in being able to draw on the important archive field recordings made by a number of people who could see the importance of putting onto tape music and speech which was in its last flowering and thereby preserving styles of music and dialect that were fast disappearing. Deserving especial mention are Peter Duddridge (RIP) who, in the early '60s, recorded both train sounds and old people reminiscing, the latter for monthly tape programmes for the elderly, blind or sick called "Hospital Roundabout" and later "Cotswold Roundabout". Unwittingly, this also recorded for posterity some fascinating and amusing stories and songs (see 222, 284, 285, 300, 301, 434, 435 and 220 for the trains). June Turner also recorded for the same programmes and her 'performers' are immortalized on 247 and 267.

Peter Kennedy (RIP) was a folk song collector of note and amassed an enormous collection of his field recordings. We cherry picked some marvellous material and the whole of his archive is now with the British Library Sound Archive. We used Peter's recordings on 332, 405, 407, 411, 416, 420 and 425. Also in this line of collecting was the late Fr Damian Webb, a charismatic priest who recorded and photographed in Britain and abroad in the 1960s and '70s (see 338 and 426).

David Fanshawe (alas, also RIP as of July 2010) recorded throughout Africa, Polynesia and elsewhere throughout the '60s and '70s and caught many musics and styles in full bloom but which were shortly to fade and disappear. He is most famous for his 'African Sanctus' choral work which embeds ethnic recordings with choir and orchestra. We were fortunate enough to work with David to assemble four albums of his original recordings from the African continent and Polynesia (see 389, 403, 414 and 418). Our world music catalogue has also been enhanced by the Asian field recordings of Caroline Swinburne on 401 and 404 and the Tibetan recordings of Robert Zollitsch on 427.

Artwork

On the Saydisc side we had an assortment of sleeve designers until SDL325 when Bob Doling of Doling Design came to our aid and created a new look and corporate logo. Matchbox benefitted from the input of David Harrison who helped with planning the blues re-issues and did some useful photography. Of course Village Thing had the imagination of the mighty Rodney Matthews to benefit it. Genny took over the artwork graphics from SDL 353 and most of the 215 album strong CD re-issue programme.

Locations (and their problems)

We always aimed to record in an uncomplicated, natural way and use good room acoustics to allow the music to flower. Where possible we used our favourite venues and the first of these was The Meeting House, Frenchay. As none of our venues was a custom made, sound insulated environment this brought difficulties in its wake. I built Rockwool filled panels to fit against the large arch windows to cut out the sound of traffic from the adjacent road. These had to be carefully manipulated into place – a two person job – before each recording and taken down before any Quaker service. The heating was very effective, but idiosyncratic, being a large black beetle stove in the middle of the room which glowed red hot when in full flight and roared loudly. But, no problem, a carefully positioned poker or lump of coal to prop the top open did the trick, but, musicians beware, keep your instruments well away if you don't want them to buckle and blister in the heat. I believe that the Meeting House now has boring electric heating (but I expect that hums!).

The Grade I Listed building that is Finchcocks in Goudhurst, Kent was the setting for most of our Amon Ra series of early music recording. This houses concert pianist Richard Burnett's amazing collection of early keyboard instruments. The wood panelled hall gave a warm acoustic and we engineered from the panelled library on the first floor (for US readers this is the second floor). Was this idyllic country residence set in acres of its own grounds free from problems? It was not. We had the small plane freak who used Finchcocks as a landmark, wind which howled under the enormous oak doors, a chimney cowl which squeaked and creaked in the wind, hundreds of sparrows cheeping on the stone ledges, guinea fowl and crows and not forgetting the bleating of the hundreds of spring lambs in the next field. We normally had a solution – the wind usually died down or changed direction at night, so start recording around midnight. Sparrows – no problem, passers by may have thought we were proclaiming a truce of some sort, but white sheets hanging on long poles from the windows seemed to deter the sparrow population. 'You're not going to are you?' anxiously enquired our vegan lutenist seeing the shotgun we had brought. No, just to scare off the crows. But the lambs – well we just had to grin and baa it.

These were non-musical problems but what of the instruments themselves and the musicians. The old wood framed pianos were notoriously unstable and needed constant tuning which meant we had to have a piano tuner with us at all times listening out for tuning problems. The worst offenders (like the lovely Fritz Viennese fortepiano) gave perhaps 20 minutes of acceptable tuning and then an hour of re-tuning by our chief resident tuner (and now Curator of Finchcocks), Alastair Laurence. Alastair is far more than a specialist tuner and has made and restored pianos for many years and has always been very enterprising in keeping the British piano making tradition alive. His latest coup was to buy the historic London makers John Broadwood and Sons (thereby reviving single-handed the entire British Piano Industry!). He now has a workshop at Finchcocks with a very big Royal Warrant over the door and tunes all the instruments for the Queen. When he has time away from his long order book he plays brilliant jazz piano and features regularly at Finchcocks recitals, amazing and surprising everyone on how well jazz goes on early pianos. When Alastair couldn't make it down from up North for our sessions then David Winston ably stepped in.

And what of artiste temperament, is this a myth? No norm on this, but I suppose Richard Burnett came closest to this stereotype. We recorded Dick in various combinations more frequently than any other artiste and his musical sensitivity and interpretations led to revelations as to how the music was originally intended to be played. When he had found his music and his glasses (which he was probably sitting on) and the piano was in tune, then the music would flood out until maybe a classic outburst along the lines of the following (the expletives have been much diluted):

Talkback from the studio: "Sorry Dick, can you go back to just before letter D"
RB: "What the bloody hell did you stop me for, that was the best I've ever played it"
Talkback: "No you had a slip"
RB: "Rubbish, you chaps should never stop me like that, you just sit up there making judgements and I'll never play it that well again."
Talkback: "Sorry, but we did need to stop you"
RB: "No you didn't – I'm coming up – you play it back to me"
Stomp, stomp, stomp up the stairs
RB: "Go on, now show me"
Playback of offending section
RB with a grin: "Oh yes – I'll do it again"

He did do it again – it was fine – and that evening after dinner he entertained us all by riding round the dining room table on his unicycle. But one could write a book about this charismatic and idiosyncratic figure – but what a musician. Our thanks to Katrina Burnett, ex–curator Bill Dow and his wife Marion who prepared lovely food for us all at unpredictable times and, of course, to Richard Burnett whose vision in collecting the instruments, seeing to their restoration, housing and preserving them and, of course, playing them so admirably.

A mention of two other frequently used venues; Fry Hall at Keynsham (RIP), once proud part of the then Cadbury Schweppes complex had a good acoustic, but had the problem of pulse clocks which gave an audible click every minute and central heating which hummed. It was feasible to have the hall clocks and heating turned off but this required a lot of forward planning and hassle on the day. The heating needed a man with a spanner to turn off a valve, but the union said that this needed a technician plus a plumber plus a foreman to carry out the job.

Forde Abbey near Chard was suggested to us by Anthony Rooley of the Consort of Musicke and we made a number of notable recordings there. We all ate with the owners, the Roper family, with delicious food prepared by Fiona Laidlaw-Smith and were accommodated in the fine bedrooms. Genny and I stayed in the room that was used by Jeremy Bentham of philosophy fame. Forde also had some noise problems which ranged from spitting logs from the open fire to chimings from the turret clock and did need us to climb on the roof on one occasion to secure the flag rope slapping against the pole.

I suppose less salubrious but necessary due to the location of the instruments was the Mickleburgh Museum in Bristol. This chaotic Aladdin's cave of all things musical housed on the top floor of the piano merchants store was cold and leaky and right next to noisy Stokes Croft. Later on we did take some instruments to Frenchay to record (SDL 346) and the fine 24" Polyphon musical box with its many discs (the thousands of pins of which I straightened personally) at Inglestone Common.

So altogether a lot of people, with great talent, imagination or a penchant for collecting have given us their time and resources to enable Saydisc to realize its objective which was stated on our first business card of 1965 or thereabouts as High Quality Records For the Specialist. I hope that posterity will be enriched and enlightened by our 35 years of active recording.

A potted history of Saydisc, The Village Thing and associated labels

Saydisc Specialized Recordings Ltd.

Gef Lucena, who left Chipping Sodbury Grammar School in 1961, started in the retail record industry by working in the newly opened Broadmead branch of the Rediffusion Record Centre in Merchant Street as an assistant, but soon became manager of the record department of Churchill and Son Limited in Park Street. Churchills, as it was popularly known, was owned by Mickleburgh, the Bristol based piano merchant, which had its main premises on Stokes Croft, close to the recently rebuilt Broadmead shopping area. Gef Lucena, however, started to find working 9 to 5 difficult because of his extramural musical interests:

> Running parallel to my time in the record shop I was performing with schoolfriend Martin Pyman as The Crofters...and it was difficult keeping up the day job. We both sang, Martin played guitar and I played mandola, autoharp and a variety of other instruments rather badly. We did a lot of TV and radio work as well as guesting at folk clubs in the South West and I was commissioned to write songs on such diverse subjects as the opening of the Severn Bridge for TWW and six songs for the then Milk Marketing Board...[1]

Meanwhile, Gef Lucena's father, Lauri, had been instrumental in setting up the Bristol Hospital Broadcasting Service, of which he also became chairman. Although hospital broadcasting is now well established, this was the first service of its kind in the UK. As Gef Lucena says, "The Crofters had their own programme ('Anything Goes') which they recorded themselves using discs and live performances and I therefore gained experience with basic recording equipment."[2]

In 1963, Gef Lucena and Martin Pyman, together with some like–minded students from The Old Vic Theatre School, formed the *Bristol Poetry and Folk Club*, which met on alternate Friday evenings in the Old Duke on King Street before the club moved to The Bathurst Hotel, on Bathurst Basin. Shortly afterwards Gef Lucena took over the running of the club when the original committee broke up, about which he explains:

> The Committee fell apart after someone walked off with the funds and there was general dissent about the running of the club and I took over until it folded sometime in 1967. The club had excellent residents of the ilk of young Fred Wedlock, Pat Small, Bev and Richard Dewar and many others and all were unrecorded in those early folk revival days.[3]

So Gef Lucena was gaining experience in using recording equipment, was heavily–immersed in the nascent Bristolian folk revival scene and was surrounded by talented and, above all, unsigned singers and musicians. Finally, because of his musical pursuits, he was looking for something other than a 9 to 5 job. All this needed was some sort of catalyst, which came in the shape of Roy Mickleburgh. Gef Lucena explains:

> Over many years Roy had assembled a kaleidoscopic collection of all things musical. Whether it was old sheet music, musical boxes, barrel organs, old brass instruments, pianolas, Roy collected it and 'displayed' his amazing and chaotic collection on the leaky, cold top floor of their store in Stokes Croft. Knowing of my interest in things traditional Roy introduced me to his collection and I was instantly hooked! Here were

sounds that were both beautiful to my ears but also in grave danger of decay and disappearance. And here was I with some basic recording knowledge and a need to give up the day job...What I didn't have was money and Roy stepped in as business partner and so in May 1965 Saydisc began its 35 years of active record production in many fields of music over some 500+ albums.[4]

Gef Lucena formed Saydisc Specialized Recordings Ltd. in May 1965, with himself, his father, Lauri, and Roy Mickleburgh as directors. The first Saydisc release was an EP by Fred Wedlock and the first LP, released shortly afterwards, was a compilation of local folk musicians called *Bristol Folks*. These were followed up with recordings of church bells, ragtime piano, more folk groups (including three EPs by the Crofters), school choirs, local jazz and even a musical staged by an amateur dramatic society. Added to this were recordings of mechanical instruments and early soundcarriers, such as musical boxes, piano rolls, wax cylinders and 78rpm records, from the Roy Mickleburgh collection.

On starting Saydisc, Gef Lucena moved from his flat in Hampton Road, Redland, back to his parents' house in Frenchay and started to use the adjoining Quaker Meeting House for recording music for Saydisc releases. Lucena explains:

> Quakers don't have music in their meetings but strangely the acoustic of the Meeting House was excellent. It was high ceilinged and the walls were largely pitch pine clad. To increase the reverb time, panels in the upper part of the room could be opened and the whole was heated by an archaic beetle stove in the middle of the room which became red hot and roared loudly unless the top was propped open with a poker. Maybe the room was as idiosyncratic as the company that was using it but was utilised to great effect in such diverse situations as recording The Mellstock Band, Maddy Prior with The Carnival Band, The Dartington String Quartet, Dave Evans, Frank Evans and many, many others. The Meeting House at Frenchay was still used by choice long after Saydisc moved to new studios at The Barton, Inglestone Common.[5]

In 1968, Gef Lucena married Genny Bultitude, one of the regular attendees of the *Poetry and Folk Club*, and the couple moved to Inglestone Common, near Badminton. At this point Genny joined Gef Lucena, Lauri Lucena and Roy Mickleburgh as a director of the company and Saydisc carried on as a limited company until 1971, when it became a partnership of Gef and Genny Lucena. At this point the company shortened its name from Saydisc Specialized Recordings Ltd. to Saydisc Records.

To backtrack a little, there were several concentrations of folk clubs in Bristol with the two main ones being in the docklands area, centred by the mid–1960s on The Bathurst Hotel, and in the then seedily–run down suburb of Clifton. It was in October 1966 that *The Troubadour* was opened in Clifton by Ray Willmott, a Bristolian who had married in Australia and had recently returned home with his wife. Many of the *Bristol Ballads and Blues* and *Bristol Poetry and Folk Club* regulars started to play at *The Troubadour* along with musicians new to Bristol. One of these latter musicians, Ian Anderson, was to become a prime mover on the Bristol (and national) folk scene and was to influence some of the future directions of Saydisc.

Anderson moved to Bristol from Weston–super–Mare in 1965 and started playing floor spots at various folk clubs and coffee houses before hooking up with Al Jones and Elliot Jackson as Anderson Jones Jackson. The trio was the first act to play *The Troubadour* and was soon recorded for a limited edition EP by Saydisc. Al Jones left for London and Anderson and Jackson continued as a duo, recording another EP for Saydisc. At this point, Anderson had started a country blues club, originally held at *The Troubadour*, but soon moved, because of its popularity, to larger premises at the Old Duke, in King Street. The club, *Folk Blues Bristol and West*, was the first in the UK to concentrate on country blues and was very well placed to take advantage of a sudden nationwide surge of interest in this music. In 1968 Ian Anderson and *Folk Blues Bristol and West* regular, Mike Cooper, suggested that Saydisc should start a label called Matchbox to release American and British country blues. Gef Lucena agreed and the first LP was recorded by Lucena at the Meeting House, Frenchay, in March and April 1968 and was called *Blues Like Showers of Rain*. Ian Anderson explains:

> We were already getting national airplay from John Peel, Mike Raven and others from the [Saydisc] EPs, and support from Alexis Korner who had written nice words in Melody Maker. During the first half of '68, as all the frontrunners of the UK country blues scene came down to the club at the Old Duke, we recorded them at the Meeting House, Frenchay on the Sunday afternoon, and when we had enough the compilation LP Blues Like Showers Of Rain went into production…With that record, everything caught fire...myself, Mike Cooper and Jo–Ann Kelly in particular began to get chased by major labels and producers.[6]

This first Matchbox LP was released in July 1968 and gained a lot of exposure for the new label, helping to draw a hardcore of blues fans, though few realise the amount of hard work that went behind a small independent label getting an album to market, which included, according to the sleeve notes on the Village Thing retrospective, *Matchbox Days*, Gef Lucena having to stick on the labels by hand.

The next Matchbox release was by Blind Boy Fuller, followed by a compilation of blues piano that included such artists as Cripple Clarence Lofton and the Mississippi Jook Band. Ian Anderson and Mike Cooper had an album, *Inverted World*, released, which was basically made up from their respective Saydisc EPs, plus some pieces newly recorded at Frenchay. This was followed by vintage blues from Kokomo Arnold, Sonny Boy Williamson, Furry Lewis, and Peetie Wheatstraw. There was also an obscure follow–up to *Blues Like Showers of Rain*, with several musicians from the first volume, including a lightly disguised Mikel Kooper, now signed to Pye.

In 1969, Saydisc started to manufacture and distribute Johnny Parth's Austrian–based Roots label, which concentrated on classic American blues. The Roots series has managed to confuse many collectors for various reasons, most of which have to do with the country of origin of the pressings. Most sleeves and records appeared to be of non–UK manufacture, though some included Saydisc matrix numbers in the record runoff. Then again, some were very obviously of UK manufacture and one even included Matchbox labels. Gef Lucena clarifies the situation:

> As regards the provenance of our Roots series, these all used Austrian metalwork and most used Austrian printed sleeves with our sticker appended. The larger selling titles had UK printed sleeves from Austrian printing film.[7]

One thing remains to be clarified, however. Each Roots LP manufactured and distributed by Saydisc was also assigned a Saydisc catalogue number, though which Roots release relates to which Saydisc catalogue number remains, for the most part, a mystery. It does, at least, explain why there were so many previously unexplained gaps in Saydisc's catalogue sequence. Saydisc also manufactured and distributed three albums from the US company, Ahura Mazda, in the UK – and one of Saydisc's budget mechanical music compilations subsequently appeared on the Ahura Mazda label in the US. Gef Lucena explains, "The three albums we released were pressed and printed in the UK from US metalwork and amended artwork."[8] Presumably these LPs were also assigned Saydisc catalogue numbers but, again, which numbers these would be remains unknown.

As the 1970s got under way, Matchbox started to release records of contemporary folk and 'old–timey' country music licensed from independent, specialist American labels, such as Rounder and Kanawha. Thus began the Matchbox Country Music Series. The last Matchbox release was in 1976, this being an LP by Dave Peabody, who had previously recorded for Village Thing, that company having closed down in 1974 (the Village Thing label was run by Ian Anderson, John Turner and Gef Lucena, releasing its first records in November 1970, of which more later). The Matchbox name was resurrected in the 1980s as the Matchbox Bluesmaster Series, which involved Johnny Parth supplying the masters and noted blues expert, Paul Oliver, providing minutely–detailed sleeve notes.

In 1973 the LP, *Music from Dartington*, was released to celebrate the 80th birthday of Leonard Elmhirst of the Dartington College of Arts. The association with Dartington led to the setting up of a new label imprint to release classical music recorded by musicians from Dartington. The label was called Amon Ra, a name that had previously been used for Saydisc's Fine Arts offshoot: Amon Ra had also in January 1972 taken over as publishers of *Blues World*, with production taken care of by David Harrison, John Lucena and Plastic Dog. After the third Amon Ra release in 1974 the label was discontinued until 1977 when it was re–launched specifically to record early music on authentic instruments from the Finchcocks collection. As Gef Lucena says of this period: "The years progressed...and the classical early music label Amon Ra based on Finchcocks music museum in Goudhurst, Kent began its long and successful life."[9]

As the 1970s progressed, Saydisc started to move in a more mainstream direction, though admittedly this was a decidedly left–field mainstream direction. There were LPs covering barbershop groups, brass bands, carillons, handbell ensembles, choirs, Cotswold dialect and stories, world music and even an LP of parlour poetry by Kenneth Williams – and on the heavy metal front there were continued releases of recordings of church bells and steam locomotives as well as several outings for Lyndon Baglin's euphonium. In the 1980s, there seemed to be a great deal of convergence between the Saydisc label and the Amon Ra imprint, in that many Saydisc releases were classically–oriented. Indeed, the Broadside Band issued albums on both labels.

The quality of the records was also an issue of prime importance with Saydisc and they were one of the first small, independent labels to routinely press all their records to classical standards using the highly–regarded Nimbus pressing company, which was located just across the River Severn in Monmouthshire. To the ultimate end of musical fidelity, Saydisc started using digital recording technologies as early as January 1983 (when SAR 9 to SAR 12 were all recorded in one fortnight long session at Finchcocks) and was the first small independent to cease releasing albums on vinyl, moving to the new CD format. As Gef Lucena says:

> We...believed that, although we did not have the resources of the major companies, we must make our recordings and presentation to be of the highest order and use the latest technologies. So, we entered the digital recording and Compact Disc field early and have proved without a shadow of a doubt that we were right.[10]

The first CD releases appeared in mid–1985 and from 1986 most Saydisc releases and all Amon Ra releases were routinely released on CD and cassette with LPs being phased out completely. Of the early days of CDs, Gef Lucena adds:

> ...from about 1985 until about 2000 many Saydisc and Amon Ra titles were released in the USA on CD, LP and MC by the mail order company Musical Heritage Society under their own imprint. This association is just being revived (Aug 2010)…In fact, in the very early days of CD production MHS could not obtain CDs and we were fortunate to have a monthly allocation of 3000 CDs from Nimbus. Also the cost of CD

production and mastering was very high. We...agreed to give MHS a third of our allo-cation in order to custom produce our material with their imprint so long as they paid us in advance. This helped us a lot with the high costs involved in the early CD days.[11]

The majority of the Amon Ra back catalogue and selected Saydisc back catalogue was reissued during 1986 and 1987. In late 1988 Saydisc stated that albums were soon to be released in DAT (Digital Audio Tape) format, though this appears to have been a bit of a red herring!

Saydisc also began a profitable association with the Past Times chain of shops, producing versions of several CDs with Past Times' own sleeve designs and logo: CD-SDL 419 was renamed *Victorian Nursery Rhymes* and CD-SDL 400 was renamed *Favourite English Songs*, whilst CD-SDL 409, CD-SDL 417, CD-SDL 398 and the four *Trad Songs of...* albums retained their original titles. Past Times also stocked other titles which sold in large quantities.

Certainly Saydisc can be seen to have been a trend setter in many areas and although other labels, such as Cornwall's Sentinel Records, have been run on similarly committed lines, no other label has ever touched Saydisc for breadth and depth of vision, commitment to fulfilling that vision and, ultimately, achievement of that vision to the extent that it ended its days providing music and, via Music Education Consultant, Christine Richards, written teaching packs for UK schools. These teaching packs were *Listen To This!*, *Percussion Around the World* and *Religions Around the World*. After retiring from active recording in 2000, Gef Lucena has since resurrected his company and to date has reissued around 215 CDs from the Saydisc, Village Thing and Amon Ra catalogues as well as releasing one or two new titles.

The Village Thing

Ian Anderson, after recording for both Saydisc and the new Matchbox imprint moved to London. He was signed by Sandy Roberton and had LPs released on major labels, Liberty and Fontana, though thanks to Philips computerising the week of his Fontana label release, only around 200 copies ever got as far as the shops (see *Bristol Folk*, available from this publisher, for the full story). Even before the Fontana LP was released, Anderson had returned to Bristol following various frustrations with his record companies. Back playing *The Troubadour* and living above the club, he wistfully bemoaned the state of the music industry as regards the humble artist. Along with local musician, John Turner, he talked about taking their recording careers into their own hands. Of the birth of Village Thing, Ian Anderson explains:

> ...after late nights at the Troubadour, we were in the habit of taking our hangovers and whichever girlfriends or club guests had stayed the night across to Splinters coffee house in nearby Clifton Down Road. Over strong coffees and Sally Lunn teacakes one day, John [Turner] and I were wondering what would be the best for the Pigsty Hill Light Orchestra's recording career and for my own future one. We'd already started using the term "Clifton Village" for the area around Waterloo Street, Princess Victoria Street and The Mall and we dreamed up this concept of an agency and record label where we could all be in complete control of our own destinies without the interference of uncomprehending "suits". So our concept was this... thing... this... ahah! The Village Thing! Born December 1969.[12]

The agency side of things quickly got off the ground and as early as April 1970, Village Thing was advertising in the music press that Ian Anderson, Keith Christmas, Pigsty Hill Light Orchestra, Sun Also Rises and Ian Hunt were available for bookings. The record label was run by Ian Anderson, John Turner and Saydisc's Gef Lucena and, although based in Bristol, the label was intended to be national in outlook and distribution, except that various talented musicians started to move to Bristol specially to be part of the local scene – as Ian Anderson said:

We've got ourselves lumbered with being a West Country record company, which we've never set out to be...It just so happens that there's been more good artists living in the West Country than anywhere else for a while.[13]

Village Thing was the archetypal cottage industry – to the extent of many recordings taking place in a cottage – with various local musicians getting involved in one way or another. Many played on each others' albums and even the record label, an idealised view of Clifton as a village, was designed 'in–house' by the Pigsty Hill Light Orchestra's Andy Leggett. Ian Anderson provides further insight into Village Thing's early operations:

Village Thing['s]...official headquarters were at Inglestone Common, a tiny hamlet in the wilds of Gloucestershire where business partner Gef Lucena of Saydisc lived and many of the initial recordings were indeed done in Gef's cottage. Later, we were able to set up in a Quaker meeting house at Frenchay on the outskirts of Bristol. Equipment was good but basic – at least one album was recorded with a pair of mics plugged straight into a Revox tape recorder, and the maximum was a pair of tape machines, multi–mics through a small mixer and a simple reverb unit. Anything more complicated than that, on the few occasions when it was needed, we took over to record at Rockfield near Monmouth. It was also very much a family of artists and musicians, as will be apparent from the way that names crop up on each other's recordings.[14]

Although, over the next year or so, most of the records released were by local, or recently imported artists, two of the first four albums were by non–Bristolian artists, Sun Also Rises and Wizz Jones. Of the first clutch of releases, Anderson explains:

The Pigsty Hill Light Orchestra became our first album, and Cardiff duo Sun Also Rises, who'd blown everybody away with spots at the Troubadour, became our second, both released 18th September 1970. Mine came up next, along with guitar legend Wizz Jones who had also fallen out of United Artists and had a half–begun album which we completed in Bristol, both released November 13th. In between we put out a promotional EP The Great White Dap, and on 25th November we promoted a London label launch at the Country Club, Haverstock Hill, with the entire label roster. We were off and running.[15]

By the third LP on the label, Ian A. Anderson's *Royal York Crescent*, released in November 1970, Bristol's Plastic Dog organisation had become involved and the record was issued with a Plastic Dog sleeve design. Ian Anderson's memories of this period run thus:

The label was being successful and so was the agency, representing not only our recording artists but other noteworthy Bristol–based names like Keith Christmas, Al Jones, Mudge & Clutterbuck and the wonderful Shelagh MacDonald. All this was being run out of the flat in Royal York Crescent. By then, John Turner had moved out and I'd married Maggie Holland, and it all got a bit much having the business in our flat. So in April 1971 we teamed up with Al Read, Terry Brace and designer Rodney Matthews of the fast growing Plastic Dog organisation who had an office above a gents' outfitters at 77 Park Street with a spare back room. The label also signed a production/ distribution deal with Transatlantic Records, which eventually proved to be Village Thing's downfall – another story.[16]

Plastic Dog published the monthly *Dogpress* magazine to advertise forthcoming attractions at the Granary rock club. This was padded out with record reviews, silly poems, adverts for local shops and a rather dubious feature called *Groupie of the Month*, which even led to a copy of *Dogpress* being waved around at a Parliamentary hearing on obscenity. To commemorate the link–up between the two agencies, the cover of the April 1971 edition was emblazoned with a photo of Al Read and Terry Brace of Plastic Dog with Ian Anderson and Maggie Holland of Village Thing. Starting from this edition, not surprisingly, *Dogpress* began to feature a larger proportion of adverts for Village Thing than hitherto, plus a page of local folk news titled, "The Village Dog's Plastic Thing".

With Rodney Matthews and Terry Brace of Plastic Dog working on many of the sleeve designs, Village Thing LPs became almost immediately identifiable. Matthews' illustrations were of gloriously caricatured people or creatures, and the label itself was modified by the inclusion of Rodney Matthews' yokel logo, complete with straw sticking out of its mouth. As Ian Anderson commented:

> We've finally got around to adopting a new logo…instead of our tatty old letraset. Needless to say it was designed by kind Uncle Rodney who has also produced some pretty amazing sleeve designs for various items in the pipeline.[17]

Not surprisingly, Terry Brace and Rodney Matthews began to fulfil the same function for Saydisc from either late 1970 or early 1971 and the first sleeve design was for the Matchbox issue, *Little Brother Montgomery 1930–1969*. On the record side the Saydisc work was mostly one of arranging supplied photographs and sleeve notes and creating an attractive layout rather than one of creating original artwork, and the real gems for Saydisc were Matthews' sleeve illustrations for several 7" LPs presenting Bristol humour and dialect, one of which showed the Three Wise Men waiting at a local bus stop. There were also a couple of uncharacteristic portraits of classical composers by Matthews for Saydisc's Amon Ra label, which is somewhat ironic because one of Matthews' tasks when a student at the West of England College of Art in 1961 had been to design a notional record sleeve for Stravinsky's *Rite of Spring*. Of the work for Saydisc, Matthews later said that they always paid promptly!

Apart from changes in the agency side, early 1971 also saw new artists signed to the Village Thing label, as Anderson remembers:

> Ralph McTell pointed Steve Tilston at the Troubadour and us, who pestered us until we took him on (actually it didn't take much pestering). Tilston moved to Bristol and brought Dave Evans, who also stayed and became one of our favourites. Local folk hero Fred Wedlock was a natural for us: his album The Folker provided perfect national press publicity when the line "Prince Phillip is The Queen in drag" to the tune of the National Anthem so offended the ladies at the EMI pressing plant we used that they refused to press it until changed – and there's no such thing as bad publicity! All these releases did well, with Tilston and Evans getting great critical success, press and radio, and Fred Wedlock selling particularly promiscuously.[18]

However, not long after the link–up with Plastic Dog, *The Troubadour*, after two years of failing to live up to the financial expectations of its new owner, was arbitrarily closed, an event that was to lead to Ian Anderson and Maggie Holland leaving Bristol and taking the administrative side of Village Thing with them. Ian Anderson explains:

> Not long after the agency merger, disaster struck when Peter Bush closed the Troubadour. The lively scene centred around it imploded, quickly reduced to people sitting in the pub across the road generally backbiting about whoever wasn't there at that point. Everything soured, and within the year, Maggie and I decided to head for somewhere fresh. She originally came from Alton in Hants, and 20 miles up the road

was a very lively scene centred on Farnham, Surrey, itself within easy striking distance of London. We moved there in 1972, taking the label admin with us and at the same time setting out as a new duo, Hot Vultures. That was the last of my seven year association with Bristol, and Farnham was where I lived for the next 16 years.[19]

This didn't represent a complete break with Bristol, however, as most subsequent LPs were still recorded in Frenchay, many with the usual cohort of local musicians. On the other hand, the move away from Bristol saw the label starting to issue a greater proportion of LPs by national, and even international, names. As Anderson says:

…a particular coup came about through me meeting and becoming friends with legendary American banjo player and songwriter Derroll Adams while touring in Belgium…Derroll, who came to Europe with Rambling Jack Elliott in the late 1950s and stayed, famously appearing in the drunken hotel room sequence in Bob Dylan's Don't Look Back film ... We brought him over to Frenchay and recorded the Feelin' Fine album with Wizz Jones and Belgian star Roland Van Campenhout, then brought him back to tour when it was released. That got us a lot of kudos (not to mention people like Rod Stewart and Long John Baldry turning up at his folk club gigs!)…[20]

Production and distribution of Village Thing LPs had been taken over by Transatlantic in July 1971, thus promising the chance of wider distribution in the UK, but sales were never that heavy, even after EMI started to distribute the label along with Transatlantic from October 1971. Most releases averaged 2,000 sales with Fred Wedlock the highest seller with approximately 20,000 sales per album.

In January 1974, a Village Thing press release stated that Ian Anderson was to leave the company with Gef Lucena taking over as the label owner, the reason given being that Anderson's current duo, Hot Vultures, was now taking up much of his time. The press release confidently stated that several albums were close to release, but it seems that not all was well in the relationship with Transtlantic and apart from the now delayed new releases and the two Wedlock LPs, the rest of the back catalogue was deleted in 1974. Gef Lucena bought the deleted stock back from Transtlantic and these were sold off via mail order at 99p each from Saydisc's Inglestone Common address. So it was that the Melody Maker, unbeknown at the time, reported both the last set of long–delayed Village Thing releases and, effectively, the label's demise in the same article.

Village Thing will be selling off their earlier records for 99p until they run out. This is because their distributors Transatlantic Records, have decided to delete a number of the early releases … Village Thing have bought them and will be making them available by mail order. The albums involved are Pigsty Hill Light Orchestra, Steve Tilston, Ian A. Anderson, Dave Evans, Wizz Jones, Hunt and Turner, Sun Also Rises, Tucker Zimmerman and Al Jones…This month the label is releasing albums by Noel Murphy, Wizz Jones and Chris Thompson, all of which have been held up for a considerable time.[21]

The Chris Thompson LP became an instant collector's item when, reputedly, only 101 of the 1,000 press run made it to the shops with the rest destroyed by Transatlantic. In a write up of the Noel Murphy LP, the Melody Maker commented that this was to be, "The last Village Thing record with Ian A. Anderson at the helm…"[22] though this was old news by this time and Murf turned out to be the last Village Thing LP altogether. A handful of titles were listed as still available in The New Records trade publication in January 1978 at a recommended retail price of £1.65 each, but that was effectively it from Village Thing, apart from Fred Wedlock's two albums, which remained available via Saydisc well into the 1980s, on a revised Village Thing label design.

Epilogue

So this year marks the 45th anniversary of Saydisc and the 40th anniversary of Village Thing. Although Saydisc is maintaining a low profile, Ian Anderson decided to commemorate Village Thing's anniversary with a CD and an all day event. The compilation CD, *Ghosts From The Basement: lost songs, dreams and folkadelia from the vaults of Village Thing, 1970–74*, is available on Ian Anderson's Weekend Beatnik label and features Wizz Jones, Derroll Adams, Al Jones, Dave Evans, The Sun Also Rises, Ian A. Anderson, Chris Thompson, Steve Tilston, Lackey and Sweeney, Tucker Zimmerman, Hunt and Turner, Dave Peabody and 'one that got away' from Dave Mudge[23].

By the time this book is available, the day–long *Ghosts From The Basement* event at Cecil Sharp House will have taken place. At time of going to print those already confirmed from the Village Thing days are Wizz Jones, Steve Tilston, Tucker Zimmerman, Ian A. Anderson, Dave Evans, Ian Hunt, Maggie Holland, Keith Christmas, Keith Warmington (from Strange Fruit) with the possibility of a cameo appearance from Sun Also Rises. Rif Mountain artists include Nancy Wallace, Jason Steel, The Owl Service, The Straw Bear Band and Pamela Wyn Shannon with further artists to be confirmed: Rif Mountain is a contemporary record label considered by Ian Anderson to have inherited the 'alternative folk' flame originally lit by Village Thing.

To add, from the author's point of view, a surreal twist, several authors with books about the golden era of British folk have also been booked, these being Colin Irwin (*In Search of Albion*), Rob Young (*Electric Eden*), Jeanette Leech (*Seasons They Change*), Will Hodgkinson (*The Ballad of Britain*) and a certain Mark Jones (*Bristol Folk* and *The Saydisc & Village Thing Discography*). To further commemorate Village Thing, Rif Mountain is compiling a tribute CD that is evidently going to include a few surprises. Seasons they change, yes, but the circle remains unbroken for all that.

Section notes

1. Gef Lucena, quoted in *Bristol Folk* (Mark Jones) Bristol Folk Publications, 2009.
2. Ibid.
3. Ibid.
4. Ibid.
5. Ibid.
6. Ian Anderson, quoted in *Bristol Folk* (Mark Jones) Bristol Folk Publications, 2009.
7. Email dated 7th November 2007.
8. Ibid.
9. Gef Lucena, quoted in *Bristol Folk* (Mark Jones) Bristol Folk Publications, 2009.
10. Saydisc's 21st anniversary catalogue.
11. Email dated 13th August 2010.
12. Email dated 9th December 2009.
13. Ian Anderson, quoted in "Focus On Folk: Bristol's cream" (Andrew Means) *Melody Maker*, 1st January 1972.
14. *Ghosts from the Basement* (sleeve notes: Ian Anderson) Weekend Beatnik, WEBE 9046, 2010.
15. Email dated 9th December 2009.
16. Ibid.
17. "Village Dog's Plastic Thing" (no author attributed) *Dogpress*, October 1971.
18. Email dated 9th December 2009.
19. Ibid.
20. Ibid.
21. "Folk News" (no author attributed) *Melody Maker*, 6th July 1974.
22. "Albums" (Colin Irwin) *Melody Maker*, 27th July 1974.
23. This author is partly-responsible for unearthing this previously-unknown Dave Mudge recording.

Discographies

Source acronyms used in lists

TNA – *The New Albums* – monthly publication (pub. Francis Antony)
TNC – *The New Cassettes/The New Cassettes and Cartridges* – monthly pub. (Francis Antony)
MM84 – *Music Master* 11th edition (pub. John Humphries: 1985)
MM13 – *The Music Master Record Catalogue* 13th edition (John Humphries: 1988)
MM89 – *Music Master Labels List '89* 9th edition (John Humphries: 1988)
MMSC3 – *Music Master Singles Catalogue* 3rd edition (John Humphries: 1990)
SC – Saydisc catalogue
All release dates/years as per Saydisc master list, pressing cards or record labels if no source is otherwise listed. Release dates for Village Thing label records courtesy of Ian Anderson.

Saydisc – the SD catalogue sequence

The SD catalogue sequence was the longest–lived catalogue sequence, the first release appearing in May 1965 with the last clutch of original releases appearing in 1999 and a slight encore in the new millennium. The sequence included 7" EPs, LPs, 7" singles, 7" 'LPs', cassettes (some items only being available in this format) and finally CDs. Through use of different suffixes, the sequence incorporated releases on the Matchbox (and Flyright/Matchbox) label between 1968 and 1976. 7" releases comprised the plain "SD" prefix, though those that played at 33⅓ instead of at 45rpm had "33" added as a prefix. LPs had "L" added to become "SDL", whilst Matchbox LPs had "M" or "R" added ("SDM" denoted modern recordings and "SDR" denoted material that had been previously issued), though there are a few mismatches between the catalogue number as appearing in the runoff and that appearing on labels and sleeves! Special releases had "X" added to become "SDX" (such as on the lone double LP, a double–length LP and, confusingly, the last Matchbox release in 1976). "B" was added to denote budget–priced releases and on one occasion "SAM" was added to denote that the LP was a sampler, this being the standard policy of Transatlantic, who acted as distributor at this point. One oddity was a one–off "SAY" prefix, though this otherwise slotted into the SD sequence. Cassette issues, when these started to appear in the 1970s, added a "C" prefix and when CDs were introduced, these added a "CD–" prefix. Just to add a final soupçon of complexity, the Roots albums pressed and distributed in the UK under their original Austrian catalogue numbers were also internally assigned "SD" catalogue numbers, as were a handful of 7" LPs contract–pressed for the Dutch Jass label, hence the existence of many gaps in the sequence between 1969 and 1972. Unfortunately, there is only partial evidence in Saydisc's records of which records were assigned which SD numbers.

By 1985, albums started to appear on CD, with cassette issues supplanting LPs with many titles now only available on cassette. The first CD releases in 1985 and 1986 were CD–SDL 325 and 327 and the budget sampler CD–SDLC 362. In late 1986 CD–SDL 357 was issued and in the first half of 1987 further back catalogue was reissued on CD in the shape of CD–SDL 326, 348, 354, 355, 359, 360 and 361. The first non–LP issue was CD–SDL 364 in 1987 and from CD–SDL 367 LP issues were discontinued completely with the majority of releases appearing in both CD and cassette formats. From CD–SDL 429, released in 1999, cassette issues were discontinued.

SD 1   ***FRED WEDLOCK: Volume One (7" EP)***

Silbury Hill	Franklin
Si Mi Quieres Escribir	Hey Nelly Nelly

Release date: 1965
Limited press of 99 copies. In generic Saydisc sleeve with artist and track credits stuck on to the front ("Silbury" is misspelled as "Sibury", trivia fans). Generic, small, red label with "Issued by The Crofters" text. Included a Roneo insert that includes the catalogue number "SD – I". Otherwise no catalogue number included on sleeve or labels.

No cat. no.   *MECHANICAL MUSIC: Christmas Carols On Disc Musical Boxes (7" EP) (see also SD 119)*

The First Nowel (A)
Come All Ye faithful (B)
Hark the Herald Angels Sing (B)
Star of Bethlehem (B)

Silent Night (C)
Good King Wenceslas (A)

Release date: 1965?
7" EP; From the Mickleburgh collection. A = 22" disc Polyphon with glockenspiel attachment, followed by a 15½" Regina; B = 15½" disc Regina; C = Symphonion 11¾" disc, followed by a Polyphon 9½" disc. This is a 1965 release by Saydisc, with no catalogue number on sleeve or label. The matrix numbers, if they help, are 16179+1 and 16180+1. The label has the "Issued by the Crofters" text. This was later reissued as SD 119 in a new sleeve design. Some of this material was included on later release, SDL 327.

No cat. no.   *VARIOUS ARTISTS: Bristol Folks*

Fiddle Medley (Bev & Richard Dewar)
She Moves Through the Fair (Anne Mavius)
Man of Constant Sorrow (Patrick Small)
Tramps and Hawkers (The Crofters)
Dona, Dona, Dona (Graham Kilsby)
Across the Hills (Paul Evans)

He Was My Brother (Paul Evans)
Fare Thee Well (Bev & Richard Dewar)
Dirty Streets (Anne Mavius)
Geordie (The Crofters)
Flora (Patrick Small)
Farewell (Graham Kilsby)

Release date: 1965
No catalogue number – matrix numbers are 16185 and 16186, which presumably puts this release after that of the EP above? Small generic label design with "Issued by The Crofters" text. Top opening sleeve. Only 99 copies pressed. All artists were singers at the Ballads and Blues and/or the Poetry and Folk Clubs of Bristol.

No cat. no.   *ST. MARY REDCLIFFE SCHOOL CHOIR: Vivaldi Gloria, etc.*

Release date: 1967?
Title unknown. Saydisc's master list gives a 1967 release; if so, why no cat. no. was assigned is a mystery.

SDL 112   *VARIOUS ARTISTS: Cylinder Jazz*

Make That Trombone Laugh (Harry Raderman's
    Jazz Orchestra)
International Cakewalk (Fred van Eps)
Hungarian Rag (New York Military Band)
At a Georgia Camp Meeting (Edison Grand
    Concert Band)
Hiawatha Rag (Ollie Oakley)
Meadow Lark (Duke Yellman & His Orchestra)

Dardanella (Harry Raderman's Jazz Orchestra)
Coconut Dance (Vess L. Ossman)
Nightime In Little Italy (Frisco Jass Band)
Bill Bailey Won't You Please Help Me Home (Burt Sheppard)
Hiawatha Rag (Edison Concert Band)
Teasing Medley (Edison Military Band)
My Sumuran Girl (Vess L. Ossman)

Release date: c1966
Subtitled "early Jazz and Ragtime recordings from 1897–1928". Small, blue, generic label design with the "Crofters" text. No cat. no: matrix numbers are an unhelpful 16199/16200. Sister–release, *Pianola Jazz* (SDL 117), gives the game away by mentioning the catalogue number of this earlier release. Cylinders from the collection of Roy Mickleburgh. The sleeve illustration was later reused, in colour, on *The Wibbly Wobbly Walk* (SDL 350). Original sleeves, printed by Trym Display Services will have gone distinctly yellow with age. Later reissued as SDL 334.

SD 113   *THE CROFTERS: Pill Ferry (7" EP)*

Pill Ferry
Whip Jamboree

23rd of June
The Card Song

Release date: 1965/1966?
7" 45rpm EP on the second red generic label design. Subtitled "and other Folk Songs sung by The Crofters". In picture sleeve with a Roneo insert stating that The Crofters were planning to record a whole EP of local songs including *The Great Nailsea Cider Bet*, though evidently Adge Cutler never finished writing this song. *Pill Ferry* is the Crofters' cover of Adge Cutler's *Pill, Pill*. The difference in respective names of the song is interesting, because this version actually predates Adge Cutler's own recording. The sleeve photo is taken from the ferry's prow just as it is approaching the slip path on the Shirehampton side. Pill Creek is in the background.

---

114   *UNKNOWN*

115   UNKNOWN

CD: CD–SDL 115 (see below)
Although it is unknown what was originally assigned this catalogue number, a CD was later issued as CD–SDL 115 – *The One Eyed Fiddler* by Paul Wilson and Ben van Weede, which was originally issued on vinyl as CP 115.

SD 116   SIOBHAN LYONS: The Patriot Game (7" EP)

The Patriot Game	Every Night
She Moved Through the Fair	Slean Libh

Release date: 1966
Sleeve also subcredited John C. Edwards as accompanist.

SDL 117   MECHANICAL MUSIC: Pianola Jazz

Skip Along	Georgia Camp Meeting
Maple Leaf	Stumbling
Blame It on the Blues	French Trot (played by Victor Ardey)
For Me and My Gal (played by Pete Wendling)	Alabama Dream
Aunt Hagars Blues (played by Billy Mayerl)	Creole Bells
I'll Dance Till De Sun Breaks Through	Old Fashioned Girl
Rose Of Washington Square	

Release date: 1966 / June 1982 (MM89)
Cassette: CSDL 117 (June 1982: MM89)   **CD:** CD–SDL 117
Subtitled "Early piano jazz and ragtime played on pianola rolls". White label test pressing with small, blue, generic Saydisc labels glued on is known to exist: existence confirmed on the short–lived third label design in green with album and track credits. Copies exist in both flipback and non–flipback sleeves. All recordings are from 65 note rolls except *Georgia Camp Meeting* (88 note Themodist) and *Old Fashioned Girl* (88 note Metrostyle). *Rose of Washington Square* (played by Pete Wendling). Original sleeves will have yellowed with age as per SDL 112.

SDL 118   NEVILLE DICKIE, QUENTIN WILLIAMS & PETE DAVIS: Ragtime Piano

Original Rags (Neville Dickie)	The Nailbreaker (Quentin Williams)
Daintiness Rag (Neville Dickie)	Ceonothus Rag (Quentin Williams)
Rosotio (Quentin Williams)	Hilarity Rag (Pete Davis)
The Cowcatcher (Quentin Williams)	Maple Leaf Rag (Pete Davis)
Paragon Rag (Neville Dickie)	Weeping Willow (Neville Dickie)
Rag–Time Dance (Neville Dickie)	The Thriller! (rag) (Neville Dickie)
	Grace and Beauty (Neville Dickie)

Release date: 1966
Subtitled "British Ragtime – Volume One", not that a Volume 2 was ever issued. White label test pressing with small, blue, generic Saydisc labels glued on known to exist. Also spotted on the fourth label design with the title on sleeve printed in gold/brown, as per original, and also in black. Q. Williams' tracks are original compositions.

SD 119   MECHANICAL MUSIC: Enchanted Carols (7" EP)

Same track listing as *Christmas Carols on Musical Disc Boxes* (no catalogue number)

Release date: prob. 1966
7" 45rpm EP on at least two label designs. This is a reissue of *Christmas Carols on Musical Disc Boxes*, which had originally been issued in generic sleeve with no catalogue number. Subtitled "Played on Old Musical Boxes".

The first issue on this catalogue number was on the large, red, generic Saydisc label without reference to The Crofters and housed in a new sleeve design. The catalogue number is included on the sleeve but not on the label. The record was still available when generic labels were discontinued for labels that included credits and catalogue numbers. All variants have 16179 matrix numbers and the new label included this number underneath the catalogue number. At some time prior to 1971 the sleeve design changed from black and white to purple tint with further changes to type face, justification and colour. On the rear of the sleeve, Saydisc contact details were added and the printer credit changed from "West Surrey Printing" to "Senol Printing".

SD 120   THE CROFTERS: Drink Up Thee Cider (7" EP)

Casn't Kill Couch	When the Common Market Comes to Stanton Drew
Champion Dung Spreader	Drink Up Thee Cider

Release date: prob. 1966
Subtitled "The Crofters Sing Adge". 7" 45rpm EP on the large blue generic label. The picture sleeve shows the Crofters at Adge Cutler's old workplace, Coates Somerset Cider Factory, Nailsea. The back of the sleeve states, "The Somerset songs of Adge Cutler Sung By The Crofters". Includes a Roneo sheet of A5 paper advertising the first Crofters EP. This EP predates Adge Cutler's own recordings of these songs. One interesting point is that the insert in the previous Crofters EP (SD–113) stated that this EP would include a song by Adge Cutler called *The Great Nailsea Cider Bet*, though evidently Adge never completed this song. The first and last tracks include Pete Davis. Pete is better known as Henry Davis, who a couple of years later joined Adge Cutler's Wurzels and later acted as their musical director.

SDL 121   MECHANICAL MUSIC: Music of the Streets

La Marseillaise/Pomone Waltz (Waldteufel)/
    Rule Britannia
Honeysuckle and the Bee/Just One Girl
    Waltz/Bicycle Barn Dance Polka
Cylinder Piano (Hicks of Bristol, 1846) four
    unidentified tunes
Hurdy Gurdy (played by Gef Lucena) Improvised
    dance tune/Unquiet Grave followed
    by Improvised dance tune
Soldiers of the Queen/Goodbye Dolly Gray/
    Let the Great Big World

Jesu Lover of My Soul/Grandfather Clock/Men of Harlech/
    Wonderful Words/Pull For the Shore
The Man Who Broke the Bank At Monte Carlo/I've Got a
    Lovely Bunch Of Coconuts/Oh Oh Antonio
Little German Home Across the Sea/Old Zip Coon/Gathering
    Sea Shells By the Sea Shore/Old Rosin the Beau
Reed Barrel Organ – two tunes
Donawallen Waltz/Little Old Mill/Ship Ahoy, Blaze Away/
    Now Is the Hour

Release date: prob. 1966
Street pianos, barrel organs and hurdy–gurdy. Re–released with modifications as SDL 340.

SDL 122?   Possibly titled Jazz Piano

SDL 123   ST. MARY REDCLIFFE SCHOOL CHOIR: Three 20th Century Cantatas

People Wherever You Are
Cantata I – The Christian Story (see below)
The Daniel Jazz – Part I

The Daniel Jazz – Part II
'People Wherever You Are'
Cantata II – The Prophesy of Isaiah

Release date: 1966
In generic sleeve: where these sleeves were used, record–specific credits and notes were added. A white label test pressing with small, red, generic Saydisc labels glued on top of white labels is known to exist. *Cantata I* credited on sleeve as both "The Christian Story" and "The Christmas Story". The St. Mary Redcliffe School Choir is conducted by Peter Fowler, who formed it in 1958. Soloists are: Roger Nicholas; Andrew Maddern; Maurice Smith; Graham Atwell; John Haly; Stephen Beasant; Thomas Bush; Richard Yandell. Music is arranged by Arthur Parkman and played by the Arthur Parkman Quintet. Recorded at T.W.W. Studios (the then local commercial television station) in December 1964 and December 1965. The St. Mary Redcliffe School Choir conducted by Peter Fowler.

SD 124   FRED WEDLOCK, BEV & RICHARD DEWAR: Virtute et Industrial

Virtute et Industrial
Broomfield Hill (Bev and Richard Dewar)
Racing Pigeon

Sovay (Bev and Richard Dewar)
Maid of Clifton (Fred Wedlock)
Bi–psychedelic Tandem (Bev and Richard Dewar)

Release date: 1966
Subtitled "Songs and Instrumentals", this came in a generic Saydisc sleeve with credits printed on front and rear. Tracks without credits include all three musicians. *Virtute et Industrial* reappeared on *Sounds of Bristol* (33SD 245). This was on the large, light blue generic label.

33SD 125   ANDERSON, JONES, JACKSON: Anderson, Jones, Jackson (7" EP)

Louise
If Your Man Gets Personal

Dan Scaggs
I'd Rather Be the Devil
Beedle Um Bum

Release date: 1966
To expand on the surnames, these were Ian Anderson, Al Jones and Elliot Jackson.

SD 126   GRAHAM KILSBY: In a Folk Mood (7" EP)

Chastity Belt
She's Like the Swallow

Man of Constant Sorrow
Keep the Willow

Release date: 1967
On the large, red, generic label deign. Picture sleeve includes the following: "... He is a very popular entertainer...As can be heard from CHASTITY BELT: a neo–Elizabethan song recorded live at the Bristol Troubadour Club. Graham's several voices are joined by Alun Jones–12 string guitar, Patrick Small–guitar and vocal, Fred Wedlock–bicycle horn and frenzied applause..." *She's Like The Swallow* was an American ballad from a collection by Maud Karpeles. *Man of Constant Sorrow* included traditional words, though with the tune revised by then local folk hero, Fred Wedlock: Al Jones played twelve string guitar on this second version of the song to be recorded for Saydisc in two years – Pat Small had originally recorded it on the *Bristol Folks* LP. *Keep the Willow* had words by Bristol writer, Berry McDonald, and music by Kilsby.

SD 127   BELLS: Bells of Britain (7" EP)

Change ringing from Bristol: St. Mary	Bristol Cathedral (8 bells)
Redcliffe (12 bells)	St. Stephen's, City (10 bells)
The Lord Mayor's Chapel (6 bells)	

Release date: either 1966 or 1967
Subtitled "vol 1, change ringing from Bristol". 7" 45rpm EP in picture sleeve with 8 page Roneo insert. This was the first record to appear with record and track credits on the label, though this particular design was fairly short–lived. The colour of this label was purple with silver lettering. This was later available on the fourth label design, still in picture sleeve and still with insert. However, the front photo had changed from black and white to having a blue tint and the lettering was of slightly different typeface. The original sleeve had been printed by West Surrey Printing Co. Ltd. whilst the new was printed by West Brothers: text on the rear changed from black to dark blue.

---

128   UNKNOWN

SD 129   THE CROFTERS: Ballad of the Severn Bridge (7" EP)

Ballad of the Severn Bridge	The Butter Churning Race
As I Walked Out One Morn	Buttercup Meadows

Release date: either 1966 or 1967
Picture sleeve. Includes a Roneo insert. Sleeve and insert advertise that The Crofters were soon to release an LP, though this was not recorded. The title track was commissioned from Gef Lucena by the local TV station, TWW: it was performed by The Crofters on the bridge and screened on the day the bridge was opened.

---

130   UNKNOWN

SDL 131   ST. MARY REDCLIFFE & TEMPLE SCHOOL CHOIR: 1967 Recital

Speak My Tongue	Humoresque (Yon)
Praise Ye the Lord (Psalm 150) (Redman)	Gloria in D major (Vivaldi)
Confitemini Domini (Constantini)	Gloria
Rejoice in the Lord Always (attr. Reford)	Laudamus Te
O Taste and See (Vaughan Williams)	Gratias Agimus Tibi
Exsultate Deo (Scarlatti)	Propter Magnam Gloriam
Nunc Dimittis in F major	Domine Deus
Zadoc the Priest (Handel)	Domine Fili Unigenite
Recession (from A Ceremony of Carols) (Britten)	Qui Tollis Peccata Mundi
	Quoniam Tu Solus Sanctus
	Cum Sancto Spiritu

Release date: 1967
In generic sleeve. Conductor, Peter Fowler, who also formed the choir in 1958; organist, John Marsh. Recorded at a concert at St. Mary Redcliffe following a highly successful tour of Germany in August 1967.

SDL 132   MECHANICAL MUSIC: Pianola Ragtime

Temptation Rag (Two Step) (65 note Imperial)	Bow–Bow Blues (88 note Universal)
Rag–Time Skedaddle (65 note Orchestrelle)	Ragtime Oriole (65 note Triumph)
Wabash Blues (88 note – no make given)	A Coon Band Contest (65 note Kohler and Campbell)
1915 Rag (88 note Perfecta)	Smokey Mokes (65 note Imperial)
The Grizzly Bear Rag (65 note – unknown make)	Ticked to Death (The Chase and Baker Co. 65 note)
Walhalla (Two Step Craze) (65 note Melographic)	Buzzer Rag (65 note Melographic)
Florida Rag (The Chase and Baker Co. 65 note)	Panama Rag (65 note Orchestrelle)

Release date: prob. 1967 / Nov. 1982 (MM89)
Cassette: CSDL 132 (Nov. 1982: MM89)   **CD:** CD–SDL 132

Volume 1 in the *The Golden Age of Mechanical Music* series. Original label design was probably the second generic label: copies exist on the later fourth label design with album and track credits. Original sleeves, printed by Trym Display Services, have probably yellowed with age, though those printed by E. J. Day will not have done.

SDL 133 — THE ST. MARY'S PLAYERS: The World Premiere Production of Bonanza 1912

Overture	Overture
Hullo There!	Paint the Town Red
Crystal Ball	Keeping Up with the Joneses
Make Hay!	Gentlemen of the Town
C'Est la Vie	Strolling Down the Strand
I'm Having the Time of My Life	Votes for Women!
Bonanza!	Airs and Graces
Farewell Monte Carlo	Rarin' to Go
	Bonanza!

Release date: 1967
In generic sleeve on small, red, generic label. Written by Kenneth Warr and Eric Ward. Recorded Live at St. Mary's Parish Hall, Fishponds, Bristol.

33SD 134 — IAN ANDERSON & ELLIOT JACKSON: Almost the Country Blues (7" EP)

Cottonfield Blues	Big Road Blues
Tom Rushen Blues	Shake Em On Down

Release date: 1968
Picture sleeve.

SD 135? — Possibly by MERRYWOOD GRAMMAR SCHOOL

Judging by the dates of the records either side, this is most likely to be a 45rpm EP by Merrywood Grammar School in Bedminster. Gef Lucena remembers recording this the day after the devastating floods that affected Bristol and other parts of the south west. The floods were July 10th 1968, so this recording took place 11th July.

SDL 136 — THE BLUE NOTE JAZZ BAND: Farewell to the Ship

Something Spanish	Edith
'Round Midnight	Creole Love Call
Mary Jane	Don't Think Twice
Just Squeeze Me	Ain't Misbehaving
Rebecca	Threepenny Bit

Release date: 1968
There are two line–ups on this LP, one recorded live at The Ship in Redcliff Hill before it was bulldozed, along with the world's first lead shot tower, to widen the road, and the other line–up on the studio recordings.

SD 137 — MIKE COOPER: Up the Country Blues (7" EP)

The Way I Feel	Send Me to the 'Lectric Chair
One Time Blues	Few Short Lines

Release date: 1968
Four track EP in picture sleeve on the large, blue, generic label design.

---

138 — See below

Two releases have been identified that may have been issued as 138, 139 or 141. One was a 45 rpm EP by a Swindon-based school choir and orchestra (which would have had a "SD" prefix) and one was an LP by the Bristol Youth Choir (which would have had a "SDL" prefix).

---

139 — See 138

33SD 140 — LAURI SAY & THE ISLAND FOLK: Songs for Singing Islanders (7" EP)

The Southern Vectis Bus Song	The Isle of Wight for Me
U.D.I. for I.O.W	The Hovercraft

Release date: 1968
Issued in two different picture sleeves. The first issue is in a generic Saydisc 7" sleeve with credits printed on the sleeve and a 33⅓ rpm sticker covering the printed 45rpm credit. The sleeve back has notes written by Say. The

later issue has a similar back, but with credits stating where the record could be bought (Teagues of Ryde and Newport). The front of the sleeve is very different with a line drawing of the island. The later press is on the fourth label design. White label copies of the first press are known to exist. "UDI", for those too young to remember, stood for "Unilateral Declaration of Independence", which Rhodesia threatened – and then carried out – at this time.

---

141   **See 138**

SDM 142   **VARIOUS ARTISTS: Blues Like Showers of Rain**

A Few Short Lines (Dave Kelly)	Say No to the Devil (Simon & Steve)
Going to Germany (Panama Limited Jug Band)	Black Snake Moan (Mike Cooper)
Nothin' In Ramblin' (Jo–Ann Kelly)	If I Had Possession (The Missouri Compromise)
Dealing with the Devil (Simon & Steve)	Rowdy Blues (Ian Anderson)
Meeting House Rag (Mike Cooper)	Black Mary (Jo–Ann Kelly)
Friday Evening Blues (Ian Anderson with Adrian	Travelling Blues (Dave Kelly)
'Putty' Pietryga & Elliot Jackson)	Cocaine Habit (Panama Limited Jug Band)
Dark Road Blues (The Missouri Compromise)	

Release date: July 1968
First Matchbox release. Original sleeves printed by Trym Display Services have not just yellowed with age, but have gone bright orange with the blue illustration turning green. Later press with E. J. Day sleeve has "Volume One" added and remains the original blue on white. The label was the first Matchbox design.

SDR 143   **BLIND BOY FULLER: Blind Boy Fuller On Down Vol. 1**

What's That Smell Like Fish (with Bull City Red)	Why Don't My Baby Write to Me?
Weeping Willow	Baby Quit Your Low Down Ways
Worn Out Engine Blues (with Sonny Terry &	Worried and Evil Man Blues
Bull City Red)	Mamie
New Oh Red (with Dipper Boy Council & Bull	If You See My Pigmeat
City Red)	Put You Back In Jail
Mean & No Good Woman (with Sonny Terry)	Where My Woman Usta Lay
Corrine What Makes You Treat Me So	
Get Your Yas Yas Out (with Sonny Terry & Bull City Red)	

Release date: 1969
In the Matchbox series. Stock copies have an "SDM" prefix in the matrix, but "SDR" prefix on labels and sleeve. The labels are on the second and final Matchbox design. LP reissued in 1974 as LP 110 by Flyright Records. The Flyright issue had a different sleeve design but retained the same title. The Saydisc "SDM" matrix number is the only matrix number in the runoff and also appears in smaller type above the Flyright number on the labels.

SDL 144?   **Possibly allocated to RL 301 based on the pressing date of the Roots LP**

SDL 145   **MECHANICAL MUSIC: The Golden Age of Mechanical Music – Vol. 2 – Story of the Polyphon**

Verlassen	Au Revoir But Not Goodbye
O Beautiful May	Tannhauser Overture
Overture 'Il Belisario'	Song of Hybrias the Cretan
The Silver Fish	Rejoice Greatly (Messiah)
Lullaby of Brahms	Shall I Be an Angel Daddy?
In the Gloaming	Hallelujah Chorus
There Is a Green Hill Far Away (Gounod)	Break the News to Mother
Chansons des Cloches	Ave Maria (Schubert)

Release date: October 1968?
Based on a 1963 Radio 3 talk. Played on 15½", 19⅝", 22" and 24½" discs, including a Le Coultre Overture Musical Box circa 1835. The track listing above is as taken from the October 1968 catalogue.

SDR 146   VARIOUS ARTISTS: Blues Piano

I Don't Know (Cripple Clarence Lofton)	Texas Heifer Blues (Springback James [Frank James])
Policy Blues (Cripple Clarence Lofton)	Stingaree Mama Blues (Springback James)
Crazy 'Bout My Baby (Blind Roosevelt Graves with Uaroy Graves, Will Ezell & unknown acc.)	Skippy Whippy (Mississippi Jook Band)
	Dangerous Woman (Mississippi Jook Band)
Bustin' the Jug (Blind Roosevelt Graves with Uaroy Graves, Will Ezell & unknown acc.)	Down By the M and O (Lee Brown with Sam Brown & unknown acc.)
	Jeff Davis Highway (Lee Brown with Sam Brown & unknown acc.)
So Cold In China (Shorty Bob Parker with Kid Prince Moore)	East Chicago Blues (Pinetop & Lindberg)
Rain and Snow (as above)	
Farish St. Jive (Little Brother Montgomery)	

Release date: 1968
White label test pressings known to exist. Both white label and stock copies have an "SDM" prefix in the matrix, but stock copies have an "SDR" prefix on labels and sleeve.

SDL 147   BRISTOL CATHEDRAL SCHOOL CHOIR: Bristol Cathedral School Choir
Track listing unknown

Release date: 1968
Marketed by the School. No file copy available at Saydisc

SDL 148?   See below
Based on release dates, two releases have been identified that may have been issued as 148, 149 or 150, these being Roots LPs, RL 306 and RL 313.

SDL 149?   See SDL 148

SDL 150?   See SDL 148

SDL 151   MECHANICAL MUSIC: The Golden Age of Mechanical Music – Vol. 3 – Wurlitzer

Most Anything Rag	Oh, You Beautiful Doll
Japanese Sandman	Happy
Tuck Me to Sleep In My Old Kentucky Home	Yankee Doodle – America
Curse of an Aching Heart	Whistling Rufus March
Bye, Bye Blackbird	Show Me the Way to Go Home
Battle Hymn of the Republic	Mammy Jinny's Jubilee
Alexander's Ragtime Band	When the Henry Clay Comes Steaming Into Mobile Bay
Over the Waves	California Here I Come
Wearing of the Green	When the Merry–Go–Round Broke Down
Cokey, Cokey Dance	Who's Sorry Now

Release date: 1969
Licensed from a US label with a 1968 original publication date.

SDL 152   MECHANICAL MUSIC: The Golden Age of Mechanical Music – Vol. 4 – Giant German Orchestrions

Amor, Amor	Stein Song
Sleep	Silver Threads Among the Gold
Razzle Dazzle Rag!	Tico–Tico
Avalon	Swinging on a Star
Deep In the Heart of Texas	12th Street Rag
Me and My Shadow	Charmaine
I'm A Jazz Vampire	Hallelujah
Barney Google	This Is the Army Mr. Jones
Kiss Me Again	Oh Suzanna
They Needed a Songbird In Heaven So God Took Caruso Away	Under the Double Eagle – March

Release date: 1969
Issued in generic Saydisc sleeve with printed credits and later issued in a different sleeve design. Licensed from a US label with a 1968 original publication date. White label test pressings known to exist.

SDL 153   MECHANICAL MUSIC: The Golden Age of Mechanical Music – Vol. 5 – Story of a Mechanical Organ

The Lost Chord	Ernani Involami, etc.
L'Etoile du Nord	Hymns incl. 'God the All Terrible'
Rigoletto Selection	Barn Dances
	The Lost Chord (reprise)

Release date: 1969
A story with musical interludes by Bruce Angrave – each track includes dialogue – about a barrel organ imported into the UK in 1865, and restored during the 1960s. The sleeve shows a lovely drawing by Angrave of a Heath Robinson–type contraption called a "Pianolautomaticarillopolyphorganenmatical box". The barrel organ is an Imhof & Muckle, No. 2296, purchased by Angrave in Portobello in the 1960s in ruinous condition and lovingly renovated.

SDL 154   VARIOUS ARTISTS: Texas – Louisiana Blues

New Road Blues (Lonnie Williams)	Ground Hog Blues (Lil' Son Jackson)
Tears in My Heart (Lonnie Williams)	Evil Blues (Lil' Son Jackson)
Single Man Blues (Frankie Lee Sims)	Cairo Blues (Lil' Son Jackson)
Don't Forget Me Baby (Frankie Lee Sims)	Rainy Morning Blues (Country Jim)
I Want My Mary (Alex Moore)	Avenue Breakdown (Country Jim)
Miss No Good Weed (Alex Moore)	Mountain Key (Jesse Thomas)
Sam's Comin' Home (Suitcase Johnson)	Same Old Stuff (Jesse Thomas)
T. P. Railer (Black Diamond)	Zetter Blues (Jesse Thomas)

Release date:
Side 1 has an incorrect matrix in the runoff groove, "SDL 134", with the "3" lightly scratched out and "5" added even more lightly; the matrix on side 2 is a stamped "SD 154" with the "L" added in 'freehand'. At least one odd UK test pressing exists in plain white sleeve, but with American stock labels glued over white labels with track details and the catalogue number H–103 (US Highway label). US issue miscredits *Cairo Blues* as "Cario Blues".

---

155   UNKNOWN

33SD 156   DAVE & TIM: Sheep (7" EP)

Robert E. Lee	Joe Collett
For the Evening	Memory Book

Release date: 1968
Picture sleeve designed by Tim Clutterbuck. Plays at 33⅓. Third label design in dark red. Sleeve includes the sub credit, "With the Downsiders". Dave and Tim became better known on the folk scene as Mudge and Clutterbuck.

---

157   UNKNOWN

SD 158   MECHANICAL MUSIC: The Street Piano (7" EP)

Colonel Bogey	Won't You Come Home Bill Bailey
Roamin' in the Gloamin'	Put Me Amongst the Girls
I Belong to Glasgow	At Trinity Church I Met My Doom

Release date: 1971 (prob. denotes a repromotion)
Subtitled "A New Selection of Popular Songs". 7" 45rpm EP in picture sleeve. Originally released on the generic label design. Later available on the short–lived third label design with record and track credits. All music from a 48 note Chiappa Ltd. street piano, with music marked and arranged by A. Tomasso, London, from the Mickleburgh collection, Bristol ('played' by Roy Mickleburgh).

SDM 159   IAN ANDERSON, MIKE COOPER: The Inverted World

One Time Blues (Mike Cooper)	Cottonfield Blues (Ian Anderson with Elliot Jackson)
Few Short Lines (Mike Cooper)	West Country Blues (Ian Anderson)
Send Me to the 'Lectric Chair (Mike Cooper)	Don't You Want to Go (Ian Anderson)
The Way I Feel (Mike Cooper)	Big Road Blues (Ian Anderson with Elliot Jackson)
Good Book Teach You (Mike Cooper)	Little Queen of Spades (Ian Anderson)
The Inverted World (Mike Cooper/Ian Anderson)	Tom Rushen Blues (Ian Anderson with Elliot Jackson)
	Beedle Um Bum (Anderson, Jones, Jackson)

Release date: 1968
White label test pressings known to exist. LP made up of tracks previously released on three EPs (33SD 125, 33SD 134 and SD 137) plus some extra tracks naughtily recorded after both had been signed elsewhere.

160	UNKNOWN

SDL 161   VARIOUS ARTISTS: Georgia Guitar 1927–38

Going Down In Galilee (Swing Along With Me) (Kokomo Arnold)
Something's Hot (Kokomo Arnold)
It Just Won't Hay (Barbecue Bob)
It's Just Too Bad (Barbecue Bob)
Poor Stranger Blues (Fred McMullen)
It's a Good Little Thing (Blind Willie McTell)
Cold Country Blues (Buddy Moss)

My Baby Don't Pay Me No Mind (Buddy Moss)
Stop Hanging Around (Buddy Moss)
Sugar Mama Blues no. 2 (Tampa Red)
Black Angel Blues (Tampa Red)
No No Blues (Curley Weaver)
Penitentiary Bound Blues (Sylvester Weaver)
Devil Blues (Sylvester Weaver)
Black Spider Blues (Sylvester Weaver)

Release date: either 1968 or 1969
White label test pressings with "SDL" matrix numbers known to exist.

SDL 162   MIKE ABSALOM: Save the Last Gherkin for Me!

Interflora Angel
Special Agent
On the Train to Huddersfield
Church St. Blues
That Friend of Mine
Devonshire Mushrooms

The Actress and the Bishop and Me
English Love Song
Pillow Chat
Confusion
Laura the Leg
One Time Blues

Release date: 1969
White label test pressings known to exist. Includes Diz Disley. All tracks published by Matchbox Music. According to the sleeve notes, this was recorded at Matchbox Studios, London...AKA Mike Absalom's front room!

SDR 163   KOKOMO ARNOLD: Kokomo Arnold

Tired of Running from Door To Door
Kid Man Blues (unknown acc.)
The Twelves
Midnight Blues (unknown acc.)
Big Leg Mama (John Russel Blues)
Your Ways and Actions (unknown acc.)
I'll Be Up Someday Black Annie

Back on the Job (with Peetie Wheetstraw)
Set Down Gal (with prob. Peetie Wheetstraw)
Southern Railroad Blues
Big Ship Blues (with prob. Peetie Wheetstraw)
Busy Bootin'
Slop Jar Blues

Release date: 1969

SDL 164   ERIC JORDAN: The Loughborough Carillon

Londonderry Air
Preludium voor Klokkenspiel
Andante
Drink to Me Only
Nocturne

Berceuse from Jocelyn
Softly Awakes My Heart
Die Lorelei
Poem
Extemporization
Humoresque
Tempo di Gavotta and Double (extract)

Release date: 1969
Subtitled "Bells of Britain Vol Two". The last piece is played by Peter Stratfold.

165	UNKNOWN

166	UNKNOWN

SDM 167   VARIOUS ARTISTS: Blues Like Showers of Rain Volume Two

Stop Breaking Down (Simon & Steve)
It Hurts Me Too (Frances McGillivray)
No Time To Lose (Little Brother Dave)
Maybelle Rag (John James)
Bread of Heaven (Steve Rye)
Whitewash Station (Panama Limited Jug Band)
Rambling Man (Frances McGillivray)
Six Feet In the Ground (Little Brother Dave)
Slow Fast Drag Trot (John James)
Corn Bread, Peas and Black Molasses (Simon & Steve)
Blues Walking Like a Man (Little Brother Dave)
Wildcat Squall (Panama Limited Jug Band)

Release date: Jul/Aug 1968
Subtitled "A compendium of the finest British country blues artists". The Frances McGillivray tracks include a lightly disguised Mikel Kooper on guitar (Mike Cooper was now signed to Pye). Bob Hall of the Brunning Sunflower Band produced the LP. The sleeve notes state that the Roots issues, RL 321, RL323 and RL 324 are all in the Matchbox Blues series.

SDR 168   VARIOUS ARTISTS: Blind Boy Fuller On Down Volume 2

Crow Lane Blues (Julius Daniels)
Walking and Looking Blues (Blind Boy Fuller)
Working Man Blues (Blind Boy Fuller)
Tricks Ain't Working No More (Buddy Moss)
Cross and Evil Woman Blues (Blind Gary Davis)
I'm Throwing Up My Hand (Blind Gary Davis)
Mississippi River (Bull City Red)
Pick & Shovel Blues (Bull City Red)
Love Me With a Feeling (Sonny Jones)
Dough Roller (Sonny Jones)
I'm a Black Woman's Man (Blind Boy Fuller No. 2 [Brownie McGhee] with Bull City Red)
Got to Find My Little Woman (Blind Boy Fuller No. 2 with Bull City Red & Jordan Webb)
Mama Mama Blues (Sleepy Joe's Washboard Band with Ralph Willis & Pete Sanders)
Shake Boogie (Jammin' Jim [Ed Harris])
Lemon Man (Dan Pickett)
Trixie (Curley Weaver)

Release date: August 1969
Subtitled "16 tracks in the Fuller tradition". Accompanying volume to Blind Boy Fuller On Down Vol. 1 (SDR 143), this has performances by both Fuller and those who he influenced. Side 2 matrix has the "R" added in freehand.

SDR 169   SONNY BOY WILLIAMSON, YANK RACHEL, ELIJAH JONES, JOE WILLIAMS: Sonny Boy and His Pals

Tell Me Baby (with Walter Davis & Big Bill Broonzy)
Honey Bee Blues (with Davis & Broonzy)
Decoration Day Blues No. 2 (with Joshua Altheimer & Fred Williams)
Love Me Baby (with Big Bill Broonzy, Blind John Davis & Alfred Elkins)
I'm Gonna Catch You Soon (with Ransom Knowling & Blind John Davis)
Miss Stella Brown Blues (with Davis, Ted Summitt & Armand Jump Jackson)
Desperado Woman Blues (with Davis, Summitt & Jackson)
Lonesome Man Blues (with Elijah Jones, Yank Rachel & unknown acc.)
I'm Wild and Crazy As I Can Be (with Jones & Rachel)
Army Man Blues (with Rachel, William Mitchell & Washboard Sam)
Tappin' That Thing (with Yank Rachel, Alfred Elkins & Washboard Sam)
Worried Blues (with Rachel, Mitchell & Washboard Sam)
.38 Pistol (with Rachel, Mitchell & Washboard Sam)
Vitamin A Blues (with Big Joe Williams & Jump Jackson)

Release date: July 1969
Side 1 label credits Williamson whilst side 2 credits Jones, Rachel and Williams. Original records provided by Dave Williams, Jack Parsons and David Ackling.

SDL 170 ?   Possibly allocated to RL 322 based on the pressing date of the Roots LP

SDL 171   Catalogue number allocated to RL 320

SDL 171 exists as matrix number in the runoff groove of RL 320, *The Great Harmonica Players Volume 1*.

SDL 172   Catalogue number allocated to RL 323

SDL 172 exists as matrix number in the runoff groove of RL 323, *Memphis Blues Vol. 1*.

SDL 173   **MECHANICAL MUSIC: The Golden Age of Mechanical Music – Vol. 6 – Honky–Tonk Nickelodeons**

Yes, We Have No Bananas	Toot, Toot, Tootsie Goodbye
America Forever	Waiting for the Robert E. Lee
Down By the Winegar Woiks	Stars and Stripes Forever
American Patrol	Yankee Dooble Blues
If You Knew Suzie	Yes Sir, That's My Baby
Love Sends a Little Gift of Roses	Five Foot Two, Eyes of Blue
Dixie	Hands Across the Sea
Sweet Georgia Brown	National Emblem March
Swinging Down the Lane	

Release date: 1969
Sleeve has the extra credits, "Seeburg, Cremorna and Empress Electric Orchestras". Music played on Seeburg H Solo Orchestrion, Cremona Orchestral K and Empress Electric Style Y. Original publication date 1967.

SDL 174?   **Possibly allocated to RL 324 based on the pressing date of the Roots LP**

---

175   **See below**
It is most likely that the majority of the unknown SD releases up to and including 215 were allocated to further Roots releases. It is also possible that the first two Ahura Mazda releases were assigned SD numbers, though no pressing cards exist for several Saydisc-pressed Roots LPs or for the first two Ahura Mazda releases.

---

176   **See 175**

33SD 177   **ORGAN MUSIC: Clifton – "Father" Willis 1873–1969 (7" LP)**

Prelude and Fugue in C major (Bach)	"Humoresque" L'Organo Primitivo (Yon)
Presto and Partita alla Lombardo from Toccata in A major (Scarlatti)	Chorale Prelude: "Nun freut euch, lieben Christen g'mein" (Bach)

Release date: 1969
7" 33⅓ rpm LP. Recordings of the organ in Big School, Clifton, played by the Director of Music, Mr. David Pettit.

---

178   **See 175**

---

179   **See 175**

33SD 180?   **Probably allocated to JASS 601 based on JASS 601 pressing date**

SDL 181   **MECHANICAL MUSIC: The Golden Age of Mechanical Music – Vol. 7 – Mechanical Opera**

Now Your Days of Philandering Are Over (Marriage of Figaro)	Overture (Semiramide)
Soldier's Chorus (Faust)	Rossini medley
Toreador's Song (Carmen)	Miscellany
Softly Awakes My Heart (Samson and Delilah)	Salut a la France (La Fille de Regimente)
Do You Know the Land? (Mignon)	Involami (Ernani)
Grand March (Tannhauser), Intermezzo (Cavaleria Rusticana)	Donizetti medley
Tit Willow, etc. (Mikado)	Miscellany
Three Little Maids (Mikado)	Miscellany
The Flowers That Bloom In the Spring (Mikado)	
Poor Wandering One (Pirates of Penzance)	
I Have A Song To Singo (Yeomen of the Guard) / Lord High Executioner (Mikado) / None Shall Part (Iolanthe)	

Release date: 1969
From the Tony Sherriff and Roy Mickleburgh collections. Musical Boxes, Barrel and Street Organs.

SDR 182   VARIOUS ARTISTS: Those Cakewalkin' Babies from Home Vol. 1

Jug Band Blues (Sara Martin with her Jug Band)
Don't You Quit Me Daddy (Sara Martin with her Jug Band)
Long Tall Mama (Bernice Edwards)
Mean Man Blues (Bernice Edwards)
Death Bell Blues (Madlyn Davis with Georgia Tom & Tampa Red)
Gold Tooth Papa Blues (Madlyn Davis with Georgia Tom & Tampa Red)
You're Going To Leave the Old Home, Jim (Lulu Jackson)
I Ain't Givin' Nobody None (Mae Glover with John Byrd)

Red Beans & Rice (Gladys Bentley)
Big Gorilla Man (Gladys Bentley)
Seaboard Blues (Lucille Bogan)
Troubled Mind (Lucille Bogan)
Deceived Blues (Annie Turner with Little Brother Montgomery & Walter Vincson)
Workhouse Blues (Annie Turner with Little Brother Montgomery & Walter Vincson)
I'm Not a Bad Gal (Memphis Minnie with Little Son Joe and unknown acc.)
It Was You, Baby (Memphis Minnie with Little Son Joe and unknown acc.)

Release date: prob. 1969
Subtitled "Country Style". White label test pressings known to exist.

183	*See 175*
184	*See 175*
185	*See 175*
186	*See 175*
187	*See 175*
188	*Probably allocated to a Roots issue (see 175) – but see also SDL 198*
189	*See 175*

SDR 190   FURRY LEWIS: Furry Lewis In Memphis

St. Louis Blues
Furry Lewis' Blues
When I Lay My Burdon Down
Kassie Jones
Going to Brownsville
Skinny Woman

See That My Grave Is Kept Clean
John Henry
Furry Lewis Rag
Careless Love
My Blue Heaven
Old Dog Blue
Spanish Flang Dang
Highway 61
Toast

Release date: prob. 1969
White label test pressings known to exist. Back of sleeve states "Continental issue Roots SL 505".

SDR 191   PEETIE WHEATSTRAW: The Devil's Son In Law (1930–36)

Ain't It a Pity and a Shame (with Charley Jordan)
Don't Hang My Clothes On No Barbed Wire Line (with Jordan)
C. And A. Blues (with Jordan)
Sleepless Nights Blues
Throw Me In the Alley (with Ike Rogers & Henry Brown)
Doing the Best I Can (with Charlie McCoy)
Rising Man Blues (with Will Weldon)
King of Spades (with poss. Jordan)

Letter Writing Blues (with Weldon)
King Spider Blues
Cocktail Man Blues
Last Dime Blues (with poss. Jordan)
Cut Out Blues
First and Last Blues
True Blue Woman
Sweet Home Blues

Release date: 1969
Reissued in 1974 as FLY LP 111 by Flyright Records in a different sleeve design and titled "Peetie Wheatstraw Vol. 1 1930 – 36". The Saydisc cat. no. is scratched out in the runoff with the Flyright catalogue number added.

SDR 192   PEETIE WHEATSTRAW: The High Sheriff from Hell (1936–38)

Low Down Rascal (with Kokomo Arnold)
When I Get My Bonus (with Arnold)
Coon Can Shorty (with Arnold)
The First Shall Be Last (with Arnold)
Deep Sea Love (with Arnold)
Remember and Forget Blues
Don't Take a Chance
Block and Tackle

When a Man Gets Down (unknown acc.)
False Hearted Woman (with Arnold & unknown acc.)
Crapshooters Blues
Sick Bed Blues
I'm Gonna Cut Out Everything (unknown acc.)
Devilment Blues (with unknown acc.)
Truckin' through Traffic (with Lonnie Johnson & unknown acc.)
Sugar Mama (with Johnson & unknown acc.)

Release date: 1969

SDL 193   MECHANICAL MUSIC: The Golden Age of Mechanical Music – Vol. 8 – The Reproducing Piano

Le Papillon op. 43 (Greig)
Ballade in G min op. 23 (Chopin)
The Lark (l'Alouette) (Glinka–Balakirev)
Jardins sous la Pluie (Debussy)
Preludes op. 28 nos. 19 & 20 (Chopin)
Preludes op. 28 nos. 23 & 24 (Chopin)
Seguidillas op. 232 no. 5 (Albeniz)

Polish Dance op. 3 no. 1 (Scharwenka)
Nocturne in Db op. 27 no 2 (Chopin)
Impromptu op 142 no. 2 (Schubert)
Wanda (Nocturne) op. 338 (Bohm)
Gavotte in A (Gluck arr. Brahms)

Release date: 1970

194	*See 175*
195	*See 175*
196	*See 175*
197	*See 175*

SDL 198   BARBECUE BOB: The Georgia Blues Vol. 1

Mississippi Heavy Water Blues
Brown Skin Gal
Waycross Georgia Blues
Going Up the Country
Mississippi Low–Levee Blues
Bad Time Blues
Meat Man Pete
Dollar Down Blues

Red Hot Mama
It's a Funny Little Thing
The Monkey and the Baboon
Darktown Gamblin' – part one
Darktown Gamblin' – part two
Jambooger Blues
It Just Won't Quit
New Mojo Blues

Release date: prob. 1970
White label test press exists with Saydisc matrix. Although the US label credits *Darktown Gamblin'* – *part one* and *Darktown Gamblin'* – *part two* as separate tracks there is no track band between these. The "9" in the matrix is indistinct, so it is possible that this could actually have been issued as SDL 188.

SDR 199   VARIOUS ARTISTS: Skoodle–Um–Skoo: Early Folk Blues Volume 1

I've Got Salvation In My Heart (Stovepipe No. 1)
Lord Don't You Know I Have No Friend Like
    You? (Stovepipe No. 1)
Cripple Creek and Sourwood Mountain – take 1
    (Stovepipe No.1)
Turkey In the Straw (Stovepipe No. 1)
Mama Don't Allow It (and She Ain't Gonna
    Have It Here) (Charlie Jackson)
Take Me Back Blues (Charlie Jackson)
Shave Em Dry (Charlie Jackson)
Coffee Pot Blues (Charlie Jackson)
Skoodle Um Skoo (Charlie Jackson)

Jonestown Blues (Banjo Joe)
Madison Street Rag (Banjo Joe)
Can You Blame the Colored Man (Banjo Joe)
Humming Blues (Joe Joe)
The Kansas City Call (Winston Holmes & Charlie Turner)
Rounders Lament (Winston Holmes & Charlie Turner)
Sheiks Special (Walter Jacobs & the Carter Brothers)
Dear Little Girl (Walter Jacobs & the Carter Brothers)
Champagne Charlie Is My Name (Billy James and His Guitar)

Release date: 1970
Subtitled "The Folk Tradition". White label test pressings known to exist.

200	**See 175**

201	**See 175**

202	**See 175**

33SD 203   **Catalogue number allocated to JASS 602**
33SD 203 exists as matrix number in the runoff groove of JASS 602 (see the "Contract pressings" section).

33SD 204   **Catalogue number allocated to JASS 603**
33SDL 204 exists as matrix number in the runoff groove of JASS 603 (see the "Contract pressings" section).

205	**See 175**

SDR 206   **VARIOUS ARTISTS: Hometown Skiffle: Early Folk Blues Volume 2**

You Shall (Beale Street Sheiks)
Jelly Roll Blues (Excelsior Quartette)
Too Long (Mississippi Sheiks)
She Showed It All (Napoleon Fletcher with
    Roosevelt Sykes & Edith Johnson)
I'm Gonna Get It (Hokum Boys)
Derbytown (Old Ced Odom & Lil 'Diamonds'
    Hardaway)
Hometown Skiffle – Part 1 (Paramount All–Stars)
Hometown Skiffle – Part 2 (Paramount All–Stars)

It's a Good Thing (Beale Street Sheiks)
Kitchen Mechanic Blues (Excelsior Quartet)
Skinner (Winston Holmes & Charlie Turner)
Slave Man Blues (Bumble Bee Slim)
Keep Your Mind On It (Hokum Boys)
Stop Truckin' & Suzi–Q (Tampa Red & the Chicago Five)
Texas Tommy (Yank Rachel with Sonny Boy Williamson
    & 'Jackson' Joe Williams)
Every Time My Heart Beats (The Delta Boys)

Release date: 1970

SDX 207/8   **VARIOUS ARTISTS: Black Diamond Express to Hell**

SDX 207 side 1:
Mother's Prayer (A. C. Forehand with Blind
    Mamie Forehand)
Sit Down Servant (Rev. J. C. Burnett & His
    Gospel Singers)
I've Got a Key to the Kingdom (Blind Willie Davis)
You Got to Walk That Lonesome Valley (Rev.
    F. W McGhee with unknown acc.)
Arise and Shine (Lonnie McIntorsh)
Christ Was Born On Christmas Morn (Cotton
    Top Mountain Sanctified Singers:
    'Half Pint' Jaxon with, prob. Punch
    Miller & unknown acc.)
Now Is the Needy Time (Daniel Brown with
    Tiny Parham & unknown acc.)
Am the Vine (Elder Otis Jones & unknown acc.)

SDX 207 side 2:
I'm So Glad Today, Today (A. C. Forehand
    with Blind Mamie Forehand)
The Angel Done Gone Down (Rev. J. C.
    Burnett & His Gospel Singers: prob.
    Sisters Grainger & Jackson)
I Saw the Light (Bull City Red with Blind Gary
    Davis)
I Want Two Wings To Veil My Face (Cotton
    Top Mountain Sanctified Singers
    ['Half Pint' Jaxon with, prob. Punch
    Johnson & unknown acc.)
How Much I Owe (Lonnie McIntorsh)
Your Enemy Cannot Harm You (Blind Willie Davis)
Beulah Land (Daniel Brown with Tiny Parham and Blind Blake)
I'm On My Way to the Kingdom Land (Bo Weavil Jackson)
When the Saints Come Marching Home (Bo Weavil Jackson)

SDX 208 side 1:
How Long (Rev. Charles White with James Butler
    & unknown acc.)
Laid Down My Burdon (Prophet B. W. West with
    congregation & unknown acc.)
I Want 2 Wings (Rev. Utah Smith with congregation)
God' Mighty Hand (Rev. Utah Smith with congregation)
Stand By Me (Sister Matthews with James Butler)
I'll Fly Away (Rev. B. C. Cambell with congregation &
    unknown acc.)
Heaven Bound Train (Rev. B. C. Cambell with congregation
    & unknown acc.)
We're Gonna Have a Good Time (Gospel Keys: Mother
    Sally Jones & Emma Daniels)

SDX 208 side 2:
I Love Travelling (Two Gospel Keys: see track 8, side 1)
I Want My Crown (Gospel Keys: as above)
What You Want the Lord To Do For You (Goldrock Gospel
    Singers)
Jesus Is With Me (Goldrock Gospel Singers)
Jesus Loves Us All (Rev. A, Johnson with unknown acc.)
I Don't Know How to Get Along Without the Lord (Rev. A.
    Miller & unknown acc.)
This Way (The Gospel Twins – no details known)
One Word (The Gospel Twins)

Release date: 1970
Double LP in single sleeve. White label test pressings known to exist.

SDL 209   MECHANICAL MUSIC: Piston Polka

Old Comrades March
Beer Barrel Polka
La Reve Passe (Soldier's Dream March)
With a Little Bit of Luck
Spoonful of Sugar
Piston Polka
Our Director
Let's Twist Again / Lily the Pink /
      Congratulations

Boccaccio Waltz
Al Jolson Medley – 8 tunes including: Dixie Melody / California
Here I Come / Me and My Gal / The Best Things In Life Are
      Free / Lullaby of Broadway / 23rd Street
Robert E. Lee
Dixieland Medley – 12 tunes including: Alexander's Rag Time
      Band / Dina / Great Big Beautiful Doll / Dixie / Sheik
      of Araby / Everybody's Doing It / That Mysterious
      Rag / Whistlin' Rufus
This Is My Song
The Last Waltz
Puppet on a String

Release date: 1970
Volume 9 in *The Golden Age of Mechanical Music* series. Music played on a 67 key, 5 register Carl Frei Dutch Street Organ.

SDL 210   I'll Dance Till De Sun Breaks Through

Alabama Skedaddle (Xylophone solo by William
      Mitcham)
I'll Dance Till De Sun Breaks Through (Archibald
      Joyce & his Orchestra)
That Mysterious Rag (Robert Carr–Jack–
      Charman–Herbert Cove with banjo by
      Olly Oakley & piano acc.)
Dill Pickles Hot Stuff Ragtime (Scala Military
      Band)
Whistling Rufus (Banjo solo by Olly Oakley,
  with piano acc. by Landon Ronald)
Unidentified Cake–Walk (from blank labelled 7",
      c. 1903)
From Soup to Nuts (Piano solo by Felix Arndt)
That Moaning Saxophone Rag (Six Brown
      Brothers – Saxophone Sextet)
Black Diamond Rag (Prince's Orchestra)

Stomp Dance (Victor Military Band)
The Cake–Walk (The Victor Minstrels)
Smoky Mokes (Metropolitan Orchestra)
Calico Rag (Piano solo by Frank E. Banta, with drums by
      Howard Kopp)
Two–Key Rag (Conway's Band)
Ragtime Frolics (Xylophone solo by Mr. R. White, with
      orchestra)
Alexander's Ragtime Band (Arthur Collins, Byron G. Harlan,
      with orchestra)
Eli Green's Cake Walk (Banjo duet by Cullen & Collins)
Bacchanal Rag (The Peerless Orchestra)
Grizzly Bear (Jack Chairman, Walter Miller, with banjo by
      Olly Oakley & piano acc.)

Release date: c1971
Subtitled "Ragtime, Cakewalks and Stomps vol. 2" and "1898–1917".

SDL 211   BELLS: Rhythm of The Bells

Six bells being raised in peal (Nunburnholme)
Grandsire Doubles without a cover bell (Norton)
Grandsire Doubles with a cover bell (Norton)
Stedman Doubles with a cover bell (Norton)
Call changes on six bells (Norton)
Plain Bob Minor (Norton)
Lowering six bells in peal (Nunburnholme)

Call Changes on eight bells (Howden)
Grandsire Triples (Howden)
Grandsire Triples (Norton)
Plain Bob Major (Howden)
Stedman Caters on the bells of Washington Cathedral, U.S.A.

Release date: 1970 / May 1979 (MM84)
Subtitled "Examples of good ringing". Produced for the Central Council of Church Bell Ringers but also marketed nationally by Saydisc. On a slightly modified label that looked more like those on records issued in the CP series. MM84 release date represents a repromotion: several more bell ringing records were repromoted in May 1979.

SDL 212   MECHANICAL MUSIC: The Limonaire Fair Organ

Track listing unknown

Release date: c1971
Recorded and marketed by A. Finbow, Stowmarket, Suffolk

SDR 213   LITTLE BROTHER MONTGOMERY: Little Brother Montgomery 1930–1969

No Special Rider Blues
Vicksburg Blues (1930)
Louisiana Blues (acc. prob. Minnie Hicks)
Frisco Hi–Ball Blues
Something Keeps a–Worrying Me
Chinese Man Blues New
Louisiana Blues part 2
Muleface Rag
Cow Cow Blues

Vicksburg Blues (c. 1954)
In the Evening (Little Brother Montgomery & His Jazz Blues Band)
Michigan Water Blues
Winding Ball Blues
Vicksburg Blues (Jeanne Carroll with the Little Brother Montgomery Trio)
Brother Red's Boogie (Little Brother Montgomery Trio)

Release date: 1971
Sleeve by Plastic Dog from photos supplied by Little Brother Montgomery. Issued outside the UK in the same sleeve design as the Roots label LP, *Rare Recordings 1930 – 1969* (RSE 3).

214	See 175

215	See 175

SDR 216   CLYDE BERNHARDT: Blowing My Top

Baby Tell Me
Jail House Blues
Cracklin' Bread
Daisy Mae
Hey Miss Bertha
Barron Boogie
Blowing My Top
It's Been a Long Time Baby
Perdido

Indiana
After Hours Blues
Don't You Think I Ought to Know
Sweet, Sweet Mama Blues
Don't Leave Me Baby
You Excite Me
Ode To Billy Joe
The Saints

Release date: 1971
Subtitled "The All Star Bands of Clyde Bernhardt". White label test pressings known to exist. Tracks 1 & 2 Bernhardt, Bill Campbell, Cecil Scott, Nathaniel Cross, Joe Scott & Slick Jones; 3 – 8 Ed Barron and His Orchestra; 10 – 17 Bernhardt, Earl Knight, Snags 'Napoleon' Allen, Thomas Barney & Sammie Scott.

SDL 217   FRANK EVANS: Stretching Forth

Thunderstruck
Dear Bill
Prince Meets Princess

Junk Shop
I Dreamt I Dwelt In New Orleans
Dear Mary K.
The Bistro Kid

Release date: 1971
With Dave Olney on bass and Ian Hobbs on drums. Track 1 is so called because it was recorded at The Barton in between power cuts caused by a heavy thunderstorm.

SD(SAM) 218   MECHANICAL MUSIC: The Golden Age of Mechanical Music

Piston Polka (Carl Frei Dutch Street Organ)
La Malchiche – March Espagnole (22" Polyphon)
Flow Gently Sweet Afton (Roller Barrel Organ)
America Forever (Empress Electric Style Y
The Blind Irish Girl and Cruiskeen Lawn
        (Orpheus Disc Piano)
Medley (Nicole Frere Forte Piano Musical Box)
Mammy Jinny's Jubilee (Automatic Harp)
Bold Gendarmes (Penny Piano)
In the Gloaming (Small Capital Musical Box) /
        Estudiantina Waltz (27" Regina M. Box)

Vienna Hearts – March (22" Polyphon)
Columbia Gem of the Ocean (Mandolin Quartet)
Rose of the Rio Grande – Foxtrot (Weber Grand Electric
        Reproducing Piano)
Example (Paillard Vaucher Fils Musical Box)
Flallergeister Waltzer (Imhof & Muckle Barrel Organ)
A Wandering Minstrel I (48 Note Street Piano)
Waiting for the Robert E. Lee (Seeburg H. Solo Orchestrion)
Blue Danube Waltz (Nicole Frere Table Model Musical Box)
Magnet and the Churn / God Save the Queen (Cabinetto
        Paper Roll Organ)

Release date: 1971
Sampler LP of new recordings and previously issued pieces from SDL 209, SDL 151 and SDL 173). Sold at 99p with the price printed on the sleeve – some sleeves overprinted with the text off–centre. Also pressed and distributed in the US by Ahura Mazda as SD 218 for the budget price of $4.98 (price also printed on the sleeve). From the Roy Mickleburgh, Tony Sherriff, Bruce Angrave, Hathaway and Bowers, and A. E. Showering collections.

SDX 219   NATURE: Antarctica

Ice movement	Rough seas
Emperor Penguins	Fur Seals
Blizzard	Cormorants
Spring	Elephant Seals
Weddell Seals	Snow Petrels
Adelie Penguins	Cape Pigeons
Skuas	Giant Petrel
	Prions, Wilson's Petrels
	Huskies

Release date: 1971
CD: CD–SDL 219
Subtitled "A Portrait in Wildlife and Natural Sound", this was a lavish set in gatefold sleeve with a 24 page booklet. Recordings from the British Antarctic Survey 1968–1971: recordings and booklet by Edwin Mickleburgh.

SDL 220   RAILWAY RECORDING: Great Western In Gloucestershire

Side 1 – Coleford Branch

0–6–0 PT. No. 3775
0–6–0 PT. No. 4689

Side 2 – Cheltenham Area

Band 1. 2–6–2T No. 4564; 'Castle' No. 7014, Caerhays Castle; 'Castle' No. 5089, Westminster Abbey; 'Grange' No. 6860, Aberporth Grange; 'Hall' No. 6999, Capel Dewi Hall; 'Hall' No. 7925, Westol Hall.
Band 2. 'Manor' No. 7816, Frilsham Manor; 2–6–2T No. 6160; 0–6–0PT No. 3775; 2–8–0 No. 3832.
Band 3. 0–4–2T No. 1440; 0–4–2T No. 1445.
Band 4. 'King' No. 6009, King Charles II; 2–8–0 No. 4706.

Release date: 1971 / Nov. 1980 (MM89)
Cassette: CSDLB 220 (Nov. 1980: MM89)   **CD:** CD–SDL 220
Recorded by Peter Duddridge. Recording information: 3775 & 4689 (5/11/65 & 12/10/65); 3775 (no date); 4564, 7014, 5089, 6860, 6999 & 7925 (6/11/63, 29/8/63, 6/7/63, & 7/8/65); 7816, 6160, 3775 & 3832 (21/10/65 & 23/11/65); 1440 & 1455 (8/8/63); 6009 & 4706 (15/12/61). By the time of the 1980 pressing the LP catalogue number had been changed to SDLB 220.

SDL 221   THE BANDS OF JIM EUROPE & ARTHUR PRYOR: Too Much Mustard

Memphis Blues	Slippery Place Rag
That Moaning Trombone	Georgia Sunset Cake–Walk
Hesitating Blues	Temptation Rag
Too Much Mustard	The African 400 (An Educated Rag)
Down Home Rag	The Ragtime Drummer
Indianola	The Ragtime Drummer (again)
The Darktown Strutters' Ball	That Rag
	The King of Rags
	Canhanibalmo Rag

Release date: c1972 / April 1981 (MM89)
CD: CD–SDL 221
Subtitled "Ragtime, Cakewalk & Stomps Vol. 3". Original copies in laminated sleeve, April 1981 copies are in non–laminated glossy sleeve. Later copies also have a glossier–finish label. Lt. Jim Europe's 369th Infantry ('Hell–Fighters') Band play on tracks 1 – 3, 6 & 7. Europe's Society Orchestra play on tracks 4 & 5. The Victory Military Band (with Pryor) play on track 8. Arthur Pryor's Band play on tracks 9 – 16.

SDL 222   SPOKEN WORD: Cotswold Characters

Miss Amy Cook of Coombe, Wotton–under–Edge	Fred Archer of Ashton–under–Hill
The late Mrs. Emily Elliott, of Frampton Mansell	The late Ned Wheeler of Lower Swell
Don and Lionel Ellis, of Chipping Campden	Mr. William Worthy Crew and the late Mrs. Mary Crew
	Howard Pritchett of Bibury

Release date: 1972
Cassette: CSDL 222   **CD:** CD–SDL 222
White label test pressing in plain white sleeve with wraparound proof sleeve known to exist. Stories, dialect and reminiscences from old people of the Cotswolds, recorded by, and with interviews by, Peter Duddridge.

SDM 223   LITTLE BROTHER MONTGOMERY: Home Again

Lonesome Mama Blues
Tremblin' Blues
Aggravatin' Blues (with Jan Montgomery)
No Special Boogie
Jan
St. Louis Blues

Home Again Blues
Dangerous Blues (with Jan Montgomery)
Up the Country
I Was So In Love With You (with Jan Montgomery)
History of Little Brother
After You've Gone (with Jan Montgomery)

Release date: 1972
Textured sleeve. Subtitled "Chicago 1972". Jan Montgomery receives a sub–credit on the sleeve.

SDM 224   VARIOUS ARTISTS: The Legacy of Tommy Johnson

Big Road Blues (Isaac Youngblood & Herb Quinn)
Bye and Bye Blues (Mager Johnson)
Maggie Campbell Blues (Arzo Youngblood)
Canned Heat Blues (John Henry 'Bubba' Brown)
Cool Water Blues (Boogie Bill Webb)
Big Fat Mama Blues (Arzo Youngblood)
Pony Blues (Houston Stackhouse & Carey 'Ditty' Mason)

I Believe I'll Make Everything All Right (Arzo Youngblood)
Show Me What You Got For Sale (Boogie Bill Webb)
Prison Bound Blues (Arzo Youngblood)
Maggie Campbell Blues (Boogie Bill Webb)
The Old Folks Doing It and the Little Ones Trying (Arzo Youngblood)
Big Road Blues (Babe Stovall, O. D. Jones & Dink Brister)
Take Your Time (Boogie Bill Webb)
Pine Top Boogie (Roosevelt Holts)
Don't You Lie To Me (Boogie Bill Webb)

Release date: 1972
Textured sleeve. White label test pressings known to exist. All tracks are songs that were in Tommy Johnson's repertoire, and all were learned by the artists here from Johnson himself.

SDM 225   VARIOUS ARTISTS: Big Road Blues

Pick and Shovel Blues (Mott Willis)
So Soon I'll Be Home (Robert Johnson)
Dresser Drawer Blues (Mott Willis)
Unknown track
Riverside Blues (Mott Willis)
Travelling Man Blues (Mager Johnson)
Mama Do Right (Willis Taylor and Mott Willis)

Maggie Campbell Blues (Roosevelt Holts)
Trashy Gang Blues (Willis Taylor and Mott Willis)
Catfish Blues (Cary Lee Simmons)
Big Road Blues (Arzo Youngblood)
Who Is That Yonder Coming Down the Road (Mott Willis)
Moustache Blues (Mager Johnson)
It Ain't Gonna Rain No More (Mott Willis)
Sundown Blues (Roosevelt Holts)
Bad Night Blues (Mott Willis)

Release date: prob. 1972
White label test pressing in plain, white sleeve known to exist, though no pressing card at Saydisc may suggest that this was not subsequently released.

SDM 226   VARIOUS ARTISTS: Blues from the Delta

Cairo Blues (James 'Son' Thomas)
Bottle Up and Go (Lee Kizart)
Big Fat Momma (Scott Dunbar)
Rootin' Ground Hog (Lovey Williams)
Rock Me Momma (James 'Son' Thomas)

Train I Ride (Lovey Williams)
It's So Cold Up North (Scott Dunbar)
Don't Want No Woman Telling Me What To Do (Lee Kizart)
Jay Bird (Scott Dunbar)

Release date: 1972
White label test pressings known to exist. Compiled by William Ferris Junior (Bill Ferris) to accompany his book, *Blues From the Delta* (November Books, London).

SDM 227   VIOLA WELLS: Miss Rhapsody

Down Hearted Blues
How Great Thou Art
See, See Rider
In the Garden
Brown Gal

His Eye Is On the Sparrow
Blues in My Heart
Power In the Blood
I Fell For You
Face to Face
Old Fashioned Love

Release date: 1972
Textured sleeve. Recorded April 22, 1972, in New York with Reuben Jay Cole, Danny Gibson, Ivan Rolle, Eddie Wright and Mrs. Grace Gregory.

SDL 228   CLYDE BERNHARDT & HIS HARLEM BLUES & JAZZ BAND: Blues and Jazz from Harlem

Good Rolling Blues
After You've Gone
Georgia On Your Mind
Lazy River

Triflin' Woman Blues
Sugar Blues
Nobody's Sweetheart
There'll Be Some Changes Made

Release date: 1972
With Charlie Holmes, Happy Caldwell, Jacques Butler, Earl Knight, Napoleon 'Snags' Allen, Jimmy Shirley and James Harewood.

SDM 229   FRANKLIN GEORGE & JOHN SUMMERS: Traditional Music for Banjo, Fiddle and Bagpipes

Londonderry Hornpipe
Boatsman (George)
Angeline (George & P. Dunford)
Pipe Medley 1: Wearing of the Green / All the
    Way to Galway
Medley: Wake Up Susan / Devil's Dream
    (with P. Dunford)
Salt River (George)
Rickett's Hornpipe (George)
Teetotaler (George)

Old Molly Hare (George & P. Dunford)
Pipe Medley II: Minstrel Boy / O'Donnell Abu (George)
Turkey In the Straw (George)
Fiddle Collection: Forked Horn Deer / Fisher's Hornpipe /
    Round Town Girls / Top of Cork Road / Arkansas
    Traveler
Cumberland Gap (George)
Nancy Ann (George)
Grey Eagle (George)
Mississippi Sawyer (with P. Dunford)

Release date: 1972
Subtitled "Matchbox Country Series Vol. 2" (Vol. 1 had an earlier release date, but a later catalogue number – SDM 231). White label test pressings known to exist. Originally released in the US on the Kanawha label with the catalogue number KANAWHA 307. UK Sleeve incorporates original design with additions by Plastic Dog.

SDM 230   VARIOUS ARTISTS: Mississippi River Blues

Lonesome Highway Blues (Lucious Curtis &
    Willie Ford with John Lomax speaking)
Guitar Picking Song (Lucious Curtis)
High Lonesome Hill (Lucious Curtis & Willie Ford)
Pay Day (Willie Ford)
Train Blues (Lucious Curtis)
Mississippi River Blues (Lucious Curtis & Willie
    Ford)
Stagolee (Lucious Curtis & Willie Ford)

Farmin' Man Blues (Lucious Curtis & Willie Ford)
Nobody's Business (Willie Ford)
Santa 'Field' Blues (Willie Ford with John Lomax speaking)
Sto' Gallery Blues (Willie Ford & Lucious Curtis)
Rubber Ball Blues (Lucious Curtis & Willie Ford)
Country Girl Blues (George Boldwin);
Time Is Gettin' Hard (Lucious Curtis & Willie Ford)

Release date: prob. 1972
Subtitled "Flyright – Matchbox Library of Congress Series: Volume One". White label test pressings known to exist. Field recordings from Natchez, Mississippi, Saturday 19 October, 1940. Field recordings by John Avery Lomax and Ruby Terril Lomax. The tracks that make up this record are analysed and discussed in *Blues World* (No. 38, Spring 1971) in the article *Natchez, Mississippi Blues*, by Bob Groom. The journal predates this UK release.

SDM 231   CLARK KESSINGER: Clark Kessinger Live at Union Grove

Trombone Rag
Dill Pickle Rag
Rose of My Heart Waltz
Round Town Girl
Whistling Rufus
Sally Goodin
Durang's Hornpipe

Arkansas Traveller
Old Joe Clark
Down Yonder
Turkey in the Straw
Golden Slippers
Billy in the Lowground
Poca River Blues

Release date: 1972
This was the first release in the Matchbox Country Series (Vol. 2 had a later release date, despite an earlier catalogue number – SDM 229). Textured sleeve. Also includes Gene Meade, guitar & Gene Parker, banjo. Originally released in the US on Kessenger's small Kanawha label with the catalogue number KANAWHA 312.

SDL 232   MECHANICAL MUSIC: Mechanical Music Hall

Miscellany:
  Burlington Bertie from Bow (A)
  After the Ball (B)
  Nellie Dean (C)
  Where Did You Get That Hat? (D)
  The Man Who Broke the Bank at Monte Carlo (E)
  K. K. K. Katie (A)
Florrie Ford:
  Flanagan (C)
  Hold Your Hand Out Naughty Boy (A)
  Down at the Old Bull and Bush (F)
Eugene Stratton:
  Lily of Laguna (G)
Miscellany:
  If It Wasn't For the 'Ouses In Between (A)
  Won't You Come Home Bill Bailey (C)
  I Do Like to Be Beside the Seaside (F)
  Ask a Policeman (D)
  Don't Have Any More, Mrs. Moore (A)
Tom Costello:
  The Ship I Love (H)
  The Ship I Love (G)
  Comrades (A)
Ellaline Terris:
  Honeysuckle and the Bee (H)
  Honeysuckle and the Bee (I)

Harry Champion:
  Any Old Iron (A)
  Boiled Beef and Carrots (A)
Miscellany:
  Cool Burgundy Ben (J)
  Just a Wee Deock and Doris (A)
  Little Dolly Daydream (I)
  Our Lodger's Such a Nice Young Man (H)
  Sister Mary Walked Like That (E)
  A Broken Doll (C)
Albert Chevalier:
  Knocked 'Em In the Old Kent Road (D)
  My Old Dutch (A)
  My Old Dutch (K)
  My Old Dutch (F)
Marie Lloyd:
  When You Wink the Other Eye (D)
  My Old Man Said Follow the Van (L)
  Wiggy Voo (H)
  The Boy I Love Is Up In the Gallery (A)
Lottie Collins:
  Ta Ra Boom De Ay (D)
  Ta Ra Boom De Ay (A)
Leo Dryden:
  Miner's Dream of Home (E)
  Miner's Dream of Home (H)
Miscellany:
  The Daring Young Man On the Flying Trapeze (A)
  Not for Joseph (J)
  Alexander's Ragtime Band (C)

Release date: 1972
Cassette: CSDL 232 (April 1981: MM89)   **CD:** CD–SDL 232 (prob. Feb. 1992: SC)
Subtitled "Saydisc's Golden Age Of Mechanical Music Volume 10". Musical Automata from the Roy Mickleburgh collection. White label test pressings known to exist. A = Keith Prowse 'Pennyano' 48 note 'penny in the slot' piano (penny piano), probably made by Chiappa; B = Excelsior Piccolo Musical Box, 12 air, 2 comb; C = 48 note Street Piano marked by Angelo Tomasso; D = 12 air cylinder Musical Box; E = Orpheus Disc Piano; F = Player Piano; G = 24½" disc Polyphon Musical Box; H = 15½" disc Regina Musical Box; I = 9½" disc Polyphon Musical Box; J = 12 air, 2 comb cylinder Musical Box with Bells; K = 10⅝" disc Symphonion Musical Box; L = 44 note Street Piano, possibly made by Rossie, marked by Angelo Tomasso.

SDL 233   THE FRANK EVANS CONSORT: In an English Manner

Summer Song
Greensleeves
Ayre by Purcell
In an English Manner
Pavane – 'Lady Long of Wraxall'
Bouree

Bach Double Violin Concerto, 1st Movement
Scarborough Fair
The Girl with the Flaxen Hair
Longing for Baia
Bach 2 Part Invention in D Minor
A Pastoral Scene
Air From the Suite No. 3 in D

Release date: 1972
CD: CD–SDL 233
White label test pressings known to exist. Arrangements and transcription by Frank Evans. Also includes Graham Sothcott, Ian Hobbs and Ian McTier. Four tracks are accompanied by the Barton String Quartet (a pseudonym for the Dartington String Quartet). There's a play on words in the title – the music is inspired by an English manor house at Wraxall, north Somerset. *Summer Song* with a shimmering backdrop from the Barton String Quartet is possibly the most wonderful single piece of music to come out of Saydisc.

SDL 234   MECHANICAL MUSIC: Parry's Barrel Organ

God Save the King / March in Blue Beard / Duke of York's March / Minuet by Vandermere (Barrel No. 4)

Lady Montgomery's Reel / Miss Murray's Strathspey / Paddy O'Rafferty / The Chartreuse (Barrel No. 4)

Devil Amongst the Taylors / Fife Hunt / Lord McDonald's Reel / Mrs. Gordon of Troop (Barrel No. 3)

La Conservatoire / Ramah Droog / Speed the Plough (Barrel No. 3)

Two unidentified titles (Barrel No. 5)

100th Psalm / Morning Hymn / Sicilian Mariners / Portuguese (Adeste Fideles) (Barrel No. 2)

Stowr Lodge /Mdm. Hillingbury / Lord Howis Reel / Highlandman – Reel / Polly Put the Kettle On (Barrel No. 1)

Evening Hymn / German Hymn / 36th Psalm / 104th Psalm (Barrel No. 2)

Three unidentified titles (Barrel No. 5)

Release date: 1973
CD: CD–SDL 234
Subtitled "Golden Age of Mechanical Music Volume 11". Includes insert.

SDM 235   GEORGE PEGRAM: George Pegram

Mississippi Sawyer
Workin' On a Building
Little Old Log Cabin In the Lane
John Henry
Where Could I Go But to the Lord
Wildwood Flower
Never Grow Old

Reubin
What a Friend We Have In Jesus
Over the Waves Waltz
Johnson's Old Grey Mule
In the Sweet Bye and Bye
Are You Washed in the Blood?
Just Because

Release date: 1973
Volume 3 in the *Matchbox Country Music Series*. Textured sleeve. White label test pressings known to exist. UK reissue of Rounder 0001. The Saydisc master list states that the prefix is "SDL" though the prefix is confirmed as "SDM". George Pegram, Clyde Isaacs, Fred Cockerham and Jack Bryant.

SDM 236   JOE VAL AND THE NEW ENGLAND BLUEGRASS BOYS: One Morning In May

Comin' On Strong
Live and Let Live
the Little Paper Boy
Do You Live What You Preach?
My Brother's Will
Where the Old Red River Flows

I Don't Believe You've Met My Baby
Dark Hollow
Come Walk With Me
One Morning In May
Ginger Brandy
What Can I Do
Sparkling Brown Eyes

Release date: 1973
Volume 4 in the *Matchbox Country Music Series*. Textured sleeve. White label test pressings known to exist. UK issue of Rounder 0003 – Includes US matrix number in runoff. Joe Val, Herb Applin, Bob French and Bob Tidwell.

SDM 237   UNKNOWN: Test pressing exists

9 unknown tracks

10 unknown tracks

Release date: see below
White label test pressing exists with K 4390/K 4416 and ST 81370 scratched out on the runoff, so most likely licensed from Kanawha, Kokomo or Rounder. Despite there being a test pressing, no pressing card at Saydisc may suggest that this was not subsequently released.

SDM 238   SNUFFY JENKINS & PAPPY SHERRILL: 33 Years of Pickin' and Pluckin'

Texas Quickstep
Mountain Top/Shout Lulu
Run, Boy, Run
Cherry Blossom Waltz
I Want My Rib
Alabama Jubilee
Nancy Rowland
Milk Cow Blues
Fifty Year Ago Waltz
Kansas City Kitty

C & NW Railroad Blues
Lonesome Road Blues
Shortenin' Bread
Model T. Blues
Coney Island
Beaumont Rag
When the Bumble Bee Backed Up to Me and Pushed
Dreamy Georgia Moon
Aunt Liza's Favourite
Wagoner

Release date: 1973
Volume 5 in the *Matchbox Country Music Series*. Textured sleeve. White label test pressings known to exist. UK reissue of Rounder 0005 – UK press still includes US matrix number in the runoff groove. Snuffy Jenkins, banjo, washboard, guitar; Pappy Sherrill, fiddle; Dick Harmon, guitar; Buddy Harmon, bass; Greasy Medlin, guitar, vocals.

SDM 239   *HAPPY TRAUM, ARTIE TRAUM, MARIA MULDAUR, JOHN HERALD, ERIC KAZ, JIM ROONEY, BILL KEITH, TONY BROWN, LEE BERG: Mud Acres – Music Among Friends*

Cowpoke
Done Laid Around
Darlin' Corey Is Gone
Titanic
Give Me Back My Fifteen Cents
Out of Joint
Jackhammer Blues
Oh, the Rain
Hobo Blues
Off to Sea Once More
Fifteen Miles to Birmingham
Out!
Lonesome Pines
Prison Wall Blues
Parting Friends
Mud Acres

Release date: 1973
Volume 6 in the *Matchbox Country Music Series*. A white label test pressing exists with ROUNDER 0011, 3001 and 17163 scratched out on the runoff. The Saydisc master list states that the catalogue prefix is "SDL", though the matrix on white label test pressing has a "SDM" prefix in line with Saydisc's policy for Matchbox releases. The US Rounder issue credits "Happy Traum, Artie Traum, Maria Muldaur, John Herald, Eric Kaz, Jim Rooney, Bill Keith, Tony Brown, Lee Berg" though it is unknown if the Saydisc issue includes the same credits. The Rounder issue has 8 track credits on side 2 but only 7 banded tracks.

SDL 240   *PHILOMUSICA OF GLOUCESTERSHIRE: Homage to Vaughan Williams*

The Old Hundredth Psalm Tune (All People that on Earth Do Dwell)
Adagio from concerto for violin in D minor
Magnificat for Contralto Solo and Women's Voices
Linden Lea
The Call from Five Mystical Songs
Whither Must I Wander from Songs of Travel
The Vagabond from Songs of Travel
Excerpt from Dona Nobis Pacem

Release date: 1973
Recorded in Down Ampney Church.

SDM 241   *HOLLOW ROCK STRING BAND: Hollow Rock String Band*

Kitchen Girl
Clog
Waltz
Dinah
Richmond Cotillion
Hog–Eyed Man
Medley: John Brown's March / Green Fields of America / Hop Light Ladies
Jawbones
Betty Likens
Cabin Creek
Folding Down the Sheets
Money Musk
Devil On a Stump
Over the Waterfall
Fiddler's Drunk and the Fun's All Over

Release date: 1973
Subtitled "Matchbox Country Music Series Vol. 8". Textured sleeve. White label test pressings known to exist. Fifteen traditional instrumental tunes, most of which were learned from Henry Reed with Alan Jabbour, Bert Levy, Bobbie Thompson and Tommy Thompson. Previously issued in the US on Kanawha as KANAWHA 311.

SDM 242   *CURLY HERDMAN: Fiddler*

Turkey In the Straw
Rachael
Moonlight Waltz
Old Joe Clark
Meigs County Reel
Under the Double Eagle
Run Rabbit Run
Dixie Howdown
Running Bear
Big Tracy
Billy In the Low Ground
Rocus's Reel

Release date: 1973
Subtitled "Matchbox Country Music Series Vol. 7". Textured sleeve, which includes Rodney Matthews' hardly used 'matchbox' logo. White label test pressings known to exist. Curly Herdman, fiddle, with Troy Herdman, Bob Tanner and Joe Tanner. Previously issued in the US on Kanawha as KANAWHA 310.

SDL 243   BELLS: Change Ringing from St. Mary Redcliffe, Bristol

Grandsire Caters – 197 changes	Little Bob Maximus – 176 changes
Stedman Cinques – 252 changes	Double Norwich Court Bob Major – 112 changes
	Erin Caters – 100 changes

Release date: 1973 / May 1979 (MM84)
Cassette: CSDL 243 (May '79 / Jan. '81: MM89)   **CD:** CD–SDL 243

Subtitled "Bells of Britain, Vol. 3". The front sleeve shows a view that had already changed drastically as the buildings on Redcliffe Hill behind St. Mary Redcliffe had already been demolished for road widening – in fact the photo is the same as used on *Bells of Britain vol. 1* (SD 127). MM84 release date represents a repromotion: several more bell ringing records were repromoted in May 1979.

SDL 244   GRAHAM COLLIER MUSIC: Portraits

And Now for Something Completely Different Part One	And Now for Something Completely Different Part Two Portraits.

Release date: 1972

Dick Pearce, Pete Hurt, Ed Speight, Geoff Castle, John Webb and Graham Collier.

33SD 245   VARIOUS ARTIST: Sounds of Bristol: A Portrait of Bristol In Sounds, Dialect and Song

Virtute et Industrial (Fred Wedlock with Bev & Richard Dewar)
Fanfare from the City Trumpeters
The Bells of St. Mary Redcliffe
Peacocks at Clifton Zoo
Opening Ceremony of the Pie Poudre Court
Great George
"Harry Brown" under Clifton Suspension Bridge
The Quarter Jacks of Christ Church with St. Ewan

An illustrated exposition of Bristol, dialect and humour by the recognized master of those arts – Geoffrey Woodruff

Release date: 1973

Side A also credits "Dialogue throughout by Geoffrey Woodruff". 7" 33⅓ rpm LP in picture sleeve. Issued in both 'sepia'–tinted and much rarer black and white sleeves. *Opening Ceremony of the Pie Poudre Court* is read by the Sergeant–at–Mace, Bristol Tolzey Court. White label test pressings known to exist. *Virtute et Industrial* was previously included on SD 124. The Harry Brown was a battered old boat, which meandered up and down the River Avon until the late 1970s.

SDLB 246   VARIOUS ARTISTS: Music from Dartington

Fanfare
Carols:
  Down In Yon Forest
  A Virgin Most Pure
Songs:
  In Praise of Arion
  Song of Hamon
Spirituals:
  The Angels Done Bowed Down
  Well, Well, Well
Nonesuch
Organ Concerto in F, Op. 4, No. 5 (Handel)
Carol: Te Haranui

Piloo Thumri
Pieces for Harpsichord:
  Tower Hill (Farnaby)
  La Volta (Byrd)
Three Movements from Missa Brevis
  Sanctus
  Benedictus
  Agnus Dei
String Quartet in D, K. 575 (Mozart)
  Slow Movement/Andante
Rounds:
  Humming Round
  Great Radnor Hills
  The Swan Sings
  Hey, Ho, Nobody At Home
  Derry Ding Ding Dason
  Non Nobis Domine (Byrd)
  Allelulia (Boyce)

Release date: 1973

Mid–price issue commemorating Leonard Elmhirst's 80th birthday. Named artists/composers: Helen Glatz; Nigel Amherst; Dulce Marshall; Nicholas Marshall; Hilary Isaacs; Rachael Pardoe; Bertha Harley; Anne Maxey; Timothy Moore; Winsom Bartlett (ret'd); Roger Yates; John Wellingham; Gordon Jones; Surendra Kamath; Anil Bhagwat; Julian Marshall; Hilary Reynolds; the Dartington String Quartet [Colin Sauer, Malcolm Latchem, Keith Lovell & Michael Evans]; Edith O'Hanrahan (former pupil); Timothy Porter (former pupil).

SDL 247 **SPOKEN WORD: Cotswold Craftsmen**

William Smith – Cotswold Sheep
Edward and Cyril Pearce – Stone Walling
Gilbert Peachey – The Cotswold Roof
Miss Victoria Smith – Gloucester Cheese
Dennis William Coates – Working with Oxen

Alec Twinning – Hurdle Making
Fred Saunders – The Wheelwright
John Millard – Cider Making
Walter Gardner – Thatching

Release date: 1973 / April 1981 (MM89)
Cassette: CSDL 247 (April 1981: MM89)   **CD:** CD–SDL 247
Recorded by June Turner. Originally issued in textured sleeve, April 1981 sleeves non–textured with a gloss finish – labels are also more glossy than originals. White label test pressings of the first press known to exist.

SDLB 248 **MECHANICAL MUSIC: Music from the West Cornwall Museum of Mechanical Music**

Weber Unika – Title not known
Piano Melodici – A Tripoli
Mechanical Singing Bird
Aeolian Orchestrelle – Smoky Smokes
Symphonium Disc Musical Box – Faust Waltz/
    Mararethe
Steck Duo Art Reproducing Piano – The Yam
    (played by Frank Milne)
Violano Virtuoso – Title not known
Imhof & Muckle Drawing Room Barrel Piano –
    Casino Tanze

Kuhl & Klatt Mandoline and Xylophone Piano – Ei Kantara
Gem Roller Organette – Sailor's Hornpipe
Marshall & Wendell Ampico Reproducing Piano – By the
    Waters of Minnetonka (played by Zez Confrey)
Aeolian 116 Note Pipe Organ – In the Hall of the Mountain King

65 Note Broadwood Player Piano – Side By Side
Cylinder Musical Box With Bells – La Suive Cavat Dieu Nous
    Eclaire Fille Cherie
Debrain Piano Mechanique – Gay Parisienne
Draper's Organette – Coming Through the Rye
Edison Amberola (Phonograph Cylinder) – Light as a Feather

Release date: 1973
Budget LP sold at £1.50. White label test pressings known to exist.

SDL 249 **QUINCICASM: Quincicasm**

Time and Motion

Trent Park Song
Winds of Change
Karen

Release date: 1973
Malcolm Bennet, Michael Ormarod, Nigel Smith and Dick Pearce with Ken Eley, Julian Marshall and Katy Zeserson.

SDM 250 **VARIOUS ARTISTS: Fort Valley Blues**

Mama You Goin' to Quit Me As Good as I Been
    to You (Allison Mathis)
Bottle Up & Go (Allison Mathis & Jessie Stroller)
Boll Weavil (Buster 'Buzz' Ezell)
Fort Valley Blues (The Smith Band)
War Song (Buster Brown)
Milk Cow Blues (Gus Gibson)
My Big Fat Hipped Mama (Charles Ellis)
Roosevelt and Hitler (part 1) (Buster 'Buzz' Ezell)

Roosevelt and Hitler (part 2) (Buster 'Buzz' Ezell)
Po' Boy Long Way From Home (Sonny Chestain)
I'm Gonna Make You Happy (Buster Brown)
Railroad Song (Gus Gibson)
Salt Water Blues (Buster 'Buzz' Ezell)
Southern Rag (James Sneed, J. F. Duffy & Alvin Sanders)
John Henry (Allison Mathis & Jessie Stroller)
Blues – When Saints Come to Town (Jessie Stroller)

Release date: 1973
Volume 2 in the *Flyright – Matchbox Library of Congress Series*. White label test pressings known to exist. Library of Congress field recordings by John Wesley Work in Georgia, in 1941, and by Willis Lawrence James and Lewis Wade Jones at Fort Valley State College, Georgia, recorded 5th to 7th March1943.

SDL 251 **WHITE ON BLACK: White On Black**

Country Roads
Snowbird
Big Yellow Taxi
Scarborough Fair
Bitter Green
Meet Me On the Corner

Carey
Nowhere Man
Bramble Cottage
Together Forever
Norwegian Wood
I Don't Know How to Love Him

Release date: 1974
Sue Franklin, Jon Knowler and Suzi Lawrence plus Al Jones, John Turner, Jon 'Wash' Hays and Richard Gould.

SDL 252   JACK ARMSTRONG: Celebrated Minstrel

Rothbury Hills
Whittingham Green Lane
Border Fray
Proudlocks Hornpipe
Redesdale
Barbara Allen
Buy Broom Bussoms
Bobby Shaftoe
Northumberland Rejoices
Kielder Burnie
Gentle Maiden
Noble Squire Dacre
Bonny at Morn
Billy Boy
Derwentwater's Farewell

Keel Row
Lass of Falstone
Peggy's Foot
Wild Hills O'Wannie
The Fair Flower of Northumberland
6 band medleys

Release date: 1974 / July 1977 (MM89)
Vol 1 in the *Saydisc Traditional Series*. Compilation from various sources, including Alan Lomax and the BBC, recorded 1944 and 1951. Includes the Northumbrian Barnstormers and the Northumbrian Minstrels Bands.

SDL 253   VARIOUS ARTISTS: Rusty Rags

Pussyfoot March (Six Brown Brothers)
You're Here and I'm Here (Europe's Society
    Orchestra)
Florida Rag (Fred van Eps & William van Eps
    with Felix Arndt)
Crazy Bone Rag (United States Marine Band)
Maori (poss. with Charles A. Prince)
Trombone Sneeze (Sousa'a Band)
Bull Frog Blues (Six Brown Brothers)
Humpty Dumpty Rag (anonymous studio band)
Beets and Turnips (poss. With Charles A. Prince)

Smiles and Chuckles (Six Brown Brothers)
Castle Walk (Europe's Society Orchestra)
Darkies' Patrol (Vass L. Ossman with poss. Landon Ronald)
The Music Box Rag (Jaudus Society Orchestra)
Alabama Jubilee (poss. with Charles A. Prince)
Rusty Rags (Vass L. Ossman with C. H. H. Booth)
Castle House Rag (anonymous studio band)
Les Copeland's Rag (poss. with Charles A. Prince)
Wild Cherries Rag (Victor Orchestra)

Release date: 1974
Subtitled "Ragtime, Cakewalks and Stomps Vol. 4 (1900 – 1917)". White label test pressings known to exist.

SDL 254   DEREK GARSIDE, WILLIAM THOMAS, HAYDN HARRIS, LYNDON BAGLIN: Foursome for Brass

Foursome for Brass (Spurgin)
An Eriskay Love Lilt (arr. Mortimer)
Fancy's Knell (Vinter)
Mary (Richardson)
Foresters Sound the Cheerful Horn (Bishop)

Concordia (Rimmer)
Butterfly Caprice (Ord–Hume)
Alla Burlesca (Vinter)
Good Night Beloved (Pinsuti)

Release date: 1974
Cassette: CSDL 254
Lyndon Baglin, Derek Garside, William Thomas and Hadyn Harris.

33SD 255   OLD PETE: Old Pete (7" LP)

Some Likely Stories

Some More Likely Stories

Release date: 1974
CD: CD–SDL 255
7" 33⅓ rpm LP in picture sleeve with three banded tracks per side. White label test pressings known to exist. Old Pete was Peter Lawrence and the protagonists in his stories always found themselves, quite innocently, in ludicrous, embarrassing, and downright libellous positions. The recent CD issue is a compilation of *Old Pete* (33SD 255) and *Isambard Kingdom Brunel* (33SD 279), credited to "Old Pete" with the subtitle, "12 comical saga'ls from our area'l incl. Isambard Kingdom Brunel with Old Pete and John Christie".

SDLB 256   **MECHANICAL MUSIC: More Music from the West Cornwall Museum of Mechanical Music**

Unknown Title
Fantasia Ballet
Unknown Title
Silver Threads Among the Gold
I Love My Baby
Unknown Title
Il Folletto
Can't Help Lovin' Dat Man
Il Bacio, Valse Brillante
Wo Sind Deine Haare, August
Bandy Bandolero
Sunny Swanee

Electric Girl
Chaqu'un ces quarelles
La Founterelle
Unknown Title
Mina Danse la Rumba
Potpourri

Release date: 1974

SDM 257   **VARIOUS ARTISTS: Out In the Cold Again**

John Henry [vocals/guitar] (Gabriel Brown)
John Henry [guitar] (Brown)
Casey Jones (Rochelle French & Brown)
Sail On, Little Girl, Sail On (French & Brown)
Out In the Cold Again (French & Brown)
Blues (Brown & French)
Tone the Bell Easy (Brown)
Motherless Child (Brown)
Franky and Albert (John French & Brown)

Po' Boy, Long Way from Home (French & Brown)
A Dream of Mine (Brown)
Blues (I Ain't Got No Mama Now) [take 1] (French & Brown)
Blues (I Ain't Got No Mama Now) [take 2] (French & Brown)
What Did the Doodle–Bug Say To the Mole? (French & Brown)
Education Blues (Brown & French)
Talking in Sebastopol (Brown & French)
Careless Love (Brown)
Uncle Bud (French & Brown)

Release date: 1975
Volume 3 in the *Flyright – Matchbox Library of Congress Series*. Includes the same insert as that issued with SDM 257. Black label test pressings known to exist. Library of Congress field recordings by Mary Elizabeth Barnacle, Zora Neale Hurston & Alan Lomax from Eatonville, Florida, June 1935.

SDM 258   **VARIOUS ARTISTS: Boot That Thing**

The Train (Booker T. Sapps)
The Fox & Hounds (Roger Matthews)
Alabama Blues [part 1] (Sapps, Matthews & Willy Flowers)
Alabama Blues [part 2] (Sapps, Matthews & Flowers)
The Weeping Worry Blues (Sapps & Flowers)

Levee Camp Holler (Flowers & Sapps)
Uncle Bud [take 1 & take 2] (Sapps, Matthews & Flowers)
Frankie and Albert (Sapps, Matthews & Flowers)
Boot That Thing (Sapps, Matthews & Flowers)
John Henry (Sapps, Matthews & Flowers)
Po' Laz'us (Sapps, Matthews & Flowers)
I'm a Pilgrim (Sapps, Matthews & Flowers)

Release date: 1975
Volume 4 in the *Flyright – Matchbox Library of Congress Series*. Includes the same insert as that issued with SDM 257. Black label test pressings known to exist. Library of Congress field recordings by Mary Elizabeth Barnacle, Zora Neale Hurston & Alan Lomax from Belle Glade, Florida, June 1935.

33SD 259   **GEOFFREY WOODRUFF: Geoffrey Woodruff Live (7" LP)**
No track credits listed – continuous dialogue

Release date: 1974
Subtitled "an entertaining demonstration of local accents". 7" 33⅓ rpm LP in picture sleeve. White label test pressings known to exist.

33SD 260   **OLD PETE: Old Pete's Christmas Story (7" LP)**
No track credits listed – continuous dialogue

Release date: 1974
7" 33⅓ rpm LP in picture sleeve. Originally recorded for Radio Bristol, this brings the Nativity up–to–date, telling the story in gentle Bristolian in terms that local children in the 1970s would understand. Odd to note is that Bristolian children would probably now need some translation: who would believe how much could be lost in one generation?

SDM 261   **DAVE PEABODY: Keep It Clean**

She's Gone	Everybody's Talking About Sadie Green
Keep It Clean	Walking Blues
No Matter How She Done It	Oh Yes!
My Friend was Arrested	Jitterbug Rag
Keep Your Hands Off Her	I Never Cried
Worried Life Blues	She's Alright with Me
Georgia Rag	Long Tall Texan

Release date: 1974 / April 1975 (TNR)
Existence confirmed of a black label test pressing. Also includes Hugh McNulty, Dave Griffiths, Diz Watson, Bill Shortt, Ian A. Anderson, Andy Leggett. RRP £2.25 on release.

SDLB 262   **THE STANSHAWE (BRISTOL) BAND: Spectrum**

Spectrum (Vinter)	Academic Festival Overture (Brahms, arr. Wright)
Variations on a Ninth (Vinter)	Suite Gothique, Op. 25 (Boellmann, arr. Ball)

Release date: 1974 / April '75 (TNR)
Cassette: CSDLB 262   **CD:** CD–SDL 262
Subtitled "The Rise to Fame of the Stanshawe (Bristol) Band". Conductor Walter Hargreaves. Original RRP £1.65.

SDLB 263   **MECHANICAL MUSIC: Poppers Happy Jazz Band and the Ruth Fairorgan**

Rheinische Lieder	Sulamit (Shimmy)
Waschermadel (Polka)	Kleine Trommelaa (Fox Trot)
Waldeslust (Waltzer Lied)	Silver Threads Among the Gold
Doruroscheus Braufahrt	Im Zigeunerlager (March) / Vaste Verkeering (March)
Title not known	Ijs Wals / Als Het Orgel Speelt
Adio La Cascina (March) / Schlager 1939 / Title not known	Annemarie (Marchpolka) / Twee Oogen Zoo Blauw (Waltzlied)

Release date: 1975
Cassette: CSDLB 263
Volume 14 in *The Golden Age of Mechanical Music* series. From the West Cornwall Museum of Mechanical Music. Mid–priced release. Side 1 = 52 Key Ruth Fairorgan; side 2 = Poppers "Happy Jazz–Band". Recorded by Ian Anderson and Maggie Holland, of which Anderson says: "SDLB 248, 256, 263...I remember being told by Gef that one of these had gained some big accolade in the world of mechanical music for its recording quality. Since all I'd done was go to the museum, listen to the instruments being cranked up, ascertain where the sound came out of them, place a stereo pair of decent condenser mics plugged directly into a Revox tape recorder, adjust levels and hit "record", it did make me wonder how awful all the other recordings of mechanical music must be!" (Email dated 10th August 2010).

SDM 264   **VARIOUS ARTISTS: Two White Horses Standin' In Line**

Rabbit In De Garden (Ace Johnson)	My Pore Mother Keeps On Praying for Me (prob. Wallace Chains & Sylvester Jones)
Mama Don't 'Low No Swingin' Out In Here (Ace Johnson & L.W. Gooden)	Smoky Mountain Blues (poss. Chains & Jones)
Worry Blues (Jesse Lockett)	Ella Speed (probably Chains & Jones)
I Wouldn't Mind Dying If Dying Was All (Smith Casey)	Long Freight Train Blues (Richard L. Lewis & Wilbert Gilliam)
When I Git Home (Roger Gill & Smith Casey)	Desert Blues (Hattie Ellis & 'Cowboy' Jack Ramsey)
Gray Horse Blues (Smith Casey)	Jack o' Diamonds (Smith Casey)
Shorty George (Smith Casey)	Mournful Blues (Smith Casey)
West Texas Blues (Roger Gill & Smith Casey)	Two White Horses Standin' In Line (Smith Casey)
Santa Fe Blues (Smith Casey)	East Texas Rag (Smith Casey)
Hesitating Blues (Smith Casey)	

Release date: June 1976 (TNR) / Oct. 1976 (MM89)
Volume 5 in the *Flyright–Matchbox Library of Congress Series*. Includes insert. Library of Congress field recordings by John Avery Lomax & Ruby Terril Lomax from Clemens State Farm, Brazoria, Texas, Sunday 16 April, 1939; Camp Four, Ramsey State Farm, Otey, Texas, Sunday 23 April, 1939; State Penitentiary, Huntsville, Texas, Thursday 11 May, 1939; Goree State Farm, near Huntsville, Texas, Sunday 14 May, 1939. RRP £2.99.

SDM 265   VARIOUS ARTISTS: Jack o' Diamonds

Jack o' Diamonds (Pete Harris)
Square Dance Calls (Pete Harris)
He Rambled (Pete Harris)
Stavin' Chain (Tricky Sam)
The Buffalo Skinners (Pete Harris)
Alabama Bound [announcement] (Pete Harris with John Lomax speaking)
Thirty Days In Jail (Pete Harris)
Stavin' Chain [different take] (Tricky Sam)
Ella Speed (Tricky Sam)
Jack and Betsy (Pete Harris)
Jack o' Diamonds [different take] (Pete Harris)

Blind Lemon's Song (Pete Harris);
The Red Cross Store (Pete Harris);
Police Special (Augustus 'Track Horse' Haggerty & prob. Jack Johnson);
Hattie Green (Augustus 'Track Horse' Haggerty & prob. Jack Johnson)
Is You Mad at Me? (Pete Harris)
It Was Early One Morning (Jack Johnson)
Up and Down Buildin' (the) K. C. Line [sic] (Little Brother)
Carrie (Pete Harris)
Standing On the Border (Pete Harris)
I Met You Mama [plus announcement] (Augustus 'Track Horse' Haggerty & Jack Johnson with John Lomax speaking)
I Feel That Old Woman Is a Jinx to Me (A. Haggerty)

Release date: 1976
Volume 6 in the *Flyright – Matchbox Library of Congress Series*. Includes insert with detailed notes. White label test pressings known to exist. Library of Congress field recordings by John Avery Lomax & Alan Lomax from Richmond, Texas, May, 1934; State Penitentiary, Huntsville, Texas, Tuesday 20th November (some definitely recorded this date and some probably) and Wednesday 21st November, 1934; some probably recorded at State Penitentiary, Huntsville, Texas, either May/June or November, 1934.

SDL 266   STAVERTON BRIDGE: Staverton Bridge

Tom Barbary
The Bold Construction Men
Eynsham Poaching Song
Request of the Poor
The Farmer In Leicester
My Lady's Coach

Captain Wedderburn's Courtship
Jocky My Son
My Master and I
The Travellers Came to Redbridge
Woman's Work Is Never Done
Wheal Rodney
We Don't Want to Live Like That

Release date: Aug. 1975 (TNR)
CD: CD–SDL 266
Lyric insert. Sam Richards, Tish Stubbs and Paul Wilson. Original RRP £2.25: it sells for somewhat more now!

SDL 267   SPOKEN WORD: Cotswold Voices

George and Dorcas Juggins – Snufftaking
Jim Hitch – Weather predictions
Bert Butler – 'Oss muckin'
William Clark – Rookstarving at twelve

George and Dorcas Juggins – 'The Express'
Walter Gardner – Old Jack, the shepherd
Godfrey Pain – 'A' ditchin' in the Fog'
Bert Butler – 'Bath Night'
George and Dorcas Juggins – Shopping expeditions to Bisley

Release date: 1975
Cassette: CSDL 267 (April 1981: MM89)   **CD:** CD–SDL 267
Recorded by June Turner. White label test pressings known to exist.

SDL 268   FRANK MANSELL: Cotswold Ballads

The Farm Dog (sung by Peter Tatham)
The Bells of Bisley (read by Frank Mansell)
Tim O'Leary (sung by Celia Carroll)
Old Inhabitants (read by Frank Mansell)
I Passed By the Fields (sung by Peter Tatham)
Cotswold Choice (read by Frank Mansell)
The Roads Go Down (sung by Celia Carroll)
The Wood (read by Frank Mansell)
In Wishanger Wood (sung by Peter Tatham)
The Spring Fox (read by Frank Mansell)
The Encounter (sung by Celia Carroll)

The Old Cricketer (read by Frank Mansell)
On Eldon Hill (read by Frank Mansell)
The Return (sung by Peter Tatham)
When the Fine Rain (sung by Celia Carroll)
Winter (read by Frank Mansell)
The Tramp In Spring (sung by Peter Tatham)
Lines For a Bereaved Libertine (read by Frank Mansell)
The Steeple It Stands (read by Frank Mansell)
The Wife (sung by Celia Carroll)
See These Hands (read by Frank Mansell)
The Cottagers Reply (read by Frank Mansell)
I'd Sooner Go Hedging (sung by Peter Tatham)

Release date: 1975
Cassette: CSDL 268   **CD:** CD–SDL 268
Read by the author with music by Peter Tatham and Celia Carroll, who both play guitar. String bass by John Turner.

SDL 269   LYNDON BAGLIN: Showcase for the Euphonium

The Swan (Le Cygne) from Carnival of Animals (Saint–Seans)	Scarborough Fair
	Prelude, Theme & Variations (Rossini)
Carnaval de Venise (Arban)	Largo (Handel)
Plaisir d'Amour (Martini)	Spanish Dance
Lucy Long	Tarantella
	Yesterday

Release date: 1975

Also includes Meinir Heulyn, Geoffrey Spratt, Gavin Ashenden and Olwyn Wonnacott. Directed by William David Thomas. Note that Olwyn Wannacott's name was misspelled on the sleeve as "Olwyn Wonncott". Several of the tracks were arranged by Gef Lucena for euphonium, two flutes and harp. The master tapes have been lost somewhere down the years, which is why this has not been released on other formats.

SDX 270   DAVE PEABODY: Come and Get It

Come on Boys, Let's Do That Messin' Around	Rock Little Baby
Statesboro Blues	Love In Vain
San Francisco Bay Blues	My Friend Whiskey
Hi–Heel Sneakers	Sweet Georgia Brown
But I Forgive You	You Can't Come In
Shut Your Mouth	Hard Man to Please
The Happy Blues	Don't You Leave Me Here

Release date: July 1976 (TNR)

Last Matchbox issue. With Hugh McNulty, Dave Griffiths, Nick Pickett, Bob Hall, Steve Rye and Jon 'Wash' Hays. Subtitled "Goodtime, Ragtime, Stomps and Blues". Dave Peabody had a residency at this point at the famous Hope and Anchor pub in Islington just as the 'pub rock' scene was getting established there. RRP £2.99.

SDLB 271   MECHANICAL MUSIC: Pipes, Barrels and Pins

That Certain Party (A)	Rigoletto Selection (I)
Country Dance from 'Nell Gwynn' (B)	Ballad – Annie Laurie (J)
Hansel & Gretel Selection (C)	The Last Rose of Summer (K)
The London to Melbourne March (D)	Unknown title (L)
Title unknown (E)	Schmetterling (M)
Dans le Bois – Mazurka (F)	Nearer My God to Thee (N)
Auld Lang Syne (G)	Bedelia (The Jersey Lily) (O)
Bye Bye Blackbird (H)	You Will See Montmartre (P)
	Ramona (Q)

Release date: 1976
Cassette: CSDLB 271   **CD:** CD–SDL 271

Subtitled "Café and Parlour entertainment of yesteryear from the West Country Museum of Mechanical Sound". The recent CD issue has standardised the original prefix. Track listing above taken from original cassette. A = Kuhl and Klatt Mandoline and Xylophone Piano; B = Aeolian 116 Note Pipe Organ; C = Symphonion 25" Disc Musical Box; D = Poppers Clarabella; E = Mills Violano Virtuoso; F = Piano Melodici; G = Gem Roller Organette; H = Steck Duo–Art Reproducing Piano played by Tom Alter; I = Ruth 52 Key Fair Organ; J = Marshall & Wendell Ampico Reproducing piano played by Levitzki; K = Manivelle Musical Box; L = Weber Unika; M = Welte Vorsetzer playing Bluthner Grand Piano; N = National Musical Cabinetto; O = Aeolian Orchestrelle; P = A. Croubois Cafe Barrel Piano; Q = Poppers Happy Jazz Band.

SDL 272   PUMPKIN PIE: Down the Cut

Birmingham Lads	Up the Kennet and Avon
Here Come the Navvies	Waterways Lament
Navvy Boots	Poor Old Horse
Push Boys Push	Operation Working Party
The Rosemary	Wild Canal
Hard Working Boater	Down the Cut
Manchester Ship Canal	

Release date: June '76 (MM89) / July '76 (TNR)
Cassette: CSDL 272

Norma King and John Mills with John Turner and Olwen Wonnacott. Rear sleeve by Terry Brace's Skyline Studios, Plastic Dog Graphics now being defunct (almost literally, the windows at 77 Park Street having recently been blown in by an IRA explosion, Rodney Matthews surviving unscathed, despite standing in front of a window). RPP £2.75.

SDL 273   VARIOUS ARTISTS: That Barbershop Style

Give Me That Barbershop Style (Combined Bristol and Reading Choruses)
Back In Dad and Mother's Day (Bristol Chorus)
Just a–Wearying for You (Bristol Chorus)
Alexander's Ragtime Band (Bristol Chorus)
Bye Bye Blues (Bristol Chorus)
Coney Island Baby (The Barrytones Quartet)
Beautiful Isle of Somewhere (Bristol Chorus)
Roses of Success (Bristol Chorus)
Battle Hymn of the Republic (Bristol Chorus)
New Ashmolean Marching Society (Reading Chorus)
Let the Rest of the World Go By (Reading Chorus)
Margie (Reading Chorus)
For All We Know (Reading Chorus)
Something (The Barrytones Quartet)
Goodbye My Lady Love (Reading Chorus)
Let's Get Together Again/Keep the Whole World Singing (Combined Bristol and Reading Choruses)

Release date: 1976
Cassette: CSDL 273

SDL 274   SOUND IN BRASS HANDBELLS: Music By Sound In Brass Handbells

Whistling Rufus
On Wings of Song
March – The Washington Post
Wiegenlied
Selection – Stephen Foster Songs
Life Let Us Cherish Medley – I've Heard It Before
Polka – Quicksilver
March – The Parade of the Tin Soldiers
Air and Variations – The Ash Grove
Original Rags
Waltz – Tales from Vienna Woods
Nola

Release date: 1976
Cassette: CSDL 274 (July 1977: MM84 / May 1979: MM89)

---

275   No pressing card at Saydisc, so possibly no release?

---

276   No pressing card at Saydisc, so possibly no release?

SDL 277   BELLS: Bells of the Norwich Diocese

Bells of The Assumption of the Virgin Mary, Redenhall – 10 bells
Bells of All Saints, Tibenham – 10 bells
Bells of S Mary and S Thomas, Wymondham – 10 bells
Bells of S Margaret, Lowestoft – 8 bells
Bells of S Michael and All Angels, Bunwell – 6 bells
Bells of S Nicholas, Gt. Yarmouth – 8 bells
Bells of S Faith, Gaywood – 6 bells
Bells of S Mary–the–Virgin, Diss – 10 bells
Bells of S Peter, Mancroft, Norwich – 12 bells
Bells of S Mary Magdalene, Pulham Market – 8 bells
Bells of S Margaret, King's Lynn – 10 bells
Bells of S Catherine, Ludham – 5 bells
Bells of S Mary the Virgin, Norton Subcourse – 6 bells
Bells of S Nicholas, Dereham – 8 bells
Bells of S Andrew, Blofield – 6 bells
Bells of S.S. Peter and Paul, Swaffham – 8 bells
Bells of S Andrew, South Lopham – 8 bells
Bells of S Michael, Aylsham – 10 bells

Release date: 1977

SDL 278   VARIOUS ARTISTS: We Sing Barbershop Too!

Baby Face (A)
Carry Me Back to Old Virginny (A)
I'd Give a Million Tomorrows (A)
Oh Suzanna (B)
If I Had the Heart of a Clown (B)
Do You Really Love Me (A)
White Christmas (A)
Ma, He's Making Eyes at Me (A)
Who Will Buy? (C)
Sonny Boy (C)
California (C)
In the Wee Small Hours of the Morning (C)
I Believe (C)
Sunrise, Sunset (C)
Born Free (C)

Release date: 1977
Three female barbershop teams: A = The Reading Barberettes; B = Minor Birds Quartet; C = Purbrook Sweet Adelines.

33SD 279   OLD PETE & JOHN CHRISTIE: Isambard Kingdom Brunel (7" LP)

Isambard Kingdom Brunel (John Christie)
The Great Britain Saga (Old Pete)
The Cabot Song (John Christie)

Silvery Pools (Old Pete)
Inventions (John Christie)
Gardening for Gran (Old Pete)

Release date: 1977
Subtitled "and other comical saga'ls from our area'l". 7" 33⅓ rpm LP in picture sleeve.

SDL 280   TISH STUBBS & SAM RICHARDS: Invitation to North America

An Invitation to North America
Callerforney
The Balaena
Betsy the Servingmaid
Canadee–io
Bold Princess Royal
The Drifter

Have Over the Water to Florida
When That I Was Weary
New York Gals
Paul Jones
Wolfe and Saunders
I Wish That the Wars Were All Over
The Banks of Newfoundland

Release date: 1977
CD: CD–SDL 280
Subtitled "The New World Seen Through English Folksong". Both were members of Staverton Bridge (SDL 266).

SDL 281   VARIOUS ARTISTS: Leicester '77 Barbershop Convention

Keep Your Sunny Side Up (A)
Who'll Take My Place When I'm Gone (A)
Back in Dad and Mother's Day (A)
Piano Roll Blues (B)
It's Opening Night on Broadway (B)
When I'm Walking with My Sweetness Down
         Among the Sugar Cane (C)
The Sweetest Song in the World (C)
There's a Ring to the Name of Rose (D)

Steamin' Down the River (E)
When Pa Was Courtin' Me (E)
Roll On Mississippi Roll On (E)
Back in Dixie Again (F)
You're Nobody's Sweetheart Now (F)
Don't Bring Lulu (G)
Are You from Dixie (G)
Dixieland Medley (H)

Release date: 1977
Side 1 labelled "Choruses" and Side 2 "Quartets". A = Great Western Chorus; B = Berkshire Barbershopper's Chorus; C = The Roker Peers of Harmony; D = Crawley Chordsmen; E = Fortunairs; F = Newtown Ringers; G = Harmony Raisers; H = Barrytones.

SDL 282   BARRY MALE VOICE CHOIR: Gloria

Viking Song
O, Could I In Song Tell My Sorrow
Dana Dana
Dychwelyd (The Return)
There Is Nothin' Like A Dame
Jock of Hazeldean
In Taberna Quando Sumus (from Carmina
        Burana)

The Song of the Saracens
Moonland
Three Hungarian Folk Songs (Seiber)
Plaisir d'Amour (Martini)
Adoramus Te (Palestrina)
My Lord What a Mornin'
Gloria (Mathias)

Release date: 1977
Cassette: CSDL 282
This was the first ever commercial LP pressed by Nimbus Records Ltd. Being their first pressing, it evidently did not fully achieve the pressing quality they aspired to.

SDL 283   CRAWLEY BARBERSHOP CHORUS: Double Gold

There's A Ring to the Name of Rosie
I'd Give a Million Tomorrows
Back In the Old Routine
Always
A Fellow Needs a Girl
Rubber Duckie
I'd Give the World to Be In My Home Town
If I Had the Heart of a Clown

In the Good Old Summertime
Ma, She's Making Eyes
Masquerade
Little Girl
Alexander's Ragtime Band
On a Wonderful Day Like Today
Who'll Take My Place
Darkness On the Delta

Release date: 1978
Cassette: CSDL 283

SDL 284   SPOKEN WORD: Steam and Harness

Howard Pritchett, Bibury – traction engines
Fred Archer, Ashton–Under–Hill – Shire horses

Emily Elliot – Severn & Thames Canal
Lily Moss and Ernie Franklin – Severn & Thames Canal
George King, Lechlade – building the Witney to Fairford
            railway branch
William Crew – 'passenger lorry'

Release date: 1978
Cassette: CSDL 284   **CD:** CD–SDL 284
Recorded by Peter Duddridge.

SDL 285   MISS DOROTHY BLAKE: Memories of Osborne

Miss Dorothy Blake recalls her childhood at Osborne House, Isle of Wight and her memories of Queen Victoria and the Royal Family (same credit on both labels)

Release date: June 1978 (MM89)
Cassette: CSDL 285   **CD:** CD–SDL 285
Recorded by Peter Duddridge.

SDL 286   VARIOUS ARTISTS: Love Is a Song

They Wrote 'Em In the Good Old Days (A)
Pal, of My Cradle Days (A)
Steamin' Down the River (A)
Pollution (B)
Lida Rose (B)
My Lady Loves to Dance (C)
I'll Take You Home Again Kathleen (C)
Something (C)

Love Is a Song (C)
Don't Bring Lulu (C)
Little Pal (C)
Whatever Happened to Mary (B)
Bye Bye Blues (B)
Little Man, You've Had a Busy Day (A)
If (A)
When Pa was Courtin' Ma (A)

Release date: 1978
Cassette: CSDL 286
Various barbershop quartets. A = The Fortunairs; B = The Five Bridge Four; C = The Barrytones.

SDL 287   FIVE IN A BAR: Lady of Fortune

Lady of Fortune
Jeepers Creepers
Just Break the News to Mother
Yesterday
The Old Woman
There Are Women
I Don't Know Why

Blue Skies
Sweet and Lovely
I Will Love You More Than Ever
Passing By
I'll Take You Home Again Kathleen
I Had a Dream Dear
Down By the Old Mill Stream
When Pa

Release date: 1978
Cassette: CSDL 287
Barbershop quartet. Includes John Turner on bass and guitar and the LP is named after one of his compositions.

SDL 288   THE BLUE NOTE JAZZ BAND: The Blue Note Jazz Band

O Gee Say Gee You Ought to See My Gee–
Gee From the Fiji Isles
Blue Feeling
Coffee Grinder
'J'
Something You Got
There'll Be Some

Importance of the Rose
Do You Know What It Means to Miss New Orleans?
High Life
L. B. Blues
T'Ain't No Sin

Release date: 1978
CD: CD–SDL 288
Originally recorded by BBC Radio Bristol for a *Jazz Tempo* programme in 1978. Roger Bennett, John Skuse, Chris Pearce, Ralph Laing, Wayne Chandler, Geoff Hancock and Crusty Martin. The recent CD issue is subtitled "The Early Days (1968 – 1978)" and also includes all bar two tracks from *Farewell to The Ship* (SDL 136), The Ship

being a famous jazz pub in Redcliffe, which was demolished for road widening along with the world's first lead shot tower. The tracks missing from *Farewell to the Ship* are *Just Squeeze Me* and *Ain't Misbehaving*.

SDL 289   SOUND IN BRASS HANDBELLS: Handbells In Harmony

Black & White Rag (Botsford)	Entry of the Gladiators (Fucik)
Intermezzo from Cav. Rusticana (Macagni)	The Girl with the Flaxen Hair (Debussy)
Jesu Joy of Man's Desiring (Bach)	The Syncopated Clock (Leroy Anderson)
Song Without Words No. 14 (Mendelssohn)	The Shepherd's Farewell (Berlioz)
Coventry Carol/Silent Night	Variations on 'Lead Kindly Light'
The Ragtime Dance (Joplin)	Savoy Christmas Medley

Release date: 1978 / May 1979 (MM84)
Cassette: CSDL 289 (May 1979: MM84)
MM84 release dates may represent a repromotion: the cassette was first available in October 1978.

SDL 290   BELLS: Bells of the Cotswolds

Burford (Oxon.) Double Norwich Court Bob Major	Bourton–On–the–Hill (Glos.) Plain Bob Minor
Bledington (Glos.) Cambridge Surprise Minor	Chipping Camden (Glos.) Grandsire Triples
Stow–On–the–Wold (Glos.) Grandsire Triples	Ebrington (Glos.) Grandsire Minor
Moreton–In–Marsh (Glos.) Kent Treble Bob Major	Ilmington (Warks.) Plain Bob Doubles

Release date: 1978 / May 1979 (MM84)
Cassette: CSDL 290 (May 1979: MM84)   **CD:** CD–SDL 290
The recent CD issue also includes the tracks from the *Bells of Bristol Vol. 1* EP (SD 127) with an amended credit on the sleeve, "+ historic recordings of Bristol bells". MM84 dates may represent a repromotion: the cassette was first available in November 1978.

SDL 291   BELLS: The Sound of the Carillon

Cuckoo Rondo	Rendezvous
Du Bist die Ruh	Cockles and Muscles
Judas Maccabaeus, chorale	Air
Last Rose of Summer	Volte
Llanfair (variations)	La Ferlaude (from J. De Gruytters Carillion Book)
Schubert Serenade	Crimond
Variations On a Gospel Tune	The Bellfounder
	Extract from Mignon

Release date: 1978 / May 1979 (MM84)
Cassette: CSDL 291 (May 1979: MM89)
Side 1 is played on the Bournville Carillon (48 bell) by Trevor Workman and side 2 is played on the Loughbourgh Carillon (47 bell) by Peter Stratford. MM84/MM89 dates are interesting: according to Gef Lucena, "The 1st cassette stocks arrived on 19/02/81, the only LP pressing was received on 20/9/78" (email dated 11th August 2010) which has to put various other dates in doubt, especially those from MM89.

CSDLB 292   MECHANICAL MUSIC: The World of Mechanical Music (cassette)

Track listing unknown

Release date: June 1978 (MM84)
Cassette: CSDLB 292
Cassette–only issue. Museum tour recital. No file copy at Saydisc. Gef Lucena says, "The 1st cassette stocks arrived on 5/5/78, there was no known promotion as this was sold virtually exclusively by the WC Museum." (email dated 11th August 2010).

SDL 293   THE RADIO BRISTOL SINGERS: So Beautiful

Laura	Blue Moon
He Was Beautiful (Cavatina)	Carnival
Let's Face the Music	Tropical Magic
Speak Low	As Time Goes By
Jungle Fantasy	Peanut Vendor
Chanson d'Amour	Birth of the Blues
Guantanamera	Yellow Bird

Release date: 1978
Mary Hale directs. Instrumental backing by Jack Toogood, Mike Hope, Norman Cole, Eddie Clayton, Eddie Jones.

SDL 294 KENNETH WILLIAMS: Parlour Poetry

Jabberwocky
Little Jim
The White Knight's Song
The Wreck of the Hesperus
The Walrus and the Carpenter
In the Workhouse: Christmas Day
The Green Eye of the Yellow God

The Pobble Who Has No Toes
Casabianca
You Are Old Father William
Billy's Rose
Hiawatha's Photographing
Come Home Father
The Dong with the Luminous Nose

Release date: 1978 / May 1979 (MM84)
Cassette: CSDL 294 (1978 / May 1979: MM84)   **CD:** CD–SDL 294
Subtitled "Comic, Patriotic and Improving Verse from the Victorian Age". MM84 dates may represent a repromotion as the LPs were pressed 3/11/78 and the cassette stock was available 29/10/78 (email dated 11th August 2010).

SDL 295 VARIOUS ARTISTS: Caister '78 Barbershop Convention

The Showboat Came to Town (A)
If the Rest of the World Don't Want You (A)
Darkness on the Delta (A)
Band Parade Medley (B)
Danny Boy (B)
If the Lord Be Willing (B)
When the Midnight Choo–choo Leaves for
        Alabam, Medley (C)
Don't Leave Me Dear Old Mammy (C)

It's Better to Leave Them Alone (D)
Bring Back Those Good Old Days (D)
Back In Dixie Again (D)
Grandma's Boy (E)
Carolina Medley (E)
Last Night Was the End of the World (E)
Don't Bring Lulu (F)
Corabelle (F)

Release date: 1979
A = Crawley Chordsmen (Crawley); B = Roker Peers of Harmony (Wearside); C = Great Western Chorus (Bristol); D = Newtown Ringers (Crawley); E = Class Distinction (Brighton & Hove); F = Harmony Raisers (Bristol).

SDL 296 STOKE ORIGINAL THEATRE: A Souvenir from Stoke

City of Smoke
Cost Keck a Boe Agen a Woe
Potters Lament
Lumpy Tums
Wedgwood Blues
The Oatcake Ceremonial

Chalk and Cheese
Alice Down the Palace
When I Was Young
Silicosis
Lobby Aria
Jolly Potters

Release date: 1979

SDL 297 MECHANICAL MUSIC: Music for the Magic Lantern

Mandoline Street Piano:
  Rule Britannia
  Pomona Waltz
Pasquale Street Piano (44 note):
  The Man Who Broke the Bank at Monte Carlo
  Oh! Oh! Antonio
Polyphon Disc Musical Boxes:
  Whistling Rufus (A)
  The Dandy Queen (B)
  The Messenger Boy (A)
Penny Piano:
  Goodbyee
Pianola:
  Ragtime Skedaddle
Chiappa Street Piano (A Tomasso, 48 note):
  Put Me Amongst the Girls
  At Trinity Church I Met My Doom
  Colonel Bogey

Mandoline Street Piano:
  Softly Awakes My Heart
  Samson and Dalila
Penny Piano:
  I've Got a Motto
Polyphon Disc Musical Box (24½"):
  Xenia, Intermezzo
  Latter Polka ('The Laughing Policeman')
Pasquale Street Piano (44 note):
  Molly O'Morgan
  He Had to Get Out and Under
  Roamin' In the Gloamin'
  Charmaine
Atlas Organette:
  Honeysuckle and the Bee
  Bicycle Barn Dance Polka
Street Piano (marked by A Tomasso, 48 note):
  Soldiers of the Queen
  Goodbye Dolly Gray
  Let the Great Big World

Release date: May 1979 (MM84)
Cassette: CSDL 297 (1980 / Jan. 1981: MM84)
Previously issued music from the Roy Mickleburgh collection. Much appeared several years later on SDL 340,

Music of the Streets. The Mandoline Street Piano is 55 note and made by D. Antonelli & Sons. Codes for Polyphon Disc Musical Boxes are as follows: A = 24½"; B = 9½". Pianola is Orchestrelle 65/88 note player attachment.

SDL 298   GROSMONT HANDBELL RINGERS: Four In Hand

Isle of Capri
Music Box Dancer
Flow Gently Sweet Afton
Country Gardens
Swallows Return
Silver Threads Among the Good
Barcarolle
Irish Jig
My Grandfather's Clock

Land of Hope and Glory
Long, Long Ago
Jesu, Joy of Man's Desiring
Bells of St. Mary's
Christmas Medley: Mary's Boy Child/Angels from the Realms of Glory/Silent Night/Deck the Hall/Away In a Manger/O Little Town of Bethlehem/The First Nowell/Auld Lang Syne

Release date: 1979
Cassette: CSDL 298 (1981)
Elizabeth Watkins; Angela Jones; John Collins; Susan Llewellyn; Sheila Parry; Sally Baylis; Ian Parry; Carolyn Inseal; Sally Griffiths; Gillian Probert; Sharon Parry.

SDL 299   NATURE: South Atlantic Islands

Early Morning Atmosphere
Coastal Scene
Paraguayan Snipe
Grass Wren
Guanaco
Southern Elephant Seal
Black–Browed Albatross
Patagonian Fox
Falkland Thrush and Thin–Billed Prion

Evening Atmosphere – Black Oystercatchers
Steamer Ducks
Red–Backed Buzzard
Military Starling
Sea Lion
Magellan Penguin
King Penguins and Gentoo Penguin Colony
Rockhopper Penguin Colony and Black–Browed Albatross
Fur Seal
Short–Eared Owl
Falkland Diving Petrels
Sooty Shearwaters – White–Chinned Petrels – Greater Shearwaters

Release date: Oct. 1979 (MM84)
Cassette: CSDL 299 (1982)   **CD:** CD–SDL 299
Subtitled "A Portrait of Falkland Islands Wild Life". Field recordings by Ian J. Strange (who also provided sounds for the Ribena, *Sounds of the Sea*, flexidisc) between 1966 and 1978. Locations are Volunteer Point, Carcass Island, Kidney Island, Staats Island, Cow Bay, New Island, Stanley, West Point Island, Mount William, Beauchene Island, Volunteer Rocks, Bird Island.

SDL 300   SPOKEN WORD: While I Work I Whistle

Ned Wheeler of Lower Swell
Jim Turner of Tetbury
Howard Pritchett of Bibury

Arthur Sallis of Dumbleton
William and Mary Crew of Elkstone
Frank Wheatcroft of Chipping Campden
Charles and Lawrence Ladbroke of Chipping Campden
Fred Archer of Ashton Under Hill
Tom Steward of Tirley

Release date: Oct. 1979 (MM84)
Cassette: CSDL 300   **CD:** CD–SDL 300
Subtitled "Songs and Humour of the Cotswolds". On the red "Special Limited Edition" label design. Songs, tales and jokes from the Cotswolds. Recorded by Peter Duddridge between 1961 and 1970.

SDL 301   MRS. EMILY ELLIOTT: Down to Earth

No track credits listed – continuous dialogue

Release date: Oct. 1979 (MM84)
Cassette: CSDL 301   **CD:** CD–SDL 301
Subtitled "The Life and Times of Mrs. Emily Elliot from 1876". From Waterley Bottom, near Wotton–under–Edge, Gloucestershire. Recorded by Peter Duddridge.

SDL 302   BELLS: Church Bells of Kent

Canterbury Cathedral – 12 bells, Grandsire Cinques
Hythe – 8 bells, Bristol Surprise Major
Leeds – 10 bells, Kent Treble Bob Royal
Chislet – 6 bells, Stedman Doubles
Ashford – 10 bells, Grandsire Caters
Brookland – 6 bells, S. Clements College Bob Minor
Lyminge – 8 bells, Double Norwich Court Bob Major

Rochester Cathedral – 10 bells, Stedman Caters
Sevenoaks, St. Nicholas – 8 bells
Beckenham – 10 bells, Plain Bob Royal
Queenborough, The Holy Trinity – 6 bells
Maidstone – 10 bells, Plain & Little Bob
Lamberhurst, St. Mary – 6 bells
Eynsford, St. Martin – 8 bells

Release date: 1979
Cassette: CSDL 302 (Jan. 1981: MM84)   **CD:** CD–SDL 302
Kent County Association of Change Ringers' Centenary record.

SDL 303   MECHANICAL MUSIC: Sublime Harmonie

Valse des Fees / Largo / Wedding Song from Lohengrin (A)
I Have a Song To Singo / Servants Chorus (both B) / two examples (C)
Selection from 'Maritana' / The Lost Chord / War March of the Priests (all A)
Example (D) / Mira O Norma (A) / Perche non Posso (E) /Sweethearts (F) / Behold the Lord High Executioner (G) / Feniculi Fenicula (A)

March of the Toreadors (A) / Ah! Non Giunge (H) / Ave Maria (A) / Cara Deh Attendini (H)
Wedding March / The Village Blacksmith / Libiamo (A)
The Legacy / The Campbells Are Coming / Kate Kearney (F)
La Serenade: Valse Espagnole / Entry March (A) / Voici le Sabre / Stride la Vampa (I)
Waltz from Faust / Hellelujah Chorus (A)

Release date: 1979
Cassette: CSDL 303 (Nov. 1980)   **CD:** CD–SDL 303 (prob. Feb. 1992)
Issued on two label designs, on the current blue label design and also on a red "Special Limited Edition" label design. A = 24½" disc Polyphon musical box; B = Excelsior Piccolo 12 air cylinder musical box; C = Nicole Freres 19½" Interchangable Cylinder, Forte Piano musical box; D = Nicole Freres 12" Cylinder, Overture Box; E = Nicole Freres 6 air cylinder musical box; F = 8 air cylinder box, makers unknown (several); G = Sublime Harmonie 8 air cylinder musical box; H = Nicole Freres 10 air cylinder musical box; I = Nicole Freres 12 air cylinder musical box.

SDL 304   NATURE: Gloucestershire Wildlife Tapestry

Spring (day)
Summer (day)
Autumn (day)
Winter (day)

Spring (night)
Summer (night)
Autumn (night)
Winter (night)

Release date: 1979
Cassette: CSDL 304 (Feb. 1981)   **CD:** CD–SDL 304 (April 2007)
Subtitled "A web of day & night natural sounds through the seasons, from woodland, meadow and wetland. Spun by Ray Goodwin". Some included a membership form and deed of covenant for joining The Gloucestershire Trust for Nature Conservation.

SDLB 305   RAILWAY RECORDING: Steam's Final Hours

48493, 45287, 73069 and 48033
45388 and 48775
44888 and 70013
48400, 48423, 48773 and 48666

45073, 48340, 45156 and 48493
Class 8F 2–8–0
44871, 44894 and 45305
45110, 70013, 44871 and 44781

Release date: Nov. 1980 (MM84)
Cassette: CSDLB 305
Recordings made during 1968 by Andrew Mellor, originally issued on Jaycee (JC013). Saydisc copies are in Jaycee sleeves with sticker on rear and Saydisc labels. Recording details: Hailwood Aintree branch (8F 48198); Pighue Lane, Liverpool (Class 5 45287); Kirkby (Class 5 73069); Lime Street (8F 48033); Hoghton, on the Preston – Blackburn line (Class 5 45388 and 8F 48775); Manchester – Southport, recorded from train (Class 5 44888 and Britannia 70013, Oliver Cromwell); Various locomotives at scene of derailment, Rose Grove, near Burnley: Approaching Manchester Victoria (Class 5 44871, 44894 and 45305); The last official steam hauled train, Liverpool – Carlisle (Class 5 45110, 44871, 44781 and Britannia 70013, Oliver Cromwell).

SDLB 306   RAILWAY RECORDING: Nocturnal Steam

Acton Grange Junction – Crewe line (8F 48198 & Class 5 45323)

Grand Junction Railway Bridge over the Mersey (unidentified 8F, Class 5 45055, unidentified 9F, etc.)

Frodsham Hill, on the Warrington – Chester line (Flying Scotsman)

Beeston, south of Leeds (Castle 7029, Clun Castle)

Pighue Lane, Liverpool (8F 48722, etc.)

On–board train between Leeds and Bradford (Jubilee 45593, Kolhapur)

Release date: 1980
Cassette: CSDLB 306
Recordings made by Andrew Mellor at evening and night during 1967 and 1968, the last two years of steam operation on British Rail metals.

SDL 307   LAUNTON HANDBELL RINGERS: Modal Melodies

The Lord of the Dance
The Ashgrove
Linden Lea (Vaughan Williams)
O Waly Waly
O Guter Mond
Brahms' Lullaby
Finlandia (Sibelius)

Nos Galan
Joy to the World (Handel)
The Cherry Tree Carol
Down With the Rosemary and Bays
A New Year Carol (Britten)
The Gloucestershire Wassail
Patapan
Little Donkey
The Little Drummer Boy
Tyrolean Cradle Song
Rocking
In the Bleak Mid–Winter (Holst)

Release date: Nov. 1980 (MM84)
Cassette: CSDL 307 (Jan. 1981: MM84)
Subtitled "'Four In Hand' style ringing on historic bells".

SDL 308   UNRELEASED – RAY GOODWIN: Fox

SDX 309   TIMOTHY DAVIES: Kilvert's Diary

Part One: Singing up the nave like a company of angels

Part Two: If gold would keep you with us we would gather a weight of gold

Part Three; It began with a lass and will end with a lass

Part Four: The strong sweet cup of life

Release date: Nov. 1980 (MM84)
Cassette: CSDX 309 (Nov. 1980: MM84)   **CD:** CD–SDL 309
Subtitled – 'He Being Dead Yet Speaketh'. Read by Timothy Davies with music by Ann Young, Ann Griffiths, Nick Oliver, Steve Glennie Smith and John Ralph. Double play length LP, hence the SDX catalogue number. Gef Lucena has the following to say about this issue on his master list: "The vinyl version was a unique "Double Play Length". Specially mastered by Gerald Reynolds of Nimbus it was a experiment that successfully squeezed 90 minutes over the LP (normal maximum depending on the sound material was around 50). The sound level on disc is very good and no problems with playing the LP were ever reported to Saydisc. However, the most perfect cutting lacquers were needed (perhaps 1 in 20 was good enough) and it evidently needed 6 cuts before successful – this perfect set was then dropped prior to growing the mother discs and cutting started again. It was not an economic way to produce LPs but proved what could be done. Nimbus then developed their own CD cutting and pressing plant which was the first in the UK by several years." The addition of the "X" to the "SD" prefix was to denote "extra long play". The CD version was cut to just under 80 minutes and therefore given the more normal "CD–SDL" prefix.

SDL 310   BELLS: Change Ringing On Handbells

Stedman Cinques
Spliced Surprise Major
London (No. 3) Surprise Royal
Little Bob Twenty–In

Grandsire Caters
Treble Bob Sixteen–In
Stedman Triples
Bristol Surprise Maximus

Release date: Mar. 1981 (MM84)
Cassette: CSDL 310 (Mar. 1981: MM84)   **CD:** CD–SDL 310

CSDLB 311   *RAILWAY RECORDING: Iron–Ore Steamers (originally cassette–only)*
See below

Release date: 1980
LP: SDLB 311 (Nov. 1980)
Recorded by Stanley White on the Storefield Quarry line, 1968. Side 1 is a medley of sounds of Andrew Barclay Nos. 11 & 19 (0–4–0) bringing loaded wagons through the woods, up the gradient to the main line and returning with empty wagons. Side 2 is recordings of 'Caerphilly' (0–6–0) from trackside and cab climbing the gradient and returning. Advertised in 1980 catalogue as cassette only, but later issued on LP.

SDL 312   *MECHANICAL MUSIC: The Gay 90's*

A Runaway Girl:
  The Singing Girl
  Land of My Home
  Far Away Over the Sea
  Society
  Soldiers In the Park (all A)
Robin Hood (selection, all B)
Florodora:
  The Shade of the Palm (A)
  Silver Star of Love (C)
  The Shade of the Palm (D
Belle of New York:
  They All Follow Me (A)
  We'll Stand and Die Together (A)
  We'll Stand and Die Together (D)
  The Purity Brigade (A)
  The Anti–Cigarette Society (A)
  The Purity Brigade (D)
The Geisha:
  Chin Chin Chinaman (A)
  The Amorous Goldfish (A)
A Greek Slave and San Toy:
  I'm a Naughty Girl (C)
  I Want to Be Popular (C)
  Rhoda and Her Pagoda (A)

A Dozen Discs from miniature to massive:
  Mister Cupid (E)
  Down the Road (F)
  Pride of the Ball, Waltz (G)
  The Birdseller (C)
  Star Light, Star Bright (H)
  Song of the Nightingale (I)
  Happy New Year Polka (J)
  Home Sweet Home (N)
  The Birdseller (D)
  Just as the Sun Went Down (M)
  Tom Titt (A)
  Soldiers of the Queen (L)
Canary and Nightingale Warble (B)
Evergreens, Stephen Foster Songs, Gay 90's Favourites:
  Old Folks at Home (D)
  Soldiers of the Queen (C)
  The Holy City (J)
  I Wish I Was In Dixie (F)
  Love's Old Sweet Song (I)
  The Last Rose of Summer (C)
  Daisy Bell (A);
Miscellany:
  Skylark, Skylark (AKA The Boys Message) (M)
  Sunshine Above (F)
  Whisper and I Shall Hear (A)
  Where Is My Boy Tonight (H)
  Queen of the Earth (A)
  Waves of the Danube (F)
  God Save the Queen (M).

Release date: Jan. 1981 (MM84)
Cassette: CSDL 312 (Nov. '80: MM84 / Jan. '81: MM89)   **CD:** CD–SDL 312
Subtitled "The World of Victorian Musical Shows & Popular Song on Twelve Disc Musical Boxes and a Pianola". Side 1 comprises "Songs from the Shows" and side 2 comprises "Popular Songs & Pieces". Instruments from the Roy Mickleburgh collection: A = 24½" Polyphon disc; B = Orchestrelle player attachment & Bechstein Grand Piano); C = 9½" disc Polyphon; D = 15½" disc Polyphon; E = 4" disc Thorens; F = 6½" disc Polyphon; G = 7½" disc Polyphon; H = 10⅝" disc Symphonion; I = 11" disc Polyphon; J = 11¾" disc Symphonion; K = 22" disc Polyphon; L = 27" disc Regina; M = 22" disc Polyphon with Glockenspiel; N = 13⅝" disc Symphonion.

SDLB 313   *RAILWAY RECORDING: Return to Steam Vol. 1*

L.M.S. 4–6–0 (Jubilee) Class nos.5596
    Bahamas and 5690 Leander
L.M.S. 4–6–0 5MT (Black Five) Class no. 44932
L.N.E.R 2–6–2 V2 Class, no. 4771 Green Arrow
L.N.E.R 4–6–2 A3 Class, no. 4772 Flying
    Scotsman
L.N.E.R 4–6–2 A4 Class, no. 4498 Sir Nigel
    Gresley
British Railways 2–10–0 9F Class, no.92203
    Black Prince

G.W.R. 4–6–0 69XX (Modified Hall) Class, no. 6998 Burton
    Agnes Hall
G.W.R. 4–6–0 68XX (Manor) Class, no. 7808 Cookham Manor
    and no. 6998
G.W.R. 4–6–0 King Class no.6000 King George V
G.W.R. 4–6–0 Castle Class, no. 4079 Pendennis Castle
G.W.R. 0–4–2T 14XX Class, no. 1420
G.W.R. 2–6–2T 61XX Class, no. 6106 and 6998 Burton Agnes
    Hall
G.W.R 0–6–0PT 57XX Class, no. 7752
Southern Railway 4–6–2 Merchant Navy Class, no. 35028
    Clan Line

Release date: April 1981 (MM84)
Cassette: CSDL 313 (April 1981: MM84)
Stereo 1973/4 recordings by Kenneth Granville Attwood. Previously issued on the Line label in 1975 (LINE 2008).

SDLB 314   MECHANICAL MUSIC: Devon Museum of Mechanical Music
Rag Melody
Nights of Gladness
Victorious Eagle
The Geisha's Life (from The Geisha)
Lady's Maid (from San Toy)
Private Tommy Atkins
Dinah
Waltz (Audran)
The Entertainer and New Rag (Audran)
Indiana

Colonel Bogey / Lady Farmer's Dance / Leichenstein Polka /
    Longest Day (medley)
Medley of small instruments
Don Caesar
Loveable and Sweet
Bye Bye Blackbird

Release date: July 1981 (MM84)
Cassette: CSDL 314 (July 1981: MM84)

SDL 315   BELLES AND BEAUS: Belles and Beaus
Bell Processional
Gloria
O Holy Night
Chorale and Alleluia (Bach)
Allemande (Vivaldi)
Trumpet Chorale (Bach)
Sleigh Ride

Change Ring
Ebb Tide
Music Box Dancer
Parade of the Wooden Soldiers
Black and White Rag
Blue Tango
Plink, Plank, Plunk
Malaguena

Release date: 1980
Subtitled "Canfield Choral Music Dept Presents the English Handbell Sounds of the Belles and Beaus, Canfield, Ohio, USA".

SDL 316   VARIOUS ARTISTS: Forest Talk
Pie Yuttin' (Keith Morgan)
The Lurcher (Dick Brice)
The New Technique (Harry Beddington)
The 'Azards O' Chimuck Szwippin' (Keith
    Morgan)
Washin' Day (Winifred Foley)
I Remember, I Remember (Dick Brice)

Up Fer the Cup (Keith Morgan)
Big Ambitions (Winifred Foley)
'Ers Zed As 'Er Could, 'Ers Zed As 'Er Should, 'Ers Zed As 'Er
    Ood, But 'Er Oon't (Dick Brice)
Varest Ship (Keith Morgan)
The Hat (Winifred Foley)
West of Severn East of Wye (Harry Beddington)
A Forester's Epitaph (Keith Morgan)

Release date: 1981
Cassette: CSDL 316   **CD:** CD–SDL 316
Subtitled "Forest of Dean Songs, Poetry & Humour". Recorded live at the Angel Hotel, Coleford.

SDL 317   LAWRENCE JAMES: Late Night Extra
I Know That You Know
It's the Talk of the Town
Goody Goody
A Kiss In the Dark
Late Night Extra
Lazy River
Glen Miller Selection:
  I Know Why
  Tuxedo Junction

I Won't Dance
All the Things You Are
Alley Cat
Love's Last Word Is Spoken
Walkin' My Baby Back Home
Burt Bacharach Selection:
  The World Is a Circle
  I'll Never Fall In Love Again
  Do You Know the Way to San Jose
  After You've Gone

Release date: July 1981 (MM84)
Cassette: CSDL 317 (July 1981: MM84)
Subtitled "Lawrence James at the Wurlitzer Theatre Organ, Buckingham Town Hall".

SDL 327   MECHANICAL MUSIC, BELLS, ETC: Enchanted Carols

The Bells of St. Mary Redcliffe, Bristol (change ringing) and Hark the Herald Angels Sing (medley from Street Piano, 15½" disc Regina Musical Box, Roller Barrel Organ, Nicole Freres cylinder Musical Box and Orpheus Disc Piano)

A Virgin Most Pure (choir with handbells from Dartington Hall)

Jingle Bells (Penny Piano) and Star of Bethlehem (15½" disc on Polyphon and Regina Musical Boxes)

Carol Medley – Angels From the Realms of Glory/Away In a Manger/O Little Town of Bethlehem/The First Nowell (Four In Hand, Grosmont Handbell Ringers)

Carol Medley – As With Gladness Men Of Old/ Glory To God In the Highest/See Amidst the Winter Snow (Sun Life Stanshawe Band)

O Come All Ye Faithful (medley from Street Piano, Parry's Barrel Organ, Nicole Freres cylinder Musical Box, Orpheus Disc Piano)

Silent Night (Sound In Brass Handbells, medley from Symphonion and Polyphon Disc Musical Boxes)

Down In Yon Forest (choir with handbells from Dartington Hall)

Good King Wenceslas (medley from 15½" disc played on Polyphon and Regina Musical Boxes, 22" disc Polyphon and Street Piano)

Carol Medley – Little Jesus Sweetly Sleep (Rocking)/Little Drummer Boy/Deck the Hall (Nos Galan)/Little Donkey (The Launton Handbell Ringers)

While Shepherds Watched Their Flocks By Night (Street Piano)/Auld Lang Syne (15½" disc on Polyphon and Regina Musical Boxes)/The Bells of St. Mary Redcliffe (change ringing)

Release date: Nov. 1981 (MM84)
Cassette: CSDL 327 (Nov. 1981: MM84)   **CD:** CD–SDL 327 (1985: SC)
Tracks taken from SDL 243; SDL 232; SDL 312; SDL 297; SDL 303; SDL 117; SDL 132; SDL 181. The Sun Life Stanshawe Band track was recorded at the session for SDL 328 but was intended specifically for this album.

SDL 328   SUN LIFE STANSHAWE BAND: Conductor's Showcase

Fanfare
Promenade
Bone Idyll
Alborado del Gracioso
Fugue In E flat
The Stars and Stripes Forever

Night Flight to Madrid
When the Boat Comes In
Ave Verum
Cranberry Corner USA
The Shepherd's Song
Leviathan
Hungarian Dance
Yodelling Brass

Release date: 1981
Cassette: CSDL 328   **CD:** CD–SDL 328
Derek Bourgeois conducts tracks 1 – 6; Cliff Sayers conducts tracks 7 & 8; Laurie Hinchley conducts tracks 9 & 10; Brian Howard conducts tracks 11 & 12; David Williams conducts tracks 13 & 14.

SDL 329   UNRELEASED – South Zeal Project

SDL 330   PRINKNASH ABBEY: Music from Prinknash Abbey

Abbey Bells & Introit – Spiritus Domini. Mode VIII
Alleluia – Emitte Spiritum tuum. Mode IV
Hymn – Christe Redemptor omnium. Mode I
Hymn – Vexilla Regis prodeunt. Mode I
Hymn – Veni Creator Spiritus. Mode III
Hymn – Adoro te devote. Mode V
Hymn – Virgo Dei Genitrix. Mode II
Offertory Verse – Ave Maria. Mode VIII
Magnificat Antiphon – Montes Gelboe. Mode I
Motet – Ave Verum Corpus. Mode VI
Antiphon – Salve Regina. Mode I
Processional – Spiritus Domini. Mode VIII

Psalm 45 – God Is for Us a Refuge and Strength
Hymn – Christ Our Saviour, from the Father
Psalm 138 – O Lord You Examine Me and Know Me
Hymn – Into the Silence of Our Hearts
Psalm 137 – I Thank You Lord with All My Heart
Hymn – Eternal Living Lord of All
Responsory – An Angel Came and Stood at the Altar
Hymn – We Praise You, Father, for Your Gifts
Anthem – We Greet You, Holy Queen
Magnificat

Release date: April 1982 (MM84)
Cassette: CSDL 330 (April 1982: MM84)   **CD:** CD–SDL 330

SDL 331 MECHANICAL MUSIC: The Road to Heaven

Old Favourites:
Abide with Me (G)
Judas Maccabaeus (F)
The Lost Chord (H)
When I Survey the Wondrous Cross (L)
How Sweet the Name of Jesus Sounds (L)
Lead Kindly Light (E)
Nearer My God to Thee (G)
Hundredth Psalm (All People That on Earth Do
     Dwell (A, B, L & C)
Redemption and Revival:
Shall We Meet Beyond the River (F)
Only an Armour Bearer (L)
I Will Sing of My Redeemer (K)
Scatter Seeds of Kindness (G)
Shall We Gather at the River (L)
Beaulah Land (I)
The Holy City (F)
The Holy City (M)
Hanover (O Worship the King) (A & B)
Christians Awake (H & L)

Rock of Ages (H, K, L & F)
Morning and Evening Hymns:
Morning hymn (A)
Morning hymn 'Awake My Soul' (B)
Evening hymn (B)
Evening hymn (C)
More Redemption and Revival:
Onward Christian Soldiers (G)
Onward Christian Soldiers (H)
Rescue the Perishing (L)
What Shall the Harvest Be (E)
We'll Work Till Jesus Comes (I)
Washed In the Blood of the Lamb (H)
Safe in the Arms of Jesus (L)
What a Friend We Have in Jesus (K)
Austria (Glorious Things of Thee are Spoken) (D, J & G)
Church Barrel Organ miscellany:
Sicilian Mariners (A)
Helmsley (A)
Luther's Hymn (B)
London New (B)
Mount Ephraim (C)
God Save the Queen (C)

Release date: Sept. 1982 (MM89) / Nov. 1982 (MM84)
Cassette: CSDL 331 (Nov. 1982: MM84)   **CD:** CD–SDL 331 (autumn 1991: SC)
Subtitled "Mechanical music for a Victorian Sunday". Instruments from the Mickleburgh collection: A = Church pipe barrel organ (Muir Wood & Co., c. 1820); B = Church pipe barrel organ (Anon. Maker, c. 1790, barrels repinned by Robson c. 1825); C = Church pipe barrel organ (Astor, c. 1800); D = Polyphon disc musical box (9½" discs); E = Symphonion disc musical box (10⅝" discs); F = Symphonion disc musical box (11¾" discs); G = Regina disc musical box (15½" discs); H = Polyphon disc musical box (15½" discs); I = Celestina paper roll organ (reed); J = Atlas Organette (reed);K = The Cabinet roller barrel organ (reed); L = Orpheus disc piano; M = Street piano, anonymous maker. MM84 includes two listings for the LP, both with different release dates!

SDL 332 TRADITIONAL: All Around England and Back Again

Helston (Cornwall) Furry Dance & Hal–an–Tow
Padstow (Cornwall) Hobby Horse Day
Castleton (Derbyshire) Oak–apple / Garland Day
Bampton–in–the–Bush (Oxfordshire) The Whit–
    Monday Morris
Abbots Bromley (Staffordshire) The Horn Dance

Antrobus (Cheshire) The Soul–cakers
Barrow–on–Humber (Lincolnshire) The Plough–Jags
Far & Near Sawrey (Cumbria) The Easter Jolly–boys
Wassailers:
    Charlie Bate, Padstow (Cornwall)
    Fred Adams, Minehead (Somerset)
    Harry & Walter Sealey, Ash Priors (Somerset)

Release date: Nov. 1982 (MM84)
Cassette: CSDL 332 (Nov. 1982: MM84)
Recordings by Peter Kennedy of folk music, traditions, dances, children's games, dialect, stories and rituals.

SDL 333 VARIOUS ARTISTS: Ringing Clear

March, Entry of the Gladiators (A)
Linden Lea (B)
Stephen Foster Selection (A)
Grandfather's Clock (C)
On Wings of Song (A)
Lord of the Dance (B)
The Girl With the Flaxen Hair (A)
Country Gardens (C)
The Ragtime Dance (A)

The Parade of the Tin Soldiers (A)
Isle of Capri (C)
Lullaby (B)
Original Rags (A)
Silver Threads Among the Gold (C)
Intermezzo from Cavalleria Rusticana (A)
Bells of St. Mary's (C)
O Waly Waly (B)
Flow Gently Sweet Afton (C)
The Syncopated Clock (A)
O Guter Mond (B)
Whistling Rufus Mills (A)

Release date: Nov. 1982 (MM84)
Cassette: CSDL 333 (Nov. 1982: MM84)   **CD:** CD–SDL 333 (autumn 1991: SC)

A = Sound In Brass; B = The Launton Handbell Ringers; C = Grosmont Handbell Ringers. Compilation of music from SDL 274, SDL 298, SDL 310 and SDL 289. Later CD issue had three extra tracks: *The Ashgrove* (The Launton Handbell Ringers); *Treble Bob Sixteen In*; *Little Bob Twenty In* (both by Change Ringing Handbell Group).

SDL 334   VARIOUS ARTISTS: Cylinder Jazz

Hungarian Rag (The New York Military Band)
Clarinet Squawk (Louisiana Five)
Dardanella (Harry Raderman's Jazz Orchestra)
Meadow Lark (Duke Yellman & His Orchestra)
Where's My Sweetie Hiding? (Merry Sparklers)
Blue–Eyed Sally (Tennessee Happy Boys)
Ain't She Sweet? (Clyde Doerr & His Orch.)

She's a Cornfed Indiana Gal (Earl Oliver's Jazz Babies)
Make That Trombone Laugh (Harry Raderman's Jazz Orch.)
Night Time In Little Italy (Frisco Jazz Band)
I'm Going to Park Myself In Your Arms (Duke Yellman & His Orchestra)
That Certain Feeling (Tennessee Happy Boys)
Do It Again (Intro. Drifting Along with the Tide) (Harry Raderman's Jazz Orchestra)
Louisville Lou (Paul Victorin's Orchestra)

Release date: Nov. 1982 (MM84)
Cassette: CSDL 334 (Nov. 1982: MM84)   **CD:** CD–SDL 334 (autumn 1991: SC)
From Edison Blue Amberol phonograph cylinders. This was a rejigged reissue of SDL 112 in a new sleeve design.

SDL 335   JIM COUZA: The Enchanted Valley

Jenny Lind Medley
Intrada and Minuet
Londonderry Air Medley
Nola
The High Cauled Cap Medley
Christine's Medley
Devil's Dream

The Enchanted Valley
La Belle Katherine Medley
Norwegian Wood
Flowers of England/The Snowflake
Los Ejes de Mi Carretta
The Perfect Cure Medley
Take Five

Release date: Aug. 1983 (MM84)
Cassette: CSDL 335 (Aug. 1983: MM84)   **CD:** CD–SDL 335 (autumn 1991: SC)
CD titled "Music for the Hammered Dulcimer". Includes Eileen Monger, Michael Punzak, Peter Kennedy, Frank Evans and Duncan Brown. In trade publications credited to "Eileen Monger" and "Eileen Monger and Jim Couza".

SDL 336   VARIOUS ARTISTS: I'll Dance Till De Sun Breaks Through

That Moaning Saxophone Rag (Six Brown Brothers)
Florida Rag (Van Eps Trio)
Bacchanal Rag (The Peerless Orchestra)
Alabama Skedaddle (Xylophone solo by William Mitcham)
Castle Walk (Europe's Society Orchestra)
From Soup to Nuts (Felix Arndt)
Smoky Mokes (Metropolitan Orchestra)
Eli Green's Cake Walk (Cullen and Collins)
The Cake Walk (Victor Minstrels)
I'll Dance Till De Sun Breaks Through (Archibald Joyce & His Orchestra)

'Tain't Nobody's Biz–ness If I Do (Charles A. Matson's Creole Serenaders)
Whistling Rufus (Olly Oakley acc. Landon Ronald)
Wild Cherries Rag (Victor Orchestra, cond. Walter B. Rogers)
Won't You Come Home Bill Bailey? (Arthur Collins with acc. prob. Fred Hager)
Stomp Dance (Victor Military Band)
Calico Rag (Frank E. Banta with Howard Kopp)
Smiles And Chuckles — A Jazz Rag (Six Brown Brothers)
On the Levee (Victor Minstrels)
Trombone Sneeze — A Humoresque Cakewalk (Sousa's Band)
Two–Key Rag (Conway's Band)

Release date: Aug. 1983 (MM89) / Nov. 1983 (MM84)
Cassette: CSDL 336 (Nov. 1983: MM84)   **CD:** CD–SDL 336 (Feb. 1992: SC)
Modified version of the album originally issued as SDL 210.

SDL 337   BELLS: The Bells of London

St. Paul's Cathedral (Stedman Cinques)
St. Vedast, Foster Lane (Cambridge Surprise Major)
St. Lawrence, Jewry (Spliced Surprise Major)
St. Giles, Cripplegate (Cambridge Surprise Maximus)
St. Clement Danes, Strand (London Surprise Royal)
St. Sepulchre, Holburn Viaduct (Stedman Caters)

St. Mary–le–Bow, Cheapside (Bristol Surprise Maximus)
St. Olave, Hart Street (Stedman Triples)
St. Michael, Cornhill (Londinium Surprise Maximus)
St. Bartholemew the Great, Smithfield (Grandsire Doubles)
Westminster Abbey (Stedman Capers)
St. Martin–in–the–Fields (Yorkshire Surprise Maximus)

Release date: Nov. 1983 (MM84)
Cassette: CSDL 337 (Nov. 1983: MM84)

SDL 338   TRADITIONAL: Children's Singing Games

England:

i) Singing Games:
King William Was King David's Son
Cock Robin Is Dead and Lies In His Grave
There Came a Gypsy Riding
We Are the Roman Soldiers
There Were Three Jolly Sailor Boys
Queen Mary Has Lost Her Golden Ring
Rosy Apple, Lemon and a Pear
Here Comes Mrs. Macaroni
Poor Mary Sat a–Weeping
There Was a Farmer Had a Dog, His Name
      Was Bobby Bingo
Mary Maloga She Lifted Her Leg
Rise Sally Walker
Sister Jane and Brother Jim
Glory, Glory, Alleluia

ii) Dipping Rhymes:
One Potato, Two Potato
Eeny Meeny Miney Mo, Put the Baby on the Po
My Mother and Your Mother Were Hanging
      Out Some Clothes
Counting In 'Shepherd's Score'

iii) Skipping:
I Am a Little Orphan
Raspberry, Strawberry, Gooseberry Jam
When I Call Your Birthday
Jelly On the Plate
Bluebells, Cockle Shells
Goodbye...When You Are Away
Cream Crackers, Penny a Packet

iv) Clapping:
Em–pom–pi
The Spaceman Said
My Mother Is a Baker
Who Stole the Shoe from the Cobbler's Shop

v) Two–ball Games:
Olicha Bolicha Sister Cololicha
Lemonade, Fizzy–pop
Mrs. Mop Bought a Shop
Gypsy, Gypsy Lived In a Tent
One, Two, Three a Plainsey
Gypsy, Gypsy Caroline
Bronco Lane Went to Spain

vi) More Singing Games:
Down By the Meadow
Queenio, Queenio Who's Got the Ball
I've Come to See You Janie Jones

Wales:
Spanish Lady
Someone Under the Bed
Jack, Jack Cross the Water
I Went to California
Coca–Cola, Pepsi–Cola
I Am a Dutch Girl
Bob Yn Ail I Mewn Ac Allan (Dusty Bluebells)
Y Llwynog A'r Ieir (The Fox Lies Sleeping)
Mari Fach Yn Crio (Mary Lies a–Weeping)
Over the Garden Wall
Mickey Mouse In His House

Southern Ireland:
We Are the Mercy Girls
I'm Shirley Temple
Under the Brown Bush
I Had German Measles
Put My Hand On Myself
The Wind
One–legged Chicken
I've Got a Girld Friend
When Suzy Was a Baby
Abe, Abe My Boy
The Irish Soldiers
Auntie Monica
The Austrian Yodeller
The Rushing Bluebells
Ish Stark Is the Mark
Here We Come Gathering Nuts In May
Keep the Sunnyside Up
Draw, Draw a Bucket of Water
Ali Baba
Three Sailors Went to Sea

Scotland:
We Are Three Wee Gallis Girls
I Lost My Love In the Kerney
German Boys Are Awful Funny
Jeannie–Bairdie
Bee–baw Babbity
Teacher, Teacher Let Me In
Cinderella at the Ball
On the Mountain Stands a Lady
Mary Had a Little Lamb, She Sat It On a Bunker
Robert Burns is Born in Here
Christopher Columba
Away Down East, Away Down West
Knees Up Mother Brown
Eeny–meeny–macharaca
Have You Ever, Ever, Ever
The Big Ship Sails Through the Illey–alley–o
Casey the Cowboy

Release date: Nov. 1983 (MM84)
Cassette: CSDL 338 (Nov. 1983: MM84)   **CD:** CD–SDL 338
Insert. Recordings made by Fr Damian Webb between 1960 and 1982.

SDL 339   WILD THYME: Wild Thyme Plays Fallibroome

The Merry Companion	The Happy Pair
Zephyrs and Flora	Miss Sayers' Allemande
Monk's March With the Wanders	Huntington's Maggot
The Topaz	Cream Pot
Bouzer Castle	Drapers Gardens
Shropshire Lass	In the Fields of Frost and Snow
Easter Thursday	Woodlark

Release date: Nov. 1983 (MM84)
Cassette: CSDL 339 (Nov. 1983: MM84)

SDL 340   MECHANICAL MUSIC: Music of the Streets

Street Piano (Pasquale & Co., 44 note) – The Man Who the Bank at Monte Carlo/ I've Got a Lovely Bunch of Coconuts/Charmaine/Oh! Oh! Antonio

Cylinder Piano (Bristol) – three unidentified tunes

Mandoline Street Piano (D. Antonelli & Sons, 55 note) – La Marseillaise/Pomone Waltz/Rule Britannia

Atlas Organette (German, 1890s) – Honeysuckle and the Bee/Just One Girl, Waltz/ Bicycle Barn Dance Polka

Street Piano (marked by A. Tomasso, 44 note) – The Bells of St. Mary's

Street Piano (marked by A. Tomasso, 48 note) – Soldiers of the Queen/Goodbye Dolly Gray/Let the Great Big World

Street Piano (Pasquale & Co., 44 note) – Molly O'Morgan/ Little Dolly Daydream/Roamin' In the Gloamin'/ He Had To Get Out and Get Under

Cylinder Piano (Bristol) – two unidentified tunes/Sailor's Hornpipe/unidentified tune

Cabinetto Paper–Roll Organ (late 19th C.) – Gathering Sea Shells By the Sea Shore/Old Zip Coon/Old Rosin the Beau

Mandoline Street Piano (D. Antonelli & Sons, 55 note) – Softly Wakes My Heart/Sweetheart/unknown tune

St. Mary's Tremelo Street Piano (Pasquale & Co., 48 note) – Little Old Mill/Now Is the Hour

Celestino Paper–Roll Organ (late 19th C.) – Jesu Lover of My Soul/Men of Harlech/Pull for the Shore

Street Piano (Chiappa Ltd., marked by A Tomasso, 48 note) – At Trinity Church I Met My Doom/Colonel Bogey

Release date: Nov. 1983 (MM84)
Cassette: CSDL 340 (Nov. 1983: MM84)   **CD:** CD–SDL 340 (June 1987: MM89)
Subtitled " Mechanical Street Entertainment", Instruments from Roy Mickleburgh's collection. A slightly different version of this LP was issued as SDL 121 under the same title. One copy found with a sticker stating, "Promotional Copy Not For Sale". On the rear was a raffle sticker, so it was given away, not sold!

SDL 341   BELLS: Carillons of Scotland

Perth:
  Scotch On the Rocks
  Mariners' Hymn (O Sanctissima)
  Esteritta
  Estudio 5 for Guitar
  See the Conquering Hero Comes
Kilmarnock:
  The Oak and the Ash
  Sailor's Song
  Duet
  Song: Sandgate Dandling
  Sarabande
  Hymn Tune: Ellers
  The Harp That Once Through Tara's Halls

Aberdeen:
  Round O'
  Charlie Is My Darling
  Tambourin
  John Anderson My Joe
  Four Variations on an Orcadian Melody
  Finale, from Petite Suite
  Waltz No. 5
  Hymn Tune: Martyrs

Release date: 1984 (MM13)
Cassette: CSDL 341 (1984: MM13)
Digital recording. Tracks 1 – 5 played on the Perth Carillon; tracks 6 – 12 played on the Kilmarnock Carillon; tracks 13 – 20 played on the Aberdeen Carillon. Raymond Aldington plays on tracks 1, 4, 6, 8, 9 & 11; Adrien Gebruers plays on tracks 2, 3, 5, 7, 10 & 12. Ronald Leith plays on tracks 13 – 20.

SDL 342   VARIOUS ARTISTS: Diamond Discs

Louisville (Sez Which–Sez How!) (Broadway Dance Orchestra)
Tessie (Stop Teasin' Me) (Fry's Million Dollar Pier Orchestra)
Nobody Knows What a Red–Head Mama Can Do (Jack Stillman & His Orchestra)
Lonely and Blue (Frank Crum & His Orchestra)
Sweet Georgia Brown (Tennessee Happy Boys)
(Oh Maw! Oh Paw!) Isn't She the Sweetest Thing? (Polla's Clover Gardens Orchestra)
Jig Walk (Earl Oliver's Jazz Babies)

Sweet Thing (Golden Gate Orchestra [California Ramblers])
Rosy Cheeks (Oreste & His Queensland Orchestra)
What Do I Care What Somebody Said? (B. A. Rolfe & His Palais d'Or Orchestra);
Oh! Doris, Where Do You Live? (Don Voorhees & His Earl Carroll Vanities Orchestra)
Anything To Make You Happy (Al Lynn's Music Masters)
Mary Ann (Louis Lilienfield & His Hotel Biltmore Orchestra)
I'm Riding To Glory (The Piccadilly Players)

Release date: Sept. 1984 (MM89)
Cassette: CSDL 342 (Sept. 1984: MM89)
Subtitled "Hot Dance Music of the '20s from Edison Diamond Discs". Discs are from Ron Jewson's collection.

SDL 343   KATHRYN TICKELL: On Kielder Side

Joan's Jig / Cut the File
Sweet Hesleyside / Hesleyside Reel
The Skate / Beeswing
Ronell's Reel / Bob Thompson's
Crooked Bawbee / J. B. Milne/Carrick Hornpipe
The Peacock Followed the Hen

Da Slockit Light
Kielder Jock / Matt's/The Stage
Jean's Reel
Johnny Cope / Tipsy Sailor
Border Spirit / A. B. Hornpipe / Billy Pigg's Hornpipe

Release date: Sept. 1984 (MM13)
Cassette: CSDL 343 (Sept. 1984: MM13)   **CD:** CD–SDL 343 (June 1987: MM13)
Subtitled "Northumbrian Small Pipes and Fiddle". Also includes Martin Matthews, Tom Gilfellon, Tristram Robson and Frankie Beegan.

SDL 344   VARIOUS ARTISTS: The Roaring 20's

If You Knew Susie (Jack Shilkret & His Orchestra, vocal, Billy Murray)
The Sheik of Araby (Pianola roll)
I'm Tellin' the Birds, Tellin' the Bees (Jack Smith with piano)
That's My Weakness Now (Pianola roll)
Canadian Capers (Paul Biese Trio)
Rose Marie (Pianola roll)
Collette (Paul Whiteman & His Orchestra, vocal, Jack Fulton, Charles Gaylord with Austin Young)
Where the Lazy Daisies Grow (Pianola roll)
Ain't Misbehaving (Jack Hylton & His Orchestra, vocal, Sam Browne)
My Inspiration Is You (Pianola roll)

The Wedding of the Painted Doll (Pianola roll)
Don't Bring Lulu (Jan Garber & His Orchestra)
Always (Pianola roll)
Where, Oh Where Do I Live? (Fred Douglas with orchestra)
The Birth of the Blues (Pianola roll)
I Miss My Swiss (Golden Gate Orchestra, vocal, Arthur Fields)
Ain't She Sweet? (Pianola roll)
Hello, Swanee, Hello! (The Syncopated Four with piano)
Ramona (Pianola roll)
Charleston (Savoy Orpheans)

Release date: Nov. 1984 (MM13)
Cassette: CSDL 344 (Nov. 1984: MM13)   **CD:** CD–SDL 344 (Feb. 1989: MM89)
Digital recording of records, pianola rolls and pianolas from Roy Mickleburgh's collection.

SDL 345   RICHARD BUTLER: The Perfect Triangle

Madame Bonaparte
Derwentwater's Farewell / Rowantree Hill
Oh Dear, What Can The Matter Be
Barrington Hornpipe / Redesdale Hornpipe
The Wild Hills of Wannies
Highland Laddie
Bracken Riggs / Happy Hours
Blow the Wind Southerly

Memories / Nancy
Johnny Armstrong / Crooked Bawbee / The Rowan Tree / Whittingham Green Lane
Proudlocks Hornpipe / Carrick Hornpipe
Chevy Chase / Come Ye Not From Newcastle?
Bonny Woodside
Bonny North Tyne / Lads of Alnwick
Gypsies' Lullaby
Rothbury Hills / Bill Charlton's Fancy

Release date: Nov. 1985 (MM13)
Cassette: CSDL 345 (Nov. 1985: MM13)   **CD:** CD–SDL 345 (May 2007)

SDL 346   MECHANICAL MUSIC: The Three Disc Symphonion

Tuxedo Polka / Old Folks at Home / After the Ball (A)
Monastery Bells / Cuckoo's Couplet / La Marjolaine, Carnival of Venice (B)
Bedouin Love Song / The Empire and the Tivoli / Vienna Hearts March (C)
Cavatina from Barber of Seville / Unidentified tune / Mandolinata (D)
Darkies Dream / Tyrolean from William Tell / Gavotte D'Amour (A)
Three unidentified titles (E)
Sailor's Hornpipe / Hail Smiling Morn / Hunting Song / Danse du Ventre Polka / Only a Pansy Blossom (F)

The Last Rose Of Summer / Liberty Bell / Intermezzo from Cavalleria Rusticana (G)
No Place Like Home / Unidentified title (H) / All's Well / Here's a Health (I) / The Last Rose of Summer (J) / Rory O'Moore / Why Are You Wandering (K)
Alpine Stars / The Rat–Catcher's Song / Love, Love from The Geisha (C)
Unidentified / The Tide / Unidentified (D)
Paradise Alley / The Blue Danube / O Promise Me (A)
The Mountain Streams / English Air / Then You'll Remember Me (L) / Unidentified (M) / Turkish Patrol March (N)

Release date: Nov. 1984 (MM13)
Cassette: CSDL 346 (Nov. 1984: MM13)
A = Three Disc Symphonion; B = Mandoline, Harp, Piccolo, Zither' Cylinder box by Le Croix & Co; C = 24½" Disc Polyphon; D = Cylinder box by Paillard, Vaucher, Fils; E = Interchangeable cylinder box by Nicole Freres; F = 15½" Disc Regina; G = Three Disc Symphonion; H = Ten air cylinder box with drums and bells; I = Six air 'Fortepiano' cylinder box by Nicole Freres; J = Six air Harp Eolianne cylinder box; K = Eight air key wound cylinder box; L = 11¾" Disc Symphonion; M = 22" Disc Polyphon with glockenspiel attachment; N = 27" Disc Regina.

SDL 347   LYNDON BAGLIN: Lyndon Baglin's Best of Brass

Marching the Blues
Childs Play
Capriol Suite
Endearing Young Charms
Dance of the Russian Sailors
Little Serenade
Fantasia On Tico Tico

Walkabout
Landscape
Cheeky Little Charleston
Brass Badinerie
The Summer Knows
Una Paloma Blanca
Dance of the Tumblers
Li'l Darlin'
Lezghinka

Release date: Sept. 1985 (MM13)
Cassette: CSDL 347 (Sept. 1985: MM13)   **CD:** CD–SDL 347 (May 2006)
Conducted by Nigel Seaman. Saydisc master lists does not include a CD version, however the existence of a CD version is confirmed.

SDL 348   EILEEN MONGER: The Lilting Banshee

King of the Fairies / The Lilting Banshee
Poll Ha'penny / Plains of Boyle / Cnoc na gClarach Slides
O South Wind / Great High Wind
The Wild Geese
Bonny Portmore
The Morning Dew / The Ivy Leaf

Limerick's Lamentation / Give Me Your Hand
The Drunken Sailor
Niel Gow's Lament for the Death of His Second Wife / Farewell to Craigie Dhu
Kerry Polkas
Fingel's Cave
Morris Tunes: Orange In Bloom (Sherborne) / Step Back (Field Town) / Idbury Hill (Bledington)
Hide and Seek

Release date: Sept. 1985 (MM89)
Cassette: CSDL 348 (Sept. 1985: MM89)   **CD:** CD–SDL 348 (Mar. 1987: MM13)
Includes Mike Billinge, Jenny McLeod and George Monger.

SDL 349   *PRINKNASH & STANBROOK ABBEYS: O Give Thanks to the Lord*

Gaudeamus (Processional)
Mass – 'Cum Jubilo' (Mass IX)
Media Vita (Prinknash)
Music from Compline
Gaudeamus (Recessional)

Keep In Your Minds
Like as the Deer (Stanbrook)
Let All Creation
Into Your Hands (Prinknash)
To the Lamb of God
O Give Thanks to the Lord (Stanbrook)
The Daughter of the King (Stanbrook)
Send Forth Your Spirit (Prinknash)
Alleluia (Prinknash)
Te Deum

Release date: Sept. 1985 (MM13)
Cassette: CSDL 349 (Sept. 1985: MM13)
Direct Metal Mastered digital recording with record manufactured in West Germany by Teldec. Latin and English chant from the monks of Prinknash Abbey and the nuns of Stanbrook Abbey, joined by the Bishops Cannings Schola. Joint recordings unless credited otherwise.

SDL 350   *VARIOUS ARTISTS: The Wibbly Wobbly Walk*

The Wibbly Wobbly Walk (Jack Charman)
Oh By Jingo, Oh By Gee (Premier Quartet)
I Miss My Swiss (Tennessee Happy Boys)
Everything's at Home Except Your Wife (Walter Van Brunt)
The Spaniard That Blighted My Life (Billy Merson)
Tickle Me, Timothy (Billy Williams)
The Little Ford Rambled Right Along (Billy Murray)
Wallaperoo (Arthur Osmond)

Love Me (Broadway Dance Orchestra);
Come Back To Georgia (Art Hickman & His Orchestra)
All By Yourself In the Moonlight (Leslie Sarony)
The Little Wooden Whistle Wouldn't Whistle (Columbia Novelty Orchestra)
Why Did I Kiss That Girl? (Savoy Havana Band)
Felix Keeps On Walking (Savoy Havana Band)
I Parted My Hair In the Middle (George Formby)
There's a Rickety Rackety Shack (Kit–Kat Band)
Down South (International Novelty Quartet)
Parade of the Wooden Soldiers (International Novelty Orchestra)

Release date: Nov 1985 (MM13)
Cassette: CSDL 350 (Nov. 1985: MM13)   **CD:** CD–SDL 350
Side 1 tracks are from Phonograph Cylinders; side 2 tracks are from 78rpm records.

SDL 351   *DAVE TOWNSEND: Portrait of a Concertina*

Lovesick Polly/Staines Morris/Three Rusty Swords
The Flat Pavane and Galliard
As Time Goes By
Down the Waggon Way/Come Ashore, Jolly Tar, Your Trousers On
John Come Kiss Me Now
The Cuckoo's Nest/The Maid of the Mill/The Gallant Hussar
Csardas

Suite in E Minor, BWV 996 (Bach)
Rosline Castle/The Golden Cross/Ratclif Cross
Peschatore Che Va Cantando/Saltarello
The Hole In the Wall/The Bashful Swain/Windsor Terrace
Benetev a Trevito

Release date: 1985 / 1988 (MM89)
Cassette: CSDL 351 (Sept. 1988: MM89)   **CD:** CD–SDL 351 (July 1988)
With Nick Hooper.

SDL 352   *THE CARDIFF POLYPHONIC CHOIR: A Christmas Cantata*

A Christmas Cantata:
  Lullay, Jesu, Lullay
  The First God Joy That Mary Had
  When Jesus Christ Was Four Years Old
  Little Jesus, Sweetly Sleep
  Rejoice O Make We Merry, Both More & Less
  I Sing of a Maiden
  By By Lullay, Thou Tiny Little Child

A Christmas Cantata (cont.):
  I Saw Three Ships Come Sailing In/Epilogue
Shiao Bao–Bao
The Angel Gabriel from Heaven Came
Ar Gyfer Heddiw'r Bore
Silent Night, Holy Night
Tua Bethlem Dref
As I Outrode This Enderes Night
Good King Wenceslas

Release date: 1985
Cassette: CSDL 352   **CD:** CD–SDL 345 (Sept: 2006)
Orchestra conducted by Richard Elfyn Jones; organist, Michael Griffiths.

SDL 353   DANIELLE PAULY: Fleur de Jura

Reve Gourmand (Waltz)	Ballade Vosgienne (Polka)
L'Epatante (Polka)	Clin d'Oeil (Java)
Ballade Matinale (March)	File Indienne (March)
Delice Catalan (Tango)	Piccolo Rag (Rag)
Rapide Digitale (Polka)	Fleur de Jura (Polka)
Carte Postale (Waltz)	Exotic Samba (Samba)

Release date: Sept. 1986 (MM89)
Cassette: CSDL 353 (June '86: MM89 / Sept. '86: MM89)   **CD:** CD–SDL 353 (Mar. 1987: MM13)
Subtitled "French Accordion Music". With Felix–Bernard Struber and his Orchestra.

SDL 354   MECHANICAL MUSIC: Mechanical Opera

Arias from Il Trovatore, Ernani, La Traviata, Rigoletto and Nabucco (Verdi)	Arias from operas by Lortzing, Mozart, Boieldieu, Thomas, Wagner, Planquette and Mendelssohn
Favourites from The Mikado, The Pirates of Penzance and H.M.S. Pinafore (Gilbert & Sullivan)	La Fille du Regiment, Linda di Chamounix, Lucia di Lammermoor (Donizetti)
Music from Faust and Carmen (Gounod; Bizet)	William Tell and Barber Of Seville (Rossini)
Les Huguenots and Robert Le Diable (Meyerbeer)	From I Puritani, La Sonnambula and Norma (Bellini)

Release date: Mar. 1986
Cassette: CSDL 354 (Mar. 1986)   **CD:** CD–SDL 354 (June 1986)
Subtitled "Opera Favourites on Musical Boxes". Music boxes used are: 24½" disc Polyphon (Penny–In–The–Slot); Le Croix 'Mandoline' Cylinder Musical Box; Paillard Vaucher Fils Cylinder Musical Box; 27" disc Regina Musical Box; Nicole Freres Interchangable Cylinder Box with 3 combs; Ducommun Girod Cylinder Musical Box; Excelsior Piccolo 12 Air Cylinder Musical Box; Nicole Freres 19 1/2" Forteppiano Interchangable Cylinder Box 1903; 48 note Penny–In–The–Slot piano; Sublime Harmony Piccolo Cylinder Musical Box; 15½" disc Regina Musical Box; 22" disc Polyphon with Glockenspiel attachment (Penny–In–The–Slot); Sublime Harmonie Piccolo Cylinder Musical Box by George Baker & Co.; Nicole Freres 10 Air Cylinder Musical Box (1841); 12 Air. 2 Comb Cylinder Musical Box.

SDL 355   MECHANICAL MUSIC: Kitten On the Keys

Bye Bye Blackbird (Fox Trot)	Doll Dance
Thora	Moon River (Waltz)
Miss Annabelle Lee (Fox Trot)	Lovable and Sweet (Fox Trot – Theme Song from 'Street Girl')
For Me and My Gal (Fox Trot)	Me and Jane In a Plane (Fox Trot)
Stars and Stripes Forever	Kitten On the Keys (Fox Trot)
Sweet Genevieve (Ballad)	Stealing (Fox Trot)
J'En Ai Marre (Fox Trot and Shimmy)	Tippy Canoe (Waltz)
Alexander's Ragtime Band	Among My Souvenirs (Fox Trot)
I Want to Be Happy (From 'No No Nanette')	The More We Are Together (One Step) (played by Laurel Pardy & Edith Murn)
	Three O'Clock In the Morning (Waltz)

Release date: June 1986 (MM89)
Cassette: CSDL 355 (June 1986: MM89)   **CD:** CD–SDL 355 (Mar. 1987: MM89)
Digital recording. Subtitled "Popular Music from Pianola Rolls". Played on pianolas from the Roy Mickleburgh collection. The original pressing was withdrawn soon after release because of an interesting mistake. Gef Lucena explains: "Here's something for the collector to track down – SDL 355 Kitten On the Keys – the first edition of the vinyl version had an amazing error – soon withdrawn when discovered but extant copies could have collector value. I only knew the title piece by its name so when I recorded this pianola roll with a wild and exciting jumble of notes I assumed that this was why it was so entitled. However, a customer soon alerted us to the fact that the roll had been rolled backwards, so we had to then hurriedly find a collector who had a copy of the roll playing in the correct direction. We found one somewhere in Leicestershire I think and recorded the roll on our way back from another recording. The LP sleeve was evidently not reprinted to credit the collector who loaned us the proper version and this was all forgotten by the time we made the CD version – so Roy Mickleburgh shows as supplying all the rolls for that recording."

Having heard both, I think that I actually prefer the wild backwards version!

CSDL 356   BELLS: Music from St. Clement Danes (cassette)

Psalm 23	*Whitsuntide:*
Advent:	Ye Now Are Sorrowful
How Shall I Fitly Meet Thee	*Eastertide:*
Christmas:	This Joyfu1 Eastertide
O magnum mysterium	*Ascension:*
Stille Nacht	Coelos Ascendit Hodie
I Saw Three Ships	Let the Bright Seraphim
Epiphany:	*Passiontide and General:*
When to the Temple Mary Went	Greater Love
Passiontide:	Toccata In B minor
Adoramus Te Jesu Christe	

Release date: June 1986 (MM13)
CD: CD–SDL 356
Not issued on LP. Issued on cassette only – later issued on CD. The side 1 break above is a 'best guess' scenario!

SDL 357   GEORGES SCHMITT: Joy to the World

O Sanctissima	Jingle Bells
Silent Night	On the Christmas Tree
O Christmas Tree	Come Along Children
Jesu Joy of Man's Desiring	The First Nowell
Rudolph the Red–Nosed Reindeer	Dance of the Santons
O Gentle Little Jesus	O Joyful Day
Come On, Shepherds	Ring, Sleigh Bells
Ave Maria	Angels from the Realms of Glory
Wake Up All You Shepherds	Song of Christmas
Joy to the World	The Holy Child Is Born

Release date: Sept. 1986
Cassette: CSDL 357 (Sept. 1986)   **CD:** CD–SDL 357 (June 1986)
Subtitled "Christmas Music for Pan Pipes and Organ". Georges Schmitt, pan–pipes, Bernard Struber, organ & Roland Bochot/Jean Garron, percussion. Music originally issued in France in 1977 and 1979.

SDL 358   VARIOUS ARTISTS, MECHANICAL MUSIC, ETC: Keep the Home Fires Burning

Here We Are, Here We Are (Wheeler & Chorus; Phonograph Cylinder)	Tramp, Tramp, Tramp (Harlan & Stanley and Chorus)
Goodbyee (Penny Piano)	Keep the Home Fires Burning (Penny Piano)
Just Before the Battle (Will Oakland & Chorus; Phonograph Cylinder)	Boys of the Old Brigade (N. M. B.; Phonograph Cylinder)
Your King and Country Want You (Helen Clarke & Chorus; Phonograph Cylinder)	Boys In Khaki, Boys In Blue (F. Wheeler & Male Chorus; Phonograph Cylinder)
The Trumpeter (Raymond Newell and Ian Swinley; 78 rpm record)	Colonel Bogey March/Keep the Home Fires Burning/Pack Up Your Troubles/It's a Long Way To Tipperary (Band of H. M. Coldstream Guards; 78 rpm record)
The Deathless Army (T. F. Kinniburgh; Phonograph Cylinder)	Roses of Picardy (Templeton Murray, pianola)
Medley (N. M. B. Flying Squadron; Phonograph Cylinder)	Passing Review Patrol (Band; Phonograph Cylinder)
	What Has Become of the Hinkey Dinky Parlay Voo (Al Bernard & Chorus; Edison Diamond Disc 1924)

Release date: Sept. 1986 (MM13)
Cassette: CSDL 358 (Sept. 1986: MM13)   **CD:** CD–SDL 358
Subtitled "The Songs and Music of the 1st World War from the Original Recordings".

SDL 359   MECHANICAL MUSIC: Musical Box Dances Played On Victorian Musical Boxes

Waltzes:
  Espana
  Redonna Sorte
  Little Sailors
  Telegramme Waltz
  The Craven
  On The Marvellous Rhine
Polkas:
  La Gracieuse
  Happy
  Les Trompettes du Regiment
  Our Little Volunteers
Miscellany:
  A Dance
  So 'ne ganze kleine Frau' — German couplet
  Impudence—Scottische
  German couplet
  Minuet by Fischer
  Pinafore Quadrille
  The Sailor's Hornpipe
Waltzes:
  See Saw
  Philomela Waltz (Strauss)
  Vals Rosita (Recuerdo de Sobrevia)
  Santiago Valse Espagnole
  La Stapleton

The Blue Danube:
  Three examples
Galops & Gavottes:
  Roulette (Galop)
  Petersburg Champagne (Galop)
  Stephanie (Gavotte)
  Air de Louis XIII (Gavotte)
  Der Glurksritter (Frauenlilt Gavotte)
Polkas:
  Angel Polka
  The Old Couples
  Anka Polka
  Le Nid de Svengali
  Bric–A–Brac
  Avec Amore
Waltzes:
  Another German Waltz
  Shop Girl
  La Guillaume
  Unidentified waltz
  Maritana
  Tyrolese Waltz
  Les Sirens
  When the Leaves Begin to Turn
  After the Ball

Release date: 1988
Cassette: CSDL 359 (Sept. 1988)   **CD:** CD–SDL 359 (June 1988)
The side 1 break above is a 'best guess'.

SDL 360   THE MELLSTOCK BAND: Under the Greenwood Tree

Arise and Hail the Joyful Day
Morgianna / The Pantaloon Quadrille
Hail Happy Morn
Kiss Me My Love and Welcome / Drops of
    Brandy (1) / Drops of Brandy (2)
Awake and Join the Cheerful Choir
The Gipsey's Hornpipe / Ashley's Hornpipe /
    The One Eyed Fiddler
See Heaven's High Portals
I'm Off to Charlestown
Awake, Awake Ye Mortals All

While Shepherds Watched
Fairy Dance / Tink a Tink
Behold The Morning Star
Moss Roses / Droll Johnny / The Flight
The Musical Lovers
Lord Nelson's Hornpipe / Enrico
Arise and Hail the Sacred Day
Rejoice This Glorious Day Is Come
The Triumph

Release date: Oct. 1986 (MM13)
Cassette: CSDL 360 (Oct. 1986: MM13)   **CD:** CD–SDL 360 (Mar. 1987: MM13)

SDL 361   THE CANTERBURY CLERKES: Fill Your Glasses

Fill Your Glasses
Push About the Bottle, Boys
When Bibo Thought Fit
Foresters, Sound the Cheerful Horn
When Gen'rous Wine Expands My Soul
Viva Tutti and Dulci Momenti
We Be Three Poor Mariners
Hark, the Hollow Woods Resounding
An Evening Rondeau
There Behold the Mighty Bowl
Life's a Bumper
Music's the Language of the Blest Above

Fear No Danger to Ensue
Peace to the Souls of the Heroes
Sportive Little Trifler, Tell Me
How Merrily We Live
Fair Aurora
Nocturne, from music for A Midsummer Night's Dream
Fear No More the Heat of the Sun
O How Sweetly Delia Sings
Breath Soft, Ye Winds
Of All the Brave Birds
Peaceful Slumberings
Time Has Not Thinned
Sleep, While the Soft Evening

Release date: Oct. 1986 (MM13)
Cassette: CSDL 361 (Oct. 1986: MM13)   **CD:** CD–SDL 361 (prob. Sept/Oct. 1986)
Digital recording. The Canterbury Clerkes are: Peter Giles, Martin Renshaw and Antony Bussell. The London Serpent Trio are: Christopher Monk, Clifford Bevan and Andrew van der Beck.

SDLC 362   VARIOUS ARTISTS: Pleasures and Treasures

March By Mr. Handel (from SAR 10)
Mira O Norma (from SDL 303)
Jean's Reel (from SDL 343)
Lezghinka (from SDL 347)
Prelude to the Suite In E major, BWV 1006a
    (from SAR 23)
Collette (from SDL 344)
John Come Kiss Me Now (from SDL 351)
Music from Compline (from SDL 349)
Le Coucou (from SAR 19)
Whistling Rufus (from SDL 333)
Limerick's Lamentation/Give Me Your Hand
    (from SDL 348)

La Quinte Estampie Real (from SAR 22)
I've Got a Lovely Bunch of Coconuts (from SDL 340)
Love at the Fair (from SDL 325)
Miss Annabelle Lee (from SDL 355)
Scherzo from the 'Spring' Sonata (from SAR 9)
The Wibbly Wobbly Walk (from SDL 350)
Jeny Lind Medley (from SDL 335)
Turkish Rondo (from SAR 6)
O Sanctissima (from SDL 357)
Reve Gourmand (from SDL 353)
Sportive Little Trifler (from SDL 361)

Release date: Sept. 1986 (MM13)
Cassette: CSDLC 362 (Sept. 1986: MM13)   **CD:** CD–SDLC 362 (Sept. 1986: MM13)
Direct metal mastered. Subtitled "A Kaleidoscope of Rare and Beautiful Music", this is a budget sampler of material previously issued on the Saydisc and Amon Ra labels. One of very few Saydisc LPs to be issued in a gatefold sleeve. A 21st anniversary budget sampler with a photo of Saydisc owners, Gef and Genny Lucena on the rear.

SDL 363   STANBROOK ABBEY: Wellsprings

Thirsting for God:
  Rorate coeli: "Drop down dew, you heavens"
  John 7:37–39
  Psalm 138
  Psalm 129
  Matthew 11:28–30
  Psalm 21
  John 19:25–30
  Good Friday Responsory: "Now is the
      judgement of this world"

Living Water:
  Melody from Roman Gradual: Easter Tuesday Introit
  Psalm 113
  Psalm 103
  John 4:4–14
  John 20:19–22 + Alleluia, Christ is risen / Iasiah 66:12.13 /
      'Sunset Over the Sea' / Psalm 22
  Psalm 83
  John 14:1–3 + Rev 22:17, 20b

Release date: Oct. 1986 (MM89)
Cassette: CSDL 363 (Oct. 1986: MM89)

CD–SDL 364   THE YORK WAITS: Music from the Time of Richard III (CD and cassette only)

England and the Low Countries:
  Quene Note
  La Spagna
  Mater Ora Filium
  L'Hom Arme
  Danse de Cleves
  Le Souvenir
France:
  Tuba Gallicalis
  Noel Nouvelet
  Anxi Bon Youre Delabonestren
  Nous voici dans la ville dit le Bourguinon
  Allcz a la Fougere

Germany:
  In Feuers Hitz
  Auf Rief Ein Huebsches Freulein
  Der Neue Bauernschwanz
  Die Katzen Pfote
  Ein Vrouleen Edel Von Naturen
  Das Jaegerhorn
Italy:
  Mercantia
  Anello
  Amoroso
  L'Amor Donna Ch'Io Te Porta
Spain:
  Bassa Con Misurias / Danza Alta
  Todos Los Biennes Del Mundo / Dindirin, Dindirin

Release date: Oct. 1997 (both formats: MM13)
Cassette: CSDL 364

SDL 365   THE FAIRER SAX: Diversions

Arrival of the Queen of Sheba (Handel)
Quatuor Pour Saxophones (Dubois):
  Ouverture: Brillante
  Doloroso
  Spirituoso
  Andante
Bransle Gentil (Praetorius)
Pavane for the Earl of Salisbury (Byrd)
Courante and Springdance (Praetorius)
Robert Burns Suite (Harvey):
  My Wife's a Winsome Wee Thing
  My Love Is Like a Red Red Rose
  Bannocks O'Bearmeal

Fugue in G Minor from Fantasia and Fugue in G minor (Bach)
Diversions (Patterson):
  Gusty
  Blowing Blue
  Sea Breeze
Aria from Suite No. 3 in D (Bach)
Moment Musicale Op.94 no.3 (Schubert)
Quartet for Saxes Op. 168 (Gardner):
  Allegro ma non troppo
  Adagio
  Finale: Allegro molto
Something Doing

Release date: Oct. 1987 (MM89)
Cassette: CSDL 365 (Oct. 1987: MM89)   **CD:** CD–SDL 365 (Oct. 1987: MM89)
Direct Metal Mastered with Teldec DMM inner sleeve, but with what appear to be UK, not German, labels.
Saxophone quartet: Anne–Louise Lane, soprano; Gabrielle Lane, alto; Karen Street, tenor; Julia Mills, baritone..

SDL 366   MADDY PRIOR WITH THE CARNIVAL BAND: A Tapestry of Carols

The Sans Day Carol
In Ducli Jubilo
God Rest You Merry Gentlemen
It Came Upon the Midnight Clear
The Holly and the Ivy
The Coventry Carol
Ding Dong Merrily On High
The Angel Gabriel

Angels From the Realms of Glory
Infant Holy
A Virgin Most Pure
Unto Us a Boy Is Born
Rejoice and Be Merry
Joseph Dearest
Personal Hodie
On Christmas Night (Sussex Carol)

Release date: Sept. 1987 (MM13)
Cassette: CSDL 366 (Sept. 1987: MM13)   **CD:** CD–SDL 366 (Sept. 1987: MM13)
Maddy Prior, vocals; Bill Badley, lute, baroque guitar, guitar, banjo, mandolin, mandocello, cittern, vocals; Andrew Davis, double bass; Giles Lewis, violin, recorders, vocals; Charles Fullbrook, small & medium tabors, basel trommel, glockenspiel, small bells, wood blocks, cowbell, triangle, antique cymbals, tambourin provencal, vocals; Andrew Watts, Flemish bagpipes, bassoon, curtal, clarinet in C, recorders, shawm, vocals.

CD–SDL 367   RIE YANAGISAWA & CLIVE BELL: Kurokami (CD)

Haru no umi
Kurokami
Disguised as a Silverer of Mirrors
Midare rinzetsu

Yugao
Esashi Oiwake
Aki no shirabe

Release date: June 1988 (MM89)
Cassette: CSDL 367
Traditional music from Japan: koto, shakuhachi, shamisen.

From the above release onwards all Saydisc records were issued on CD (and most on cassette) with production of LPs discontinued. Release date from here on refers to both CD and cassette issues unless release dates are known to be different.

CD–SDL 368   JING YING SOLOISTS: Evening Song

Autumn Moon
Ducks Quacking
Love Song of the Grassland
Singing The Night Among Fishing Boats
The Fishing Song
The Marriage of Chan Xian–Yuen

Moonlight Over the Spring River
Happy Reunion
Bamboo Flute Song from the Village
Variations On Yang City Tune
Meditating On the Past
Moon Over Guan–shan

Release date: Oct. 1987 (MM89)
Cassette: CSDL 368

CD–SDL 369   MONKS & NUNS OF PRINKNASH & STANDBROOK ABBEYS: Christmas Chant

Sequence: Laetabundus

Extracts from Matins:
 Invitatory: Christus Natus Est. Ps. 94
 Hymn: Christe Redemptor
 Melody from Ely MS
 Antiphon: Dominus Dixit Ps. 2
 Lesson: Isaiah. Ch.9. vv 1–6
 Responsory: Verbum Caro
 Marian Anthem: Alma Redemptoris Mater
Mass Chants:
 Introit: Dominus Dixit: Midnight Mass
 Kyrie Missa IV: Cunctipotens
 Gloria
 Gradual: Omnes de Saba Epiphany

Alleluia: Dawn Mass
Offertory: Laetentur: Midnight Mass
Sanctus
Agnus Dei
Communion: In Splendoribus: Midnight
Mass
Short Hymns & Chants:
 Hymn: Angelus Ad Virginem
 Anthem: Ecce Nomen
 Antiphon: Quem Vidistis
 Antiphon: Angelus Ad Pastores
 Antiphon: Hodie
 Recessional: Puer Natus

Release date: prob. autumn 1988 (SC)
Cassette: CSDL 369 (Oct. 1988: MM89)

CD–SDL 370   VARIOUS ARTISTS: Whistle Away Your Blues

Whistle Away Your Blues (Jay Whidden Band)
Mon Paris (Jay Whidden Band)
Why Robinson Crusoe Got the Blues (Savoy
      Havana Band)
When it's Night Time in Italy (Casino Dance
      Orchestra)
Sunny Havana (New Princes Toronto Band)
To Know You Is to Love You (Jack Hylton Band)
Dreamy Honolulu (Jack Hylton Band)
Today's a Sunny Day for Me (Lloyd
      Shakespeare Band)

Laughing Marionette (Lloyd Shakespeare Band)
Here I Am Broken Hearted (Lou Gold Band)
Little Old Church In the Valley (Layton & Johnstone)
Carolina Moon (Norman Blair)
Just Plain Folk (Norman Blair)
Gonna Get a Girl (The Admirals)
White Wings (Will Oakland)
Side By Side (Sam Lanin)
I Love a Lassie (Harry Lauder)
The Wedding of Lauchie McGraw (Harry Lauder)
A Wee Deoch an' Doris (Harry Lauder)

Release date: May 1988 (MM89)
Cassette: CSDL 370

CD–SDL 371   SNEAK'S NOYSE: Christmas Now Is Drawing Near

Christmas Now Is Drawing Near – Advent:
 Oh, Christmas Now Is Drawing Near at Hand
 We've Been Awhile a–Wandering
 The Waits
Sweet Jesus Born – The Nativity:
 Lully, Lulla, Thou Little Tiny Child
 Good People All, This Christmastime
 Sweet Was the Song the Virgin Sang
Down In Yon Forest – Christmas Legends:
 As I Sat On a Sunny Bank
 Down In Yon Forest
 The Holly and the Ivy
 Joseph Was an Old Man
 Cold Was the Day When In a Garden Bare
Tomorrow Shall Be My Dancing Day – Carol(e)
      Roots:
 English Dance (instrumental)
 Angelus ad Virginem
 Hail Mary Full of Grace

Tomorrow Shall Be My Dancing Day
The Furry Day Carol (instrumental)
Cold Winter Is Come – Plenty and Poverty:
 The Boar's Head In Hand Bear I
 Fy, Nay, Prithee John (instrumental)
 Cold Winter Is Come
 Deck the Halls with Boughs of Holly
 All Hail to the Days
 As It Fell Out Upon One Day
Remember O Thou Man – The Christian Message:
 Remember, O Thou Man
 On Christmas Night All Christians Sing
 This Is the Truth Sent from Above
God Send You A Happy New Year – Farewell to Christmas:
 The Old Year Now Away Is Fled
 Here We Come a–Wassailing
 God Bless You Merry, Gentlemen
 Oh, Christmas Now (instrumental reprise)

Release date: autumn 1988 (SC) / Oct. 1986 (MM89)
Cassette: CSDL 371 (1988: MM89)
October release date in MM89 is incorrect, as several other release dates seem to be in this publication.

CD–SDL 372   BONNIE SHALJEAN: Farewell to Lough Neaghe

Pibddawns Y Tant / Yr Ysgubau / Y Blodau
Roslin Castle / The Lea–Rig
Captain O'Neil / Colonel O'Hara / Sir Festus Burke
Bryd One Brere / Foweles In the Frith / Edi Beo Thu Hevene Quene / Sumer Is Icumen In
The Late Hour / The Clock's Back Reel
Meillionen
Maille Bheag O
The Kilburn Jig / Diarmuid's Well / The Wild Irishman
Childgrove / Daphne / 'Twas Within a Furlong of Edinburgh Town / The Oak and the Ash
Farewell to Lough Neaghe

Pant Corlan Yr Wyn / Pibddawns Jones / Pwt Ar Y Bys
Her Mantle So Green / In Aonar Seal
Port 4th / Air By Fingal No. 1 / Air By Fingal No.3 / Port 5th
When She Cam Ben She Bobbit
Planxty Drew / Mary O'Neill / Edmond MacDermott Roe / The Maids of Derry
Caismeachd Mhic Iain 'Ic Sheumais / Marbhna Cathaoir Mhic Cába
An Páistín Fionn / Seán O'Duibhir An Ghleanna
Port Priest / Port Atholl
I Was Not ... Since Martinmas / An Muileann Dubh / The Highlandman / Kissed His Mother
Cumha Mhic Guidhir / Táim I Mo / Chodhladh Is Ná Duisigh Mé
Maggy Lauther / Bonie Jean Makis / Meikill Of Me

Release date: Sept. 1988 (MM89)
Cassette: CSDL 372

CD–SDL 373   THE YORK WAITS: Music from the Time of the Spanish Armada

The Queenes Visiting of the Campe at Tilsburie
The Spanish Pavan / Galliard — La Gamba
Crimson Velvet
La Doune Cella / La Shy Myze / La Bounette
The Obtaining of the Great Galleazzo
Browninge My Dere / Browninge Fantasy
Les Bransles Gays
The Delight Pavan / Galliard to Delight Pavan
Staines Morris
The Quarter Brawles

Pavana / Galiarda / Coranto
Watkins Ale
Robin Is to the Greenwood Gone
Wilson's Fantasie
The Spanish Lady / The Cushion Dance
Dulcina / All You That Love Good Fellowes
Eighty–Eight or Sir ffrancis Drake
Les Bransles de Champagne
The Carman's Whistle / Under and Over / Pepper Is Black / Millfield / Roowe Well Ye Marynors

Release date: July 1988 (MM89)
Cassette: CSDL 373

CD–SDL 374   NIGEL EATON AND FRIENDS: The Music of the Hurdy Gurdy

Il Pastor Fido (Vivaldi) Sonata:
  Moderato
  Allegro: Tempo di Gavotta
  Affetuoso: Aria
  Allegro
  Giga: Allegro
The Crocodile 3/8 Bourree
Lady Diamond, New Jig
The Bourree with No Name
Satins Blanc
Malashevska

Les Amusements D'Une Heure, Sonata 3 (Baton):
  Gayement
  Gigue
  Gracieusement
  Bourree
  Two Hornpipes
  Bourree / The Crocodile
  Laridé
  Queen Adelaide, The Man In the Brown Hat
  Scottische, Gloryflower
  Bourree

Release date: autumn 1988 (SC)
Cassette: CSDL 374

CD–SDL 375   BRISTOL BACH CHOIR: Welcome Yule

Welcome Yule (Joubert)
A Hymn to the Virgin (Britten)
Virga Jesse (Bruckner)
A Spotless Rose (Howells)
The Rose (Paynter)
Lully, Lulla (Leighton)
Come to Bethlehem (Warlock)
This Have I Done for My True Love (Holst)
What Sweeter Music (Bennett)

Carol of the Bells (arr. Leontovich)
Long, Long Ago (Beaumont)
He Smiles Within His Cradle (arr. Willcocks)
Ding Dong! Merrily On High (arr. Burt)
Wexford Carol (arr. Rutter)
There Is No Rose of Such Virtue (Joubert)
Stille Nacht (Gruber arr. Cashmore)
O Magnum Mysterium (Poulenc)
Hodie Christus Natus Est (Poulenc)

Release date: 1988
Cassette: CSDL 375
Original issue subtitled "Seasonal Choral Music". Conducted by Glyn Jenkins.

CD–SDL 376   TRADITIONAL: Disappearing World

The Meo, Laos	The Basques, French Pyrenees
The Mehinacu, Brazil	The Wodeabe, Sahel
The Mongols, Mongolia	The Shilluk, Sudan
The Rendille, Kenya	The Tuareg, Sahara
Vlach Gypsies, Hungary	The Panare, Venezuela
The Pathans, Khyber	Marrakech, Morocco
The Masai, Kenya / Tanzania	The Sakuddei Siberut, Indonesia
Kataragama, Sri Lanka	The Tuvinians, Tuva
Dervishes, Kurdistan	

Release date: 1989
Cassette: CSDL 376
Produced in conjunction with Granada Television and The British Library National Sound Archive.

CD–SDL 377   VIRAM JASANI, GURDEV SINGH & USTAD LATIF AHMED KHAN: Rags, Malkauns and Megh

Rag Malkauns:
  Bilampit Khyal
  Tal–Tintal (16 beats)

Rag Megh:
  Alap
  Gat in Ektal (12 beats)
  Gat in Tintal (16 beats)

Release date: 1989
Cassette: CSDL 377
Sitar, sarod, tabla.

CD–SDL 378   BELLS: Church Bells of England

St. Mary Redcliffe, Bristol (Little Bob Maximus)	St. Mary–le–Bow, Cheapside (Bristol Surprise Maximus)
St. Paul's Cathedral (Stedman Cinques)	St. Olave, Hart Street (Stedman Triples)
St. Vedast, Foster Lane (Cambridge Surprise Minor)	St Michael, Cornhill (Londinium Surprise Maximus)
St. Lawrence, Jewry (Spliced Surprise Major)	St. Bartholomew the Great, Smithfield (Grandsire Doubles)
St. Giles, Cripplegate (Cambridge Surprise Maximus)	Westminster Abbey (Stedman Caters)
St. Clement Danes, Strand (London Surprise Royal)	St. Martin–in–the–fields (Yorkshire Surprise Maximus)
St. Sepulchre, Holborn Viaduct (Stedman Caters)	St. John the Baptist, Burford, Oxon. (Double Norwich Court Bob Major)
	St. Leonard, Bledington, Glos. (Cambridge Surprise Minor)
	St. David, Moreton–in–Marsh, Glos. (Kent Treble Bob Major)

Release date: 1989
Cassette: CSDL 378
Sixteen famous peals from London, the Cotswolds, and elsewhere with tracks originally issued on SDL 243, SDL 290 and SDL 337.

CD–SDL 379   THE ENGLISH GUITAR QUARTET: Romantic Guitar Quartets

Songs Without Words (Mendelssohn):
  No. 45 (Op. 102 No. 3)
  No. 7 (Op. 30 No. 1)
  No. 35 (Op. 67 No. 5)
  No. 44 (Op. 102 No. 2)
  No. 21 (Op. 53 No. 3)
Mazurka No. 35 (Op. 56 No. 3) (Chopin)
Mazurka No. 37 (Op. 59 No. 2) (Chopin)

Mazurka No. 32 (Op. 50 No. 3) (Chopin)
String Quartet No. 2 (Borodin:
  Notturno
"Arpeggione" Sonata (Schubert):
  Allegro moderato
  Adagio
  Allegretto

Release date: 1990
Cassette: CSDL 379

CD–SDL 380   VARIOUS ARTISTS: The Golden Years of Music Hall

Who Were You With Last Night? (Mark Sheridan)
The Tower of London (The Beefeater) (Dan Leno)
My Old Dutch (Albert Chevalier)
The Twenty–Third (Little Tich)
Look What Percy's Picked Up In the Park (Vesta Victoria)
Little Willie's Woodbines (Billy Williams)
I'm Henery the Eighth (Harry Champion)
I'm Shy, Mary Ellen, I'm Shy (Jack Pleasants)
Hello! Hello! Who's Your Lady Friend? (Harry Fragson)
Jolly Good Luck to the Girl Who Loves a Soldier (Vesta Tilley)

A Little of What You Fancy (Marie Lloyd)
And That's That (George Robey)
I Was a Good Little Girl Till I Met You (Clarice Mayne & "That" [James W. Tate])
Burlington Bertie from Bow (Ella Shields)
Sailing (George Formby)
Roamin' In the Gloamin' (Sir Harry Lauder)
Nellie Dean (Gertie Gitana & Chorus)
Broke the Bank at Monte Carlo (Charles Coborn)
Down at the Old Bull and Bush (Florrie Forde)
I Belong to Glasgow (Will Fyffe)
That's Where the Soldiers Go (Lily Morris)
It's a Great Big Shame (Gus Elen)
Love 'Em and Leave 'Em Alone (Hetty King)

Release date: 1990
Cassette: CSDL 380

CD–SDL 381   FINE ARTS BRASS ENSEMBLE: The Lighter Side of the Fine Arts Brass Ensemble

William Tell Overture
Pavane
Nellie's Nutcracker
Chanson de Matin
Puttin' On the Ritz
Top Hat, White Tie and Tails
Alexander's Ragtime Band
Prelude to Te Deum

Brass Quintet (Divertimento No.5) Op.67:
  Fanfares and Questions
  Lament and Hymn
  Scherzino
  Funeral March
  Quodlibet en Rondeau
Jesu Joy of Man's Desiring
Washington Post March

Release date: 1990
Cassette: CSDL 381

CD–SDL 382   THE CITY WAITS: Pills to Purge Melancholy

Sometimes I Am a Tapster New
Honest Shepherd Since You're Poor
Blowzabella my Bouncing Doxie
As Oyster Nan Stood By Her Tub
There Was a Lass of Islington
Poor Celia Once Was Very Fair
Oh Fie! What Mean I Foolish Maid
What Life Can Compare with the Jolly Town Rakes
I Hate a Fop That at His Glass
Would Ye Have a Young Virgin of Fifteen Years
Weep All Ye Nymphs, Your Floods Unbind
A Soldier and a Sailor, a Tinker and a Taylor
Then Jockey Wou'd a Wooing Away

With My Strings of Small Wire
How Vile Are the Sordid Intrigues of the Town
Like a Ring Without a Finger
Through the Cold Shady Woods
When for Air I Take My Mare
Young Collin, Cleaving of a Beam
One Sunday at St. James's Prayers
There Was an old Woman Liv'd Under a Hill
Oh! My Panting, Panting Heart
Now Listen A While, and I Will Tell
Oh Mother, Roger with His Kisses
Do Not Rumple My Top–knot
Come Jug My Honey, Let's to Bed

Release date: 1990
Cassette: CSDL 382
Lewd songs and low ballads.

No cat. no. Fred Wedlock, Volume 1

No cat. no. Christmas Carols on Disc Musical Boxes

No cat. no. Bristol Folks

SDL 112 Cylinder Jazz

SD 113 The Crofters, PIll Ferry

SD 116 Siobhan Lyons, The Patriot Game

SDL 117 Pianola Jazz

SDL 118 Ragtime Piano

SD 119 Enchanted Carols (original sleeve design)

SD 119 Enchanted Carols (modified sleeve design)

SD 120 The Crofters, Drink Up Thee Cider

SDL 121 Music of the Streets

SDL 123 St. Mary Redcliffe School Choir, Three 20th Century Cantatas

SD 124 Fred Wedlock/Bev & Richard Dewar, Virtute et Industrial

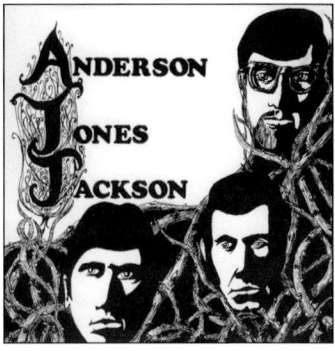

33SD 125 Anderson Jones Jackson

SD 126 Graham Kilsby, In a Folk Mood

SD 127 Bells of Britain vol. 1 (original sleeve design)

SD 127 Bells of Britain vol. 1 (modified sleeve design)

SD 129 The Crofters, Ballad of the Severn Bridge

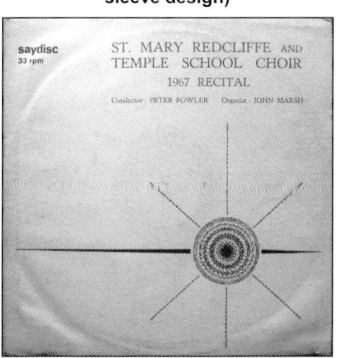

SDL 131 St. Mary Redcliffe and Temple School Choir, 1967 Recital

SDL 132 Pianola Ragtime

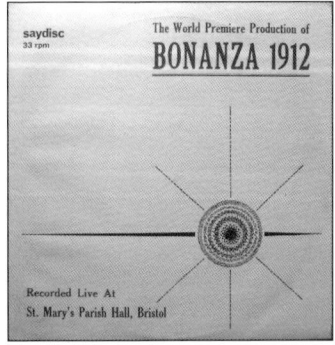

SDL 133 Bonanza 1912

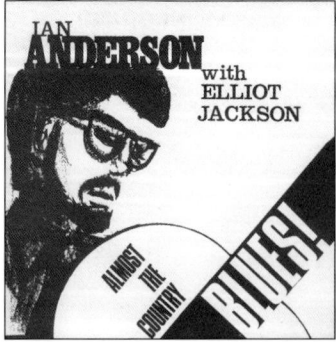

33SD 134 Ian Anderson with Elliot Jackson, Almost the Country Blues

SDL 136 The Blue Notes Jazz Band, Farewell to the Ship

SD 137 Mike Cooper, Up the Country
Blues!

33SD 140, Lauri Say & the Island Folk
(original sleeve design)

33SD 140, Lauri Say & the Island Folk
(later sleeve design)

SDM 142 Blues Like Showers of Rain
(original sleeve design)

SDM 142 Blues Like Showers of Rain
(modified sleeve design)

SDR 143 Blind Boy Fuller, Blind Boy
Fuller on Down Vol. 1

SDL 145 Story of the Polyphon (poss.
second sleeve design)

SDR 146 Blues Piano Vol. 1

SDL 151 Wurlitzer (poss. second
sleeve design)

SDL 152 Giant German Orchestrons
(orig. issued in sleeve like SDL 123)

SDL 153 Story of a Mechanical Organ
(poss. second sleeve design)

SDL 154 US label stuck on UK white
label test press

33SD 156 Dave & Tim (Mudge & Clutterbuck), Sheep

SD 158 The Street Piano

SDM 159 Mike Cooper/Ian Anderson, The Inverted World

SDL 162 Mike Absalom, Save the Last Gherkin for Me!

SDR 163, Kokomo Arnold

SDL 164 The Loughborough Carillon

SDM 167 Blues Like Showers of Rain Volume Two

SDR 168 Blind Boy Fuller on Down Vol. 2

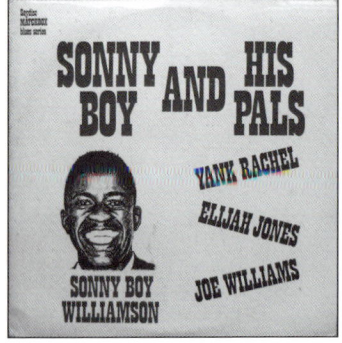

SDR 169 Sonny Boy and His Pals

SDL 173 Honky Tonk Nickelodeons

33SD 117 Clifton – "Father" Willis

SDL 181 Mechanical Opera

SDR 182 Those Cake Walking Babies from Home

SDR 190 Furry Lewis, Furry Lewis In Memphis

SDR 191 Peetie Wheatstraw, The Devil's Son in Law

SDR 192 Peetie Wheatstraw, The High Sheriff from Hell

SDL 193 The Reproducing Piano

Prob. SDL 198 or poss. SDL 188 US label stuck on UK white label

SDR 199 Skoodle–Um–Skoo

SDR 206 Home Town Skiffle

SDX 207/SDX 208 Black Diamond Express to Hell (2–LP)

SDL 209 Piston Polka

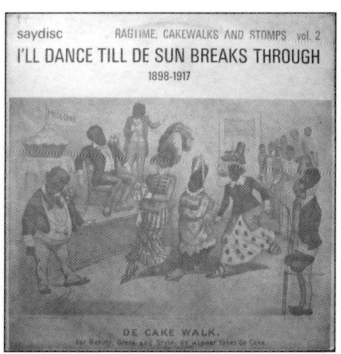

SDL 210 I'll Dance Till de Sun Breaks Through

SDL 211 The Rhythm of the Bells

SDR 213 Little Brother Montgomery

SDR 216 Clyde Bernhardt, Blowing My Top

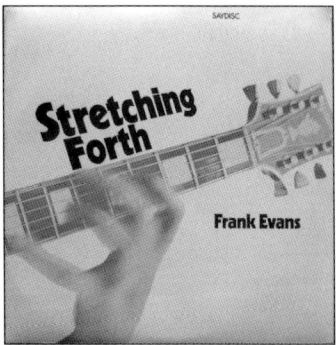

SDL 217 Frank Evans, Stretching Forth

SD(SAM) 218 The Golden Age of Mechanical Music

SDX 219 Antarctica

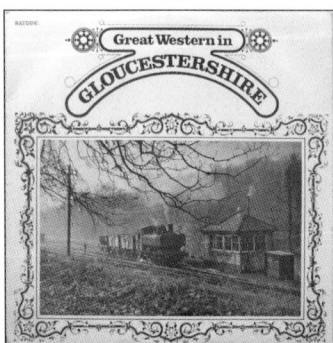

SDL 220 Great Western in Gloucestershire

SDL 221 The Bands of Jim Europe & Arthur Prior, Too Much Mustard

SDL 222 Cotswold Characters

SDM 223 Little Brother Montgomery, Home Again

SDM 224 Tommy Johnson, The Legacy of Tommy Johnson

SDM 226 Blues from the Delta

SDM 227 Viola Wells, Miss Rhapsody

SDL 228 Clyde Bernhardt, Blues & Jazz from Harlem

SDM 229 Traditional Music for Banjo, Fiddle & Bagpipes

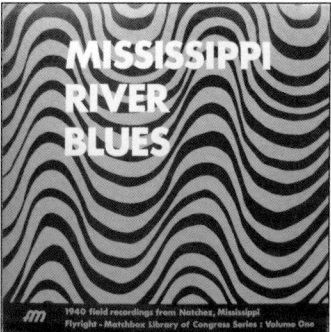

SDM 230 Mississippi River Blues

SDM 231 Clark Kessinger, Live at Union Grove

SDL 232 Mechanical Music Hall

SDL 233 The Frank Evans Consort, In an English Manner

SDL 234 Parry's Barrel Organ

SDM 235 George Pegram

SDM 236 Joe Val, One Morning in May

SDM 238 Snuffy Jenkins & Pappy Sherrill

SDM 239 Mud Acres

SDL 240 Philomusica of Gloucestershire

SDM 241 Hollow Rock String Band

SDM 242 Curly Herdman, Fiddler

SDL 243 Change Ringing from St. Mary Redcliffe, Bristol

SDL 244 Graham Collier Music, Portraits

33SD 245 Sounds of Bristol

SDLB 246 Music from Dartington

SDL 247 Cotswold Craftsmen

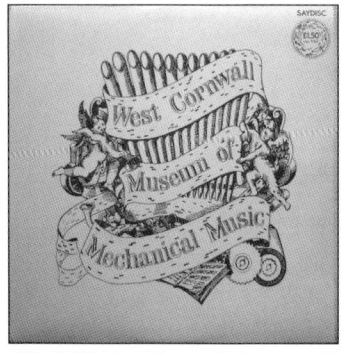

SDLB 248 West Cornwall Museum of Mechanical Music

SDL 249 Quincicasm

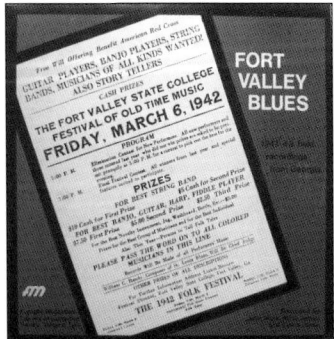

SDM 250 Fort Valley Blues

SDL 251 White on Black

SDL 252 Jack Armstrong, Celebrated Minstrel

SDL 253 Rusty Rags

SDL 254 Foursome for Brass

33SD 255 Old Pete

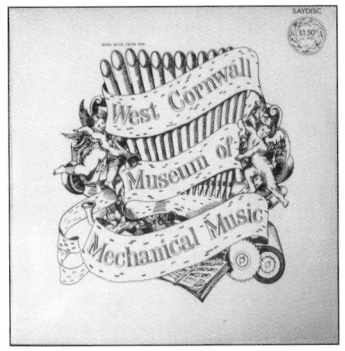

SDLB 256 More Music from the West Cornwall Museum of Mech. Music

SDM 257 Out in the Cold Again

SDM 258 Boot that Thing

33SD 259 Geoffrey Woodruff, 'Live'

33SD 260 Old Pete, Old Pete's Christmas Story

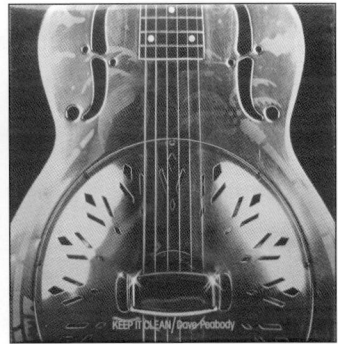

SDM 261 Dave Peabody, Keep It Clean

SDLB 262 Stanshawe (Bristol) Band, Spectrum

SDLB 263 Poppers Happy Jazz Band & the Ruth Fairorgan

SDM 264 Two White Horses Standing in Line

SDM 265 Jack O' Diamonds

SDL 266 Staverton Bridge

SDL 267 Cotswold Voices

SDL 268 Cotswold Ballads

SDL 269 Lyndon Baglin, Showcase for the Euphonium

SDX 270 Dave Peabody, Come and Get It

SDLB 271 Pipes, Barrels and Pins

SDL 272 Pumpkin Pie, Down the Cut

SDL 273 That Barbershop Style

SDL 274 Sound in Brass Handbells, Music By Sound in Brass Handbells

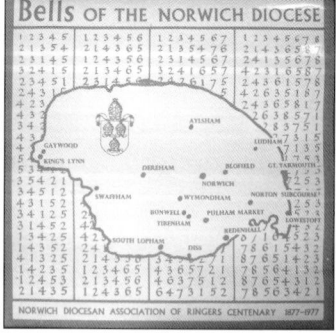

SDL 277 Bells of the Norwich Diocese

SDL 278 We Sing Barbershop Too!

22SD 279 Old Pete & John Christie, Isambard Kingdom Brunel

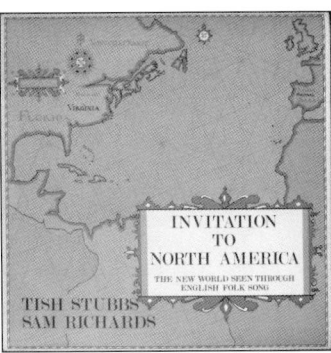

SDL 280 Tish Stubbs & Sam Richards, Invitation to North America

SDL 281 Leicester '77 Barbershop Convention

SDL 282 Barry Male Voice Choir, Gloria

SDL 283 Crawley Barbershop Chorus, Double Gold

SDL 284 Steam and Harness

SDL 285 Miss Dorothy Blake, Memories of Osborne

SDL 286 Love is a Song

SDL 287 Five in a Bar, Lady of Fortune

SDL 288 Bluenote Jazz Band

SDL 289 Sound in Brass, Handbells in Harmony

SDL 290 Bells of the Cotswolds

SDL 291 The Sound of the Carillon

CSDLB 292 World of Mechanical Music (second inlay design)

SDL 293 The Radio Bristol Singers, So Beautiful

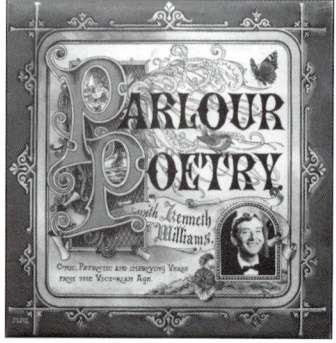

SDL 294 Kenneth Williams, Parlour Poetry

SDL 295 Caister '78 Barbershop Convention

SDL 296 A Souvenir from Stoke

SDL 297 Music for the Magic Lantern

SDL 298 Grossmont Handbell Ringers, Four in Hand

SDL 299 South Atlantic Islands

SDL 300 While I Work I Whistle

SDL 301 Down to Earth

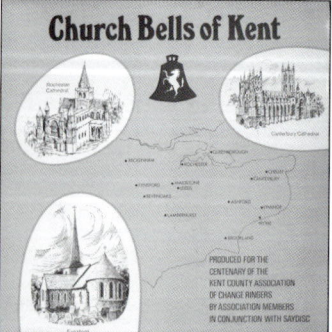

SDL 302 Church Bells of Kent

SDL 303 Sublime Harmonie

SDL 304 Gloucestershire Wildlife Tapestry

SDLB 305 Steam's Final Hours

SDLB 306 Nocturnal Steam

SDL 307 The Launton Handbell Ringers, Modal Melodies

SDX 309 Kilvert's Diary

SDL 310 Change Ringing on Handbells

SDLB 311 Iron–Ore Steamers (orig. cassette only as CSDLB 311)

SDL 312 The Gay 90's

SDLB 313 Return to Steam

SDLB 314 Devon Museum of Mechanical Music

SDL 315 Belles and Beaus

SDL 316 Forest Talk

SDL 317 Lawrence James, Late Night Extra

SDL 318 Bioscope Memories

SDLB 319 Return to Steam Vol. 2

SDL 320 Norman Goodland, My Old Chap

SAY 321 Johnny Morris, Geminee Geminii

CSDL 322 Geoffrey Woodruff, Entertains (originally cassette only)

SDL 323 Ronald Curtis, Bye Bye Blues

SDL 324 Ronald Curtis, Yes, I Remember It Well

SDL 325 Jing Ying Soloists, Like Waves Against the Sand

SDL 326 Alain Presencer, The Singing Bowls of Tibet

SDL 327 Enchanted Carols

SDL 328 Sun Life Stanshawe Band, Conductor's Showcase

SDL 330 Music from Prinknash Abbey

SDL 331 The Road to Heaven

SDL 332 All Around England and Back Again

SDL 333 Ringing Clear

SDL 334 Cylinder Jazz

SDL 335 Jim Couza, The Enchanted Valley

SDL 336 I'll Dance Till de Sun Breaks Through

SDL 337 The Bells of London

SDL 338 Children's Singing Games

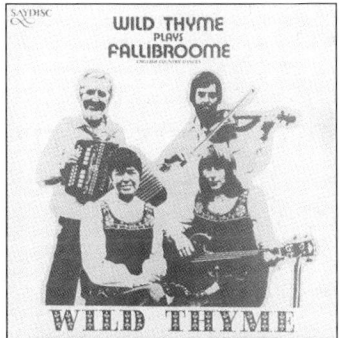

SDL 339 Wild Thyme, Plays Fallibroome

SDL 340 Music of the Streets

SDL 341 Carillons of Scotland

SDL 342 Diamond Discs

SDL 343 Kathryn Tickell, On Kielder Side

SDL 344 The Roaring 20's

SDL 345 Richard Butler, The Perfect Triangle

SDL 346 The Three Disc Symphonion

SDL 347 Lyndon Baglin, Best of Brass

SDL 348 Eileen Monger, The Lilting Banshee

SDL 349 Prinknash & Standbrook Abbeys, O Give Thanks to the Lord

SDL 350 The Wibbly Wobbly Walk

SDL 351 Dave Townsend, Portrait of a Concertina

SDL 352 Cardiff Polyphonic Choir, A Christmas Cantata

SDL 353 Danielle Paully, Fleur du Jura

SDL 354 Mechanical Opera

SDL 355 Kitten on the Keys

CSDL 356 Music from St. Clement Danes (cassette only)

SDL 357 Georges Schmitt, Joy to the World

SDL 358 Keep the Home Fires Burning

CD–SDL 359 Musical Box Dances (Original CD sleeve)

SDL 360 The Mellstock Band, Under the Greenwood Tree

SDL 361 The Canterbury Clerkes, Fill Your Glasses

SDLC 362 Pleasures and Treasures

SDL 363 Stanbrook Abbey, Wellsprings

CD-SDL 364 The York Waits, Music from the Time of Richard III

SDL 365 The Fairer Sax, Diversions

SDL 366 Maddy Prior with the
Carnival Band, A Tapestry of Carols

CD–SDL 367 Rie Yanagisawa & Clive
Bell, Kurokami (original sleeve)

CD–SDL 368 Jing Ying Soloists,
Evening Song (original sleeve)

CD–SDL 369 Prinknash & Standbrook
Abbeys, Christmas Chant

CD–SDL 370 Whistle Away Your Blues

CD–SDL 371 Sneak's Noyse,
Christmas Now is Drawing Near

CD–SDL 372 Bonnie Shaljean,
Farewell to Loch Neaghe

CD–SDL 373 The York Waits, Music
from the Time of the Spanish Armada

CD–SDL 374 Nigel Eaton, The Music
of the Hurdy Gurdy (original slv.)

CD–SDL 375 Bristol Bach Choir,
Welcome Yule

CD–SDL 376 Disappearing World
(original sleeve)

CD–SDL 377 Rags, Malkauns and Megh (original sleeve)

CD–SDL 378 Church Bells of England

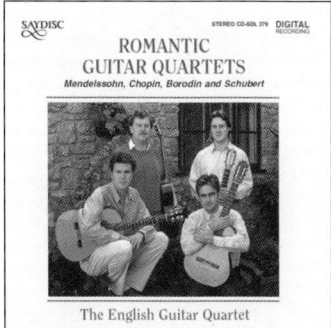

CD–SDL 379 The English Guitar Quartet, Romantic Guitar Quartets

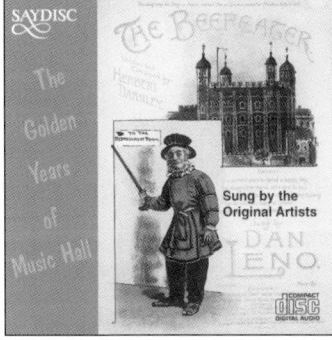

CD–SDL 380 The Golden Years of Music Hall

CD–SDL 381 Fine Arts Brass Ensemble, The Lighter Side of

CD–SDL 382 The City Waits, Pills to Purge Melancholy

CD–SDL 383 Maddy Prior etc, Sing Lustily & with Good Courage

CD–SDL 384 Joji Hirota, Rain Forest Dream

CD–SDL 385 The Musical Life of Samuel Pepys

CD–SDL 386 The English Guitar Quartet, Baroque Guitar Quartets

CD–SDL 387 Arabesque, Traditional Arabic Music

CD–SDL 388 Caliche, Music of the Andes

CD–SDL 389 Spirit of African Sanctus
(original sleeve)

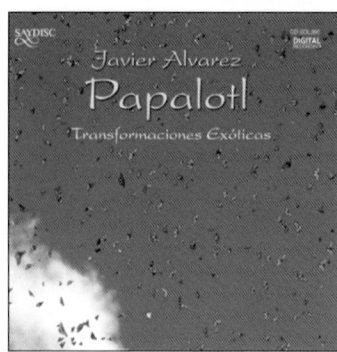

CD–SDL 390 Javier Alvarez, Papalotl

CD–SDL 391 Ray Fisher, Traditional
Songs of Scotland

CD–SDL 392 The Theatre Organ

CD–SDL 393 The Broadside Band,
English Country Dances

CD–SDL 394 Roger Winfield,
Windsongs (original sleeve)

CD–SDL 395 Lucie Skeaping etc.,
Raisins & Almonds (original sleeve)

CD–SDL 396 Vocal Traditions of
Bulgaria (original sleeve)

CD–SDLC 397 A Musical Banquet
(original sleeve)

CD–SDL 398 The York Waits, Old
Christmas Return'd

CD–SDL 399 The English Guitar
Quartet, Spanish Guitar Quartets

CD–SDL 400 The Broadside Band,
English National Songs

CD–SDL 401 Rajasthani Folk Music

CD–SDL 402 Jo Freya, Traditional Songs of England (original sleeve)

CD–SDL 403 Spirit of Polynesia (original sleeve)

CD–SDL 404 North Indian Vocal Music (original sleeve)

CD–SDL 405 Sea Songs & Shanties (original sleeve)

CD–SDL 406 Siwsann George, Traditional Songs of Wales

CD–SDL 407 Songs of the Travelling People

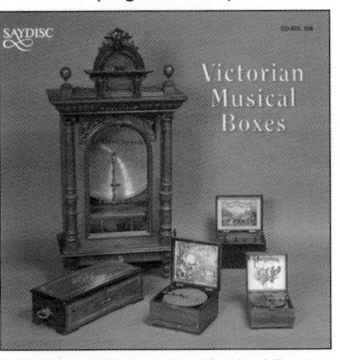

CD–SDL 408 Victorian Musical Boxes

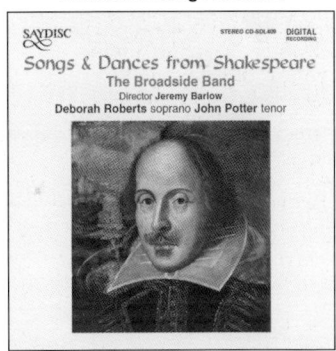

CD–SDL 409 The Broadside Band, Songs & Dances from Shakespeare

CD–SDL 410 Sally Dexter, etc., Songs of Thomas Hardy's Wessex

CD–SDL 411 Traditional Songs of Ireland

CD–SDL 412 Robin Huw Bowen, Harp Music of Wales

CD–SDL 413 Cockney Kings of Music Hall

CD–SDL 414 Spirit of Micronesia

CD–SDL 415 Music for the Arabian Dulcimer and Lute

CD–SDL 416 Bagpipes of Britain & Ireland

CD–SDL 417 A Celtic Christmas

CD–SDL 418 Spirit of Melanesia (original sleeve)

CD–SDL 419 The Broadside Band, Old English Nursery Rhymes

CD–SDL 420 Traditional Dance Music of Ireland

CD–SDL 421 Vocal Traditions of Albania (original sleeve)

CD–SDL 422 Prinknash & Standbrook Abbeys, Compline and Other Chant

CD–SDL 423 Prinknash & Standbrook Abbeys, Chants & Psalms

CD–SDLC 424 Catalogue included a free sampler CD in plain PVC sleeve

CD–SDL 425 English Customs and Traditions

CD–SDL 426 Traditional Songs and Dances of Sardinia

CD–SDL 427 Tibetan Folk Music

CD–SDL 428 Roger Winfield, Voices of the Wind

CD–SDL 429 Carillon Bells of Britain

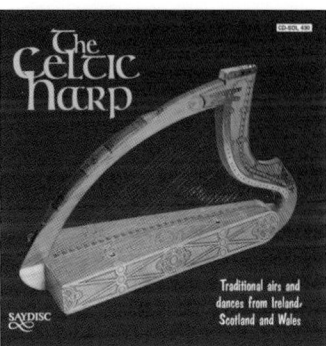

CD–SDL 430 The Celtic Harp

CD–SDL 431 Cry You Mountains, Cry You Fields

CD–SDL 432 Knut Buen, Hardanger Fiddle Music of Norway

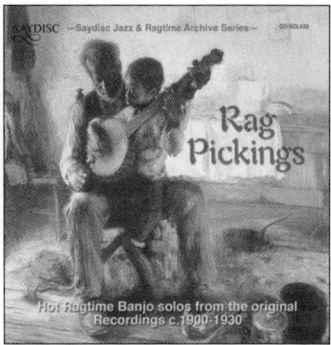

CD–SDL 433 Rag Pickings

CD–SDL 434 Gloucestershire Characters

CD–SDL 435 George Swinford of Filkins

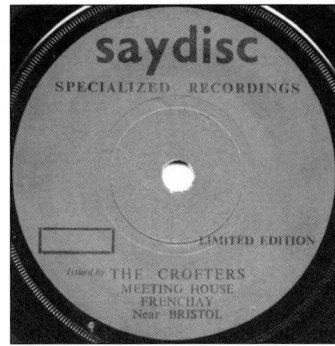

1965 to 1966: same size label used on 7" and LP releases

1966 to 1968: same size label used on 7" and LP releases

1968 to 1969: 7" version

1968 to 1969: LP version

1968: Matchbox label

1968 or 1969 to 1976: Matchbox (early examples prone to age–spotting!)

1969 to 1979: same design but different sizes on 7" and LP releases

1973 to 1976: Flyright–Matchbox label

1979: Special Limited Edition label

1979 to 1982: same design but different sizes on 7" and LP releases

1982 to 1987: final label design

RL 301 Blind Lemon Jefferson, Volume 1

RL 302 Mississippi Blues Vol. 1

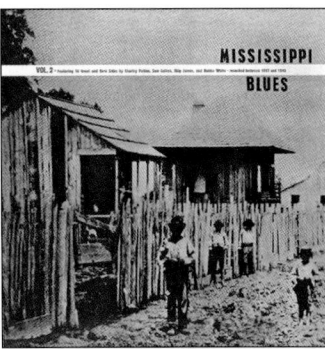

RL 303 Mississippi Blues Vol. 2

RL 304 Nearer My God To Thee

RL 305 Tommy McClennan, Cross Cut Saw Blues

RL 306 Blind Lemon Jefferson, Volume 2

RL 307 The Memphis Area

RL 308 Frank Stokes

RL 309 Blues from Georgia

RL 310 Missouri and Tennessee

RL 311 Harmonicas Washboards Fiddles & Jugs

RL 312 Texas Country Music Vol. 1

RL 313 Down South

RL 314 Mississippi Blues Vol.3

RL 315 Texas Country Music Vol. 2

RL 316 The Country Fiddlers

RL 317 Lucille Bogan & Walter Roland, Alabama Blues

RL 318 The East Coast States

RL 319 Up and Down the Mississippi

RL 320 The Great Harmonica Players Volume 1

RL 321 The Great Harmonica Players Volume 2

RL 322 The Memphis Jug Band

RL 323 Memphis Blues Vol. 1 (with Saydisc sticker)

RL 324 Blind Willie McTell, King of the Georgia Blues Singers (with sticker)

RL 325 Alabama Country Blues (with Saydisc sticker)

RL 326 The East Coast States Vol. 2 (with Saydisc sticker)

RL 327 Texas Country Music Vol. 3 (with Saydisc sticker)

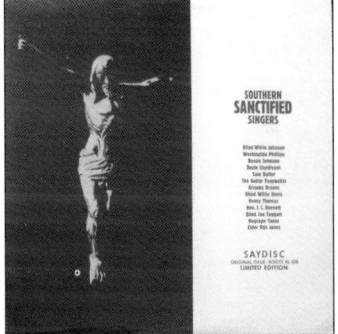

RL 328 Southern Sanctified Singers (with printed Saydisc credits)

RL 329 Memphis Blues Vol. 2 (with printed Saydisc credits)

RL 330 Tommy Johnson & Ishman Bracey (with printed Saydisc credits)

RL 331 Blind Lemon Jefferson: Volume 3

RL 332 Cream of the Crop

RL 333 Kings of Memphis Town

RL 334 Country Blues Obscurities Vol. 1

RL 335 Texas & Louisiana Country

RL 336 Cannon's Jug Stompers

RL 337 Memphis Jug Band, Volume 2

RL 338 Rev. F. W. McGee

RL 339 Delta Blues

RL 340 Country Blues Obscurities Vol. 2

SL 502 Son House, The Vocal Intensity of Son House

SL 506 The Bluegrass Specials, The Train that I Ride

RSE 1 Son House

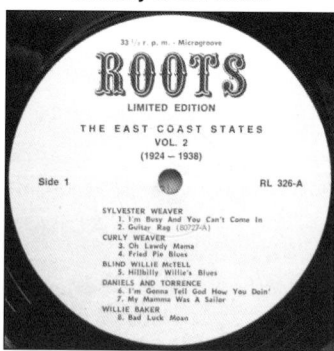

Roots label design (RL 337 was on the current Matchbox label design)

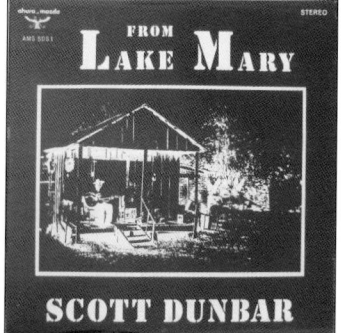

AMS SDS 1 Scott Dunbar, From Lake Mary

AMS 2002 Robert Pete Williams, Robert Pete Williams

AMS 2003 Harmonica Williams with Little Freddie King

Label for AMS SDS 1: AMS 2002/2003 were on the normal Saydisc label

VTS 1 Pigsty Hill Light Orchestra, Presents (aka PHLOP!)

VTS 2 Sun Also Rises, The Sun Also Rises

VTS 3 Ian A. Anderson, Royal York Crescent

VTS 4 Wizz Jones, The Legendary Me

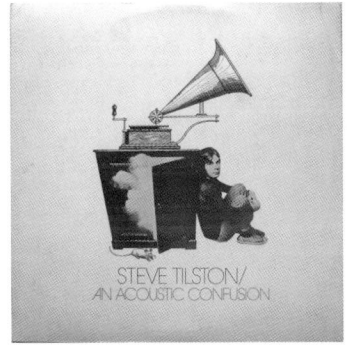

VTS 5 Steve Tilston, An Acoustic Confusion

VTS 6 Dave Evans, The Words In Between

VTS 7 Fred Wedlock, The Folker

VTS 8 Pigsty Hill Light Orchestra, PIggery Jokery

VTS 9 Ian A. Anderson, A Vulture Is Not a Bird You Can Trust

VTS 11 Hunt and Turner, Magic Landscape

VTS 12 Tight Like That, Hokum

VTS 13 Tucker Zimmerman

VTS 14 Dave Evans, Elephantasia

VTSAM 15 Us

VTSAM 16 Matchbox Days

VTS 17 Derroll Adams, Feelin' Fine

VTS 18 Ian A. Anderson, Singer Sleeps as Blaze Rages

Y8VTS 18 – Ian A. Anderson, Singer Sleeps 8-track cartridge

VTS 19 Al Jones, Jonesville

VTS 20 Fred Wedlock, Frollicks

VTS 21 Chris Thompson

VTS 22 Dave Peabody, Peabody Hotel

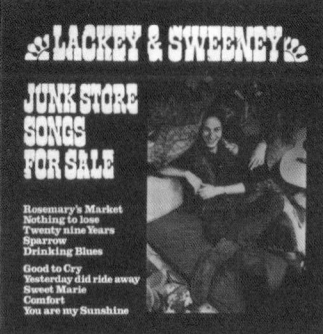

VTS 23 Lackey and Sweeney, Junk Shop Songs for Sale

VTS 24 Wizz Jones, When I Leave Berlin

VTS 25 Noel Murphy, Murf

VTSX 1000 Various, The Great White Dap

Andy Leggett's original sketch on which the label design was based

1970 to 1971: original label design

1971 to 1974: second label design with Rodney Matthews logo

1980s: simplified label design (only used on Fred Wedlock LPs)

SAR 1 Dartington String Quartet, Shostakovich

SAR 2 David Stone & Allan Schiller, Delius

SAR 3 Richard Burnett, A Graf Fortepiano Recital

SAR 4 Swiss Baroque Soloists

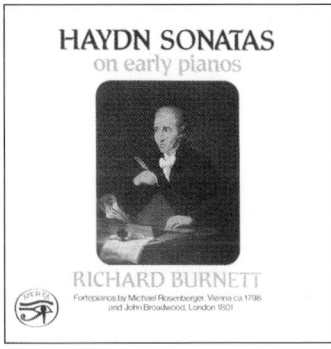

SAR 5 Richard Burnett, Haydn Sonatas

SAR 6 Richard Burnett, The Finchcocks Collection

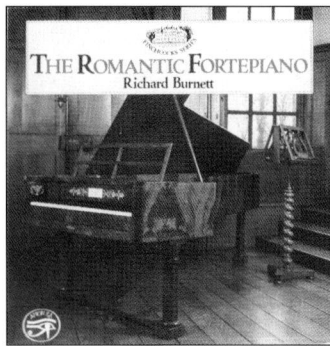

SAR 7 Richard Burnett, The Romantic Fortepiano

SAR 8 Richard Burnett, Clementi

SAR 9 Richard Burnett & Ralph Holmes, Beethoven

SAR 10 Alan Hacker, Clarinet Collection

SAR 11 Preston's Pocket, Music for Two Flutes

SAR 12 Richard Burnett & Ralph Holmes, Hummel

SAR 13 Howard Shelley, Schubert Sonatas

SAR 14 London Baroque, English Music of the Eighteenth Century

SAR 15 Ian Partridge & Richard Burnett, Beethoven Songs

SAR 16 Richard Burnett & Ralph Holmes, Beethoven Violin Sonatas

SAR 17 Alan Hacker & Salomon String Quartet, Mozart Clarinet Quintets

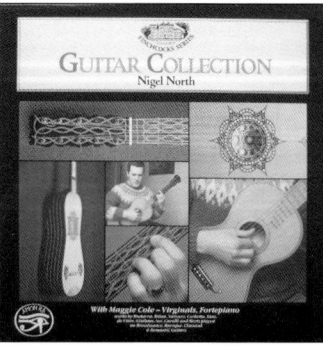

SAR 18 Nigel North, Guitar Collection

SAR 19 Stephen Preston & Lucy Carolan, Flute Collection

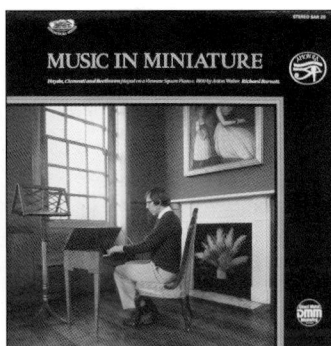

SAR 20 Richard Burnett, Music in Miniature

SAR 21 Stephen Preston etc., Weber Flute Trio & Sonatas

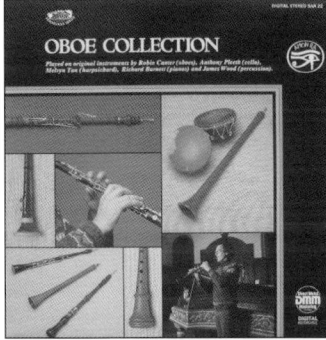

SAR 22 Robin Cantor, etc., Oboe Collection

SAR 23 Nigel North, Bach Lute Music

SAR 24 New London Chamber Choir, Requiem, etc.

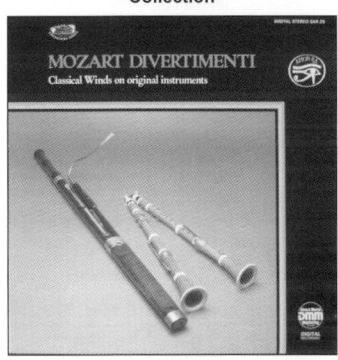

SAR 25 Classical Winds, Mozart Divertimenti

SAR 26 Classical Winds, Beethoven Wind Music

SAR 27 Maggie Cole, Scarlatti Sonatas

SAR 28 The Broadside Band, John Playford's Popular Tunes

CD–SAR 29 Fretwork, In Nomine (CD only)

CD–SAR 30 The Clarion Ensemble, Trumpet Collection (CD only)

SAR 31 Richard Burnett etc., Mozart Piano Quartets

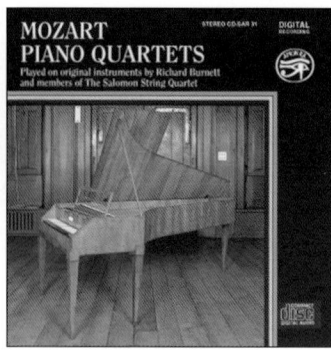

CD-SAR 31 Mozart Piano Quartets (CD in new sleeve design)

CD-SAR 32 Richard Burnett, Gottschalk Piano Music (orig. sleeve)

CD-SAR 33 LIsa Beznosiuk & Nigel North, Concord of Sweet Sounds

CD-SAR 34 Robin Canter & London Baroque, Mozart Music for Oboe

CD-SAR 35 Frances Eustace, Bassoon Collection

CD-SAR 36 Frances Kelly, Harp Collection

CD-SAR 37 Alan Hacker, etc., Brahms Clarinet Trio & Sonatas

CD-SAR 38 Alan Hacker, etc., Mendelssohn Works for Clarinet, etc.

CD-SAR 39 American Baroque, Telemann (original sleeve)

CD-SARC 40 Musica Miscellanea (original sleeve)

CD-SAR 41 Ian Partridge & Richard Burnett, Schubert Winterreise

CD–SAR 42 Le Nouveau Quatuor, Thomas Arne Instrumental Works

CD–SAR 43 Robert Woolley, Carlos Seixas Harpsichord Sonatas

CD–SAR 44 Le Nouveau Qautuor, C.P.E. Bach Trio Sonantas

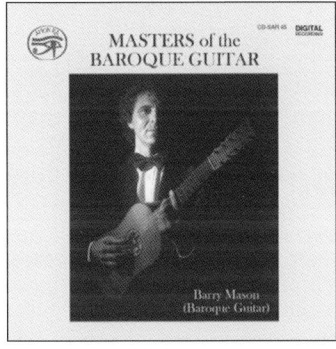

CD–SAR 45 Barry Mason, Masters of the Baroque Guitar

CD–SAR 46 Red Byrd, etc., Elizabethan Christmas Anthems

CD–SAR 47 Le Nouveau Quatuor, etc,. Vivaldi Chamber Concertos

CD–SAR 48 Richard Burnett, The Piano Music of John Field

CD–SAR 49 The Orlando Consort, Philippe de Vitry and the Ars Nova

CD–SAR 50 Glenda Simpson & Barry Mason, Now What Is Love?

CD–SAR 51 Musica Antiqua of London, The Field of the Cloth of Gold

CD–SAR 52 The Cambridge Baroque Camerata, Rare Baroque Flute, etc.

CD–SAR 53 Alison Stephens, Sue Mossop, etc., Music for Mandolin

CD–SAR 54 Richard Burnett & Fitzwilliam String Quartet, Schumann

CD–SAR 55 Rose Consort of Viols, etc., John Dowland's Lachrimae

CD–SAR 56 New London Chamber Choir, The Brightest Heaven, etc.

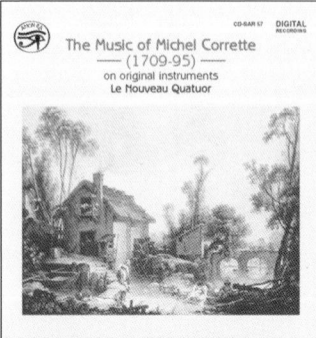

CD–SAR 57 Le Nouveau Quatuor, The Music of Michel Corrette

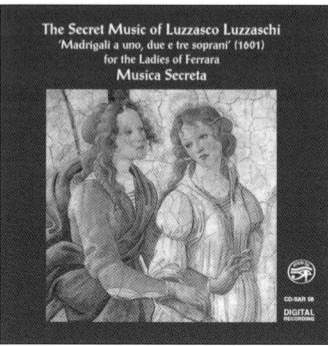

CD–SAR 58 Musica Secreta, The Secret Music of Luzzasco Luzzaschi

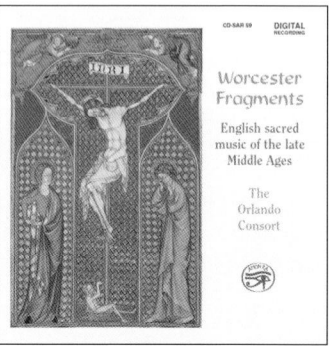

CD–SAR 59 The Orlando Consort, Worcester Fragments

CD–SAR 60 Robin Canter & Paul Nicholson, J.S. Bach: Music for Oboe

CD–SAR 61 Musica Secreta, Barbara Strozzi

CD–SAR 62 A Golden Treasury of Elizabethan Music

CD–SAR 63 A Golden Treasury of Mediaeval Music

CD–SAR 64 A Golden Treasury of Historic Pianos

CD–SAR 65 A Golden Treasury of Renaissance Music

CD–SAR 66 A Golden Treasury of
Georgian Music

CD–SAR 67 Richard Burnett, The
Romantic Piano

CD–SAR 68 A Golden Treasury of
Baroque Music

CD–SAR 69 A Golden Treasury of
Ancient Instruments

CD–SAR 70 A Golden Treasury of
Flute Music

SARB 01 The Dartington String
Quartet, Quartet Cameos

CD–SAR 1001 Richard Burnett's
Musical Tour

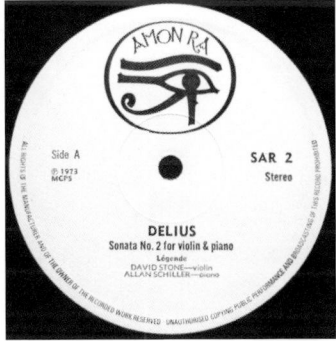

1973 to 1987: Amon Ra label design

1980s label with Teldec's DMM logo &
West German manufacturing credits

MSE 201 Papa Harvey Hull & Long Cleve Reed, etc.

MSE 202 Walter "Buddy Boy" Hawkins 1927 – 29

MSE 203 Bo Weavil Jackson (Sam Butler) 1926

MSE 204 Ragtime Blues Guitar 1928 – 30

MSE 205 Peg Leg Howell (1928 – 29)

MSE 206 Texas Alexander Vol.1 (1927 – 28)

MSE 207 Skip James 1931

MSE 208 Coley Jones & the Dallas String Band (1927 – 29)

MSE 209 Great Harp Players (1927 – 30)

MSE 210 Leroy Carr 1928

MSE 211 Tommie Bradley – James Cole Groups 1930 – 32

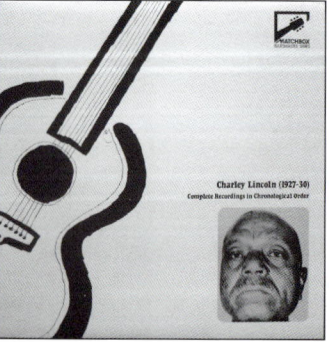

MSE 212 Charley Lincoln (1927 – 30)

MSE 213 Memphis Harmonica Kings 1929 – 30

MSE 214 Texas Alexander Vol. 2 (1928 – 29)

MSE 215 Ramblin' Thomas 1928 – 32

MSE 216 Country Girls 1926 – 29

MSE 217 Rufus & Ben Quillian 1929 – 31

MSE 218 Harmonica Showcase

MSE 219 Atlanta Blues 1927 – 30

MSE 220 Texas Alexander Vol. 3 (1929 – 30)

MSE 221 Peg Leg Howell Vol. 1 (1926 – 27)

MSE 222 Sanctified Jug Bands (1928 – 30)

MSE 223 St Louis Bessie: (Bessie Mae Smith) (1927 – 30)

MSE 224 Texas Alexander Vol. 4

MSE 1001 Blind Lemon Jefferson
1926 – 29

MSE 1002 Frank Stokes 1927 – 29

MSE 1003 Blind Blake 1926 – 29

MSE 1004 Big Bill Broonzy 1927 – 32

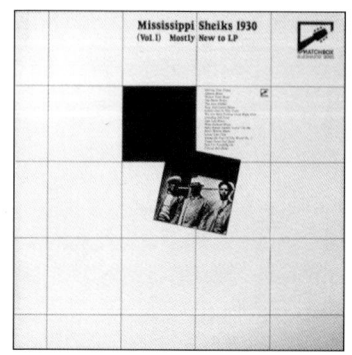

MSE 1005 Mississippi Sheiks 1930
(Vol. 1)

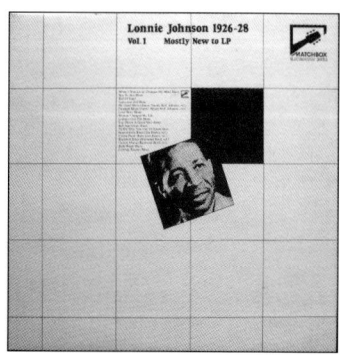

MSE 1006 Lonnie Johnson Vol. 1
1926–28

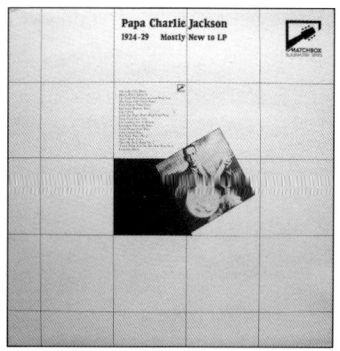

MSE 1007 Papa Charlie Jackson
1924 – 29

MSE 1008 Memphis Jug Band
(1927 – 34)

MSE 1009 Barbecue Bob (Robert
Hicks)1927 – 30

MSE 1010 Bobbie Leecan & Robert
Cooksey (1926 – 27)

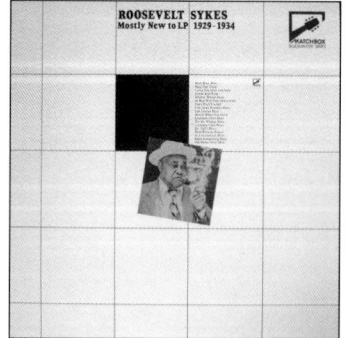

MSE 1011 Roosevelt Sykes 1929 – 34

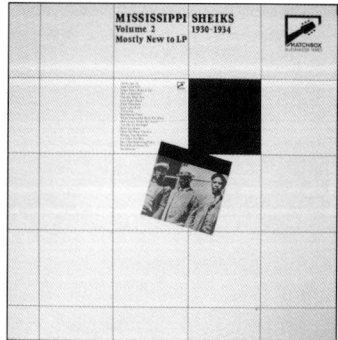

MSE 1012 Mississippi Sheiks
Volume 2 1930 – 34

MSEX 2001/2002 Songsters & Saints Vol. 1

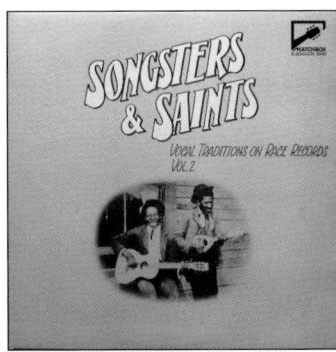

MSEX 2003/2004 Songsters & Saints Vol. 2

Matchbox Bluesmaster label design

CD–KS 1001 Listen To This! Key Stage 1 (original book jacket)

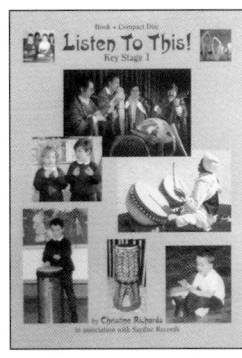

CD–KS 1001 Listen To This! Key Stage 1 (updated book jacket

CD–KS 1002 Listen To This! Key Stage 2 (original book jacket)

CD–KS 1002 Listen To This! Key Stage 1 (updated book jacket)

CD–KS 1003 Listen To This! Key Stage 3 (book jacket)

CD–KS 1004 Percussion Around the World (book jacket)

Percussion Around the World (wall chart)

CD–KS 1005 Religions of the World (book jacket)

Religions of the World (wall chart)

CP 103 Mike Cooper Jazz Band, Blue Turning Grey Over You

CP 105 The Choir & Instrumentalists of Queen Elizabeth Hospital Bristol

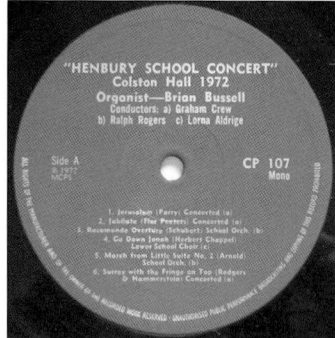

CP 107 Henbury School Concert

CP 108 Ecclesfield Handbell Ringers

CP 109 Lindsay Peck with the Friary Folk Group, Reality from Dream

CP 111 Barbershop Bonanza

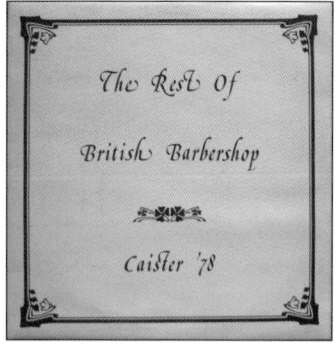

CP 112 The Rest of British Barbershop – Caister '78

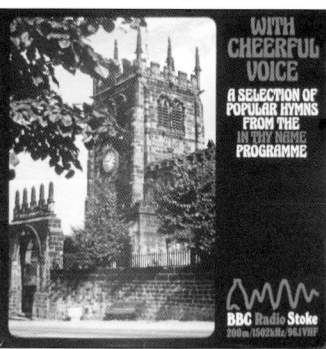

CP 113 With Cheerful Voice

CP 114 Fumble, Rumble with Fumble

CP 115 Paul Wilson & Ben van Weede, The One Eyed Fiddler

CP 116 Countryside Calling

CP 117 Vale of Arrow Choir

CP 118 Rhymney Valley Festival Schools Orchestra

CP 119 In Every Corner Sing

CP 122 Lydbrook Silver Band

CP 123 Greater Manchester Radio Chorale, Manchester Carols

CP 128 Gnosall Handbell Ringers, The Sound of Bells Volume 2

CP 129 Kennet and Avon Handbell Ringers

CP 131 Vale of Arrow Choir, Songs for All Seasons

CP 132 Belles & Beaus Handbell Ringers, Ring In England

CP 136 Tongwynlais Temperance Band, Crazy Music

BUP 1 Evening Post Carol Concert 1983

LYN 3248 Sounds of the Sea

A melange of Saydisc and Amon Ra cassettes illustrating three different eras of cassette inlay design. *Conductors Showcase*, by the Sun Life Stanshawe Band, represents the first era, with many cassettes not even enjoying a graphic and displaying only text (see also CSDL 322). *Memories of Osborne*, *The Gay 90s* and *Fleur du Jura* represent the next era, when graphic designer, Bob Doling, of Doling Design, created a corporate Saydisc image with new logo and dual red lines enhancing all new records and cassettes, with back catalogue also getting a makeover when new stock was required. The rest of the cassettes shown represent the final era: whilst still being recognisably Saydisc or Amon Ra releases, the constraints of a strict corporate image were laid aside when expedient to make each cassette release more individualistic. Cassette issues, more often than not, also included foldout inserts with comprehensive notes.

Friends Meeting House, Frenchay, Bristol

Ian Anderson recording at Frenchay, 1968

The Jing Ying Soloists recording at Frenchay

Above and below: Mike Cooper recording at Frenchay, 1968

Roy Mickleburgh in his 'museum', Stokes Croft, Bristol

Gef and Genny Lucena at The Barton, 1969, with Ferrograph mono recorder

Outside The Barton, 1980s

Chipping Manor, Wootton-under-Edge

Gef & Genny Lucena's 21st anniversary

Finchcocks playback session. (L to R) Martin Renshaw (organ tuner), Richard Burnett, Alexander Dow, Bill Dow (curator); seated: David Wilkins and Gef Lucena

Finchcocks Museum, Goudhurst

Classical Winds recording at Finchcocks

Forde Abbey

Musica Secreta at Forde Abbey

Above: part of the photoshoot for Ian Anderson's *Royal York Crescent*. Several Village Thing records were recorded here and Village Thing musicians in the photo are (L to R) Andy Leggett (with dog), John Turner (with hat, at back), Ian "Heavy Drummer" Turner (with Bongos), Maggie Holland (almost obscured by Turner), Ian Hunt and Ian Anderson.

Ian Anderson at Rockfield, 1971, with (L to R) Ian Hunt, Kipps Brown, Pick/Pique Withers (on floor), Kingsley Ward, Pete Descindis: Brown, Withers and Descindis were currently members of Spring

Ian Anderson, 1967

Anderson Jones Jackson, 1967

Fred Wedlock and chums

Frank Evans

White on Black

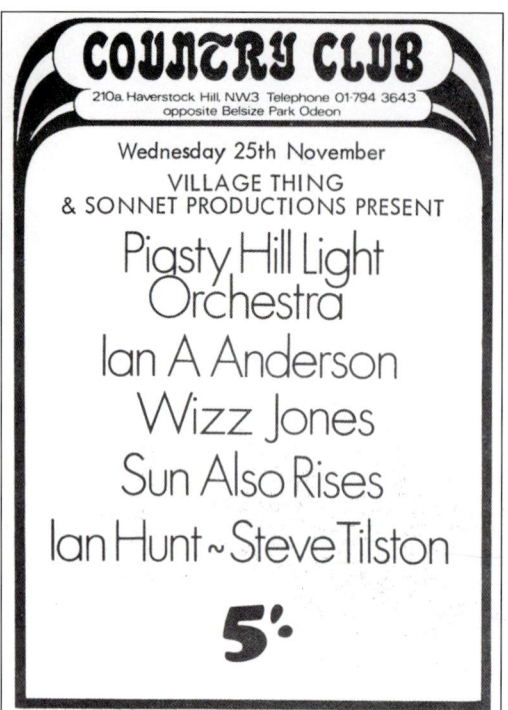

Above, left: flier for Village Thing's London launch. Above, right: Village Thing concert flier with Rodney Matthews graphics. Below: fliers advertising the first four Village Thing LPs.

Sun Also Rises
publicity shot

Sun Also Rises on TV

Bill Lackey and Kathy Sweeney

Fred Wedlock and Mike Evans at the Stonehouse

Tucker Zimmerman

Hunt and Turner with Keith
Warmington and Richie Gould
at the Stonehouse

Strange Fruit at the Ashton
Court Festival

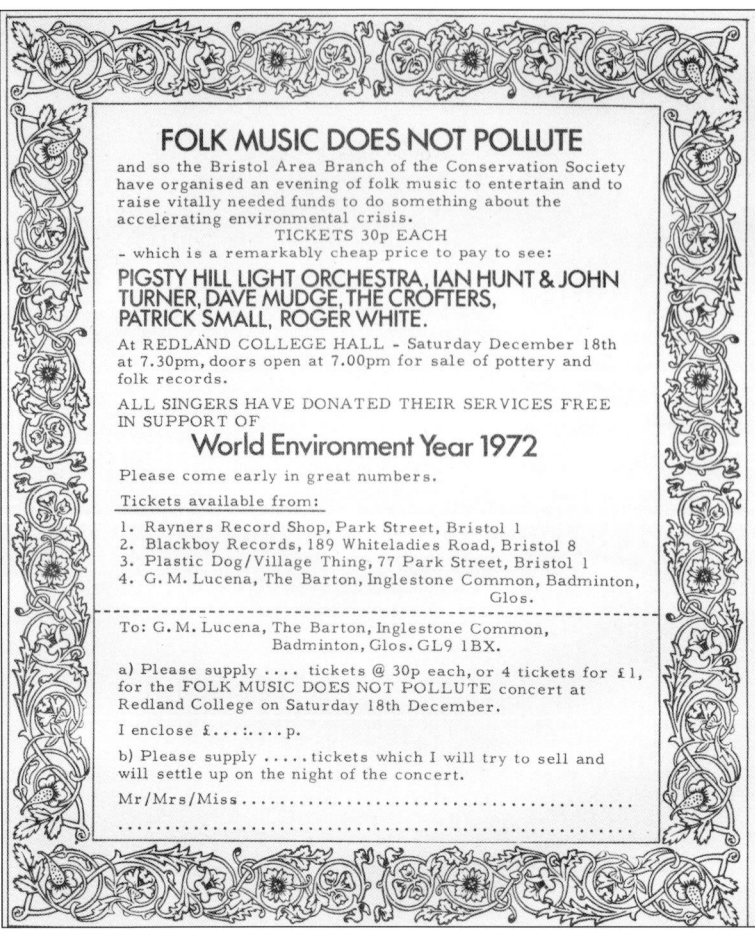

Gig flier, Village Thing button badge and LP promotional stickers.

CD–SDL 383   MADDY PRIOR WITH THE CARNIVAL BAND: Sing Lustily and with Good Courage

Who Would True Valour See (Tune: Monk's Gate)
Rejoice Ye Shining Worlds (Tune: from Harmonia Sacra c.1760)
O Thou Who Camest from Above (Tune: Wilton)
Lo He Comes with Clouds Descending (Tune: Helmsley)
How Firm a Foundation (Tune: American trad.)
O for a Thousand Tongues to Sing (Tune: Lyngham)
As Pants the Hart (Tune: Martyrdom)
The God of Abraham Praise (Tune: Leoni)
Instrumental: The Twenty–Ninth of May or The jovial Beggars – The Dancing Master 1686
Light of the World (Tune: Hull)
All Hail the Pow'r of Jesus' Name (Tune: Diadem)
Lord, In the Morning (Tune: Walsall)
Away with Our Sorrow and Care (Tune: Hymn of Eve)
Christ the Lord Is Ris'n Today (Tune: Easter Morn)
O Worship the King (Tune: Hanover)
And Can It Be? (Tune: Sagina)

Release date: autumn 1990
Cassette: CSDL 383

CD–SDL 384   JOJI HIROTA: Rain Forest Dream

Ubiquity
Purple Spring
Celebration of Harvest
Malaysian Image
Satellite Express
Rain Forest Dream
Demon Dance
Pacific Samba

Release date: autumn 1990
Cassette: CSDL 384

CD–SDL 385   RICHARD WISTREICH & ROBIN JEFFREY: The Musical Life of Samuel Pepys

Gavott
Jan 16 1660 – Arise, arise, ye subterranean winds
July 22 1664 – Lucifero
Dec 9 1665 – Beauty retire
May 17 1661 – Cloris Yielding
Oct 30 1665 – Hero's Complaint
Nov 15 1666 – Verse in G minor (solo organ)
Nov 16 1666 – Inconstancy return'd
Allemande (solo guitar)
Mar 5 1667 – Newcastle – Heart's Ease – St. Martin's
A Dream Henry Lawes
Pavan John Jenkins
Lord, I have sinn'd Pelham Humirey
And art thou griev'd John Blow
Sept 2 1666 – Down to the very centre of the earth
Feb 12 1667 – Orpheus Hymn
Jan 24 1667 – First Brawles / Second Brawles
Perche quando Giovanni Draghi
Such moving sounds

Release date: autumn 1990
Cassette: CSDL 385

CD–SDL 386   THE ENGLISH GUITAR QUARTET: Baroque Guitar Quartets

Concerto Grosso Op. 3 No. 1 (Handel):
  Allegro
  Lento
  Presto
Passacaglia and Fugue (BWV 582) (Bach):
  Passacaglia
  Fugue
Sonata da Camera Op. 2 No. 6 (Corelli):
  Allemanda
  Corrente
  Giga
  Allegro
  Andante
  Allegro
Sonata da Chiesa Op. 3 No. 1 (Corelli):
  Grave
  Allegro
  Vivace
  Allegro
Suite No. 1 from The Fairy Queen (Purcell):
  Prelude
  Rondeau
  Jig
  Hornpipe
  Dance for the Fairies

Release date: Feb. 1991
Cassette: CSDL 386

CD–SDL 387   ARABESQUE: Traditional Arabic Music

Longa	Sama'l Thaqil
Taksim Hussayni	Sidi Blal
Ansam	Cerga
Redili Guelbi	Alwan Mizan
Hiwar	Bab Arraja

Release date: prob. autumn 1991 (SC)
Cassette: CSDL 387
Led by Hassan Erraji, a blind ud player.

CD–SDL 388   CALICHE: Music of the Andes

Festival de las Flores	Volver a un Tiempo Nuevo
Amanecer Andino	Vientos del Sur
Recuerdos del Lago	El Pillán
El Cóndor Pasa	Papel de Plata
N'Guillatún	Oasis
El Pájaro Campana	Llorando se Fué

Release date: autumn 1991
Cassette: CSDL 388

CD–SDL 389   DAVID FANSHAWE: Spirit of African Sanctus

Acholi Bwala Dance (A)	Acholi Enanga (A)
Call to Prayer (B)	Dingy Dingy Dance (A)
Egyptian Wedding (B)	Rain Song of Latigo Oteng (A)
Islamic Prayer School Camel Drivers' Songs (C)	Bunyoro Madinda (A)
Reed Pipe and Grass Cutting Song (C)	Bwala Dance (A)
Courtship Dances (C)	Rowing Chant of the Samia (A)
Four Men On a Prayer Mat (C)	Song of Lamentation (A)
Zebaidir Song with Rebabah (C)	Masai Milking Song (D)
Hadandua Cattle Boy's Song (C)	Song of the River, Karamoja (A)
Hadandua Love Song and Bells (C)	Karamajong Childrens' Song (A)
Zande Song of Flight and Frogs (C)	Turkana Cattle Song (D)
Tamboura Song (A)	Luo Ritual Burial Dance (D)
Edongo Dance (A)	War Drums (C)
Busoga Fishermen (A)	Call to Prayer (B)
Bowed Harp (A)	Acholi Warriors and Bwala Dance (A)
Toso Fishermen (A)	Aluar Horns (A)

Release date: prob. autumn 1991 (SC)
Cassette: CSDL 389
Complete versions of recordings used in *African Sanctus* (released on Philips in 1975) plus further recordings from Fanshawe's collection, all recorded between 1969 and 1973. A = Uganda; B = Egypt; C = Sudan; D = Kenya.

CD–SDL 390   JAVIER ALVAREZ: Paplotl

Acuerdos por Diferencia (Hugh Webb, harp)	Mannam (Inok Paek, kayagum)
Temazcal (Luis Julio Toro, maracas)	Asi el Acero (Simon Limbrick, steel pan)
Papalotl (Philip Mead, piano)	

Release date: 1992
Cassette: CSDL 390
Subtitled "Transformaciones Exótica". Electroacoustic creations by Mexican composer Javier Alvarez. Released out of sync with surrounding catalogue numbers due to recording complexities.

CD–SDL 391   RAY FISHER: Traditional Songs of Scotland

Night Visiting Song
Wark o' the Weavers (acc. John Kirkpatrick)
Lady Keith's Lament (acc. Martin Carthy)
The Gallowa Hills (acc. Colin Ross)
Coulter's Candy (acc. Colin Ross)
Willie's Fatal Visit (acc. Martin Carthy)
Twa Recruiting Sergeants (acc. Martin Carthy, John Kirkpatrick)
Floo'ers o' The Forest (acc. Colin Ross)
MacGinty's Meal and Ale (acc. John Kirkpatrick)
Baron o'Brackley
Gipsy Laddies
Lang Biding Here (acc. Colin Ross)
Jute Mill Song (acc. Colin Ross)
Hie, Jeannie Hie (acc. John Kirkpatrick)
Johnny My Man
My Laddie's Bedside (acc. Martin Carthy)
What Can A Young Lassie (acc. Martin Carthy)
Nicky Tams (acc. John Kirkpatrick)

Release date: autumn 1991 (SC)
Cassette: CSDL 391

CD–SDL 392   RONALD CURTIS & LAURENCE JAMES: The Theatre Organ

Whispering (A)
Lullaby Of the Leaves (A)
Alone (A)
Five Foot Two, Eyes of Blue (A)
Autumn Concerto (A)
Lover (A)
Only Make Believe / Why Do I Love You (A)
Caribbean Honeymoon (A)
A Nightingale Sang In Berkeley Square (A)
Only a Rose (A)
Top Hat, White Tie and Tails (A)
Funiculi Funicula (A)
What a Perfect Combination (A)
Over the Rainbow (A)
Falling In Love with Love (A)
Bye Bye Blues (A)
I Know That You Know (B)
It's the Talk of the Town (B)
Goody Goody (B)
A Kiss In the Dark (B)
Lazy River (B)
Glen Miller Selection (B)
 I Know Why
 Tuxedo Junction
I Won't Dance (B)
All the Things You Are (B)
Alley Cat (B)
Love's Last Word Is Spoken (B)
Walkin' My Baby Back Home (B)
After You've Gone (B)

Release date: prob. autumn 1991 (SC)
Cassette: CSDL 392
A = Ronald Curtis at the Compton Theatre Organ, Paramount Organ Studios; B = Laurence James at the Wurlitzer Theatre Organ, Buckingham Town Hall. Reissue of tracks from SDL 317 and SDL 323.

CD–SDL 393   THE BROADSIDE BAND: English Country Dances

1st edition 1651:
  Cuckolds All a Row
  Shepheards Holyday or Labour In Vaine
  Newcastle
  The Beggar Boy
  Picking of Sticks
  Faine I would If I could or Parthenia
  Gathering Peascods
  The Night–Peece or The shaking of the Sheets
3rd edition 1657:
  Chelsey Reach or Buckingham–House
4th edition 1670:
  Jameko
  Epping Forest
6th edition (supplement) 1679:
  Well–Hall
7th edition 1686:
  The Fits Come On Me Now or The Bishop of Chester's Jigg
7th edition (supplement) 1687:
  Mad Robin
9th edition 1695:
  Red–House
  Mr. Beveridge's Magot
Part II 1696 (supplement to 9th edition):
  The Geud Man of Ballangigh, To a New Scotch Jigg
11th edition 1701:
  Childgrove
  Woolly and Georgey
  Portsmouth
  White–Hall Minuett
12th edition 1703:
  Bloomsberry Market

Release date: Feb. or Mar. 1992
Cassette: CSDL 393

CD–SDL 394   ROGER WINFIELD: Windsongs

North Wind
South Wind
East Wind
West Wind
Windsong 1
Windsong 2
Windsong 3
Windsong 4

Release date: Feb. or Mar. 1992 (SC)
Cassette: CSDL 394
Aeolian harps.

CD–SDL 395   *LUCIE SKEAPING & THE BURNING BUSH: Raisins and Almonds*

Yo m'enamori d'un aire
Tum Balalaika
Chassidic Melody No. 24 (instrumental)
Tsen kopikes
Adio querida
Puncha, puncha
Sha! Shtil!
Una matica de ruda
Chassidic Melody No. 13 (instrumental)
Di alte kashe

Avrix mi galanica
Gey ikh mir shpatsirn
Una hija tiene el rey
Di mezinke oysgegebn
Mi padre era de Francia
Oyfn pripetchik
Chassidic Melody No. 10 (instrumental)
La rose enflorece
Rozhinkes mit mandlen
Zog nit keynmol

Release date: early 1992 (SC)
Cassette: CSDL 395

CD–SDL 396   *TRADITIONAL: Vocal Traditions of Bulgaria*

Mari Maro / Yanka Rupkina (Stoyan Velichkov)
Snoshti Vecher U Vas Byah (Men's folk group, Hadjidimovo)
Polegnala Bela Pshenitza (Linka Gergova & Menka Aronova, Bistritsa)
Momne Le Mari Hubava (Folk song group, Kutela, and Dimiter Pethovskl)
Vido Dva Vetra Veyat (Folk song group, Sapareva Banya)
Zaidi Mi Rayo (Kalinka Vulcheva & Stoyan Velichkov)
Dosto, Mome Dosto (Folk group, Breznitsa)
Shto Yubavo Sofliskoto Pole (Dimiter & Vladimir Mitev, Vladaya)
Zamurknaya Petstotin Aiduka (Turmachkite folk

song group, Plana)
Senkya Pada (Purva Barenkova, Pakovitsa)
Bre Nikola Nikola (Folk group, Radovetz)
Devoiko Mari Hubava (Vesselin Djigov, Kutela, and Stephan Zachmanov)
Rechenski Kamuk Reka Zaglavya (Folk song group, Nedelino)
Rasti Bore (Folk group, Bansko)
Zazhena Se Niva (Hadka Dimitrova, Kosharevo)
Pominalo E Devoiche (Folk song group, Kalishte)
Rodilo Se Muzhko Dete (Dimiter & Vladimir Mitev)
Sluntzeto Trepti Zauda (Yanka Rupkina, Gospodin Stanev and Kostadin Varimezov)
Pusni Ma Maicho (Folk song group, Zhultusha)
Doide Mi Obed Pladnina (Folk song group, Dolen)
Done Ide Ot Manastir (Folk group, Balanovo)

Release date: autumn 1992
Cassette: CSDL 396
From the archives of Bulgarian State Radio

CD–SDLC 397   *VARIOUS ARTISTS: A Musical Banquet*

Baroque Flute (from CD–SAR 52)
Guitar Quartet (from CD–SDL 379)
Folk Hymn (from CD–SDL 383)
South America (from CD–SDL 388)
Flemish Polyphony (from CD–SAR 56)
Mandolin (from CD–SAR 53)
Jewish Music (from CD–SDL 395)
French Baroque (from CD–SAR 57)
Italian Renaissance (from CD–SAR 58)
Folk Dance (from CD–SDL 393)
Aeolian Harps (from CD–SDL 394)
Harmonic singing (from CD–SDL 376)
Welsh Harp (from CD–SDL 372)

Latin Plainsong (from CD–SDL 369)
Muslim Chant (from CD–SDL 389)
French Song (from CD–SAR 51)
Historic Piano (from CD–SAR 48)
Mediaeval Motet (from CD–SAR 49)
Musical Boxes (from CD–SDL 359)
Bulgarian Song (from CD–SDL 396)
Portuguese Baroque (from CD–SAR 43)
Renaissance Town Band (from CD–SDL 364)
Scottish Song (from CD–SDL 391)
Arabic Music (from CD–SDL 387)
French Harp (from CD–SAR 36)

Release date: autumn 1992
Cassette: CSDLC 397
Budget priced sampler, subtitled "A Sampler of Musical Treats from Saydisc and Amon Ra".

CD–SDL 398   THE YORK WAITS WITH RICHARD WISTREICH & ROBIN JEFFREY: Old Christmas Return'd

Gabriel from Heven–King
Es ist ein ros entsprungen / En natus est
    Emanuel / In dulci jubilo
The Seven Joys of Mary
Joseph, lieber Joseph mein
Nous voici dans la ville / Il est né / Les Anges
dans nos campagnes / Touro–louro–louro! Lou
    gau canto
Den haghel ende die calde snee / Gaudete,
    Christus est natus

The Old Year Now Away Is Fled
Almain: The Night Watch
Quittez pasteurs
Remember, O Thou Man
Pavan: Heigh–ho Holyday / Galliard: The New–Yeeres Gift
Drive the Cold Winter Away
Pavan: The Cradle / Galliard: The new–Yeeres gift
Er ist een kindeken geboren op d'aard / The Sans Day Carol
The Gloucestershire Wassail

Release date: autumn 1992
Cassette: CSDL 398

CD–SDL 399   THE ENGLISH GUITAR QUARTET: Spanish Guitar Quartets

From Suite Española (Albéniz):
  Sevilla
  Cadiz
  Asturias
  Castilla
Three Mexican songs
From Concerto for two organs (Soler):
  Allegro
  Andante

Tempo de Minué
From La Vida Breve (Falla):
  Spanish Dance No. 1
Six Pavans (Milan)
Spanish Dances (Granados):
  No. 3
  No. 5
  No. 10

Release date: 1992
Cassette: CSDL 399

CD–SDL 400   THE BROADSIDE BAND WITH JOHN POTTER & LUCIE SKEAPING: English National Songs

I The Late Renaissance:
  Greensleeves
  Gather Ye Rosebuds While Ye May
  When the King Enjoys His Own Again
  The Northern Lass
II The Baroque Period:
  Harvest Home
  Sally In Our Alley
  The Roast Beef of Old England
  The Vicar of Bray
  Rule Britannia
III Late Baroque / Galant:
  God Save the King

Nancy Dawson
The Miller of the Dee
The British Grenadiers
A Hunting We Will Go
IV Classical and Early Romantic:
  Drink to Me Only with Thine Eyes
  The Chapter of Kings
  The Lass of Richmond Hill
  Begone Dull Care
  Tom Bowling
  Early One Morning
  Home, Sweet Home

Release date: Feb./Mar. 1993
Cassette: CSDL 400

CD–SDL 401   VARIOUS ARTISTS: Rajasthani Folk Music

Langas:
  Note Patterns (A)
  Shepherds' Music (B)
  Bhairavi (B)
  Rano (B)
  Roupnager Su Raj or "Heli" (C)
  Nagaji (C)

Mehandi or "Henna" (D)
Kotal Ghurhlo (D)
Manganiyars:
  Sorath (E)
  Kalyan (F)
  Khamayachi (E)

Release date: 1991
Cassette: CSDL 401
A = Habib Khan; B = Habib Khan & Ramjan Khan; C = Askar Khan, Gani Khan, Habib Khan & Ramjan Khan; D = Master Sikander, Habib & Ramjan Khan; E = Chanan Khan & Ramjan Khan; F = Bartak, Chanan & Ramjan Khan.

CD–SDL 402   JO FREYA: Traditional Songs of England

All Things Are Quite Silent
As I Set off to Turkey
As Sylvie was Walking
General Wolfe
Though I Live Not Where I Love
A Sailor's Life
Rounding the Horn
Lord Franklin
The Unquiet Grave
The Broomfield Wager
There Was a Lady All Skin and Bone

Geordie
Maids When You're Young Never Wed an Old Man
Bold William Taylor
Lovely Joan
A Blacksmith Courted Me
The Carnal and the Crane
The Green Cockade
Fourpence a Day
The Streams of Lovely Nancy
Sweet England

Release date: 1993
Cassette: CSDL 402
Also includes Fi Fraser, Paul Burgess, violin, Flos Headford, Dave Townsend, Nigel Eaton, Nick Hooper, Kathryn Locke and The Rose Consort of Viols. Musical arrangements by Gef Lucena.

CD–SDL 403   VARIOUS ARTISTS: Spirit of Polynesia

Aitutaki Drum Dance (Cook Is.)
Himene Tarava (Rapa Iti, Austral Is.)
Poipoi – Taro Pounding (Austral Is.)
Song of Papa Teora (Austral Is.)
Himene Ruau (Rapa Iti (Austral Is.)
Bird Dance Hula (Hawaii)
Haka Maori Welcome, N.Z. (Australia)
Song of Papa Kiko (Easter Is.)
Kai Kai of Mama Amelia (Easter Is.)
Hoko War Dance (Easter Is.)
Meke Wesi Spear Dance (Fiji)
Tau'a'alo (Tonga)
Fangufangu Nose Flute (Tonga)
Faikava Love Song (Tonga)
Chiefs and Orators Sasa (W. Samoa)
Tagi Lullaby (W. Samoa)
Tawhoe – Oar Dance (Tokelau)
Copra Bugle Call (Tokelau)
Mokaone's Harmonica (Niue)
Song of Anili (Niue)

Frigate Bird Dance, Nauru (Australia)
Funafuti Chorus, Tuvalu (Australia)
Imenetuki – Gospel Chant (Cook Is.)
Mire of Eamaki (Cook Is.)
Ute – Cutting Nuts (Cook Is.)
Tapa Cloth Beating (Cook Is.)
Palmerston Shanties (Cook Is.)
Imenetuki (Pukapaka, (Cook Is.)
Mako of Mama Lulutangi (Pukapuka, Cook Is.)
Canoe Racing and Wresling (Pukapuka, Cook Is.)
Children's Games (Pukapaka, Cook Is.)
Akatikatika Drum Dance (Pukapuka, Cook Is.)
Mako Chant (Pukapuka, Cook Is.)
Haka Tapatapa (Marquesas Is.):
  a) Pig Dance (Nuku Hiva, Marquesas Is.)
  b) Ruu Chant (Fatu Hiva, Marquesas Is.)
Himene Tarava (Tahiti)
Himene Nota (Bora Bora)
Otea Drum Dance (Tahiti)

Release date: 1993
Cassette: CSDL 403
Field recordings by David Fanshawe.

CD–SDL 404   VARIOUS ARTISTS: North Indian Vocal Music

Khyal in Raga Bhairav (Hafeez Ahmed Khan)
 Thumri in Raga Bhairav (Neela Bhagwat)
 Khyal in Raga Bhupal (Hafeez Ahmed Khan)

Thumri in Raga Bhairai (Neela Bhagwat)
Khyal in Deshkar (Neela Bhagwat)

Release date: 1994
Cassette: CSDL 404
Field recordings by Caroline Swinburne, who also provided the recordings for CD-SDL 401.

CD–SDL 405 VARIOUS ARTISTS: Sea Songs and Shanties

Stormy Weather Boys (A)
Rio Grande – Shanty (B)
Mister Stormalong – Shanty (A)
Warlike Seamen (The Irish Captain) (C)
The Worst Old Ship (Waiting For the Day) (A)
The Yarmouth Fishermen's Song (D)
Maggie May (A)
Caroline and Her Young Sailor Bold (E)
Whisky Johnny – Shanty (A)
What Shall We Do with a Drunken Sailor? (B)
Can't You Dance the Polka? – Shanty (A)
The Sailor's Alphabet – Shanty (F)
Haul Away Joe – Shanty (A)

Cruising Round Yarmouth (D)
Windy Old Weather (A)
Farewell and Adieu (We'll Rant and We'll Roar) (B)
High Barbaree (A)
The Liverpool Packet (G)
Little Boy Billee (A)
Johnny Todd (A)
The Banks of Claudy (C)
The Bold Princess Royal (A)
Jack Tar On Shore (D)
The Smuggler's Boy (A)
The Smacksman (H)
Hanging Johnny – Shanty (A)

Release date: 1994
Cassette: CSDL 405
Field recordings by Peter Kennedy. A = Bob Roberts; B = Fishermen's Group, Cadgwith, Cornwall; C = Bob & Ron Copper; D = Harry Cox; E = Sarah Makem; F = Clifford Jenkins; G = Bill Barber; H = Tom Brown.

CD–SDL 406 SIWSANN GEORGE: Traditional Songs of Wales

Adar Man Y Mynydd
Y Gwcw Fach
Can Merthyr
Miner's Life
Blodau'r Flwyddyn
Hen Ferchetan
Hiraeth
Can Y Cardi
Cainc Yr Aradwr
Titrwm Tatrwm

Yr Hen Wr Mwyn
Yr Eneth Gadd Ei Gwrthod
Bachgen Bach O Dincer
Mae'r Ddaear Yn Glasu
Ar Fore Dydd Nadolig
Clywch Clywch
Llangollen Market
Can Y Bugail
Lisa Lan
Marwnad Yr Ehedydd

Release date: 1994
Cassette: CSDL 406
Subtitled "Caneuon Traddodiadol Cymru". Also includes Robin Huw Bowen, Ceri Matthews, Iolo Jones, Julie Murphy, Roger Plater, Nigel Eaton and Catrin Defis.

CD–SDL 407 VARIOUS ARTISTS: Songs of the Travelling People

Won't You Buy My Sweet Blooming Lavender?
    (Janet Penfold)
Come A' Ye Tramps an' Hawkers (Davie
    Stewart)
The Blarney Stone (Margaret Barry)
The Berryfields of Blair (Belle Stewart)
The Muckin' O' Geordie's Byre (Jimmy McBeath;
    Willie Kelby)
The Choring Song (Jeannie Robertson)
The Beggar Wench (Davie Stewart)
A Blacksmith Courted Me (Phoebe Smith)
Barnyards o' Delgaty / Gin I Were Where the
    Gadie rins (Willie Kelby)
On the Bonny Banks o' the Roses (Duncan
    McPhee)
The Bard of Armagh (Margaret Barry)
Dandling Song / Bonny Lassie–o / Cuckoos's
    Nest (Jeannie Robertson)
I Am a Romany (Phoebe Smith)

Devonshire Time and two gipsy hornpipes (Frank
    O Connor)
Higher Germanie (Phoebe Smith)
The Little Beggarman (Paddy Doran)
Kathleen (Margaret Barry)
The Lady o' the Dainty Doon–By (Jeannie Robertson)
The Tenpenny Bit / She Moves Through the Fair (Our
    Wedding Day) (Belle Stewart)
The Poor Smuggler's Boy (Angela Brasil)
Aul' Jockey Bruce o' the Fornet (Davie Stewart)
Tuning Up (mouth music) / Paddies Lay Down / Mandi Went
    To Poove the Grys / The Leaving of Glen Urquhart
    (Carolyne Hughes, Charlie Lindsay)
Twa Heids Are Better Than Yin (Kathie Stewart)
The Moss O' Burreldale / The Gay Gordons (march)
    (Jimmy McBeath, Willie Kelby)
The Overgate (Jeannie Robertson)
Macpherson's Rant / Macpherson's Lament (Donald and
    Albert Stewart, Davie Stewart)

Release date: 1994
Cassette: CSDL 407
Field recordings by Peter Kennedy.

CD–SDL 408   MECHANICAL MUSIC: Victorian Musical Box

Polyphon March / The Victoria Cross / Frou–
    Frou – At Supper Song (A)
The Merry Coppersmith–March / The Sweet
    Story Olden / The Honeybee / The
    Old Folks at Home / Kathleen
    Mavourneen (B)
The Little Chatterbox / Tyrolese Song / Air from
    Stabat Mater (A)
Sailor's Hornpipe / Home Sweet Home / Eileen
    Alannah / La Matchiche (C)
Walk–March of Friesach / Drinking, Drinking,
    Drinking / Shepherd's Dance from
    Henry VIII (A)
National Songs of Britain: The British Grenadiers/

Rule Britannia / Bluebells of Scotland / The Gay
    Gordons/ Men of Harlech / Land of My Fathers (D)
Seven Victorian Musical Toys and Snuff Boxes
Unidentified tune / 'Dance a Cachucha' from The Gondoliers /
    Home Sweet Home (E)
Under the Double Eagle / It Never Troubles Me / Monastery
    Bells (F)
Lazily, Drowsily / Two unidentified tunes (G)
The Bells Go Ringing for Sarah / Sweet Spirit Hear My Prayer
    / Pretty Gemima Don't Say No (H)
The Last Rose of Summer / Adjets Kraten / Lorelie / Les
    Grelots (I)
Two unidentified tunes / The Glad Trumpet / The Soldier's
    Tears (J)

Release date: 1994
Cassette: CSDL 408
A = Large Polyphon musical box; B = Small Polyphon musical boxes; C = Medium Polyphon musical box, Polyphon with glockenspiel attachment; D = Nicole Frere fortepiano, Regina and Polyphon musical boxes; E = Nicole Freres musical boxes; F = Regina musical box; G = Excelsior piccolo cylinder box, Paillard Vaucher Fils cylinder box; H = 12 air, 2 comb cylinder box with bells; I = Le Croix cylinder musical box; J = Cylinder musical boxes (unknown).

CD–SDL 409   THE BROADSIDE BAND: Songs and Dances from Shakespeare

Full Fathom Five Thy Father Lies
Where the Bee Sucks, There Suck I
O Mistress Mine Where Are You Roaming?
The Poor Soul Sat Sighing (The Willow Song)
It Was a Lover, and His Lass
Sellengers Round
Scottish Jigge
Hoboken Brawl 'Brawl'
Staines Morris
How Should I Your True Love Know
Tomorrow Is St Valentine's Day
And Will He Not Come Again
In Youth When I Did Love
The Woosell Cock, So Black of Hue
O Sweet Oliver
When Daffodils Begin to Peer
Jog On, Jog On, the Footpath Way
When That I Was and a Little Tiny Boy
Kemp's Jig Love's Labour's Lost
Passamezzo Pavan

Bergamasca
QM Dumpe
As You came from That Holy Land
I Loathe That I did Love
Bonny Sweet Robin
Come Live with Me
There Dwelt a Man in Babylon
Farewell Dear Love
Fortune My Foe
The Earl of Essex Measure
La Volta
The Sinkapace Galliard
Coranto
Take, O Take Those Lips Away
Sigh No More Ladies
Hark, Hark, the Lark
Lawn as White as Driven Snow
Get Ye Hence
When That I Was and a Little Tiny Boy

Release date: 1995
Cassette: CSDL 409
Director, Jeremy Barlow. With Deborah Roberts and John Potter.

CD–SDL 410   SALLY DEXTER, JULIE MURPHY, IAN GILES, ANDY TURNER WITH THE
MELLSTOCK BAND: Songs of Thomas Hardy's Wessex

The Foggy Dew
Jockey to the Fair / Dame Durden
The Mistletoe Bough
Cupid's Garden
Queen Eleanor's Confession
The Spotted Cow
The Seeds of Love
The Barley Mow
The Prentice Boy
I Have Parks, I Have Hounds
Break o'the Day

The Sheepshearing Song
The Tailor's Breeches
The Downhills of Life
I Wish, I Wish
Joan's Ale
The Outlandish Knight
Such a Beauty I Did Grow
The Banks of Allan Water
King Arthur Had Three Sons
The Light of the Moon

Release date: 1995
Cassette: CSDL 410

CD–SDL 411   VARIOUS ARTISTS: Traditional Songs of Ireland

An Doro Féinne (The McPeake Trio)
The Moorlough Shore (Jim O'Neill)
The Wild Colonial Boy (Margaret Barry)
My Singing Bird (The McPeake Trio)
The Whistling Thief (Seamus Ennis)
The Factory Girl (Margaret Barry)
When You Go to the Fair (Má Théid
Tú Un Aúnaigh) (Hudie Devaney)
The Jug of Punch (The McPeake Trio)
Moses Ritoolarilay (Margaret Barry)
Keening Song (Kitty Gallagher)
The Verdant Braes of Skreen (McPeake Trio)
Her Mantle So Green (Jim O'Neill)
Wedding Day (Margaret Barry)
Bhríd Og Ní Mháille (Hudie Devaney)

As I Roved Out (Seamus Ennis)
The Factory Girl (Sarah Makem)
Brian O Linn (Thomas Moran)
The Hawk and the Crow (Liam O Connor)
She Moves Through the Fair (Our The Wild Mountain Thyme
(The McPeake Trio)
The Blackbird / The Rights of Man (Francis McKearn)
The Turfman from Ardee (Margaret Barry)
The Nursemaid (An Bhanaltra) (Kitty Gallagher)
Monaghan Fair (Frank McPeake)
The Magpie's Nest (Annie Jane Kelly)
Dance to Your Daddy / Cucanandy–Nandy / What Would You
Do? (Elizabeth Cronin)
Siubhan Ni Dhuibhir (The McPeake Trio)

Release date: 1995
Cassette: CSDL 411
Field recordings by Peter Kennedy.

CD–SDL 412   ROBIN HUW BOWEN: Harp Music of Wales

Ar Hyd y Nos
Moel yr Wyddfa / Nos Galan
Pibddawns y Gof / Dyn y Geg
Llwyn Onn
Polca Saiforella
Dafydd y Garreg Wen
Pwt–ar–y–bys

Meillionen o Feirionnydd
Hwylio Adref
Gorymdaith Gw'yr Harlech
Y Llinyn Arian
Pant Corlan yr W'yn
Merch Megan / Wyres Megan
Cader Idris

Release date: 1995
Cassette: CSDL 412

CD–SDL 413   VARIOUS ARTISTS: Cockney Kings of Music Hall

If It Wasn't for The 'ouses In Between (Gus Elen)
Any Old Iron? (Harry Champion)
The Future Mrs. 'awkins (Albert Chevalier)
Wait A Minute (Tom Woottwell)
Meat! Meat! (Fred Earle)
And the Fog Grew Thicker & Thicker (Ernie
Mayne)
The Coster's Christening (Duncan and Godfrey)
And His Day's Work Was Done (George Brooks)
I've Only Been Married A Week (Charles Austin)
The Penny Whistler (Fred Lay)
I'm Getting Ready for My Mother–In–Law (Harry
Champion)
I've Only Come Down for the Day (Sam Mayo)

The Germans Are Coming, So They Say (Harry Bedford)
Inquisitive Kiddie (Ben Albert)
Down the Road (Gus Elen)
The Day That I Become A Millionaire (Harry Ford)
The May–Day Fireman (Dan Leno)
Mamma's Darling Boy (Herbert Campbell)
Man! (Harry Randall)
My Next Door Neighbour's Garden (Herbert Darnley)
Won't Yer Buy Some Beer? (Nat Travers)
The King of Karactacus (Rich and Rich)
Right as Ninepence (Albert Chevalier)
Should Husbands Work? (Charles Coborn)
Boiled Beef and Carrots (Harry Champion)

Release date: 1995
Cassette: CSDL 413

CD–SDL 414   VARIOUS ARTISTS: Spirit of Micronesia

Te Kamei – standing dance (Kiribati)
Te Kamei Batere (Kiribati)
"Tibwereri" (Kiribati)
Te Katake Chant (Kiribati)
Te Bino – sitting dance (Kiribati)
Te Orobaoki – strike the box! (Kiribati)
Te Karuo – love song (Kiribati)
Toddy Cutting Songs (Kiribati)
Te Kawawa / Te Kamei (Kiribati)
Aeroplane Song (Marshall Is.)
Morning Star Choir (Marshall Is.)
Presentation of Food (Marshall Is.)
Jebua Stick Dance (Marshall Is.)
"Beet!" (Marshall Is.)
Sunday Morning Service (Marshall Is.)
Micro Palm – copra boat (Marshall Is. / Kosrae)
Seamen's Dance (Kosrae)
Kepia / Dokia – stick dance (Pohnpei)
Ordination Song (Chuuk)
Navigators of Pulusuk (Chuuk)
Death of Titilap (Chuuk)
Conche / outrigger / storm (Chuuk)
Puluwat Hymn (Chuuk)
Navigators of Puluwat (Chuuk)
Men's Standing Dance (Chuuk)
Launching a Canoe (Yap)
Dances of Satawal (Yap)
Songs of Lamotrek (Yap)
Song for Sick People (Yap)
Star–Path Chant (Yap)
Night Revelry (Yap)
Ulithi Sailing Chant (Yap)
Chants and Dances of Yap (Yap)
"Wul" Bird (Palau)
Palauan Chant (Palau)
Birds of Helen Reef (Palau)

Release date: 1995
Cassette: CSDL 414
Field recordings by David Fanshawe.

CD–SDL 415   HASSAN ERRAJI: Music for the Arabian Dulcimer and Lute

Badru Zuhur
Nida Insan
Zubida
Altaf
Taqsim Ajam Kabir
Moulana
Salaam
Taqsim Ráad
Munawaat Ahlam

Release date: 1995
Cassette: CSDL 415

CD–SDL 416   VARIOUS ARTISTS: Bagpipes of Britain and Ireland

The Irish Uillean Pipes:
  Maidrin Rua
  The Blackthorn Stick / Saddle The Pony
  Juanita
  Mrs McLeod's Reel
  The Lark In the Morning (Felix Doran)
  Pigeon On the Gate / Miss Monaghan's (Felix Doran)
  The Brown Thorn (Seamus Ennis)
  The Boyne Hunt (Seamus Ennis)
  The Dear Irish Boy (Willie Clancy)
  Rowsome's Slip Jig (Willie Clancy)
The Northumbrian Small–Pipes:
  Lewis Proudlock's Hornpipe
  Peter Baillie's Pig
  Maggie's Foot
  Maa Bonny Lad (with Isla Cameron)
  Money Musk
  The Fair Flower of Northumberland
  The Jenny Bell Polka
Wild Hills O' Wannies
Whittingham Green Lane / Ward's Brae
The Redesdale Hornpipe
The Lads of Alnwick
Bonny at Morn / Billy Boy / The Earl of Derwentwater's Farewell
Keel Row
The Scottish Highland Pipes (Alex Stewart):
The Burning Sands of Egypt
My Lodging Is On the Cold, Cold Ground
The De'il's I' the Kitchen / London Society
Loch Duich
Manchester Hornpipe / Maggie Dickie's / De'il Among the Tailors / Reel o' Tulloch / Wind That Shakes the Barley / Rights of Man
Bonnie Annie / The Duke of Roxburgh's Farewell to Black Mount
By Loch Etive's Side / High Road to Gareloch
Leaving Ardtornish / Port Askaig
Duncan Macrae of Kintail's Lament

Release date: 1996
Cassette: CSDL 416
Tracks featuring the Irish Uillean Pipes are by The McPeake Family Trio unless stated; Northumbrian Small–Pipes played by Jack Armstrong; Scottish Highland Pipes played by Alex Stewart.

CD–SDL 417   TRADITIONAL: A Celtic Christmas

Calennig – Wales
Tàladh Chriosda – Scotland (Isle of Barra)
The Wren Hornpipe / The Christmas Eve /
   Winter Apples –Ireland
Oikan Ayns Bethlehem – Isle of Man
Hunting the Wren:
   a) The King – Wales
   b) Can Hela'r Dryw – Wales
   c) Shelg Y Drean – Isle of Man
   d) Wren – Boys of Dun / Wren Boys' Song –
      Ireland
Kanomp Nouel – Brittany
Dublin Tune – Ireland

Mari Lwyd: Can y Fari Lwyd / Cariad Cywir – Wales
Da Day Dawns / Christmas Day i da Moarnin / The Papa Stour
   Sword Dance – Scotland (Shetland)
The Tree of Life – Cornwall
Carval ny drogh vraane – Isle of Man
The Gower Wassail – Wales
Plygain: Wel dyma'r borau gorau i gyd – Wales
Arise and Hail the Glorious Star – Cornwall
The Seven Rejoices of Mary – Ireland
Ffarwel Gwyr Aberffraw – Wales
Leanabh an àigh – Scotland (Isle of Mull)
Highland Pipe Medley – Scotland

Release date: 1996
Cassette: CSDL 417
Winter ritual song and traditions from Brittany, Cornwall, Ireland, Isle of Man, Scotland and Wales.

CD–SDL 418   VARIOUS ARTISTS: Spirit of Melanesia

Sepik Flutes Kanengara (Papua New Guinea)
Pan Pipes of Buma (Solomon Is.)
Club Dance – Meke Iwau (Fiji)
Meke Rara Nakelo (Fiji)
Meke Sea–sea – standing dance (Fiji)
Vakamalolo – sitting dance (Fiji)
Nabua Methodist Church Choir (Fiji)
New Year Celebrations (Fiji)
Grog Song Lakeba (Fiji)
Singera String Band (Vanuatu)
Naghol Land Diving (Vanuatu) Kanengara
Lifou Mouth Pipes (New Caledonia)
Spirit Song U'ula (Solomon Is.)
Shell Money Making (Solomon Is.)
Spirit Song "ia ia ia" (Solomon Is.)
Gilo Stones (Solomon Is.)
Pan Pipes "The Awakening" (Solomon Is.)
Funeral Song (Solomon Is.)

Karop Pipes, Mouth Harp, Dance (Torres Strait Is.)
Yule Island Festivities (Papua New Guinea)
Mount Hagen Singsing (Papua New Guinea)
Mendi Girls Chant Alipuli (Papua New Guinea)
Wagi Brothers Bamboo Band (Papua New Guinea)
Rymoka String Band (Papua New Guinea)
Karawari Initiation (Papua New Guinea)
Sepik Flutes Sangriman, Kamanibit (Papua New Guinea)
Timbunke Garamut Drums (Papua New Guinea)
Wundubu Bangu Ceremony (Papua New Guinea)
Singsing Apunivur (Papua New Guinea)
Kanengara War Dance (Papua New Guinea)
Bisorio House Building Kilao War Party (Papua New Guinea)
Singsing Bodif Headhunting (Papua New Guinea)
Waskuk Yam Harvesting (Papua New Guinea)
Misa Yaroma Wewak (Papua New Guinea)
Mariway Flutes "Secret Place" (Papua New Guinea)

Release date: 1998
Cassette: CSDL 418
Field recordings by David Fanshawe.

CD–SDL 419   THE BROADSIDE BAND: Old English Nursery Rhymes

Girls and Boys:
 Girls and Boys Come Out to Play
 Polly Put the Kettle On / Lucy Locket
 Jack and Jill Went Up the Hill
 Tom, He Was a Piper's Son
 Little Boy Blue, Come Blow Your Horn
 Little Miss Muffet, She Sat On a Tuffet
 Oh Dear What Can the Matter Be?
Round the Mulberry Bush – Games and Dances:
 Here We Go Round the Mulberry Bush
 Oranges and Lemons
 Oats and Beans and Barley Grow
 The Farmer's In His Den
 Dance to Your Daddy
 A Ring o' Roses
Hey Diddle Diddle – Riddles and Nonsense:
 Hey Diddle Diddle / Humpty Dumpty
 I Had Four Brothers Over the Sea
 I Saw a Ship a–Sailing
 There Was a Man Lived In the Moon
 If All the World Were Paper
The Lion and the Unicorn – The High and Mighty:
 Lavender's Blue
 Sing a Song of Sixpence
 I Had a Little Nut Tree
 Oliver Cromwell Lay Buried and Dead
 Old King Cole Was a Merry Old Soul
 Grand Old Duke of York / Lion and the Unicorn

Ding Dong Bell – Cats and Mice:
 Ding Dong Bell, Pussy's In the Well
 Hickory Dickory Dock
 Three Blind Mice
 There Were three Little kittens
 I Love Little Pussy
 Pussy Cat, Pussy Cat, Where Have You Been?
 Three Mice Went Into a Hole To Spin
A Frog He Would A Wooing Go – Fortune and Fate:
 My Daddy Is Dead, But I Can't Tell You How
 A Jolly Fat Frog Lived In the River
 The North Wind Doth blow
 Who Killed Cock Robin?
 A Frog He Would a Wooing go
Little Bo Peep – Sheep:
 Mary Had a Little Lamb
 Baa Baa Black Sheep
 Little Bo Peep
Hot Cross Buns – Food:
 Hot Cross Buns
 Little Jack Horner
 Dame Get Up and Bake Your Pies
 Pat a Cake, Pat a Cake, Baker's Man
 Oh, What Have You Got for Dinner Mrs Bond?
Hush A Bye Baby – Bedtime:
 Hush a Bye Baby On the Tree Top
 Dance a baby Diddy
 Hey Diddle Dumpling, My Son John
 Twinkle Twinkle Little Star
 Sleep, Baby Sleep
 Boys and Girls to Play (instrumental version)

Release date: 1996
Cassette: CSDL 419

CD–SDL 420   VARIOUS ARTISTS: Traditional Dance Music of Ireland

Reels: Sally Gardens, Mason's Apron (A)
Slip Jig: Gurty's Frolic (B)
Hornpipe: Louis Quinn's (C)
Reel: David's Delight (D)
Hornpipe: The Sweep's (E)
Reels: Bunker Hill, Tommy Whelan's (A)
Quadrille: Please Give a Penny to the Poor Old
    Man (B)
Reel: Stormy Weather (B)
Reel: The Gosson That Bate His Father (F)
Reels: The Copperplate, The Boys of the Spuds
    (Bunch of Keys) (A)
Reel: Carracastle Lasses (George White's) (G)
Jigs: Biddy the Bowl Wife, I Lost My Love and I
    Care Not, King of the Cannibal Islands
    (Cumberland Reel) (H)
Reel: New Lough Isle Castle (bagpipe style) (B)
Reel: Marry When You're Young (B)
Reel: Lords Gordons (B)
Reels: The Boys of the Lough, The Lark (A)
Reel or Hornpipe: Down the Glen (E)

Hare Among the Heather, Woman of the House (G)
Hornpipes: Paddy O'Brien's (the second known as
    Cooley's) (C)
Reels: McKenna's, Tinker's Apron and Antrim Reel (H)
Reel or Hornpipe: The Red–Haired Boy (D)
Jigs: O'Malley's, The Luck Penny (A)
Reel: The Salamanca (B)
Reel: The First of May (B)
Hornpipes: The Trumpet, The Locomotive (A)
Reel: The Banks of the Ilen (E)
Polka: The Dark Girl Dressed In Blue (B)
Reel: The Floggin (B)
Hornpipes: Johnson's, The Golden Eagle (A)
Reel: Mason's Apron (D)
Hornpipe: The Independent (C)
Jigs: Paddy's Own, The Launch (Off She Goes) (I)
Reel: Music at the Gate (J)
Reel: The Basket of Oysters, Jig: Jackson's Rum Punch (K)
Jigs: O'Brien's Fancy, Garret Barry's (A)
Reel: The Boys of Ballisadare (Dublin Lasses) (G)
Hornpipes: The Passing Cloud and Ryan's (A)

Release date: 1997   **Cassette:** CSDL 420
Field recordings by Peter Kennedy. A = Jimmy Hogan Trio; B = Johnny Doherty; C = Jimmy Hogan; D = Tom
Turkington; E = Paddy Taylor; F = Sean Maguire; G = Michael Gorman & Margaret Barry; H = McCusker Brothers
Ceilidh Band; I = Paddy Breen; J = Seamus Ennis; K = Johnny Pickering.

CD–SDL 421   VARIOUS ARTISTS: Vocal Traditions of Albania

Shqiptaria bashkë gjithmonë
Një thëllëzë e shkruar prilli
Smarte moj!
Këngë vaji
Në gjumë isha dhe u zgjova
Këngë popullore qytetare
Në majë të shelgut
Kam shtëpinë me rasa
Larg nga vendi i bardhë flori
Fyell i Tanës
Bec Patani
Ra një lot dhe lagu syt

Më muar malli më muar
Djalë të bukur të bëri nëna
Vajta një ditë në pazar
Qaj moj zemër, qaj
Zani i Nanës
Këngë për Meço Bonen
Ymer Aga
Lan vasha në gurë të lumit
Moj Kosovë, trimneshë dardane
Medet o Riza, medet
Dasmorë sot asht tan Shqipnija

Release date: 1997
Cassette: CSDL 421
Recordings from Albanian State Radio.

CD–SDL 422   STANBROOK ABBEY, PRINKNASH ABBEY: Compline and Other Chant

Latin Plainchant (Monks of Prinknash Abbey):
  Abbey Bells and Introit – Spiritus Domini
          Mode VIII
  Alleluia – Emitte Spiritum tuum Mode IV
  Hymn – Christe Redemptor omnium Mode I
  Hymn – Vexilla Regis prodeunt Mode I
  Hymn – Veni Creator Spiritus Mode VIII
  Hymn – Adoro te devote Mode V
  Hymn – Virgo Dei Genitrix Mode II
  Offertory Verse – Ave Maria Mode VIII
  Magnificat Antiphon – Montes Gelboe Mode I
  Motet – Ave Verum Corpus Mode VI

English Chant (Monks of Prinknash Abbey):
  Psalm 45 – God is for us a refuge and strength
  Hymn – Christ our Saviour, from the Father (Christmas)
  Psalm 138 – O Lord you examine me and know me
  Hymn – Into the silence of our hearts
  Psalm 137 – I thank you Lord with all my heart
Compline:
  Compline (Latin) (The Monks of Prinknash Abbey)
  Compline (English) (The Nuns of Stanbrook Abbey)

Release date: April 1997
Cassette: CSDL 422
Compilation of material from "Music from Prinknash Abbey" (SDL 330) and "O Give Thanks to the Lord" (SDL 349)

CD–SDL 423   STANBROOK ABBEY, PRINKNASH ABBEY: Chant and Psalms

Latin Chant (Prinknash and Stanbrook):
  Gaudeamus (Processional)
  Mass – Cum Jubilo:
    Kyrie
    Gloria
    Sanctus
    Agnus Dei
  Media Vita
  Gaudeamus (Recessional)
English Chant (Prinknash and Stanbrook):
  Keep In Your Minds
  Like As the Deer (Stanbrook)
  Let All Creation
  Into Your Hands (Prinknash)
  To the Lamb of God
  O Give Thanks to the Lord (Stanbrook)
  The Daughter of the King (Stanbrook)
  Send Forth Your Spirit (Prinknash)
  Alleluia (Prinknash)
  Te Deum

'Thirsting for God':
  Rorate coeli: "Drop down dew, you heavens" Traditional
      Advent chant
  John 7:37–39 "If any one thirst, let him come to me"
  Ps 62 (63) "O God, you are my God, for you my soul is
      thirsting"
  Ps 138 (139) "O Lord, you search me and you know me"
  Ps 21 (22) "My God, my God, why have you forsaken me?"
  Good Friday Responsory: "Now is the judgement of this world"
'Living Water':
  Ps 113 (114) "Alleluia! Christ the Lord has conquered death"
  Ps 137 (138) "In the presence of the angels, I will bless you,
      O Lord"
  John 4:4–14 "A spring of water welling up to eternal life"
  Isaiah 12 "With joy you will draw water from the wells of
  salvation"
  Easter Canticle: "Alleluia, Christ is risen, alleluia"
  Ps 22 (23) "The Lord is my shepherd"

Release date: April 1997
Cassette: CSDL 423
Compilation of material from *O Give Thanks to the Lord* (SDL 349) and *Wellsprings* (SDL 363).

CD–SDLC 424   VARIOUS ARTISTS: Free Sampler of Saydisc and Amon Ra albums

British traditional songs
Traditional dance & Thomas Hardy music
Customs, shanties, folk hymns, travellers,
    favourite songs
Childrens' games & rhymes, bagpipes
Harps, dulcimers & hurdy gurdies
World Music – Africa, Pacific
World Music – China, Japan, Arabia
World Music – India, Eastern Music
World Music – Various
Musical boxes
Nostalgia + mechanical music
Nostalgia + mechanical music (cont)
The Music of Christmas Past

The Music of Christmas Past (cont)
Latin & English Chant, Bells
Guitar & saxophone quartets
Education Packs for schools
Keyboards, trumpets, oboes
Harps, mandolins, guitars, flutes
Mediaeval music
Renaissance, Elizabethan & Tudor music
Elizabethan & Tudor music (cont.)
Flemish and Italian Renaissance music
Baroque music on original instruments
Classical period music on original instruments
Romantic period music on original instruments
Singing bowls, windharps, percussion, electroacoustic

Release date: 1997

The CD was not available for sale but was included free with Saydisc's 1997 catalogue – track listing above as credited in the catalogue. 100,000 copies and catalogues were sent out. 78 minutes on 27 tracks. Each track comprises several snippets from different recordings, covering most of the currently available catalogue. Manufactured in Austria.

CD–SDL 425   VARIOUS ARTISTS: English Customs and Traditions

Helston Furry & Hal–an–tow (Cornwall, May 8th)
Padstow Hobby Horse (Cornwall, May 1st)
Castleton Garland Day (Derbyshire, May 29th)
Bampton Morris (Oxfordshire, Whit–Monday)
Headington Morris (Oxford, Morris Dance Tunes)
Abbots Bromley Horn Dance (Staffs., Sept.)
Antrobus Soulcakers (Cheshire, end Oct.)
St. Clement's Day Song (Hammerwich,
    Staffordshire, Nov 23rd)

The Singing of the Travels (Christmas Mummers at
    Symondsbury & Eype, Dorset)
As I Sat On a Sunny Bank (Camborne, Cornwall)
The Cherry Tree Carol (Cinderford, Gloucestershire)
The Bitter Withy (Tarrington, Herefordshire)
Lazarus (Bromsberrow Heath, Herefordshire)
West Country Wassailers
John Barleycorn (Haxey, Lincs sung before Jan 6th)
Shrove Tuesday (Warminster, Wilts 1954)
The Gower Wassail

Release date: 1997
Cassette: CSDL 425

Field recordings by Peter Kennedy, this was a remake of SDL 332, though with revisions

CD–SDL 426   VARIOUS ARTISTS: Traditional Songs and Dances of Sardinia

Pastoral sounds from Lotzorai / Nonmi giamedas
    Maria (Male quartet from Nuoro)
La Povera Cecchina / I Colori dell' Arcobaleno /
    Il Treno (Children of Nuoro)
Ballo tondo (Nuoro folk dance group)
Vanto alla Fidanzata (Dorgali folk song group)
Ave Maria (Children of Nuoro)
Folk dance music / Ballo (Tres passos) (Monni
    Salvatore Pudrana, Baunei/Dorgali)
Su Sa Corte De Su Re / Sas Cozzulas de
    Jubanna / Ite Bella Pizzinna
    (Children of Nuoro)

Folk dance music (Blind accordion player, Santa Maria
    Navoresse)
Three Sardinian love songs (Dorgali folk song group)
Un Vaso di Porcellana / I Tre Tamburi / La Bella Villana
    (Children in Lotzorai)
Passu tozzau, Dyllu (Nuoro folk dance group)
Sas Rundine e S'Oddéu / Quell' Uccelletto / Le Rondinelle
    / La Formicuzza (Children of Nuoro)
Folk dance music (Accordion player, Santa Maria Navoresse)
La Solitudine / Gioco Topolino / Madama Le Frulle Frulle /
    Siamo Sette Cavaglieri (Children in Lotzorai/
    Outside Case populari, Dorgali)

Release date: 1998
Field recordings by Fr Damian Webb.

CD–SDL 427   VARIOUS ARTISTS: Tibetan Folk Music

Yarkyi Dakmo (Lhasa)
Gö Thang Kar Dungi Dungdro Chen (Nagchu)
Shaglen (Central Tibet)
Bal Lu (Nagchu)
Dar Tson Nanga (Sertal)
Gyu Nor (Sertal)
Pang Shong Yar La (Zhigatse)
Toe–shey Sugze Yag La (Lhasa)
Kham folk song (Kham)
Zachig Zanyi (Kham)
Nangma Sonam Yangchen (Lhasa)
Lhashig Bumo Gonpay Gyen (Sertal)
Nangma Tala–shipa (Lhasa)

Mana Mar Nor Gyi Sacha (Nagchu)
Lak Shue Pay Druk La Harta Che (Zhigatse)
Nya Lam Thangla (Lhasa)
Tsa Lu (Nagchu)
Shing Yagrelo(Sertal)
Garlu Leydro (Lhasa)
A Ngon Nam (Sertal)
Nye Phayul Nagshö (Nagchu)
Toe Dingri Mangshey(Zhigatse)
Nga Yi Tseway Chungdri (Central)
Tse De Yenche Rey (Sertal)
Nye Sol Lu Len (Sertal)
Toe–shey Daway Shon Nu (Lhasa)

Release date: 1999
Subtitled "Traditional songs & instrumental music from the roof of the world".

CD–SDL 428   ROGER WINFIELD: Voices of the Wind

Voices of the Wind

Release date: 1998
Subtitled "Roger Winfield's Aeolian Harps". This is one continuous track.

CD–SDL 429   BELLS: Carillon Bells of Britain

Carillon of St. Nicholas's Church:
  Round O' (from Abdelazer) (Ronald Leith)
  Charlie Is My Darling (R. Leith)
  Tambourin (R. Leith)
  John Anderson My Joe (R. Leith)
  Finale, from Petite Suite (R. Leith)
The Bournville Carillon:
  Cuckoo Rondo (Trevor Workman)
  Judas Maccabaeus, Chorale (T. Workman)
  Last Rose of Summer (T. Workman)
  Llanfair (Variations) (T. Workman)
  Variations On a Gospel Tune (T. Workman)
Carillon of St. John's Kirk, Perth:
  Scotch On the Rocks (Raymond Aldington)
  Mariners' Hymn (O Sanctissima) (A. Gebruers)
  Esteritta (A. Gebruers)
  Estudio 5 for Guitar (R. Aldington)
  See the Conquering Hero Comes (A. Gebruers)

The Loughborough Carillon:
  Rendezvous (Peter Stratfold)
  Cockles and Mussels (P. Stratfold)
  La Ferlaude (from J.de Gruytters Carillon Book) (P. Stratfold)
  Crimond (P. Stratfold)
  Entracte from Mignon (P. Stratfold)
Carillon of St. Marnock's Church, Kilmarnock:
  The Oak and the Ash (R. Aldington)
  Duet (R. Aldington)
  Song: Sandgate Dandling (R. Aldington)
  Hymn Tune: Ellers (R. Aldington)
  The Harp That Once Through Tara's Hall (Adrian Gebruers)
Domestic Clocks:
  'Westminster' and 'Cambridge' Chimes and Cuckoo Clock
The Chime of the Church of St. Clement Danes, London:
  Oranges and Lemons ('The Bells of St. Clements')

Release date: 1998
Compilation of material from *Sound of the Carillon* (SDL 291) and *Carillons of Scotland* (SDL 341).

CD–SDL 430   VARIOUS ARTISTS: The Celtic Harp

Kerry Polkas (Monger)
Her Mantle So Green / Im Aonar Seal (Shaljean)
Poll Ha'penny / Plains of Boyle / Cnoc na
          gClarach Slides (Monger)
Bonny Portmore (Monger)
Captain O'Neill / Colonel O'Hara / Sir Festus
          Burke (Shaljean)
The Wild Geese (Monger)
The Kilburn Jig / Diarmuid's Well / The Wild
          Irishman (Shaljean)
King of the Fairies / The Lilting Banshee (Monger)
Pibddawns y Gof / Dyn y Geg (Bowen)

Dafydd y Garreg Wen (Bowen)
Pant Corlan yr Wyn (Bowen)
Meillionen o Feirionnydd (Bowen)
Gypsy Hornpipe / Pwt–ar–y–bys (Bowen)
Roslin Castle / The Lea–Rig (Shaljean)
Fingal's Cave (Monger)
When She Cam' Ben She Bobbit (Shaljean)
I Was Not .. Since Martinmas/ An Muileann Dubh / The
          Highlandman Kissed His Mother (Shaljean)
Port Priest / Port Atholl (Shaljean)
Airs By Fingal (Shaljean)
Maggy Lauther/ Bonie Jean Makis Meikill of Me (Shaljean)

Release date: c. Mar.1999
Compilation of material from Eileen Monger's *The Lilting Banshee* (SDL 348), Bonny Shaljean's *Farewell to Lough Neaghe* (CD–SDL 372) and Robin Huw Bowen's *Harp Music of Wales* (CD–SDL 412).

CD–SDL 431   VARIOUS ARTISTS: Cry You Mountains, Cry You Fields

Kaba e rëndë Kolonjare
Do të marrë shaminë dhe do shkoj në varrë
Një behar tërë behar
Djalka shkonte në dyqan
Këngë kaba Kolonjare
Pse ma mban kokën mënjanë
Pastoral improvisation
Kolonjë, e bukur Kolonjë
Pa seç ja thotë qyqja
Valle e gajdes

Këngë për Riza Cerovën
Ditën e Shën Gjergjit
Melodi e mëngjezit
Kënga e Tiko Kapedanit
Valle popullore
Vogëlushe e vogël, sa fort që të dua
Qani male, qani fusha
Esmerkë më ishe
Kaba kurbeti

Release date: 1999 (1998?)
Subtitled "Traditional songs & instrumental music from south east Albania".

CD–SDL 432   KNUT BUEN: Hardanger Fiddle Music of Norway

Klonkaren, halling
Myllargutens bruremarsj
Myllargangar etter Halvor Flatland
Siklebekken, springar
Maltstein, gangar/Kivlemøyane etter
        Myllarguten
Gangar
Springar
Lokkaren
Forsteinaren
Filleveren, gangar
Fyrispel

Kivlemøyane, gangar
Håvards draum, springar
Kivlegangar
Sigurd Jondalen, springar
Leirlid'n, gangar
Margit Hjukse, lydarslått
Rosa, lydarslått etter Lars Fykerud og Svein Løndal
Gangar etter Lars Fykerud
Huldregubben i Gaustafjell, lydarslått
Fykerudvrengja etter Olav Løndal
Fanitullen, lydarslått
Fykerud's farvel til Amerika

Release date: autumn 1999

CD–SDL 433   VARIOUS ARTISTS: Rag Pickings

Poppies (Joe Roberts)
Rag Pickings (Fred Van Eps)
Camptown Carnival (Olly Oakley)
Sunflower Dance (Vess L. Ossman)
Ross Double Shuffle (E. Ross)
My Sumurun Girl (Fred Van Eps)
Peach Blossoms (Olly Oakley)
Lost Arrow (Fred Van Eps)

Ragtown* (Olly Oakley)
Dixie Medley (Fred Van Eps)
Sunflower Dance (Olly Oakley)
Banjo Frolic* (Fred Van Eps)
The Ragtime Major* (Olly Oakley)
Medley of Southern Melodies (Fred Van Eps)
Queen Of Diamonds (Olly Oakley)
Lumbrin Luke (Olly Oakley)

Release date: May 2007
Subtitled "Hot Ragtime Banjo solos from the original Recordings c. 1900 – 1930". The titles marked with an asterisk were modified to prevent offence being caused by the original titles – which itself caused offence!

CD–SDL 434   SPOKEN WORD: Gloucestershire Characters

Fred Smith of Daglingworth – stone walling
Fred Archer of Ashton–under–Hill – cider apples
Mollie Harris of Eynsham, Oxfordshire – sheep
        dagging'
Charlie Whitfield of Walham near Gloucester –
        elver fishing, life by the river

William Jones of the Forest of Dean – Old Joulter
Amy Cooke of Coombe, Wotton–under–Edge – eating snails
George King of Lechlade – mop hiring fairs
Jack Fisher of Winchcombe – delivering mail on horseback
Mrs Vaughan of Fawley near Ross–on–Wye – living without
        'the 'lectric'

Release date: June 2007
Field recordings, mostly recorded in the early to mid–1960s, by Peter Duddridge.

CD–SDL 435   SPOKEN WORD: George Swinford of Filkins
No track credits listed – continuous dialogue

Release date: June 2007
Field recordings, from 1962, by Peter Duddridge. Recollections of a Gloucestershire mason, collector and craftsman, born c. 1866.

Matchbox – SD series summary listing

Full details of the following records can be found in the previous section.

SDM 142	VARIOUS ARTISTS: Blues Like Showers of Rain
SDR 143	BLIND BOY FULLER: Blind Boy Fuller On Down Vol. 1
SDR 146	VARIOUS ARTISTS: Blues Piano
SDM 159	IAN ANDERSON, MIKE COOPER: The Inverted World
SDR 163	KOKOMO ARNOLD: Kokomo Arnold
SDM 167	VARIOUS ARTISTS: Blues Like Showers of Rain Volume Two
SDR 168	VARIOUS ARTISTS: Blind Boy Fuller On Down Volume 2
SDR 169	SONNY BOY WILLIAMSON, ETC: Sonny Boy and His Pals
SDR 182	VARIOUS ARTISTS: Those Cakewalkin' Babies from Home Vol. 1
SDR 190	FURRY LEWIS: Furry Lewis In Memphis
SDR 191	PEETIE WHEATSTRAW: The Devil's Son In Law (1930–36)
SDR 192	PEETIE WHEATSTRAW: The High Sheriff from Hell (1936–38)
SDR 199	VARIOUS ARTISTS: Skoodle–Um–Skoo
SDR 206	VARIOUS ARTISTS: Hometown Skiffle
SDX 207/8	VARIOUS ARTISTS: Black Diamond Express to Hell (2–LP)
SDR 213	LITTLE BROTHER MONTGOMERY: Little Brother Montgomery 1930–1969
SDR 216	CLYDE BERNHARDT: Blowing My Top
SDM 223	LITTLE BROTHER MONTGOMERY: Home Again
SDM 224	VARIOUS ARTISTS: The Legacy of Tommy Johnson
SDM 225	VARIOUS ARTISTS: Big Road Blues
SDM 226	VARIOUS ARTISTS: Blues from the Delta
SDM 227	VIOLA WELLS: Miss Rhapsody
SDM 229	FRANKLIN GEORGE & JOHN SUMMERS: Traditional Music for Banjo, Fiddle & Bagpipes
SDM 230	VARIOUS ARTISTS: Mississippi River Blues (Flyright – Matchbox)
SDM 231	CLARK KESSINGER: Clark Kessinger Live at Union Grove
SDM 235	GEORGE PEGRAM: George Pegram
SDM 236	JOE VAL AND THE NEW ENGLAND BLUEGRASS BOYS: One Morning In May
SDM 237	UNKNOWN: Test pressing exists
SDM 238	SNUFFY JENKINS & PAPPY SHERRILL: 33 Years of Pickin' and Pluckin'
SDM 239	HAPPY TRAUM, ETC: Mud Acres – Music Among Friends
SDM 241	HOLLOW ROCK STRING BAND: Hollow Rock String Band
SDM 242	CURLY HERDMAN: Fiddler
SDM 250	VARIOUS ARTISTS: Fort Valley Blues (Flyright – Matchbox)
SDM 257	VARIOUS ARTISTS: Out In the Cold Again (Flyright – Matchbox)
SDM 258	VARIOUS ARTISTS: Boot That Thing (Flyright – Matchbox)
SDM 261	DAVE PEABODY: Keep It Clean
SDM 264	VARIOUS ARTISTS: Two White Horses Standin' In Line (Flyright – Matchbox)
SDM 265	VARIOUS ARTISTS: Jack o' Diamonds (Flyright – Matchbox)
SDX 270	DAVE PEABODY: Come and Get It

Roots

The Roots label was a specialist blues label run by Johnny Parth and pressed in Austria. As the 1960s blues boom took hold in the UK, many UK record shops supplied Roots label LPs at premium import prices – for example Peter Russell's Hot Record Store, in Plymouth, advertised Roots LPs at 52/6 in its December 1968 catalogue – quite expensive when UK–manufactured LPs generally ranged from around 30/– to 35/– at this point. However, in 1969, having set up the Matchbox imprint as a blues label, Saydisc began to press and distribute Roots LPs in the UK, thus bringing the price down by quite a few shillings over the import price. The majority of the LPs were housed in the original sleeve designs with original labels, often printed in the UK from Austrian film, and many had a Saydisc sticker stuck on the sleeve, whilst others included a printed Saydisc credit. Some releases seem to have included a Roneo insert with detailed track and artist credits.

It is probable that not all of the following Roots LPs were manufactured and distributed by Saydisc, but verifying exactly which were not is difficult. Therefore, the following list errs on the side of caution and almost certainly lists a few LPs not manufactured by Saydisc. The June 1969 Matchbox and Roots catalogue included RL 320, 321, 323 and 324 and stated that, "The release of all future Roots Records will be made by Saydisc/Matchbox for sale to G.B. and Eire only", going on to say that back numbers and overseas orders should be made to the Austrian address." Saydisc ceased manufacturing and distributing Roots LPs in the UK in 1972.

Saydisc has pressing cards for RL 301, RL 306, RL 313, RL 320 through to RL 334, RL 337, RSE 1, SL 504 and SL 506. However, the lack of a pressing card does not mean that Saydisc did not press some of the others, RL 335 and RL 336 being cases in point with sleeves stating, "Roots Records are manufactured and distributed in Britain by Matchbox Records Ltd." A couple of Matchbox releases also seem to have been leased to Roots, with SDR 213 listed as Roots RSE 3, though this may not have been subsequently issued by Roots. SDR 190, however, was issued by Roots as SL 505. To add even more complexity, RL 337 appeared on the Matchbox label design, rather than on the Roots label design, and SL 506 appeared on the Saydisc label design. It is possible that one or two more SL or RSE albums were issued by Saydisc, but only those where pressing cards exist have been included: Saydisc seems to have been cherry picking here!

RL 301   BLIND LEMON JEFFERSON: Blind Lemon Jefferson Volume 1

Wartime Blues	Booster Blues
Booger Rooger Blues	Dynamite Blues
Corinna Blues	Eagle Eyed Mama
Black Horse Blues	Right of Way Blues
Maltese Cat Blues	Black Snake Dream Blues
D. B. Blues	Black Snake Moan
Dry Southern Blues	Chock House Blues
Rambler Blues	Prison Cell Blues
Rabbit Foot Blues	See That My Grave Is Kept Clean – No. 2

Release date:
Subtitled on label "1926–1929". Includes a Roneo insert with original recording details.

RL 302   VARIOUS ARTISTS: Mississippi Blues Vol. 1

Snake Doctor Blues (Jelly Jaw Short)	Mississippi Moan (Isiah Nettles)
C & O Blues (Blind Joe Amos)	Cypress Grove Blues (Skip James)
Early Mornin' Blues (William Harris)	The Jinx Blues – No. 2 (Son House)
Signifying Blues (Sam Collins)	Black Train Blues (Bukka White with Washboard Sam)
Mean Black Moan (Charley Patton & Henry Sims)	Barefoot Blues (Jelly Jaw Short)
Jesus Is a Dying–Bed Maker (as above)	Left Alone Blues (Ishman Bracey with Charlie McCoy)
Rolling Stone, part 1 & 2 (Robert Wilkins)	Blue Harvest Blues (Mississippi John Hurt)
	Kind Hearted Woman Blues (Robert Johnson)

Release date:
Subtitled on label "1927–1942".

RL 303   **VARIOUS ARTISTS: Mississippi Blues Vol. 2**

Prayer of Death, pts. 1 & 2 (Charley Patton)
Heart Like Railroad Steel (Charley Patton)
Jersey Bull Blues (Charley Patton)
Lord, I'm Discouraged (Charley Patton)
Love My Stuff (Charley Patton)
Hank It On The Wall (Charley Patton)
34 Blues (Charley Patton)

Dark Cloudy Blues (Sam Collins)
Pork Chop Blues (Sam Collins)
How Long "Buck" (Skip James)
22–20 Blues (Skip James)
Pinebluff Arkansas (Bukka White)
Shake 'Em On Down (Bukka White)
District Attorney Blues (Bukka White)
Parchman Farm Blues (Bukka White)

Release date:.
Above track listing includes a 'best guess' as to where the side 1 break is.

RL 304   **VARIOUS ARTISTS: Nearer My God to Thee**

Sinking of the Titanic (Richard 'Rabbit' Brown)
The Royal Telephone (Sister Mary Nelson)
Mother's Love (Joe & Emma Taggart)
Jonah In the Belly of the Whale (Rev. F. W. McGee)
Lift Him Up That's All (Washington Phillips)
Praying On the Old Damp Ground (Mississippi John Hurt)
Sweet Heaven Is My Home (Arizona Dranes)
You'll Need Somebody on Your Bond (Blind Willie Johnson)

Ain't No Grave Can Hold My Body Down (Bozie Sturdivant)
Blessed Be Thy Name (Mississippi John Hurt)
With His Stripes We Are Healed (Rev. F. W. McGee)
It's All Right Now (Arizona Dranes)
Religion Is Something Within You (Blind Joe Taggart)
He Arose From the Dead (Blind Lemon Jefferson)
Be Ready When He Comes (Skip James)
When the Saints Go Marching In (Barbecue Bob)

Release date:
Subtitled on label "Sanctified Singers, Preachers & Congregations" and "1926–1942". Includes a Roneo insert with original recording details.

RL 305   **TOMMY McCLENNAN: Cross Cut Saw Blues**

Baby, Don't You Want to Go?
I'm Goin', Don't You Know
She's Just Good Huggin' Size
My Little Girl
My Baby's Doggin' Me
She's a Good–Looking Mama
New Sugar Mama
Down to Skin and Bones

Katy Mae Blues
Love with a Feeling
Drop Down Mama
Black Minnie
Elsie Blues
Cross Cut Saw Blues
You Can't Read My Mind
It's a Crying Pity

Release date:
Subtitled on sleeve and label "1939–1941". Includes a Roneo insert with original recording details.

RL 306   **BLIND LEMON JEFFERSON: Blind Lemon Jefferson Vol 2**

I Want to Be Like Jesus In My Heart
All I Want Is That Pure Religion
Jack o' Diamonds Blues No. 1
Old Rounders Blues
Easy Rider Blues
Match Box Blues No. 2
Match Box Blues No. 4
See That My Grave Is Kept Clean
'Lectric Chair Blues

Piney Woods Moany Mama
Low Down Mojo Blues
Competition Bed Blues
Sad News Blues
Christmas Eve Blues
Happy New Year Blues
Yo Yo Blues
Fence Breakin' Yellen' Blues
Cat Man Blues

Release date:
Subtitled on label "1925–1929". Includes a Roneo insert with original recording details.

RL 307 VARIOUS ARTISTS: The Memphis Area

Madison Street Rag (Cannon's Jug Stompers)
Hollywood Rag (Cannon's Jug Stompers)
Broken–Hearted, Ragged and Dirty Too
  (Sleepy John Estes)
Black Mattie Blues (Sleepy John Estes)
Nobody Knows What the Good Deacon Does
  (Hambone Willie Newbern)
Tappin' That Thing (Burse & Stephen)
Come Along, Little Children ('Poor Jab')
It Won't Be Long Now – take 2 (Frank Stokes)

Garage Fire Blues (Memphis Minnie)
Bad Lucks' My Buddie (Noah Lewis' Jug Band)
Stack o' Dollars (Sleepy John Estes)
My Black Gal Blues (Sleepy John Estes)
Roll and Tumble Blues (Hambone Willie Newbern)
Nashville Stonewall Blues (Robert Wilkins)
Police Sergeant Blues (Robert Wilkins)
Kansas City Blues (Memphis Jug Band)

Release date:

Subtitled on sleeve and label "1927–1932". Includes a Roneo insert with original recording details. Label includes German copyright text.

RL 308 FRANK STOKES: Frank Stokes

You Shall
Sweet to Mama
Half a Cup of Tea
Beale Town Bound
Mr. Crump Don't Like It
Chicken You Can Roast Behind the Moon
Bedtime Blues

Mistreatin' Blues
Nehi Mama Blues
Stomp That Thing
Ain't Goin' to Do Like I Used to Do
South Memphis Blues
Bunker Hill Blues
Memphis Rounders Blues

Release date:

Subtitled on sleeve and label "With Dan Sane and Will Batts". Subtitled on label "1927–1929". Tracks 1 to 6 & 11 are by The Beale Street Sheiks (Stokes & Dan Sane). Track 7 has an unknown accompanist. Tracks 12 & 13 are by Frank Stokes & Will Bates.

RL 309 VARIOUS ARTISTS: Blues from Georgia

Cold Wave Blues (Barbecue Bob)
Beggin' for Love (Barbecue Bob)
Jesus' Blood Can Make Me Whole (Barb. Bob)
Ugly Papa (Charlie Lincoln)
If It Looks Like Jelly (Charlie Lincoln)
Chain Gang Trouble (Charlie Lincoln)
Hard Luck Blues (Charlie Lincoln)
Gamblin' Charley (Charlie Lincoln)

Stole Rider Blues (Blind Willie McTell)
Mr. McTell Got the Blues (Blind Willie McTell)
Low Rider's Blues (Blind Willie McTell)
Rock and Gravel Blues (Peg Leg Howell)
Walkin' Blues (Peg Leg Howell)
Turtle Dove Blues (Peg Leg Howell)
Fo' Day Blues (Peg Leg Howell)
New Prison Blues (Peg Leg Howell)

Release date:

Subtitled on label "1926–1931". Includes a Roneo insert with original recording details.

RL 310 VARIOUS ARTISTS: Missouri and Tennessee

Raidin' Squad (Charley Jordan)
Got Your Water On (The Two Charlies)
Don't Put Your Dirty Hands On Me (The
  Two Charlies)
Biddle Street Blues (Henry Spaulding)
Lonesome John (Stovepipe No. 1)
Fisher's Hornpipe (Stovepipe No. 1)
She's Got a Mean Disposition (Henry Townsend)
A Woman Gets Tired of the Same Man All the
  Time (Stovepipe No. 1/David Crockett)

Hambone Willie's Dreamy–Eyed Woman's Blues (Hambone
  Willie Newbern)
Way Down In Arkansas (Hambone Willie Newbern)
My Money Never Runs Out (Banjo Joe)
Staggering Blues (Rosie Mae Moore)
Little Sarah (James 'Yank' Rachel)
T–Bone Steak Blues (James 'Yank' Rachel)
Crazy 'Bout My Black Girl (Charlie Pickett)
Evergreen Money Blues (Memphis Jug Band)

Release date:

Subtitled on label "1924–1937". Includes a Roneo insert with original recording details.

RL 311   VARIOUS ARTISTS: Harmonicas, Washboards, Fiddles, Jugs

Apaloosa Blues (Bobby Leecan's Need–More Band)
Peaches in the Springtime (Memphis Jug Band)
Feed Your Friend (Memphis Jug Band)
I Whipped My Woman (Memphis Jug Band)
I Packed My Suitcase (Memphis Jug Band)
Believe I'll Go Back Home (Jack Kelly's Jug Band)
Ko–Ko–Mo Blues (Jack Kelly's Jug Band)
Jazz Gypsy Blues (Banjo Joe)

Nobody's Business If I Do (Tommie Bradley)
Mistreated the Only Friend You Had (James Cole)
I Can Deal Worry (King David's Jug Band)
Sweet Potato Blues (King David's Jug Band)
String Band Blues (Kansas City Blues Stompers)
Pig Meat Blues (Whistler's Jug Band)
Black Cat Bone Blues (Leecan & Cooksey)
Dirty Guitar Blues (Leecan & Cooksey)

Release date:
Subtitled on label "1926–1933". Includes a Roneo insert with original recording details.

RL 312   VARIOUS ARTISTS: Texas Country Music Vol. 1

Arkansas (Henry Thomas)
Sunshine Special take 1 (Blind Lemon Jefferson)
Hot Mattress Stomp (Bernice Edwards)
Before Long (J. T. 'Funny Paper' Smith)
Jail Break Blues (Texas Tommy)
No Job Blues (Ramblin' Thomas)
Back Knawing Blues (Ramblin' Thomas)
Frisco Blues (Billikin Johnson & Neal Roberts)

Sweet Mama Blues (Coley Jones)
Dallas Rag (Dallas String Band)
When the War Was On (Blind Willie Johnson)
Praise God I'm Satisfied (Blind Willie Johnson)
Section Gang Blues (Texas Alexander)
No More Women Blues (Texas Alexander)
Sittin' On a Log (Texas Alexander)
Sweet Patuni (Jesse James)

Release date:
Includes a Roneo insert with original recording details.

RL 313   VARIOUS ARTISTS: Down South (Louisiana – Mississippi – Alabama – Florida)

Never Let the Same Bee Sting You Twice (Richard 'Rabbit' Brown)
Home Wreckin' Blues (Shreveport Home Wreckers)
Hard Hearted Mama Blues (Kid Cole)
Niagra Falls Blues (Kid Cole)
Milkcow's Calf Blues No. 2 (Robert Johnson)
Deep Blue Sea Blues (Tommy McClennan)
Fo' Clock Blues (Fiddlin' Joe Martin, Son House & Willie Brown)
Going to Fishing (Fiddlin' Joe, W. Brown & L. Williams)

Big Rock Jail (Barefoot Bill)
If You Want a Good Woman (Wiley Barner)
Hard–Headed Woman Blues (Clifford Gibson)
Levee Camp Moan (Clifford Gibson)
Save Your Money – Let These Women Go (Jaybird Coleman)
Man Trouble Blues (Jaybird Coleman)
Black Snake (Tallahassee Tight)
Depression's Gone From Me Blues (Blind Blake)

Release date:
Subtitled on label "1927–1941".

RL 314   VARIOUS ARTISTS: Mississippi Blues Vol.3

Out On Santa Fe–Blues (Arthur Petties)
I Want You To Know (Bo Carter)
Jake Leg Blues (Poor Boy Lofton)
My Mean Baby Blues (Poor Boy Lofton)
Jail Bird Love Song (Mississippi Sheiks)
Yodelin' Fiddlin' Blues (Mississippi Sheiks)
I'm Through With You (Big Joe McCoy)
When You Said Goodbye (Big Joe McCoy)

Drunken Hearted Man – take 2 (Robert Johnson)
Let's Go Riding (Mr. Freddie Spruell)
My Baby Left Me (Robert Petway)
Cotton Pickin' Blues (Robert Petway)
Stack O'Lee Blues (Mississippi John Hurt)
Dangerous Woman (Mississippi Jook Band)
Mozelle Blues (Tommy McClennan)
Mr. So and So Blues (Tommy McClennan)

Release date:
Subtitled on label "1928–1942". Includes a Roneo insert with original recording details.

RL 315   *VARIOUS ARTISTS: Texas Country Music Vol. 2*

Charmin' Betsy (Henry Thomas)
The Elders He's My Man (Coley Jones)
If It Had Not Been for Jesus (Blind W. Johnson)
Sunrise Blues (Will Day)
Corn–Bread Blues (Texas Alexander)
Long Lonesome Day Blues (Texas Alexander)
Blues ('Little Brother')
Family Trouble Blues (Andrew Hogg)

Corpus Blues (Little Hat Jones)
Wild Jack Blues (Billikin Johnson & Neal Roberts)
The Soul of Man (Blind Willie Johnson)
Take Your Stand (Blind Willie Johnson)
T. P. Window Blues (Jack Ranger)
It Wouldn't Be So Hard (Whistlin' Alex Moore)
Packin' Trunk Blues (Leadbelly)
All Out and Down (Leadbelly)

Release date:
Subtitled on label "1927–1937". Includes a Roneo insert with original recording details.

RL 316   *VARIOUS ARTISTS: The Country Fiddlers*

The Moore Girl (Andrew & Jim Baxter)
Walking Blues (Chasey Collins)
Highway No. 61 Blues (Jack Kelly's South
     Memphis Jug Band)
Georgia Crawl (Henry Williams & Eddie Anthony)
Lonely One In This Town (Mississippi Sheiks)
Sittin' On Top of the World (Mississippi Sheiks)
J. C. Johnson's Blues (T. C. Johnson & 'Blue
     Coat' Tom Nelson)
Blue Coat Blues ('Blue Coat' Tom Nelson)

Rustlin' Man (State Street Boys)
Too Tight Blues (Peg Leg Howell & His Gang)
Peg Leg Stomp (Peg Leg Howell & His Gang)
Violin Blues (T. C. Johnson Boys)
Seen Better Days (Texas Alexander)
Frost Texas Tornado Blues (Texas Alexander)
Fattenin' Frogs (Mobile Strugglers)
Memphis Blues (Mobile Strugglers)

Release date:
Evidently, Roots' Austrian printers refused to print this sleeve because of the 'offensive' picture of Johann Strauss crossed out with a big red X.

RL 317   *LUCILLE BOGAN & WALTER ROLAND: Alabama Blues*

My Georgia Grind
Sloppy Drunk Blue
Alley Boogie
T. N. & O. Blues
Hungry Man's Scuffle
You Got to Die Some Day
Lonesome Midnight Blues
My Man Is Boogan Me

Pig Iron Sally
Tired As I Can Be
Sweet Man, Sweet Man
Reckless Woman
Down In Boogie Alley
Man Stealer Blues
Stew Meat Blues
Skin Game Blues

Release date:
Subtitled on sleeve and label "1930–1935". Includes a Roneo insert with original recording details.

RL 318   *VARIOUS ARTISTS: The East Coast States (Georgia – Carolinas – Virginia)*

Ball and Chain Blues (Peg Leg Howell & Jim Hill)
Away from Home (Peg Leg Howell & Jim Hill)
Salty Dog (Kokomo Arnold)
Wild About My Loving (Lonnie Coleman)
St. Louis Blues (Sylvester Weaver/Walter
     Beasley)
Bottleneck Blues (as above)
Railroad Blues (Will Bennett)
Gravy Server (Buddy Moss)

Bamalong Blues (Andrew & Jim Baxter)
Furniture Man (Lil' McClintock)
Don't Think I'm Santa Claus (Lil' McClintock)
Gonna Tip Out Tonight (Pink Anderson & Simmie Dooley)
Crooked Woman Blues (Blind Boy Fuller)
Somebody's Been Talking (Blind Boy Fuller)
My Gal's Dome Quit Me (Luke Jordan)
Ragtime Crazy (William Moore)

Release date:
Subtitled on label "1927–1940". Includes a Roneo insert with original recording details. The side 2 runoff on the copy viewed says, "Made in Austria".

RL 319   VARIOUS ARTISTS: Up and Down the Mississippi

Mystery of the Dunbar's Child (Richard 'Rabbit' Brown)
I'm Not Jealous (Richard 'Rabbit' Brown)
Jail House Fire Blues (Buddy Boy Hawkins)
Shaggy Dog Blues (Buddy Boy Hawkins)
You Can't Keep No Brown (Bo Weavil Jackson)
Pig Meat Papa (Mae Glover & John Byrd)
Bedside Blues (Jim Thompkins)
Mind Reader Blues (Bertha Lee & Charley Patton)

Friar's Point Blues (Robert Lee McCoy)
You Scolded Me and Drove Me from Your Door (Mississippi Bracey)
I'll Overcome Someday (Mississippi Bracey)
Hitch Me to Your Buggy (Will Weldon)
Grief Will Kill You (Little Buddy Doyle)
Bad in Mind Blues (Little Buddy Doyle)
California Desert Blues (Lane Hardin)
Henry's Worried Blues (Henry Townsend)

Release date:
Subtitled on label "1926–1940". Includes a Roneo insert with original recording details.

RL 320   VARIOUS ARTISTS: The Great Harmonica Players Volume 1

Mean Low Blues (Blues Birdhead)
Harmonica Blues (Blues Birdhead)
McAbee's Railroad Piece (Palmer McAbee)
Lost Boy Blues (Palmer McAbee)
Roubin Blues (William Francis & Richard Sowell)
John Henry Blues (as above)
Middlin' Blues (George 'Bullet' Williams)
Chickasaw Special (Noah Lewis)

Careless Love (Slim Barton & Eddie Mapp)
I'm Hot Like That (Slim Barton & Eddie Mapp)
Ice Water Blues (De Ford Bailey)
Davidson County Blues (De Ford Bailey)
Meddlin' with the Blues (The Two of Spades)
Harmonica Blues (The Two of Spades)
Ah'm Sick and Tired of Tellin' You (To Wiggle That Thing) (Jaybird Coleman)
Black Snake Blues (Whistlin' Pete and Daddy Stovepipe)

Release date: July 1969 (SC)
Subtitled on label "1925–1929". Sleeve includes Austrian printing credits. Unlike most records in this series, the labels are clearly of UK manufacture and the runoff includes the SDL 171 matrix along with the Roots matrix number. Listed as available from Saydisc at 41/– in the January 1970 catalogue.

RL 321   VARIOUS ARTISTS: Great Harmonica Players Volume 2

Cow Cow Blues (Jed Davenport plus unk. acc.)
How Long How Long Blues (as above)
Dollar Blues (Martin & Robert)
Hock My Shoes (Martin & Robert)
Poor Convict Blues (Slim Barton & James Moore)
The Cockeyed World (Minnie Wallace with Her Night Hawks)
Field Mouse Stomp (as above)
Mountain Blues (Jimmy Smith)

Royal Palm Blues (Leecan & Cooksey)
Ain't She Sweet (Leecan & Cooksey)
Smokey Blues (Ellis Williams plus unknown acc.)
Buttermilk Boys (Ellis Williams plus unknown acc.)
I Want It Awful Bad (Joe Williams with prob. Jed Davenport)
Mr. Devil Blues (Joe Williams with prob. Jed Davenport)
Tough Luck (Robert Lee McCoy with Big Joe Williams & Sonny Boy Williamson)
Harmonica & Washboard Breakdown (Sonny Terry & Oh Red)

Release date: August 1969 (SC)
Subtitled on label "1927–1940". Listed as available from Saydisc at 41/– in the January 1970 catalogue.

RL 322   THE MEMPHIS JUG BAND: The Memphis Jug Band

Stingly Woman Blues
Memphis Jug Blues
Sunshine Blues
I'm Looking for the Bully of the Town
State of Tennessee Blues
Beale Street Mess Around
I'll See You In the Spring
Snitchin' Gambler Blues

Papa Long Blues
She Stays Out All Night Long
A Black Woman Is Like a Black Snake
Mississippi River Waltz
I Can't Stand It
Dirty Butter
The Old Folks Started It
Memphis Yo Yo Blues

Release date:
Subtitled on sleeve and label "1927–1929". Sleeve includes a printed Saydisc credit.

RL 323　　　VARIOUS ARTISTS: Memphis Blues Vol. 1

Prater Blues (Johnson Boys)
'Tain't Nobody's Business (Frank Stokes)
I raised My Window (Ollie Rupert)
Ain't Gonna Be Your Low Down Dog (as above)
She Could Toodle–Oo (Hambone Willie Newbern)
Everybody Help the Boys Come Home (William
　　　& Versey Smith)
Mr. Furry's Blues (Furry Lewis)
Mistreatin' Mama (Furry Lewis)

I Couldn't Help It (Allen Shaw);
Worry Blues (Tom Dickson);
Poor John Blues (Sleepy John Estes)
Whatcha Doin'? (Sleepy John Estes)
School Girl Blues (Rosie Mae Moore)
Bootlegging Blues (Jim Jackson)
Move That Thing (Memphis Jug Band)
You Got Me Rollin' (Memphis Jug Band)

Release date: July 1969 (SC)
Subtitled on label "1927–1934". Sleeve has a Saydisc sticker stating, "Saydisc Records as originally presented by Roots Records, Austria". The runoff includes the SDL 172 matrix along with the Roots matrix number. Includes a Roneo insert with original recording details, plus the copy viewed includes both June 1969 and January 1970 Matchbox and Roots catalogues. Listed as available from Saydisc at 41/– in the January 1970 catalogue.

RL 324　　　BLIND WILLIE McTELL: King of the Georgia Blues Singers (1929–1935)

Come On Around To My House Mama
Razor Ball
Rollin' Mama Blues
Lord Have Mercy If You Please
Don't You See How This World Made a Change?
My Baby's Gone
Weary–Hearted Blues
Runnin' Me Crazy

We Got to Meet Death One Day
Dying Gambler
God Don't Like It
Bell Street Blues
Lay Some Flowers On My Grave
Ticket Agent Blues
Cold Winter Day
Your Time to Worry

Release date: August 1969 (SC)
Subtitled on sleeve and label "1929–1935". Includes a Roneo insert with original recording details. The sleeve has a Saydisc sticker attached stating, "Saydisc Records as originally presented by Roots Records, Austria". Listed as available from Saydisc at 41/– in the January 1970 catalogue.

RL 325　　　VARIOUS ARTISTS: Alabama Country Blues

Barefoot Bill's Hard Luck Blues (Barefoot Bill)
One More Time (Barefoot Bill)
I Don't Like That (Pillie Bolling & Barefoot Bill)
She's Got a Nice Line (as above)
Shrimp Ma　(Red Hot Ole Man Mose)
Sundown Blues (Daddy Stovepipe)
Stove Pipe Blues (Daddy Stovepipe)
Beat You Doing It (Clifford Gibson)

Carry It Right Back Home (Ed Bell)
She's a Fool Gal (Ed Bell)
Fat Mouth Blues (Ben Curry)
Red Cross Blues (Sonny Scott)
Cane Break Blues (Birmingham Jug Band)
Kickin' Mule Blues (Birmingham Jug Band)
It's a Fight Like That (Blind Bogus Ben Covington)
Boodle–De–Bum Bum (Blind Bogus Ben Covington)

Release date:
Subtitled on label "1924–1933". Includes a Roneo insert with original recording details. The sleeve has a Saydisc sticker attached stating, "Saydisc Records as originally presented by Roots Records, Austria". Listed as available from Saydisc at 41/– in the January 1970 catalogue.

RL 326　　　VARIOUS ARTISTS: The East Coast States Vol. 2

I'm Busy and You Can't Come In (S. Weaver)
Guitar Rag (Sylvester Weaver)
Oh Lawdy Mama (Curly Weaver)
Fried Pie Blues (Curly Weaver)
Hillbilly Willie's Blues (Blind Willy McTell)
I'm Gonna Tell God How You're Doin' (Julius
　　　Daniels & Bubba Lee Torrence)
My Mamma Was a Sailor (as above)
Bad Luck Moan (Willie Baker)

Pretty Mama Blues (Joe Linthecome)
Travelin' Man (Virgil Childers)
Preacher and the Bear (Virgil Childers)
Poor Boy a Long Ways from Home (Barbecue Bob)
K. C. Railroad Blues (Andrew & Jim Baxter)
Traveling Coon (Luke Jordan)
Pick Poor Robin Clean (Luke Jordan)
Cocaine Blues (Luke Jordan)

Release date:
Subtitled on sleeve "(Georgia – Carolina – Virginia)". Subtitled on label "1924–1938". Includes a Roneo insert with original recording details. Sleeve has a Saydisc sticker attached stating, "Saydisc Records as originally presented by Roots Records, Austria". Listed as available from Saydisc at 41/– in the January 1970 catalogue.

RL 327   VARIOUS ARTISTS: Texas Country Music Vol. 3

Cross the Water Blues (Little Hat Jones)
Cherry Street Blues (Little Hat Jones)
Blue Goose Blues (Jesse 'Babyface' Thomas)
No Good Woman Blues (as above)
Fourteenth Street Blues (Blind Percy & His
     Blind Band)
Corn Liquor Blues (Lewis Black)
Awful Moanin' Blues, pts. 1 & 2 (Texas Alexander)

Water Bound Blues (Texas Alexander)
Goin' Back To My Baby (Texas Bill Day)
Back Door Blues ('Bo' Jones)
Leavenworth Prison Blues ('Bo' Jones)
Ninth Street Stomp (Bernice Edwards)

Christmas Time Blues (Black Ace)
Trinity River Blues (Oak Cliff T–Bone)
Black Gal – No. 2 (Joe Pullum)

Release date:
Subtitled on label "1927–1937". Sleeve has a Saydisc sticker stating, "Saydisc Records as originally presented by Roots Records, Austria". Includes Roneo insert. Available from Saydisc at 41/– in the January 1970 catalogue.

RL 328   VARIOUS ARTISTS: Southern Sanctified Singers

Go with Me to That Land (Blind Willie Johnson)
A Mother's Last Word to Her Daughter
     (Washington Phillips)
The Great Reaping Day (Bessie Johnson)
I Want My Crown (Bozie Sturdivant)
Christians Fight On (Sam Butler)
Your Enemy Cannot Harm You (Rev. Edward
     W. Clayborn)
In That Day (Arizona Dranes)
When the Saints Go Marching In (Blind Willie Davis)

Jonah In the Wilderness (Henry Thomas)
I've Got the Key To the Kingdom (Washington Phillips)
Put Your Trust in Jesus (Rev. J. C. Burnett)
Heaven Is My View (Sam Butler)
I'll Be Satisfied (Blind Joe Taggart)
There's a City Built of Mansions (Nugrape Twins)
The Gospel Train Is Coming (The Guitar Evangelist)
Holy Mountain (Elder Otis Jones)

Release date:
Subtitled on label "1926–1942". Sleeve is Austrian, though the sleeve includes a printed Saydisc credit. The copy viewed included the January 1970 Matchbox and Roots catalogue plus a Roneo insert with original recording details. Listed as available from Saydisc at 41/– in the January 1970 catalogue.

RL 329   VARIOUS ARTISTS: Memphis Blues Vol. 2

Squat It (Memphis Minnie)
Someday I'll Be In the Clay (Kansas Joe McCoy)
Highway 61 Blues – No. 2 (Jack Kelly's South
     Memphis Jug Band)
Number Nine Blues (Blind Clyde Church)
Pneumatic Blues (Blind Clyde Church)
Mad Dog Blues (Rosie Mae Moore)
Hard Scufflin' Blues (Little Buddy Doyle)
Renewed Love Blues (Little Buddy Doyle)

Sweet Mama (Sleepy John Estes & Yank Rachel)
Good Looking Girl Blues (Furry Lewis)
Country Woman (Will Batts)
Money Never Runs Out (Canon's Jug Stompers)
Prison Wall Blues (Canon's Jug Stompers)
Blues Everywhere I Go (Casey Bill Weldon)
Somebody's Got to Go (Casey Bill Weldon)
1931 Depression Blues (The Three Stripped Gears)

Release date:
Subtitled on label "1927–1939". Sleeve includes a printed Saydisc credit.

RL 330   TOMMY JOHNSON & ISHMAN BRACEY: The Famous 1928 Tommy Johnson – Ishman Bracey Session

Cool Drink of Water Blues (Tommy Johnson
     with Charlie McCoy)
Big Road Blues (as above)
Bye–Bye Blues (Tommy Johnson)
Maggie Campbell Blues (as track 1, above)
Canned Heat Blues (Tommy Johnson)
Lonesome Home Blues (Tommy Johnson)
Lonesome Home Blues (different take) (as above)
(Missing track – see notes)
Big Fat Mama Blues (Tommy Johnson)

Saturday Blues (Ishman Bracey with Charlie McCoy)
Left Alone Blues (as above)
Leavin' Town Blues (as above)
My Brown Mamma Blues (as above)
Trouble–Hearted Blues (Ishman Bracey)
Trouble–Hearted Blues (different take) (Ishman Bracey)
The Four Day Blues (Ishman Bracey)

Release date:
Subtitled on sleeve "Complete For The First Time – In Chronological Order". Sleeve includes a printed Saydisc credit. *Louisiana Blues* by Tommy Johnson was recorded August 31st, 1938 but no pressings seem to exist, so this does not appear – though it is noted in the track listing where it fits into the running order.

RL 331   *BLIND LEMON JEFFERSON: Blind Lemon Jefferson Volume 3*

Lemon's Worried Blues
Mean Jumper Blues
Balky Mule Blues
Long Lastin' Lovin'
How Long How Long (with unknown acc.)
Oil Well Blues
Tin Cup Blues
That Black Shake Moan No. 2
Big Night Blues

Peach Orchard Mama
Mosquito Moan
Southern Woman Blues
Bakershop Blues
Pneumonia Blues
Long Distance Moan
That Crawlin' Baby Blues
Bootin' Me Bout'

Release date:
Subtitled on label "1928–1929". Sleeve includes a printed Saydisc credit.

RL 332   *VARIOUS ARTISTS: Cream of the Crop*

Shetland Pony Blues (Son House)
Make Me a Pallet On Your Floor (Willie Brown)
Sic 'Em Dogs On (Bukka White)
Po' Boy (Bukka White)
Kitchen Range Blues (William Harris)
Go I'll Send Thee (Dennis Crumpton & Robert
     Summers)
Everybody Ought to Pray Sometime (as above)
Why Do You Moan? (Bo Weavil Jackson)

The Pony Blues (Son House)
The Jinx Blues – No. 1 (Son House)
Mississippi Swamp Moan (Alfred Lewis)
Workin' On the Railroad (Walter 'Buddy Boy' Hawkins)
Yellow Woman Blues (Walter 'Buddy Boy' Hawkins)
James Alley Blues (Robert 'Rabbit' Brown)
Wasn't That Doggin' Me (The Beale Street Sheiks)
Rockin' On the Hill Blues (The Beale Street Sheiks)

Release date: 1960s
Subtitled on label "1926–1942".

RL 333   VARIOUS ARTISTS: Kings of Memphis Town

Falling Down Blues (Furry Lewis)
Mean Old Bedbug Blues (Furry Lewis)
Why Don't You Come Home Blues (Furry Lewis)
Furry's Blues (Furry Lewis)
Kassie Jones – Part 1 & 2 (Furry Lewis)
Alabama Blues (Robert Wilkins)
Long Train Blues (Robert Wilkins)

Downtown Blues (Frank Stokes with unknown acc.)
Hunting Blues (The Beale Street Sheiks)
The Girl I Love, She Got Long Curly Hair (Sleepy John Estes
     with Jab Jones & James 'Yank' Rachel)
Diving Duck Blues (as above)
Street Car Blues (as above)
Expressman Blues (as above)
Sleep On, Mother Sleep On (Lonnie McIntorsh)
The Lion and the Tribes of Judah (Lonnie McIntorsh)

Release date: 1960s
Subtitled on sleeve and label "1927–1930". Sleeve includes a printed Saydisc credit.

RL 334   *VARIOUS ARTISTS: Country Blues Obscurities Vol. 1*

When that Great Ship Went Down (William &
     Versey Smith)
The Coon Crap Game ('Big Boy' George Owens)
Poor Girl (Smith & Harper)
Insurance Policy Blues (Smith & Harper)
Quill Blues (Big Boy Cleveland)
The Moanin' Blues (John D. Fox & Sam Collins)
Fare Thee Blues – Part 1 & 2 (Johnnie Head)

Greyhound Blues ('Bill' Wilber with Willie Lofton)
Friday Moan Blues (Alfred Lewis)
The Crowing Rooster (Walter Rhodes with 'Pet' & 'Can')
Real Estate Blues (Will Bennett)
(Who's Gonna Do Your) Sweet Jelly Rollin' (Whistlin' Rufus)
Miss Handy Hanks (Archie Lewis [as 'Handy Archie'])
Fence Breakin' Blues (Shreveport Home Wreckers)

Release date:
Subtitled on label "1926–1936". Sleeve includes a printed Saydisc credit.

RL 335   VARIOUS ARTISTS: Texas and Louisiana Country

Bed Springs Blues (Blind Lemon Jefferson)
Struck Sorrow Blues (Blind Lemon Jefferson)
Saturday Night Spender Blues (as above)
Empty House Blues (Blind Lemon Jefferson)
Leavin' Home (Willie Reed)
Billikin's Weary Blues (Texas Bill Day & Billikin
      Johnson with poss. Alex Moore &
      Coley Jones)
Wandering Blues (Gene Campbell)
Robbin' & Stealin' Blues (Gene Campbell)

Sun Beam Blues (Billikin Johnson & Fred Adams with Willie
      Tyson & Octave Gaspard)
Interurban Blues (as above)
Drunkard's Special (Coley Jones)
Hard to Rule Woman's Blues (Willard 'Ramblin'' Thomas)
Sawmill Moan (Willard 'Ramblin'' Thomas)
No Baby Blues (Willard 'Ramblin'' Thomas)
Ramblin' Mind Blues (Willard 'Ramblin'' Thomas)
Whoopee Blues (King Soloman Hill)

Release date:
Subtitled on label "1927–1932". UK sleeve stating, "Roots Records are manufactured and distributed in Britain by Matchbox Records Ltd."

RL 336   CANNON'S JUG STOMPERS: Cannon's Jug Stompers

Minglewood Blues
Pig Ankle Strut
Feather Bed
Cairo Rag
Bugle Call Rag
Viola Lee Blues
Riley's Wagon

Last Chance Blues
Fourth and Beale
Tired Chicken Blues
Walk Right In
Mule Get Up In the Alley
Jonestown Blues
Pretty Mama Blues
Bring It with You When You Come

Release date: 1971
Subtitled on sleeve and label "1928–1930". UK sleeve stating, "Roots Records are manufactured and distributed in Britain by Matchbox Records Ltd." All tracks by Canon's Jug Stompers, except: tracks 1 & 2, side 1, by Gus Cannon & Elijah Avery; tracks 3 to 6, side 1, by Gus Cannon, Elijah Avery and (probably) Hosea Woods; tracks 1 & 2, side 2, by The Beale Street Boys (Gus Cannon & Hosea Woods).

RL 337   MEMPHIS JUG BAND: Memphis Jug Band Volume 2

Memphis Boy Blues
Bob Lee Junior Blues
Sugar Pudding
Whitewash Station Blues
Stealin, Stealin'
I Can Beat You Plenty (That Hand You Tried
      to Deal Me)
Tired of You Driving Me
K.C. Moan

Oh Ambulance Man
Jim Strainer Blues
Cave Man Blues
Meningitis Blues
Got a Letter From My Darlin'
You May Leave But This Will Bring You Back
I Got Good Taters
She Done Sold It Out

Release date: 1971
Subtitled on sleeve " 1927–1934". Very obviously a UK press in UK sleeve. Sleeve does not include a Saydisc credit, but the record, with RL catalogue number, is on the Saydisc Matchbox label design.

RL 338   REV. F. W. McGEE: Rev. F. W. McGee

Testifyin' Meetin'
Holes In Your Pockets
I Looked Down the Line & I Wondered
Jesus the Lord Is a Saviour
Three Ways – Part 1
Three Ways – Part 2
Death May Be Your Pay Check
Sin Is to Blame for It All

Jesus the Light of the World
He's Got the Whole World In His Hand
The Half Ain't Never Been Told
The Scarlet Thread In the Window
The Crooked Made Straight
Babylon Is Falling Down
Rock of Ages, with Scripture lesson
I've Seen the Devil

Release date: 1971
Subtitled on label "1927–1930". Most tracks have unknown accompanists. Track 8 includes Elsa Henry Reid.

RL 339   **VARIOUS ARTISTS: Delta Blues**

Ramblin' On My Mind (Robert Johnson)
Come On In My Kitchen (Robert Johnson)
Phonograph Blues (Robert Johnson)
Cross Road Blues (Robert Johnson)
Little Queen of Spades (Robert Johnson)
Drunken Hearted Man (Robert Johnson)
Stop Breakin' Down Blues (Robert Johnson)
Love In Vain (Robert Johnson)

Mississippi Bo Weavil Blues (Charley Patton)
Four O'Clock Blues (Skip James)
Drunken Spree (Skip James)
Illinois Blues (Skip James)
How Long Blues (Skip James)
Sundown (Son House)

Release date: 1971
Subtitled on label "1929–1969".

RL 340   **VARIOUS ARTISTS: Country Blues Obscurities Vol. 2**

Free Women Blues (Jelly Roll Anderson)
Dice's Blues (Bob Campbell)
Shotgun Blues (Bob Campbell)
Don't Leave Me Blues (Spider Carter)
Broke Down Engine (Lonnie Clark)
Down In Tennessee (Lonnie Clark)
Sing Song Blues (Bob Coleman)
Lonesome Midnight Dream (Willie Harris)

Hop Head Blues (Smoky Harrison)
Iggly Oggly Blues (Smoky Harrison)
Bug Juice Blues (Kid Prince Moore)
Honey Dripping Papa (Kid Prince Moore)
Midnight Blues (William Moore)
Fast Stuff Blues (George Thomas)
Don't Kill Him In Here (George Thomas)
Charleston Contest – part 1 (Too Tight Henry)

Release date: 1972
Subtitled on label "1927–1936". This is pure guesswork as to where the split between side 1 and side 2 is.

SL 504   **SON HOUSE: The Vocal Intensity of Son House**

Son's Blues
Yonder Comes My Mother
Shetland Pony Blues

Preachin' the Blues
Empire State Express
Grinnin' In Your Face
Sun Goin' Down

Release date: 1969
Printed Saydisc credit on sleeve. Label states "King of the Mississippi Blues Singers" and "Recorded in Rochester New York 1969".

SL 505   **Continental issue of Saydisc/Matchbox SDR 190**

SL 506   **THE BLUEGRASS SPECIALS: The Train I Ride**

Orange Blossom Special
You Don't Love Me
The Bugle
You Are My Flower
Russian Ride
Victory Rag
The Train I Ride

Soldier's Joy
Foggy Mountain Breakdown
Home Sweet Home
Down the Road
Shuckin' the Corn
Silver Bells
The Battle of New Orleans

Release date: 1970
UK press in UK sleeve with Saydisc label design.

RSE 1   **SON HOUSE: Son House**

Shetland Pony Blues
Camp Hollers
Delta Blues (acc. Leroy Williams)
Special Rider Blues
Low Down Dirty Dog Blues
Depot Blues
The Key of Minor (acc. Alan Lomax)

American Defence
Am I Right Or Wrang
Walking Blues
County Farm Blues
The Pony Blues
The Jinx Blues – Part 1
The Jinx Blues – Part 2

Release date: 1972
UK sleeve with UK credits, but label has German copyright text. Subtitled "The Legendary 1941–1942 Recordings In Chronological Sequence". Track 2 includes Fiddlin' Joe Martin & Willie Brown.

RSE 3   **Continental issue of Saydisc/Matchbox SDR 213 (though not released?)**

Ahura Mazda

Three Ahura Mazda LPs were issued by Saydisc in the UK and, as with the Roots label records, these were manufactured in the UK, in this instance from US metalwork, with amended artwork for the sleeves. It is highly likely that one or more of these LPs were assigned Saydisc catalogue numbers, but, as with the Roots LPs, which numbers these might be remains unknown. The last LP listed here was originally a Saydisc UK release that was distributed in the US by Ahura Mazda.

AMS SDS 1   *SCOTT DUNBAR: From Lake Mary*

Who Been Foolin' You	That's Alright, Mama
Little Liza Jane	Easy Rider
Memphis Mail	Richard Daley Blues
Vickburg Blues	Sweet Mama Rollin' Stone
Forty–Four Blues	Blue Yodel
	Goodnight Irene

Release date: 1970

Sleeve states, "This Ahura Mazda production is manufactured and marketed in Great Britain by: Saydisc Specialized Recordings Ltd." The record includes the AMS SDS catalogue number in the runoff with PRP 21711/PRP 21712 scratched out. The copy viewed includes a Roneo transcription of an interview with Dunbar, dated February 27, 1970, with the Ahura Mazda record label address (P.O. Box 15582, New Orleans, Louisiana 70115) stamped on several pages. It is unlikely that this was included in any stock copies.

AMS 2002   *ROBERT PETE WILLIAMS: Robert Pete Williams*

Farm Blues	Railroad Blues
Rub Me Until My Love Come Down	Tombstone Blues
Freight Train Blues	Sweep My Floor
Got Me a Way Down Here	You Used to Be a Sweet Cover Shaker Woman But You Ain't
Matchbox Blues	No More
	Vietnam Blues

Release date: 1971

Record manufactured in the UK with normal Saydisc label design and AMS catalogue number. Runoff does not include the AMS catalogue number, but includes the original Ahura Mazda PRP 27151/PRP 27152 catalogue numbers. The inner sleeve included with the US issue advertised that the Scott Dunbar LP (AMS SDS1) was available in UK, Eire, Europe, Australia and New Zealand from Saydisc for 39/11 (near enough £2).

AMS 2003   *HARMONICA WILLIAMS WITH LITTLE FREDDIE KING: Harmonica Williams with Little Freddie King*

Baby Don't You Know	Born Dead
Juke Boy	The King's Special
Sideways	Williams' Special
Declaration Day	Highway 82
	Williams' Goodbye

Release date: 1971

Sleeve and record manufactured in the UK with normal Saydisc label design and AMS catalogue number. Runoff includes only the original Ahura Mazda PRP 31981/PRP 31982 catalogue numbers. Songs are published in the UK by Village Thing. Also includes; Newton S. Greer, A. B. Bruer and Rudy Taylor.

SD 218   *The Golden Age of Mechanical Music (US–only issue)*
Track listing same as for SD(SAM) 218

Release date: 1971

Distributed by Ahura Mazda for the US market with a price of $4.98 printed on the sleeve. The copy viewed looks very like a UK pressing, with the SD (SAM) matrix number in the runoff groove, but with a different label design to the UK issue, so this was presumably pressed in the US from UK metalwork.

The Village Thing

Village Thing records were issued on three label designs all told, though strictly speaking the company had long since shut up shop when the last of these designs was introduced in the 1980s: only the two Fred Wedlock LPs were available on the final yellow label design, this via Saydisc. The first two labels incorporated a background of an idealised view of Clifton as a village, as drawn by Andy Leggett from the Pigsty Hill Light Orchestra. The first label design included the label name in ornate type face and this design was used on all records up to and including VTS 7: this label design was also used on the *Great White Dap* EP and the Strange Fruit single. The second label design replaced the ornate type face with a Rodney Matthews logo and this was used on all subsequent releases. Several albums, such as *Royal York Crescent*, *Pigsty Hill Light Orchestra Presents*, *The Folker* and *An Acoustic Confusion* have been spotted on both first and second label design.

The first two LPs were issued in September 1970 and the last crop of releases were advised by the music press in July 1974 at the same time as it was announced that Transatlantic was deleting the majority of items in the Village Thing catalogue. Ian Anderson had already left Village Thing earlier in the year, Gef Lucena having taken over as label head. Lucena bought back the unsold stock from Transatlantic and sold the albums off via mail order at 99p each. There must have still been quite a stock of some titles left in the late 1970s, because in January 1978 several Village Thing albums were listed in *The New Records* trade publication as being available, priced at £1.65 each: those albums listed as still available were *The Sun Also Rises*, *Royal York Crescent*, *The Words In Between*, *A Vulture Is Not a Bird You Can Trust* and *Magic Landscape*.

Three albums were issued on cassette and 8–track cartridge (release advised for the Derroll Adams and Fred Wedlock tapes in the November 1973 edition of *The New Cassettes and Cartridges* trade publication: the Ian A. Anderson tapes seem to have gone unannounced, in this trade release at least). More titles were planned for issue in these formats but none were forthcoming. The tape issues were manufactured and distributed by Precision Tapes, part of the Pye empire (Precision Tapes undertook the same role with many other companies, such as Transatlantic, Charisma, Peg, Warner Brothers, DJM and so on). Both tape formats were priced at £2.45.

VTS 1 **PIGSTY HILL LIGHT ORCHESTRA: The Pigsty Hill Light Orchestra Presents**

Cushion Foot Stomp	T'Aint No Sin
Funny Side of the Street	Sleepy Time Blues
Silk Pyjamas	My Pet
Company Policy	Nothing Else Will Do Babe
On Sunday	Sporting Life Blues
Second Fiddle	Men of Harlech

Release date: 18th Sept.1970
Barry Back, Dave Creech, John Turner, and Andy Leggett, assisted by Ian Hunt and Julie Bridson with a cameo appearance by Ian A. Anderson on snores and rattling teacups.

VTS 2 **SUN ALSO RISES: The Sun Also Rises**

Until I Do	Tales of Jasmine and Suicide
Wizard Shep	Flowers
Part of the Room	Song of Consolation
Green Lane	Suddenly It's Evening
	Death

Release date: 18th Sept. 1970   **CD:** VTS 202
Included an insert. Graham and Anne Hemmingway. Also includes John Turner and Andy Leggett, and Leggett also designed the front sleeve illustration for which he got a free copy.

The Saydisc/Village Thing CD issue includes *Fafnir and the Knights*, originally included on *Us* (VTSAM 15). Also issued on CD by Lion Records, USA. Also issued 18th March 2008 on 180 gram vinyl by Wah Wah of Barcelona.

VTS 3   IAN A. ANDERSON: Royal York Crescent

No Way to Get Along	Silent Night No. 2
Please Re–adjust Your Time	Mr Cornelius
Goblets and Elms	The Maker/The Man In the High Castle/The Last Conjuring
Shining Grey	Ginger Man
The Worm	Working Man
Hero	

Release date: 13th Nov. 1970

Included a lyric insert: the original was printed in green ink on primrose–yellow but the printing on all later pressings changed to black ink on bright yellow. On catalogue long enough to appear on the second label design. Some second label copies were exported to Germany where they were distributed by the Autogram label: these had stickers attached with Autogram credits and also included a poster that, oddly, included a write–up of Anderson's Fontana LP, *Book of Changes*. Original copies and those sold via Autogram are in matt sleeves but later UK pressings are in gloss, laminated sleeves. Also includes Ian Hunt, John Turner, Ian Turner, Andy Leggett, Pete Siddons and Sun Also Rises.

Royal York Crescent, as seen in the back sleeve photo, was a rather run–down road in the Clifton area of Bristol where lived many musicians and artists in the late 1960s and early 1970s (Stackridge lived a couple of roads up in West Mall). The road is now one of the most exclusive and expensive addresses in Bristol!

VTS 4   WIZZ JONES: The Legendary Me

See How the Time Is Flying	Beggar Man Keep Your Lamp Trimmed and Burning
The Legendary Me	Dazzling Stranger
When I Cease to Care	If Only I'd Known
Nobody Told You So	Slow Down to My Speed
	Stick a Little Label On It

Release date: 13th Nov. 1970

Also includes Reina Sutcliffe, Ralph McTell, Pete Berryman and John Turner. Ron Geesin engineered on several tracks that had already been recorded prior to Village Thing picking up the option of an album. *Stick a Little Label On It* was recorded live at Bristol's Troubadour Club.

VTS 5   STEVE TILSTON: An Acoustic Confusion

I Really Wanted You	Sleepy Time on Peel Street
Simplicity	Prospect of Love
Time Has Shown Me Your Face	Green Toothed Gardener
It's Not My Place to Fail	Normandy Day
Train Time	Rock and Roll Star

Release date: May 1971   **CD:** VTS 205

Original copies have a matt–finish sleeve, whilst later copies on the second label design have a laminated front sleeve. Also includes Dave Evans, Keith Warmington, John Turner and Pete Finch. White label copies exist with two extra tracks that were finally left off the LP: these were *What Would You Be* and *She Sits Wondering*. White label test pressings also exist of the LP as issued.

The recent Saydisc/Village Thing CD includes two extra tracks, *The Price of Life* and *Show a Little Kindness*. Also released on CD by Riverman Music, South Korea. Also issued 18th March 2008 on 180 gram vinyl by Wah Wah of Barcelona.

VTS 6   DAVE EVANS: The Words In Between

The Words In Between	Now Is the Time
Rosie	Doorway
Grey Lady Morning	City Road
Insanity Rag	Circular Line
Magic Man	Sailor

Release date: Oct. 1971

Also includes Keith Warmington, Pete Airey, and Adrienne Webber.

The album has recently been reissued on Ian Anderson's Weekend Beatnik label (WEBE 9039) with extra tracks from *Elephantasia*.

VTS 7　　　FRED WEDLOCK: The Folker

The Folker	Spencer the Rover
British Bobby	Skinheads
Moreton Bay	Bristol Buses
Thees Got'n Wur Thee Casn't Back'n, Asn't	Bruton Town
	Lurn Theeself Fawk

Release date: Oct. 1971　　　**CD:** VTS 207
Cassette: ZCVTS 7　　　**8–track cartridge:** Y8VTS 7

This was the last LP to appear on the first label design: on catalogue long enough to be issued on the second and short–lived third label designs. White label test pressings exist with the final part of *Learn Theeself Fawk* including a short piece about the Queen being Prince Philip in drag. The ladies at EMI's pressing plant refused to press the LP until this was removed. However, it seems that the LP reverted to the original master tape for later pressings as there is confirmed existence of normal copies with the original track on all three label designs. It now appears that copies without the offending piece of music are the rare copies instead of being the majority! Also includes Mike Evans, Ian Hunt, The Deaf Clifton Sunflower (really Ian Anderson – have another listen to the bit that goes "Woke up dis mornin', whooooo, lawdy mama...") and the Pigsty Hill Light Orchestra. Cassette and 8–track cartridge issues listed in the November 1973 edition of *The New Cassettes and Cartridges* trade magazine, priced at £2.45.

The recent CD issue is a 2–CD set and also includes the *Frollicks* LP (VTS 20), the *Volume One* EP (no cat. no.) and *Virtute et Industrial* (originally on SD 124 and later included on 33SD 245, *Sounds of Bristol*).

VTS 8　　　PIGSTY HILL LIGHT ORCHESTRA: Piggery Jokery

Sadie Green	Basin Street Blues
Motorway Song	Meet Me Where They Play the Blues
High Society	Desperate Dan
The Wiltshire Plumbers Saga	The Silly Organ Story
Sweet Miss Emmaline	Shim Sham Shimmy
Let Your Linen Hang Low	Royal Garden Blues

Release date: 10th Dec. 1971

This was the first LP to appear on the second label design. Live from The Room at the Top Club, Redruth. Includes Andy Leggett, David Creech, Barry Back and occasional member, Bill Cole. Both Andy Leggett and Barry Back appear on the sleeve resplendent in Plastic Dog t–shirts – Andy Leggett still has his.

VTS 9　　　IAN A. ANDERSON: A Vulture Is Not a Bird You Can Trust

One More Chance	Well.....Alright
Black Uncle Remus	Time Is Ripe
Policeman's Ball	Wishing the World Away
Edges	One Too Many Mornings
The Survivor	Number 61

Release date: 14th Jan. 1972

Also includes Ian Hunt, John Turner, Keith Warmington, Pick (spelled "Pique" here) Withers, Kipps Brown, and Pete Descindis. Recorded at Rockfield in September 1971, which explains how three–quarters of Neon label mellotron–heavy, progressive band Spring appears on the LP (Withers, Brown and Descindis). Pat Moran, another member of Spring, sang on Anderson's next album.

VTS 10　　　DAVE MUDGE: Mudge – NOT COMPLETED

Not released. Some acoustic tracks with Keith Christmas were recorded at 12A, Royal York Crescent, Clifton, and a sleeve illustration of a singing hippo was drawn by Rodney Matthews – a play on Flanders and Swann, as in, "Mudge, Mudge, glorious Mudge". The hippo drawing was later used on the *Us* compilation, VTSAM 15. As Ian Anderson says, "...the album was intended to be part acoustic and part band – so the likelihood was maybe Rockfield for [the band tracks]" (email dated 22nd May 2010). Somewhere down along the years the master tape went missing. Maggie Holland's diary sheds some light on a possible reason for the recordings being abandoned, which was that that Dave Mudge became ill with hepatitis.

VTS 11   **HUNT AND TURNER: Magic Landscape**

Hold Me Now	Living Without You
Silver Lady	Man of Rings
We Say We're Sorry	Older Now and Younger Then
Magic Landscape	Morning for Eve
Mr. Bojangles	Rockfield Rag

Release date: 22nd Sept. 1972   **CD:** VTS 211

Also includes John Merrett, and Rodney Matthews from Bristol's unsigned progressive rock band, Squidd.

Recently reissued on CD by Saydisc/Village Thing, by Lion Records, USA. and by Riverman Music, South Korea. Also issued 18th March 2008 on 180 gram vinyl by Wah Wah of Barcelona.

VTS 12   **TIGHT LIKE THAT: Hokum**

Mississippi Mud	Death Letter
What Makes My Baby Cry?	Muskrat Ramble
Twentieth Century Rag	Selling Our Stuff
How Do You Want Your Rolling Done?	Spider John
Everybody Loves My Baby	Don't Put Your Hands On Me
West End Rag	Coney Island Washboard
If I Had a Talking Picture of You	

Release date: 22nd Sept. 1972

Textured sleeve. Tight Like That was Dave Peabody, Hugh McNulty, Dave Griffiths, and Bill Shortt. Also includes Andy Leggett.

VTS 13   **TUCKER ZIMMERMAN: Tucker Zimmerman**

Another Normal Day	She's an Easy Rider
Freeway	Amusement Park
A Friend Like You	Back on the Road Again
Left Hand of Moses	Canary Island Rain
No Love Lost	Keep That Fire Burning

Release date: 22nd Sept. 1972

Originally issued in Germany on the Autogram label.

VTS 14   **DAVE EVANS: Elephantasia**

Only Blue	St. Agnes Park
Elephantasia	Beauty Queen
Lady Portia	Ten Ton Tasha
That's My Way	Earth, Wind, Sun & Rain
On the Run	Take Me Easy

Release date: 6th Oct. 1972

Also includes Keith Warmington, John Merrett, Rodney Matthews, and Steve Swindells. Swindells later released a solo LP and went on to spells in Pilot and the Hawkwind alter–ego band, Hawklords.

VTSAM 15   **VARIOUS ARTISTS: Us**

Only Blue (Dave Evans)	One More Chance (Ian A. Anderson)
West End Rag (Tight Like That)	Another Normal Day (Tucker Zimmerman)
Beggarman (Whizz Jones)	Sweet Miss Emmaline (The Pigsty Hill Light Orchestra)
The Folker (Fred Wedlock)	Fafnir and the Knights (Sun Also Rises)
I Really Wanted You (Steve Tilston)	Hold Me Now (Hunt & Turner)

Release date: 1st Sept. 1972

Originally sold at 99p. The catalogue number includes the "SAM" prefix, in line with Transatlantic policy for samplers. Record re–mixed by Gef Lucena and David Wilkins. *Fafnir and the Knights* was previously unreleased. Mint copies are very few and far between because the sleeve was printed blue over a silver background without any laminate sealant being applied. The sleeves tended to peel and scuff even if you just looked at them.

VTSAM 16   VARIOUS ARTISTS: Matchbox Days

Bulldog Blues (Mike Cooper)	Travellin' Blues (Dave Kelly)
Stop Breaking Down (Prager, Rye and Hall)	Cocaine Habit (The Panama Limited Jug Band)
Nothin' in Ramblin' (Jo–Ann Kelly)	Cottonfield Blues (Ian A. Anderson)
Searchin' the Desert (Al Jones)	Rambling Man (Frances McGillivray)
Maybelle Rag (John James)	The Inverted World (Mike Cooper & Ian A. Anderson)
Dark Road Blues (The Missouri Compromise)	Spoonfull (Wizz Jones)

Release date: 1st Sept. 1972
Originally sold at 99p.

This has been reissued on CD with extra tracks on Ace/Big Beat (CDWIKD 168).

VTS 17   DERROLL ADAMS: Feelin' Fine

Darling Corey	Love Song
Apprenticed In London	Mr. Rabbit
Freight Train Blues	Deep Ellum Blues
Wildwood Flower	Blue Ridge Mountains
The Sky	Chattering Jaw
Muleskinner Blues	The Valley

Release date: Dec. 1972
Cassette: ZCVTS 17   **8–track cartridge:** Y8VTS 17
The inner sleeve is printed on one side. Includes Danny Adams, Wizz Jones and Roland van Campenhout. Cassette and 8–track cartridge issues listed in the November 1973 edition of *The New Cassettes and Cartridges* trade magazine, both priced at £2.45. Ian Anderson says of this album, "As one of the VT albums of which I'm most proud, I'm really annoyed with myself that I failed to notice my producer credit got missed off the cover until after it was out!" (email dated 22 May 2010).

VTS 18   IAN A. ANDERSON: Singer Sleeps as Blaze Rages

Hey, Space Pilot	Paint It Black
Marie Celeste On Down	Pretty Peggyo
Spider John	The Western Wind
A Sign of the Times	Out of the Side
Paper and Smoke	Shirley Temple Meets Hawkwind

Release date: Dec. 1972
Cassette: ZCVTS 18   **8–track cartridge:** Y8VTS 18
Textured sleeve. Also includes Roland van Campenhout, Maggie Holland, Poto Ciddons, Mike Cooper, Pat Moran and Mike Cooper's Machine Gun Company (Les Calvert, Ian Foster, and Bill Boazman). An earlier version of *Paint It Black* had previously been included on Anderson's *Book of Changes* LP on Fontana.

To find out the story behind the title, you'll have to buy *Bristol Folk* (available from www.bristol–folk.co.uk), in which publication Ian Anderson tells the story in his own words.

VTS 19   AL JONES: Jonesville

Jeffrey Don't You Touch	Ice Age
Get Out of My Car	Time to Myself
Tell the Captain	To London With You
Bernard's Exit	Most Chickens Are Mild and Friendly Or Would Like to Be
High and Dry	Caught In a Storm
Earthworks	Black Cat
	The Wild Rover

Release date: July 1973
Also includes Pete 'Boris' Moody, Tony Fennell, Dave Gillis and Graham Smith.

By the time this book is published, this should have been released on CD with bonus tracks on the Weekend Beatnik label.

VTS 20   FRED WEDLOCK: Frollicks

The Vicar and the Frog	Vatican Rag
Robin Hood	Robin Head
Handier Household Help	Lovely Like Me
Salvation Army Lassie	Superman
Examinations Rag	Talking Folkclub Blues
Oh Sha La La	Wild Rover

Release date: c. Dec. 1973
The record was on catalogue long enough to be issued on the short–lived third label design. White label copy in proof, wraparound sleeve known to exist. This was recorded live at the Stonehouse Folk Club, Bristol. Also includes Ian Hunt, Barry Back, Richard Gould and Martin Runnacles.

Recently issued on CD by Saydisc/Village Thing along with *The Folker* and bonus Saydisc tracks as VTS 207 tracks (see VTS 7 above).

VTS 21   CHRIS THOMPSON: Chris Thompson

Hugo Spellman	London Blues
The Song of Wandering Aengus	Her Hair Was Long
De Debil Take De Blue–Tail Fly	Young Lust
The River Song	Love

Release date: c. Feb. 1974
Most copies were reputedly destroyed by distributor, Transatlantic records with only 101 copies surviving. The album was recorded between 1971 and 1973 with Keshav Sathe and Clem Atford from Magic Carpet, and Ed Deane from the Woods Band. Also included are Brian Dunning and The Kings of Rhythm (E.J. Peters, Nial Toner and Vince Gurran). Although having a publication date of 1973, the release was delayed by what a January 1974 press release described thus, "The Chris Thompson LP which Village Thing advertised as a November release has yet to reach the shops due to advanced bungling at the pressing stage. Having got through that, it is now of course affected by 3–Day working, vinyl shortages etc and thus may be at least another month or two delayed."

The LP was reissued on CD with bonus material on Scenescof Records of Massachusetts, though these are almost as hard to find as is the LP. There is the distinct possibility that this may receive a UK CD issue in the near future.

VTS 22   DAVE PEABODY: Peabody Hotel

Turn On the Light	Jug Band Superstars
Right Now	Searching the World for You
Scared at Night	Long Time Loser Blues
Mistaken Identity	Blue Ridge Breakdown
Ain't Nobody's Business if I Do	Last of the Goodtime Guys
Aviator Special	Walking the Dog

Release date: 5th Oct. 1973
Included an insert. A promotional sticker for the LP can be seen on the tea–chest bass on the front of Dave Peabody's *Come and Get It* (Saydisc Matchbox SDX 270). White label test pressings known to exist. Also includes Dave Griffiths, Bill Shorrt, Hugh McNulty, Don Weller (later in East of Eden and the Count Basie Band), Bill Lackey and Kathy Sweeney. Village Thing having shut up shop by then, Dave Peabody's next two LPs were issued on Saydisc's Matchbox imprint, the second, in 1976, being the last LP issued on Matchbox.

VTS 23   LACKEY AND SWEENEY: Junk Store Songs for Sale

Rosemary's Market	Good to Cry
Nothing to Lose	Yesterday Did Ride Away
Twenty Nine Years	Sweet Marie
Sparrow	Comfort
Drinking Blues	You Are My Sunshine

Release date: 5th Oct. 1973
Also includes John Turner, Joe Kucera and Canton Trig's Graham Smith.

VTS 24   **WIZZ JONES: When I Leave Berlin**

Living Alone	When I Leave Berlin
Pastures of Plenty	Frankie
First Girl I Loved	Skip Rope Song
She's Only Waiting	Winter Song
Cluck Old Hen	Freudian Slip

Release date: July 1974
Includes Lazy Farmer (John Bidwell, Sandy Jones and Jake Walton), Don Coging and Bert Jansch.

VTS 25   **NOEL MURPHY: Murf**

As I Roved Out	Zoological Gardens
Rambling Robin	Carrickfergus
Love is Pleasure	The Leather Bottle
Me and Bobbie McGhee	The Limerick Rake
The Curragh of Kildare	The Old Man's Tale
The Flowers of Edinburgh/Chief O'Neill's	Meet On the Ledge
Favourite	Is Love Pleasing

Release date: July 1974
Includes Andy Pay, John Land, John Turner, Dennis O'Rourke, Ian Hunt, Mike Evans, Dave Doyle, Andy Leggett, Brendan Whitmore, Lady Fred and Dave Herbert. This was the last Village Thing label LP and its long–delayed release coincided with Transatlantic deleting most of the other items on the label. The other albums were sold off from Gef Lucena's Inglestone Common address for 99p each. A few remaining titles were relisted in trade magazines in January 1978, otherwise, apart from the two Fred Wedlock LPs, that was it for Village Thing, until the digital age, that is.

7" releases

VTSX 1000   **VARIOUS ARTISTS: The Great White Dap EP (7" EP)**

Time Is Flying (Wizz Jones)	Silent Night No. 2 (Ian A. Anderson)
Tales of Jasmine and Suicide (Sun Also Rises)	'Taint No Sin (Pigsty Hill Light Orchestra)

Release date: 13th Nov. 1970 (Sounds) / 23rd Oct. 1970 (Ian Anderson)
Subtitled "A Long Slow Single". 7" EP in picture sleeve. Plays at 33⅓. All sold for the astoundingly low price of 9/6d (47½p).

VTSX 1001   **STRANGE FRUIT: Cut Across Shorty / Shake That Thing (7" single)**
Release date: 2nd July 1971
Mono.

VTSX 1002   **IAN A. ANDERSON: One More Chance / Policeman's Ball (7" single)**
Release date: early 1972
Mono. The b–side was from "A Vulture Is Not a Bird You Can Trust" (VTS 9), whilst the a–side was a shortened and remixed version with, as Ian Anderson says, "...a chorus and passage of superfluous noodling excised" (email dated 22nd May 2010).

Amon Ra

Amon Ra started life as a fine arts business before being recast as, firstly a publishing company, publishing Bob Groom's *Blues World* magazine, and then as a record company. The first releases featured resident professional musicians from the Dartington College of Arts but the label was put on hold in 1974. In 1977 the label was relaunched around the Finchcocks collection of original instruments to specialise on authentic performances on period instruments.

In 1982 Amon Ra records began to be digitally recorded, first using the German Telefunken company for pressing before moving back to Nimbus in Monmouthshire. From 1986 all Amon Ra releases were routinely released on CD and cassette with LPs being phased out completely, the last back catalogue LP stock being sold off on special offer in late 1988 and early 1989. The first CD releases in 1985/6 were CD–SAR 13, 15, 16, 17, 18, 19, 21 and 23. Further Amon Ra back catalogue items were reissued on CD and cassette starting in late 1986 (CD–SAR 14, 22, 24, 25, 26) and the first half of 1987 (CD–SAR 10, 11, 12, 27 and 28). From CD–SAR 66 in late 1998 albums were issued on CD only.

SARB 01 — THE DARTINGTON STRING QUARTET: Quartet Cameos

Andante from Quartet in A minor, Op. 29 (Schubert)

Minuet and Trio from Quartet in D minor, K421 (Mozart)

Andante Cantabile from Quartet No. 1 in D, Op. 11 (Tchaikovsky)

Intermezzo from Quartet in A minor, OP. 13 (Mendelssohn)

Scherzo from Quartet in E–flat, D. 87 or Op. 125 No. 1 (Schubert)

Nocturne from Quartet No. 2 in D (Borodin)

Scherzo from Quartet No. 1 in C (Shostakovich)

Allegretto from Quartet in G, Op. 54 No. 1 (Haydn)

Canzonetta from Quartet in E flat Op. 12 (Mendelssohn)

'Serenade' from Quartet in F, Op. 3 No. 5 (Haydn)

Release date: 1974   **CD:** CD-SAR 101 (May 2007)
Budget–priced issue. White label test pressings known to exist.

SAR 1 — THE DARTINGTON STRING QUARTET: Shostakovich String Quartets Nos. 4 & 9

String Quartet No. 4:
 Allegretto
 Andantino
 Allegretto – Finale: Allegretto

String Quartet No. 9:
 Moderato con moto
 Adagio
 Allegretto

Release date: 1973   **CD:** CD-SAR 1 (Sept. 2006)
White label test pressings known to exist. The Quartet comprised Colin Sauer, Malcolm Latchem, Keith Lovell & Michael Evans, who were all teachers at Dartington College of Arts. Gef Lucena adds the following: "The Dartington String Quartet were one of Britain's finest quartets (and who also formed the section leaders of the then Bristol Sinfonia). Amongst the good reviews in journals around the world was one from a publication called something along the lines of What's On In Devon which amused us and which described the Quartet as "One of the finest string quartets in South Devon" – praising with faint damn or what!" (Email dated 14th August 2010).

SAR 2 — DAVID STONE, ALLAN SCHILLER: Delius Sonatas Nos 2 & 3 for Violin & Piano – Legende

Sonatas No 2 for Violin & Piano
Legende

Sonata No 3 for Violin & Piano

Release date: 1973   **CD:** CD-SAR 1 (Sept. 2006)
David Stone, violin; Allan Schiller, piano. Voted "Record Of the Month" by Hi–Fi News on its original release.

SAR 3 — RICHARD BURNETT: A Graf Fortepiano Recital

Papillons (Schumann)

Harmonies Poetiques et Religieuses (Liszt)

Piano Sonata in A minor, D. 537 (Schubert)

Nocturne in E minor, Op. 72 (Chopin)

Nocturne in C sharp minor, Op. posthumous (Chopin)

Release date: 1977
Restored Fortepiano by Conrad Graf of 1826 from the Finchcocks collection. From this issue onwards, Amon Ra specialised in authentic performances on period instruments.

SAR 4   SWISS BAROQUE SOLOISTS: Swiss Baroque Soloists

Sonata in D major for Fortepiano concertante, German Flute and Violoncello (J.C. Bach)

Sonata in G major for Harpsichord, German Flute and Violoncello (Richter)

Sonata in G major for Harpsichord, German Flute and Violoncello (conc.)

Sonata in G major for German Flute and Thorough Bass (Stanley)

Release date: 1976
This was leased directly from the artist for release by Amon Ra, one of only three leased items on the label.

SAR 5   RICHARD BURNETT: Haydn Sonatas On Early Pianos

Sonata No. 35 in A flat major:
  Moderato
  Menuett
  Rondo: presto
Sonata No. 41 in A major:
  Allegro moderato
  Menuet al Rovescio
  Finale: presto

Sonata No. 60 in C major:
  Allegro
  Adagio
  Allegro molto
Sonata No. 61 in D major:
  Andante
  Finale: presto

Release date: 1979
Cassette: CSAR 5   **CD:** CD–SAR 5
Nos. 35 & 41 played on Viennese Fortepiano by Michael Rosenberger, c.1798; Nos. 60 & 61 played on English Pianoforte by John Broadwood and Son, 1801. Both from the Finchcocks collection.

SAR 6   RICHARD BURNETT: The Finchcocks Collection of Historic Keyboard Instruments

A Toye (Farnaby)
Almand in G (Croft)
Prelude in E (Bach)
Sonata no. 7 in A (Arne):
  Presto
  Andante
  Allegro
Voluntary no. 1 in C (Stanley):
  Adagio
  Andante
Works for Musical Clock (Haydn):
  Minuet in C
  Vivace in C
  'Der Kaffeeklatsch'
  March in D
  Presto in G
Adagio for Glass Harmonica K.356 (Mozart)
Bagatelle in C op. 119 no. 2 (Beethoven)
Sonata op. 5 no. 5 (J.C. Bach):
  Prestissimo

Sonata in B flat op. 23 (Dussek):
  Allegro con spirito
German Dance in D, D.783 no. 2: from 12 Landler D.790 no. 5 in B minor: from 4 Komische Landler D.354 no. 2 in B minor & no. 4 in D (Schubert)
Sonata in D ('La Chasse') (Clementi):
  Allegro
Nocturne in E minor (Field)
Waltz in A flat op. 42 (Chopin)
Venetian Gondola Song in F min. (Songs without Words op. 30 no. 6) (Mendelssohn)
Turkish Rondo (Mozart)

Release date: 1982
Cassette: CSAR 6   **CD:** CD–SAR 6 (prob. April 1988)
Virginals, English bentside spinet, fretted clavichord, two manual harpsichord, chamber organ, square piano, grand piano by Rosenberger, square piano by Broadwood, grand piano by Fritz, grand piano by Clementi, London, small cabinet piano by Clementi, grand piano by Graf, grand piano by Collard & Collard.

SAR 7   RICHARD BURNETT: The Romantic Fortepiano

Ten variations on a theme from Gluck's Armida
    (Hummel)
Andante Spianato from op.22 (Chopin)
Dances (Schubert):
  Ländler—D.145 nos.2, 3, 4, 5
  Ecossaisen—D.421 nos. l, 2, D. 145 nos. 1, 2, 3
  'Letzte Walzer'—D.146 nos. 20 & 1 8.42

Kinderscenen op. 15 (Schumann):
  1. Von fremden Ländern und Menschen
  2. Curiose Geschichte
  3. Hasche–Mann
  4. Bittendes Kind
  5. Glückes genug
  6. Wichtige Begebenheit
  7. Träumerei
  8. Am Kamin
  9. Ritter vom Steckenpferd
  10. Fast zu ernst
  11. Fürchtenmachen
  12. Kind im Einschlummern
  13. Der Dichter spricht
Five variations on a theme of Rode op.33 'La Ricordanza'
    (Czerny)

Release date: 1982
Cassette: CSAR 7   **CD:** CD–SAR 7
Fortepiano by Conrad Graf, Vienna 1826.

SAR 8   RICHARD BURNETT: Clementi Late Piano Works

Sonata in G minor Op. 50 No. 3 'Didone
    abbandonata – Scena tragica':
Introduzione: Largo patetico e sostenuto
Allegro, ma con expressione: diliberando,
    e meditando
Adagio dolente
Allegro agitato, e con disperazione

Twelve Monferrinas Op. 49

Release date: 1983
Cassette: CSAR 8   **CD:** CD–SAR 8
Finchcocks series, vol. 4. Richard Burnett, Grand Pianoforte, Clementi & Co., London 1822.

SAR 9   RALPH HOLMES, RICHARD BURNETT: Beethoven The Violin Sonatas

Sonata for Piano and Violin Op. 24 in F major
    ("Spring")
Allegro
Adagio molto espressivo
Scherzo: allegro molto
Rondo: allegro ma non troppo

Sonata for Piano and Violin Op. 30 No. 2 in C major
  Allegro con brio
  Adagio cantabile
  Scherzo: allegro
  Finale: allegro

Release date: 1983
Cassette: CSAR 9   **CD:** CD–SAR 9
Finchcocks series, vol. 5. Ralph Holmes, violin; Richard Burnett, Fortepiano.

SAR 10   ALAN HACKER: Clarinet Collection

She Moves Through the Fair (Trad)
Sinfonia from 'Su le Sponde del Tebro' (Scarlatti)
L'hiver (Telemann)
March by Mr. Handel (Handel)
Adagio Cantabile (Vanhal)
Minuet from Divertimento K439b (Mozart)
Variations for Clarinet and Piano Op.33 (Weber)

Duo for Clarinet and Piano Op.15 (Burgmüller)
Phantasy Pieces Op.73 (Schumann)
Romanza from 'La Forza del Destino' (Verdi)
Macedonian folk tune (Trad)

Release date: 1983
Cassette: CSAR 10   **CD:** CD–SAR 10 (autumn 1987)
Subcredited to Richard Burnett. Alan Hacker, Chalumeau (speculative reconstruction), copy of 2 keyed Baroque clarinet in D of J. Denner, 5 keyed boxwood C clarinet by Bland & Weller, London late 18th century, 9 keyed boxwood Bb clarinet by Bilton, London early 19th century, Modern reconstruction of a Stadler/Lodz basset clarinet, Clarinet in Bb by Louis after 19th century Boehm system design, London 1920s, Clarinet in A by Louis after 19th

century Boehm system design, London 1920s, Modern C clarinet by Noblet, Paris; Richard Burnett, English bentside spinet attr. Cawton Aston c.1700, 2 manual harpsichord by Jacob Kirckman, London 1756, Fortepiano by Michael Rosenberger, Vienna c. 1800, Fortepiano by Conrad Graf, Vienna 1826, Fortepiano by Carl Henschker, Vienna c. 1845.

SAR 11 PRESTON'S POCKET: Music for Two Flutes

Trio Sonata in G, BWV 1039 (Bach):
 Adagio
 Allegro ma non presto
 Adagio e piano
 Presto
Sonata Op. 2 no. 5 (Handel):
 Larghetto
 Allegro
 Adagio
 Allegro

Trio no. 1 (Haydn):
 Allegro moderato
 Andante
 Vivace
Voi che sapete (Mozart)
Variations on Paisielo's 'Nel cor piu' (Drouet)
Valse des Fleurs, Op. 87 (Kohler)

Release date: 1983
Cassette: CSAR 11   **CD:** CD–SAR 11 (autumn 1987)
Finchcocks series, vol. 7. Stephen Preston, baroque flure, classical flute; Lisa Beznosiuk, baroque flute, classical flute; Jane Coe, baroque cello; Robert Woolley, two manual harpsichord, fortepiano, pianoforte.

SAR 12 RALPH HOLMES, RICHARD BURNETT: Hummel

Sonata Op. 50 in D:
 Allegro con brio
 Andante
 Rondo pastorale
Sonata Op. 5 no. 3 in Eb:
 Allegro moderato

 Adagio e cantabile
 Rondo con moto
 Nocturne Op. 99

Release date: 1983
Cassette: CSAR 12   **CD:** CD–SAR 12 (June 1986)
Subtitled "Sonata Op. 50 in D, Sonata Op. 5 no. 3 in Eb, Nocturne Op. 99". Ralph Holmes, violin; Richard Burnett, fortepiano.

SAR 13 HOWARD SHELLEY: Schubert Sonatas

Sonata Op. 78 in G, D.894:
 Molto moderato e cantabile
 Andante
 Menuetto: allegro moderato

Sonata Op. 78 in G (cont.):
 Allegretto
Sonata Op. Posthumous 143 in A minor, D.784:
 Allegro giusto
 Andante
 Allegro vivace

Release date: Feb. 1985
Cassette: CSAR 13   **CD:** CD–SAR 13
Finchcocks series, vol. 9. Fortepiano by Johann Fritz, Vienna, c. 1814.

SAR 14 LONDON BAROQUE: English Music of the 18th Century

Sonata op. 5 No. 2 in C min/maj for harpsichord,
  two violins & cello (Avison):
 con giubilo
 con tenerezza
Harpsichord Sonata No. 2 in E min (Arne):
 andante
 adagio
 allegrissimo
Trio Sonata op. 2 No. 3 in F (Handel):
 adagio
 allegro
 adagio
 allegro

Trio Sonata No. 2 in G (Arne):
 largo
 con spirito
 largo
 allegro
Sonata op. 9 No.1 in A for violin, cello & basso continuo (Abel):
 moderato
 vivace
Harpsichord Concerto op. 10 No. 4 in C min (Stanley):
 vivace
 andante affetuoso
 presto

Release date: 1984
Cassette: CSAR 14   **CD:** CD–SAR 14 (Feb. 1985)

SAR 15   IAN PARTRIDGE, RICHARD BURNETT: Beethoven Songs

An die Hoffnung op. 32
Neue Liebe, neues Leben op. 75 no. 2
Ich liebe dich WoO 123
Mailied op. 52 no. 4
Busslied op. 48 no. 5
Der Zufriedene op. 75 no. 6
Resignation woO 149
Der Kuss op. 128
Adelaide op. 46

An die ferne Geliebte op. 98
Der Wachtelschlag WoO 129
Aus Goethes Faust op. 75 no. 3
Andenken WoO 136
Wonne der Wehmut op. 83 no. 1
Sehnsucht op. 83 no. 2
Mit einem gemalten Band op. 83 no. 3

Release date: 1984/1985?
Cassette: CSAR 15   **CD:** CD–SAR 15 (1985: SC)
Ian Partridge, tenor; Richard Burnett, fortepiano by Rosenburger, Vienna, c. 1800.

SAR 16   RALPH HOLMES, RICHARD BURNETT: Beethoven Violin Sonatas

Sonata For Piano and Violin Op. 47 in A
   major ("Kreutzer"):
Adagio sostenuto
Andante con Variazioni

Finale presto
Sonata for Piano and Violin Op. 30 no. 3 in G major:
Allegro assai
Tempo di Minuetto, ma molto moderato e grazioso
Allegro vivace

Release date: 1984
Cassette: CSAR 16   **CD:** CD–SAR 16

SAR 17   ALAN HACKER, SALOMON STRING QUARTET WITH LESLEY SCHATZBERGER: Mozart Clarinet Quintets

Clarinet Quintet in A (K 581):
 Allegro
 Larghetto
 Menuetto

Allegretto con Variazioni
Clarinet Quintet fragment in Bb (K 516c) (Compl. by Druce):
 Allegro
Quintet fragment in F for clarinet in C, basset horn and string
   trio (K 580b) (Completed by Druce):
 Allegro

Release date: 1984
Cassette: CSAR 17   **CD:** CD–SAR 17 (autumn 1985)

SAR 18   NIGEL NORTH: Guitar Collection

Fantasia del quarto tono (Mudarra)
Romanesca: o guardame las vacas (Mudarra)
Branle de Poictou (pub. le Roy, Ballard)
Pimontoyse (pub. le Roy, Ballard)
Fantasia del quarto tono (Milan)
La Cancion del Emperador: Mille Regres
   (Josquin) (Narvaez)
Fantasia que contrahaze la harpa en la manera
   de Luduvico (Mudarra)
Sinfonia a 2 (Corbetta)
Passacalles (Sanz)
Canarios (Sanz)
Suite in D minor (de Visee):
 Prelude
 Allemande
 Courante
 Sarabande
 Gigue

Grande Ouverture Op. 61 (Giuliani)
Introduction and variations on a theme of Mozart ("Oh Cara
   armonia" from the Magic Flute) op. 9 (Sor)
Variations de Beethoven arrangees pour Piano et Guitare
   Op. 169 (Carulli)
Lied ohne Worte (Mertz)

Release date: autumn 1985
Cassette: CSAR 18   **CD:** CD–SAR 18 (1985: SC)
Virginals and fortepiano: Maggie Cole. Other instruments include Renaissance guitar, Vihuela, 5 course Venetian

---

guitar c. 1640 w. Virginals by Onofrio Guarracino, Italy 1668, 5 course guitar by Dias (?) c. 1590, Fabricatore 1818, Panormo 1828 and 1843, French guitar c. 1825, fortepiano by Michael Rosenberger, Vienna c. 1800.

SAR 19   STEPHEN PRESTON WITH LUCY CAROLAN: Flute Collection

Le Coucou (Daquin)

Air de Mr de Luly (sic) / Sonata in D (arr. Le
      Romain; Quantz):
  Soave
  Allegro
  Presto
La De Drummond / Sonata in E minor (Duphly; Devienne):
  Allegro
  Adagio
  Allegro ma non troppo

Fantaisie Brillant Sur "La Fée Aux Roses" (De Halevy) (Tulou)
Home Sweet Home Charles Nicholson (1795 – 1837)
Gute Nacht (Schubert, arr. Boehm)

Release date: 1985
Cassette: CSAR 19

CD: CD–SAR 19

SAR 20   RICHARD BENNETT: Music In Miniature

Sonata in A (Haydn):
  Andante
  Menuet and trio
  Finale
Pieces for Musical Clock (Haydn):
  Nos. 17 in C, 10 in C, 5 in C, 12 in C, 13 in F,
      17 in F, 19 in C, 23 in C, 27 in G
Sechs Leichte Variationen (Haydn)

From Six Progressive Sonatinas Op. 36 (Clemanti):
  Sonatina no. 1 in C: Allegro, Andante, Vivace
  Sonatina no. 2 in C: Allegretto, Allegretto grazioso, Allegro
  Sonatina no. 3 in G: Spiritoso, Un poco adagio, Allegro
Ecossaise in E flat (Beethoven)
Ecossause in G (Beethoven)
Waltz in D (Beethoven)
Allemande in A (Beethoven)
Rondo in C Op. 51 No. 1 (Beethoven)

Release date: autumn 1985
Cassette: CSAR 20

CD: CD–SAR 20 (spring 2004)

Played on a Viennese Square Piano, c. 1800 by Anton Walter. Direct metal mastering with record pressed in West Germany with the LPs ordered from Teldec 20th May 1985.

SAR 21   STEPHEN PRESTON, JENNIFER WARD CLARKE, RICHARD BURNETT: Weber Flute Trio and Sonatas

Trio for flute, cello and piano J.259:
  Allegro moderato
  Scherzo: Allegro vivace
  Schafers Klage: Andante espressivo
  Finale: Allegro
Sonata for flute & piano no. 1 in F major J.99:
  Allegro
  Romanze: Larghetto
  Rondo: Amabile

Sonata for flute and piano no. 3 in D major J.101:
  Air russe: Allegretto moderato
  Rondo: Presto
Sonata for flute and piano no. 4 in E flat major J.102:
  Moderato
  Rondo vivace
Sonata for flute and piano no. 6 in C major J.106:
  Allegro con fuoco
  Largo
  Polacca

Release date: 1985
Cassette: CSAR 21

CD: CD–SAR 21 (1985: SC)

Finchcocks series, vol. 17. Stephen Preston, flute; Jennifer Ward Clarke, cello; Richard Burnett, fortepiano. Direct metal mastering with record pressed in West Germany. Track listing moved around for the CD issue.

SAR 22   ROBIN CANTER: Oboe Collection

Alborada (trad. Spanish)
Etenraku (trad. Japanese)
Traditional Turkish
An Dro Nevez (trad. Breton)
La Quinte Estampie Real (Anon)
Variations on 'Les Folies d'Espagne' (Marais)
Sonata in G minor (C.P.E. Bach):
  Adagio
  Allegro
  Vivace

Morceau de Salon (Kalliwoda)
Sonatina No. 2 in G major (Walmisley)
Gran Concerto sopra motivi dell Opera 'I Vespri Siciliani'
    di Verdi (Pasculli)

Release date: 1985
Cassette: CSAR 22   **CD:** CD–SAR 22 (late 1986: SC)
Finchcocks series, vol. 18. Robin Canter, dulzaina, hichiriki, bombarde, zurna, treble shawm, baroque oboe, classical oboe, romantic oboe, modern oboe; James Wood, traditional drums, bell, nakers; Anthony Pleeth, cello; Melvyn Tan, 2 manual harpsichord; Richard Burnett, fortepiano, grand piano. Direct metal mastering with record pressed in West Germany with Teldec inner sleeve.

SAR 23   NIGEL NORTH: Bach Lute Music

Suite (Partita) in E major BWV 1006a (Bach):
 Prelude
 Loure
 Gavotte en Rondeau
 Menuets 1 & 2
 Bourree
 Gigue
Prelude in C minor BWV 999 (Bach)
Fugue in G minor BWV 1000 (Bach)

Suite in G minor BWV 995 (Bach):
 Prelude, Tres vite
 Allemande
 Courante
 Sarabande
 Gavottes 1 & 2
 Gigue

Release date: 1985
Cassette: CSAR 23   **CD:** CD–SAR 23

SAR 24   NEW LONDON CHAMBER CHOIR: Pierre de la Rue / Josquin des Prez

Missa pro defunctis (de la Rue):
 Introit
 Kyrie
 Sicut cervus / Tract
 Offertory
 Sanctus
 Lux aeterna
 Agnus Dei

Mass: Hercules Dux Ferrariae (des Prez):
 Kyrie
 Gloria
 Credo
 Sanctus
 Agnus Dei
La Deploration de Johannes Ockeghem: "Nymphes des
  bois" (des Prez)

Release date: 1986
Cassette: CSAR 24   **CD:** CD–SAR 24 (Dec. 1986: SC)
James Wood conducts. Direct metal mastering with record pressed in West Germany.

SAR 25   CLASSICAL WINDS: Mozart Divertimenti

Divertimento no. 1:
 Allegro
 Menuetto (Allegretto)
 Adagio
 Menuetto
 Rondo (Allegro)
Divertimento no. 2:
 Allegro
 Menuetto
 Larghetto
 Menuetto
 Rondo (Allegro)

Divertimento no. 3:
 Allegro
 Menuetto
 Adagio
 Menuetto
 Rondo (Allegro assai)
Divertimento no. 4:
 Allegro
 Larghetto
 Menuetto
 Adagio
 Rondo (Allegretto)

Release date: 1986
Cassette: CSAR 25   **CD:** CD–SAR 25 (Nov. 1986: SC)

SAR 26   CLASSICAL WINDS: Beethoven Wind Music

Octet Op. 103:
 Allegro
 Andante
 Menuetto: Allegro
 Rondo: Andante (Rondino WoO25)
 Finale: Presto

Sextet Op. 71:
 Adagio, Allegro
 Adagio
 Menuetto: Quasi Allegretto
 Rondo: Allegro

Release date: 1986
Cassette: CSAR 26   **CD:** CD–SAR 26 (Dec. 1986: SC)
Finchcocks series, vol. 21. Paul Goodwin, oboe; Clare Shanks, oboe; Colin Lawson, clarinet; Margaret Archibald, clarinet; John Hadden, horn; Mary Knepper, horn; Frances Eustace, bassoon; Andrew Watts, bassoon. Direct metal mastering. No mention of country of manufacture and this does not look like a West German press. Gef Lucena has the following to say about the DMM issues: "Intriguing: SAR19 to 31 incl. ALL have Direct Metal Mastering @ Teldec logo emblazoned on the front of the sleeve and credited on the back of the sleeve under the cat. no. The label also has the DMM logo, 'Made in West Germany' and plain inner sleeve for 19, 20, 21, 24, 25. The label also has the DMM logo, 'Made in West Germany' and printed inner sleeve from Teldec with DMM logo and description of process in 4 languages for 22, 23. All the above have a credit on the back of the sleeve 'Record pressed in W. Germany by Teldec-Press'. However: 26, 27, 28 and 31 have same DMM logo on front and Direct Metal Mastering on back but all say 'printed and made in England' on the back of the sleeve and 'Made in England' on the label. Plain inner sleeves for 26, 27 and 28 BUT 31 has an inner sleeve with the large DMM logo and description of the process in English only and the giveaway 'Pressed by PR Records England'. I recall we went to PR Records for a while – presumably they had the franchise from Teldec to press with, I imagine, the mastering done in Germany."

SAR 27   MAGGIE COLE: Scarlatti Sonatas

Sonata Kk 380 in E major	Sonata Kk 551 in Bb major
Sonata Kk 381 in E major	Sonata Kk 263 in E minor
Sonata Kk 27 in B minor	Sonata Kk 264 in E major
Sonata Kk 446 in F major	Sonata Kk 318 in F sharp major
Sonata Kk 141 in D minor	Sonata Kk 319 in F sharp major
Sonata Kk 550 in Bb major	Sonata Kk 417 in D minor

Release date: 1986
Cassette: CSAR 27   **CD:** CD–SAR 27 (Jan. 1987: SC)
Harpsichords by Jacob Kirckman, London 1756 (tracks 1 to 7); Adlam Burnett after Ruckers, Antwerp 1638 (tracks 8 to 12).

SAR 28   THE BROADSIDE BAND: John Playford's Popular Tunes

Greenwood / Heart's Ease / Excuse Me	Partenia / Corant 'La Chabott' / Jocobella
Lady Cahtherine Ogle / The Scotchman's Dance	Paul's Steeple
/ Never Love Thee More / Miller's Jig	The Lady Nevils Delight / The Whisk [Wish] / A New Rigaudon
The Granadees March / Sarabande	An Italian Rant / Bouzer Castle
Lady Hatton's Almaine / Prins Robbert Masco –	Childgrove / Mr. Lane's Minuet / Up With Aily / Cheshire
Prince Rupert's March / Daphne;	Rounds / Hunt the Squirrel
Lilli Burlero	

Release date: 1986 (SC)
Cassette: CSAR 28   **CD:** CD–SAR 28 (Mar. 1987: SC)
Jeremy Barlow (director), renaissance and baroque recorders, flageolets, harpsichord, regal; Alastair McLachlan, baroque violin; Rosemary Thorndycraft, bass viol, lyra viol, hurdy gurdy; George Weigand, lute, mandore, cittern, arch–cittern. Direct metal mastering.

CD–SAR 29   FRETWORK: In Nomine

In Nomine à 4 no. 1 for 4 viols (Tallis)	In Nomine à 4 no. 2 for 4 viols (Tallis)
In Nomine à 5 'Crye' for 5 viols (Tye)	O lux beata Trinitas à 3 for 3 viols, lute (Preston)
In Nomine à 5 'Trust' for 5 viols (Tye)	In Nomine à 4 for 4 viols (Johnson)
Solfaing Song à 5 for 5 viols, lute (Tallis?)	In Nomine à 5 for 5 viols (Parsons)
Fa la sol à 3 for 3 viols (Cornysh)	Ut re mi fa sol la à 4 for 4 viols (Parsons)
In Nomine à 4 for 4 viols (Baldwin)	In Nomine à 5 for 5 viols (Ferrabosco the elder)
Fantasia à 5 for 5 viols (attr. Tallis, reconstr.	Lute fantasia, no 5 (Ferrabosco the elder)
Milsom)	Fantasia à 4 for 4 viols, lute (Ferrabosco the elder)
In Nomine à 5 for 5 viols, lute (Bull)	Libera nos, salva nos à 5 for 5 viols, lute (Tallis?)
In Nomine à 4, no. 2 for 4 viols (William Byrd)	In Nomine à 4 for 4 viols (Taverner)
Fantasia à 3 no. 3 for treble viol, lute (Byrd)	
In Nomine, anonymous setting for lute (Taverner)	

Release date: 1987
Cassette: CSAR 29

Subtitled "16th C. English music for viols including the complete consort music of Thomas Tallis". Richard Campbell, Julia Hodgson, Elizabeth Liddle, Richard Boothby, William Hunt, Christopher Wilson. No LP issue.

CD–SAR 30   THE CLARION ENSEMBLE: Trumpet Collection

From "Modo per Imparare a sonare di Tromba" (Fantini)
Et e pur dunque vero (Monteverdi)
Canzona a canto (Frescobaldi)
To arms, heroic Prince (Purcell)
Si suoni la tromba (Scarlatti)
Arietta and Waltzer (Bishop)
Lo L'udia (Donizetti)
Post Horn Galop (Koenig)
Thine For Ever (Bishop)
Fantaisie sur l'opera Rigoletto de Verdi (Arban)
Cousins (Clarke)
Legende (Enesco)

Release date: spring 1988
Cassette: CSAR 30 (autumn 1987)
Deborah Roberts, soprano; Jonathan Impett, historic brass; Susan Addison, sackbut, trombone; Helen Verney, cello; Paul Nicholson, keyboards. No LP issue.

SAR 31   RICHARD BURNETT & MEMBERS OF THE SALOMON QUARTET: Mozart Piano Quartets

Piano Quartet in G minor K478:
  Allegro
  Andante
  Rondo
Piano Quartet in E flat major K493:
  Allegro
  Larghetto
  Allegretto

Release date: 1987
Cassette: CSAR 31   **CD:** CD–SAR 31
Direct metal mastering. Fortepiano by Rosenberger, Vienna, c. 1798; Simon Standage, violin by Mariani, Brescia, c. 1650; Trevor Jones, viola by Rowland Ross, 1980, after Stradivari; Jennifer Ward Clarke, cello, attrib. Dom Nicolo Amati, Bologna, c. 1730. This was the last Amon Ra issue to appear on LP.

CD–SAR 32   RICHARD BURNETT: Gottschalk Piano Music

Le Bananier – chanson negre
La Savane – ballade creolo
Le Mancenillier – serenade
Souvenir de Porto Rico – marche des Gibaros
Romance
Chanson du Gitano
Polka in B flat
Polka in A flat
Suis Moi – caprice
Manchega – etude de concert
La Gallina – danse cubaine
Minuit a Seville – caprice
Souvenirs d' Andalousie – caprice concert
Mazurk
Berceuse
Ballade no. 6
The Dying Poet – meditation

Release date: autumn 1988   **Cassette:** CSAR 32
Of the release date, Gef Lucena says, "ordered 5/5/88 – no doubt sold by Finchcocks as soon as pressed with general release in the autumn as normally did not release in June or July" (email dated 14th August 2010).

CD–SAR 33   LISA BEZNOSIUK, NIGEL NORTH: Concord of Sweet Sounds

Sonata in G minor Op.2a No.3 (Locatelli):
 Largo
 Allegro / Largo
 Allegro
Sonata in C major BWV 1033 (Bach attrib.):
 Andante
 Allegro
 Adagio
 Menuetto 1 & 2
Sonata in A minor W. 128 (C.P.E. Bach):
Andante
Allegro
Vivace
Gran Duetto Concertante Op. 52 (Giuliani):
 Andante sostenuto
 Menuetto (Allegro vivace)
 Rondo militare (Allegretto)
Waltzes (from Op. 9) (Schubert arr. Diabelli)
Potpourri (Beethoven arr. Diabelli)
Waltzes (from Op. 9) (Schubert arr. Diabelli)

Release date: 1988   **Cassette:** CSAR 33
Lisa Beznosiuk, One keyed boxwood flute, 8 keyed ebony flute; Nigel North, 13 course lute, 6 string guitar.

CD–SAR 34   ROBIN CANTER WITH LONDON BAROQUE: Mozart Music for Oboe

Quartet in F, K.370:
Allegro
Adagio
Rondeau: Allegro
Quintet in C minor, K.516b (arr.):
Allegro
Andante
Menuetto

Allegro
Divertimento in D, K.251:
Marcia Alla Francese
Molto Allegro
Menuetto
Andantino
Menuetto (Tema con Variazioni)
Rondeau: Allegro assai

Release date: autumn 1988   **Cassette:** CSAR 34

CD–SAR 35   FRANCES EUSTACE: Bassoon Collection

Sonata I (Bertoli)
Sonatas I and II from Vierfaches Musikalisches
        Kleeblatt (Speer)
Sonata in C major (Fasch):
 Largo
 Allegro
 Andante
 Allegro
Sonata V for two bassoons (de Boismortier):
 Moderement
 Courante
 Musette

Gigue
Sonata in G minor Op. 24 No. 5 (Devienne):
 Allegro con espressione
 Adagio
 Rondeau
Sonata in Bb major KV 292 (Mozart):
 Allegro
 Andante
 Rondo
The Trout with apologies to Schubert (Schubert)
Romance Op. 62 1909 (Elgar)

Release date: autumn 1988   **Cassette:** CSAR 35
Andrew Watts, Dulzian (Speer), bassoon (Boismortier); Jennifer Ward Clarke, Cello by William Forster 1791,
England (Fasch, Devienne, Mozart, Schubert); Paul Nicholson, Chamber organ by John Avery, London 1793
(Bertoli, Speer), Harpsichord by Adlam Burnett after Ruckers, Antwerp 1638 (Fasch), Fortepiano by Michael
Rosenberger, Vienna c. 1800, (Devienne, Mozart, Schubert), Grand pianoforte by John Broadwood, London 1846
(Elgar).

CD–SAR 36   FRANCES KELLY: Harp Collection

Lais from the Roman de Tristan: En morant de
        si douche mort: La u jou fui deafens
        la mer: A vous, Tristan, amis verse
L'autrier pastoure seoit: Lai de la pastourelle
        (Je Druues)
Patientiam muess ich hen: Patientia: Mein
        Fleiss und Mueh (Senfl)
Je requier a tous amoureux: Je veuil chanter
        de cuer joyeux (Dufay)
Ricercar Terzo: Partite sopra Fidele (Mayone)
Ancidetemi pur, Per l'Arpa (Trabaci)

Lesson IV Allegro: Minuet (Parry)
Musical Relicks of the Welsh Bards (Jones):
 Rhyban Morfydd
 Merch Megan
 Olan Feddwdod mwyn
 Blodeu'r Grug
 Confet Gruffydd ap Cynan
 Rhyban Morfydd
Fantaisie Op. 35 (Spohr)
The Manly Heart: A Favourite Air by Mozart (Arr.Naderman)
Une Chatelaine en sa Tour (Faure)

Release date: late 1989 (SC)   **Cassette:** CSAR 36
Medieval Harp – Martin Haycock 1984 (tracks 1 & 2); Gothic Harp – Geoff Ralph 1979 (tracks 3 & 4); Double Harp
– Martin Haycock 1983 (tracks 5 & 6); Triple Harp – Martin Haycock 1985 (tracks 7 & 8); Single Action Pedal Harp
– Anon c. 1800 (tracks 9 & 10); Double Action 'Concert' Harp – Salvi (Electra) c. 1969 (track 11).

CD–SAR 37   ALAN HACKER, JENNIFER WARD CLARKE, RICHARD BURNETT: Brahms
        Clarinet Trio Sonatas

Trio in A minor Opus 114 for Clarinet, Cello
        and Piano:
 Allegro
 Adagio
 Andantino grazioso
 Allegro
Sonata No. 1 in F minor Opus 120 for Clarinet
        and Piano:

Allegro appassionato
Andante un poco adagio
Allegretto grazioso
Vivace
Sonata No. 2 in Eb for Clarinet and Piano:
 Allegro amabile
 Appassionato, ma non troppo Allegro
 Andante con moto – Allegro

Release date: late 1989 (SC)   **Cassette:** CSAR 37
Alan Hacker, clarinets; Jennifer Ward Clarke, 'cello; Richard Burnett, pianoforte.

CD–SAR 38   ALAN HACKER, LESLEY SCHATZBERGER, RICHARD BURNETT:
Mendelssohn

Konzertstück No. 2 in D minor op. 114 for
  clarinet, basset horn and piano:
Presto – Prestissimo
Andante
Allegretto grazioso – Adagio – Presto e con
  fuoco
Rondo Capriccioso op. 14
Songs Without Words:
  op. 67 no. 2 in F sharp minor
  op. 62 no. 6 in A
  op. 53 no. 4 in F
  op. 67 no. 4 in C
Sonata in E flat (1824) for clarinet and piano:

Adagio – Allegro moderato
Andante
Allegro moderato
Songs Without Words:
  Venetian Gondola Song in A minor op. 62 no. 5
  Venetian Gondola Song in A (1842)
  17 Variations Serieuses op. 54
Konzertstück no. 1 in F minor op. 113 for clarinet,
    basset horn and piano:
  Allegro con fuoco
  Andante
  Presto

Release date: late 1989 (SC)   **Cassette:** CSAR 38
Subtitled "Works for Clarinet, Bassett Horn & Piano". Alan Hacker, clarinets; Lesley Schatzberger, basset horns; Richard Burnett, pianos.

CD–SAR 39   AMERICAN BAROQUE: Telemann Paris Quartets

Concerto No.2 in D major:
  Allegro
  Affettuoso
  Vivace
Sonata No. 1 in A major:
  Soave
  Allegro
  Andante
  Vivace

Sonata No. 2 in G minor:
  Andante
  Allegro
  Largo
  Allegro
Concerto No.1 in G major:
  Grave–allegro–grave–allegro–largo
  Presto–largo
  Allegro

Release date: autumn 1988   **Cassette:** CSAR 39
This was leased directly from the artist for release by Amon Ra, one of only three leased items on the label.

CD–SARC 40   VARIOUS ARTISTS: Musica Miscellanea

Divertimento K251: Marcia alla francese (Mozart)
Flute Sonata in C BWV 1033 Allegro (Bach)
Piano Quartet in Eb K 493 Allegretto (Mozart)
To Arms Heroic Prince (Purcell)
Greenwood, Heart's Ease, Excuse Me
  (Playford)
Libera nos, salva nos a 5 (Tallis)
Harpsichord sonata Kk381 in E (Scarlatti)
Missa pro defunctis: Introit (De La Rue)
Violin sonata Op 50 in D – Rondo pastorale
  (Hummel)

Flute Sonata in D – Allegro (Quantz)
Sonata 5 for two bassoons (Boismortier)
Clarinet quintet in A K581 – Larghetto (Mozart)
Piano sonata in A min D784 – Allegro vivace (Schubert)
Flute concerto No 2 in D – Vivace (Telemann)
Harpsichord concerto Op 10 No 4 – Andante (Stanley)
Sinfonia a 2 (Corbetta)
Wind sextet Op 71 – Menuetto (Beethoven)
Die Nebensonnen (Schubert)
Le Mancenillier (Gottschalk)

Release date: autumn 1988   **Cassette:** CSARC 40 (Oct. 1988: MM89)
Budget priced sampler of previously released Amon Ra tracks.

CD–SAR 41   IAN PARTRIDGE & RICHARD BURNETT: Schubert – Winterreise

Gute Nacht	Die Post
Die Wetterfahne	Der greise Kopf
Gefrorne Tränen	Die Krähe
Erstarrung	Letzte Hoffnung
Der Lindenbaum	Im Dorfe
Wasserflut	Der stürmische Morgen
Auf dem Flusse	Täuschung
Rückblick	Der Wegweiser
Irrlicht	Das Wirtshaus
Rast	Mut
Frühlingstraum	Die Nebensonnen
Einsamkeit	Der Leiermann

Release date: autumn 1988   **Cassette:** CSAR 41
Ian Partridge, tenor; Richard Burnett, fortepiano by Conrad Graf, Vienna c. 1820.

CD–SAR 42   LE NOUVEAU QUATUOR: Thomas Arne Instrumental Works

Trio Sonata in D (VII Sonatas) Op. 3 no. 5:	Trio Sonata in G (VII Sonatas) Op. 3 no. 2:
Largo	Largo
Andante	Con spirito
Largo ed amoroso	Largo
Allegro	Allegro
Trio Sonata in B minor (VII Sonatas) Op. 3 no. 6:	Sonata in F (VIII Sonatas or Lessons for the Harpsichord)
Largo	no. 1:
Allegro	Andante
Larghetto	Adagio
Allegro	Allegro
Concerto in C (solo harpsichord)	Trio Sonata in E minor (VII Sonatas) Op. 3 no. 7:
Add. MS 16155 of Six Favourite Concertos) no. 1:	Siciliana largo
Largo ma con spirito	Andante
Fuga: allegro	Largo ma non staccato
Allegro	Jigg: allegro ma non troppo
Minuetto — allegro	Allegro

Release date: autumn 1989   **Cassette:** CSAR 42
Subtitled "Trio sonatas and harpsichord solos".

CD–SAR 43   ROBERT WOOLLEY: Carlos Seixas Harpsichord Sonatas

Sonata in D minor (25 Sonatas no. 7):	Minuet
(Allegro)	Sonata in C minor (80 Sonatas no. 12):
Minuet	(Andante)
Sonata in D minor (80 Sonatas no. 27):	Allegro
Allegro	Sonata in G major (80 Sonatas no. 47):
Minuet	(Allegro)
(Allegro)	Sonata in D minor (80 Sonatas no. 24):
Sonata in A major (80 Sonatas no. 57):	(Allegro)
Allegro	Sonata in B flat major (80 Sonatas no. 78):
Adagio	(Allegro)
Allegro assai	Minuet
Sonata in F sharp minor (25 Sonatas no. 14):	Sonata in E flat major (80 Sonatas no. 32):
(Allegro)	Moderato
Minuet	Sonata in G minor (80 Sonatas no. 50):
Sonata in E major (80 Sonatas no. 34):	Allegro
(Presto)	

Release date: autumn 1989   **Cassette:** CSAR 43
Harpsichord by Joaquin José Antunes, Portugal 1785.

CD–SAR 44   LE NOUVEAU QUATUOR: C.P.E. Bach – Trio Sonatas

Trio io B minor H 567 W 143:
 Allegretto
 Andante
 Vivace
Trio in G major H 568 W 144:
 Adagio
 Allegro
 Presto
Trio in D minor H 569 W 145:
 Allegretto

 Largo
 Allegro
Trio in A major H 570 W 146:
 Allegretto
 Andante
 Vivace
Trio in C major H 571 W 147:
 Allegro
 Adagio
 Allegro

Release date: autumn 1989   **Cassette:** CSAR 44

CD–SAR 45   BARRY MASON: Masters of the Baroque Guitar

Fandango (de Murzia)
Españoletas (Sanz)
Clarines y Trompetas (Sanz)
Pavanas (Sanz)
Folia (Sanz)
Musette (de Visee)
Ricercata (Pellegrini)
Corrente (Pellegrini)
Sarabande (Pellegrini)
Battaglia Francese (Pellegrini)
Preludio (Corbetta)

Ciaccona (Corbetta)
Suite in D minor (de Murzia):
 Prelude
 Gavotte
 Minuet
 Sarabande
 Gigue
Ruggiero (Calvi)
Corrente (Calvi)
Passamezzo (Calvi)
Aria di Firenze (Calvi)

Release date: 1990   **Cassette:** CSAR 45

Guitar by Klaus Jacobsen, London 1977 after Voboam, France, mid–17th century. This was leased directly from the artist for release by Amon Ra, one of only three leased items on the label.

CD–SAR 46   RED BYRD & THE ROSE CONSORT OF VIOLS: Elizabethan Christmas Anthems

Verse anthem: This is the record of John
        (Gibbons)
Christe qui lux (Byrd)
Verse anthem: Sing unto God (Tomkins)
Upon my lap (Peerson)
Fantasy 2 in 1 (Byrd)
Verse anthem: O Ye Little Flock (Amner)

Fantasy: Browning (Byrd)
Consort song: Sweet was the song the virgin sung (Anon)
Pavan: The Cradle / Galliard: Lullabie (Holborne)
The Starre Anthem (Bull)
Consort Song: Lullaby (Byrd)
In Nomine (Gibbons)
Verse Anthem: See, see, the Word is Incarnate (Gibbons)

Release date: 1990   **Cassette:** CSAR 46

CD–SAR 47   LE NOUVEAU QUATUOR WITH ANDREW WATTS: Vivaldi Chamber Concertos

Concerto in F for flute, violin, bassoon and
        continuo (RV 100):
 Allegro
 Adagio
 Allegro
Concerto in D minor for flute, violin, bassoon
        and continuo (RV 96):
 Allegro
 Largo
 Allegro
Concerto in D for flute, violin & continuo (RV 84):
 Allegro
 Andante
 Allegro

Sonata in C minor for violin, cello and continuo (RV 83):
 Allegro
 Largo
 Allegro
Concerto in G minor for flute, violin, bassoon and continuo
        (RV 106):
 Allegro
 Largo
 Allegro
Concerto in D for flute, violin, bassoon and continuo (RV 91):
 Allegro
 Largo
 Allegro non molto

Release date: 1990   **Cassette:** CSAR 47

Andrew Watts, bassoon.

CD–SAR 48   RICHARD BURNETT: The Piano Music of John Field

Nocturne no. 1 in E flat
Nocturne no. 5 in B flat
Sonata in E flat, op. 1 no. 1: Allegro moderato / Rondo allegro
Nocturne no. 6 in F
Nocturne no. 4 in A
Nocturne no. 2 in C minor
Nocturne no. 3 in A flat
Nocturne no. 11 in E flat

Nocturne no.12 in G
Grand Pastorale in E
Variations in A minor on a Russian Air for four hands
The Bear Dance (in E flat) for four hands
Andante in C minor for four hands
Variations in B flat on a Russian Air 'Kamarinskaya'
Variations in D minor on a Russian Song
Nocturne no 14 in C

Release date: autumn 1991   **Cassette:** CSAR 48
Subcredit to Lorna Fulford. 1 & 2 played on Fortepiano by Johann Fritz, Vienna c. 1815; 3 played on Grand pianoforte by Clementi & Co., London 1822; 4, 5, 6 & 7 played on Fortepiano by Michael Rosenberger, Vienna c. 1800; 8, 9 & 10 played on Cabinet piano by Clementi & Co., London c. 1825; rest played on Fortepiano by Conrad Graf, Vienna 1826. Lorna Fulford also plays on 11, 12 & 13.

CD–SAR 49   THE ORLANDO CONSORT: Phillipe de Vitry and the Ars Nova

Vos quid admiramini / Gratissima virginis species
Se je chant
Apta caro / Flos virginum
Tribum que non abhorruit / Quoniam secta latronum
O canenda vulgo / Rex quem metrorum
Colla iugo subdere / Bona condit
Petre Clemens / Lugentium siccentur
Trahunt in precipicia / Quasi non ministerium / Ve qui gregi

Almifonis melos / Rosa sine culpe spina
Douce playsence / Garison selon nature
Tuba sacre fidei / In arboris
In virtute / Decens carmen
Impudenter circumivi / Virtutibus laudabilis
Aman novi probatur / Heu, fortuna subdola
Floret cum vana gloria / Florens vigor
Firmissime fidem / Adesto Sancta Trinitas
Flos ortus / Celsa cedrus
Servant regem / O Philippe
Cum statua Nabucodonasor / Hugo, Hugo, princeps invidie

Release date: Feb. 1991   **Cassette:** CSAR 49
Subtitled "14th Century Motets". Robert Harre–Jones, countertenor; Charles Daniels, tenor; Angus Smith, tenor; Donald Greig, baritone.

CD–SAR 50   GLENDA SIMPSON & BARRY MASON: Now What Is Love?

Now What Is Love? (Jones)
It is a sunshine mix'd with rain:
  Guardatevi Olà (Rossi)
  Occhi Belli (Anon)
  Toccata Prima (Piccinini)
  Se piu del canto mio (Striggio)
It is a thing will soon decay:
  Go Crystal Tears (Dowland)
  Solus cum Sola (Dowland)
  Grief Keep Within (Danyel)

It is a gentle pleasing pain:
  Enfin la beaute (Moulinié)
  Ma bergere non legere (Bataille)
  Cesses mortels de soupirer (Guedron)
Where pleasures and repentance dwell:
  Love Arms Himself (Purcell)
  If Love's a Sweet Passion (Purcell)
  Suite in D (Matteis)
  O Lead Me (Purcell)
  Hark the Echoing Air (Purcell)

Release date: spring 1991   **Cassette:** CSAR 50
Subtitled "Aspects of Love in the 17th Century". Glenda Simpson, mezzo–soprano; Barry Mason, lute, Baroque guitar and chitarrone.

CD–SAR 51   MUSICA ANTIQUA OF LONDON: The Field of the Cloth of Gold

Kyng Harry VIII Pavyn / Pavane Les Quercarde (Anon)

L'Amour De Moi / L'Amour De Moi (Anon; Brugier)

La My / Tris (Isaac; Lloyd)

Le Cuer est Bon / Reprise (de Sermisy; Susato)

Pavane et Galliarde d'Angleterre (Gervaise)

Adieu My Hertes Lust / La Belle Fyne / Farewell My Joye (Cornish; Cornish; Cooper)

Allons Fere Nos Barbes / En Vray Amour (Compere; Henry VIII)

Fa La Sol (Cornish)

De Mon Triste Deplaisir / Pastime With Good Company (Richefort; Henry VIII)

Baisez Moi / J'ay Le Rebours / Pavane / Au Joli Bois (Willaert; Certon; Attaignant; non Pap)

Four Consort Pieces (Henry VIII; rest Anon)

Dont Vient Cela / Basse Danse et Reprise / Dont Vient Cela (de Sermisy; Susato; Crecquillon)

Fantasia Con e Senza Pause (van Wilder)

Pavane La Bataille (Susato)

Release date: prob. autumn 1991 (SC)   **Cassette:** CSAR 51

CD–SAR 52   NEIL McLAREN & THE CAMBRIDGE BAROQUE CAMERATA: Rare Baroque Flute Concertos

Concerto in G (Tartini):
 Allegro non molto
 Andante
 Allegro
Concerto in E minor (Quantz):
 Allegro ma non tanto
 Affetuoso
 Vivace

Concerto in D, Op. 11 No.1 (Naudot):
 Allegro
 Largo
 Allegro
Concerto in G (Benda):
 Allegro
 Largo
 Presto

Release date: autumn 1991   **Cassette:** CSAR 52

CD–SAR 53   ALISON STEPHENS, SUE MOSSOP, POPPY HOLDEN, RICHARD BURNETT: Music for Mandolin

Duetto IV (from six duos pour deux violons ou deux mandolines avec une basse ad libitum) (Barbella):
 1st movement
 A Charming Shepherdess in the country
 The God Bacchus infuses mirth in a German Woman and induces her to digest her wine by dancing
Sonatina in C min (Beethoven)
Sonatina in C (Beethoven)
Adagio in E (Beethoven)
Theme and Variations in D (Beethoven)

Komm, liebe Zither, komm (Mozart)
Zufriedene (Contentment) (Mozart)
Grande Sonata per il clavicembalo con mandolins o violins obbligato (Hummel):
 Allegro con spirito
 Andante moderato siziliano
 Rondo
Suite No.3 op.98 (Calace):
 Adagio
 Marziale allegretto
 Minuetto
 Scherzoso

Release date: autumn 1991   **Cassette:** CSAR 53

Alison Stephens, mandolin; Sue Mossop, mandolin; Poppy Holden, soprano; Richard Burnett, fortepiano.

CD–SAR 54   RICHARD BURNETT & THE FITZWILLIAM QUARTET: Schumann

Piano Quintet in E Flat Major, Op. 44:
 Allegro brillante
 In modo d'una Marcia – Un poco largamente
 Scherzo: Molto vivace
 Allegro ma non troppo
Sonata for Violin and Piano No. 1 in A Minor, Op. 155:
 Mit leidenschaftlichem Ausdruck

 Allegretto
 Lebhaft
Piano Quartet in E Flat Major, Op. 47:
 Sostenuto assai – Allegro ma non troppo
 Scherzo: Molto vivace
 Andante cantabile
 Finale: Vivace

Release date: autumn 1991   **Cassette:** CSAR 54

Richard Burnett, Viennese Graf fortepiano of 1822; Fitzwilliam String Quartet, on original instruments.

CD–SAR 55   ROSE CONSORT OF VIOLS: John Dowland's Lachrimae or Seven Tears

"Flow my teares" Second book of Songs
Lachrimae Antiquae
"Come, Heavy Sleep" First book of Songs
Lachrimae Antiquae Novae
"Sorrow Stay" Second book of Songs
Lachrimae Gementes
"In Darkness Let Me Dwell" A Musical Banquet

Lachrimae Tristes
"From Silent Night" A Pilgrim's Solace
Lachrimae Coactae
"Go Cristall Teares" First book of Songs
Lachrimae Amantis
"I Saw My Lady Weep" Second book of Songs
Lachrimae Verae

Release date: autumn 1992   **Cassette:** CSAR 55

Includes subcredits for Caroline Trevor and Jacob Heringman. Alison Crum, treble and alto viols; John Bryan, tenor viol; Susanna Pell, small bass viol; Elizabeth Liddle, consort bass viol; Sarah Groser, great bass viol. With Caroline Trevor, alto; Jacob Heringman, renaissance lutes.

CD–SAR 56   NEW LONDON CHAMBER CHOIR: The Brightest Heaven of Invention

O admirabile commercium (Regis)
Factor orbis (Obrecht)
Preter rerum seriem (des Prez)
Nato canunt omnia (Brumel)

Salve crux (Obrecht)
In hydraulis (Busnois)
Ave regina celorum (Dufay)
Anthoni usque limina (Busnois)

Release date: 1992   **Cassette:** CSAR 56

Flemish polyphony.

CD–SAR 57   LE NOUVEAU QUATUOR: The Music of Michel Corrette (1709 – 95)

Sonata in D minor:
 Allegro
 Adagio
 Allegro
Sonata in D major:
 Allegro moderato
 Aria (Affettuoso)
 Giga (Allegro)
Sonata in D major:
 Allegro
 Largo
 Allegro
Sonata in E minor 'Les amusements d'
          Apollon chez le roi Admete':
 Allegro
 Affettuoso
 Presto
Sonata in A major:
 Allegro

Aria I – Aria II
 Allegro
Sonata in F major:
 Allegro
 Adagio
 Presto
Sonata in D minor:
 Adagio
 Corrente (Allegro)
 Allegro
Sonata in G major:
 Fuga (Allegro)
 Andante
 Allegro
Sonata in E minor:
 Allegro
 Adagio
 Fuga (Allegro)

Release date: 1992   **Cassette:** CSAR 57

CD–SAR 58   MUSICA SECRETA: The Secret Music of Luzzascho Luzzaschi

Occhi del pianto mio
Aura soave
T'amo mia vita
O primavera
Toccata del quarto tuono
I' mi son giovinetta
O dolcezz'amarissime d'Amore
Ch'io non t'ami cor mio

Toccata No. 12 (Piccinini)
Non sa che sia dolore
Deh vieni ormai cor mio
Stral pungente d'Amore
Canzon à 4
Ricercare
Cor mio
Troppo ben può

Release date: 1992   **Cassette:** CSAR 58

Deborah Roberts, Tessa Bonner and Suzie Leblanc, sopranos; Mary Nichols, alto; Paula Chateauneuf, lute, chitarrone; John Toll, harpsichord.

CD–SAR 59   ORLANDO CONSORT: Worcester Fragments

Alleluya moduletur
O sponsa dei electa
Alleluya Nativitas
Sanctus
Ave virgo mater
Salve sancta parens
Thomas gemma Cantuarie primula
Super te Ierusalem
Munda Maria
Sponsa rectoris omnium
O Maria virgo pie
Candens crescit lilium
Gloria

O quam glorifica
Fulget celestis curia
Senator regis curie
Inviolata integra mater
Dulciflua tua memoria
Virgo regalis
Puellare gremium
Beata viscera
Prolis eterne genitor
Lux polls refulgens aurea
De supernis sedibus
Quam admirabilis

Release date: 1993   **Cassette:** CSAR 59

CD–SAR 60   ROBIN CANTER: J. S. Bach: Music for Oboe

Sonata in G major BWV 1027:
  Adagio
  Allegro ma non tanto
  Andante
  Allegro moderato
Sonata in G minor BWV 1030b:
  Andante
  Siciliano: Largo e dolce
  Presto — Allegro

Sonata in Eb major BWV 1031:
  Allegro moderato
  Siciliano
  Allegro
Sonata in G minor BWV 1020:
  Allegro
  Adagio
  Allegro

Release date: 1993   **Cassette:** CSAR 60

CD–SAR 61   MUSICA SECRETA: Barbara Strozzi – La Virtuosissima Cantatrice

Merce di voi
Noiosa lontananza: Dimmi dove sei
Le tre Gratie a Venere
Gl'occhi superbi
Amor dormiglione
Begli occhi
Anima del mio core

Sete pur fastidioso
I baci
Sino alla morte
Mordeva un bianco lino
Godere e tacere
Canto di bella bocca
Libertà: Non ci lusinghi più

Release date: 1994   **Cassette:** CSAR 61

Deborah Roberts, soprano; Suzie le Blanc, soprano; Mary Nichols, alto; Kasia Elsner, theorbo (by Klaus Jokobsen, 1991, after Tieffenbrucker); John Toll, harpsichord (by Ransom, London, 1990, after 17th Century Italian models).

CD–SAR 62   VARIOUS ARTISTS: A Golden Treasury of Elizabethan Music

Dance: Sellengers Round (Anon)
Verse Anthem: This Is the Record of John
          (Gibbons)
Dance: Bergamasqa (Anon)
Viol consort: In nomine à 5 (Parsons
Song: Coventry Carol (Anon)
Lute solo: Passamezzo Pavan (Anon)
Verse Anthem: Sing Unto God (Tomkins)
Dance: The Spanish Pavan / Galliard – La
          Gamba (Anon)
Song: Go Cristall Teares (Dowland)
Virginals solo: A Toye (Farnaby)
Dance: La Doune Cella (Anon)
Viol consort: Pavan—Lachrimae Coactae
          ("forced tears") (Dowland)
Song: Greensleeves (Anon)

Dance: Crimson Velvet (Anon)
Song: There dwelt a man in Babylon (Anon)
Dance: Almain — The Night Watch (Holborne)
Song: Come Live With Me (Anon)
Lute solo: Bonny Sweet Robin (Anon)
Recorder consort: Pavan — Heigh–ho Holyday (Holborne)
Consort Song: Sweet Was the Song the Virgin Sung (Anon)
Dance: Staines Morris (Anon)
Viol consort: Libera nos, salva nos à 5 (Tallis)
Song: Fortune My Foe (Anon)
Dance: Dulcina / All You That Love Good Fellowes (Anon)
Song: The Poor Soul Sat Sighing (The Willow Song) (Anon)
Viol consort: Fantasy à 5: Browning (Byrd)
Recorder consort: Pavan — The Cradle (Holborne)
Song: Farewell Dear Love (Jones)
Dance: La Bounette (Anon)

Release date: autumn 1995   **Cassette:** CSAR 62
Compilation of previously available Amon Ra recordings. 1 & 3 by The Broadside Band; 2, 7 & 20 by Red Byrd & The Rose Consort of Viols; 4 & 22 by Fretwork; 5 by Sneak's Noyse; 6 & 18 by George Weigand; 8, 11, 14, 16, 19, 21, 24, 27 & 29 by The York Waits; 9 by Caroline Trevor & The Rose Consort of Viols; 10 by Richard Burnett; 12 & 26 by The Rose Consort of Viols; 13, 17 & 28 by John Potter & The Broadside Band; 15 & 25 by Deborah Roberts & The Broadside Band; 23 by John Potter, Deborah Roberts & The Broadside Band.

CD–SAR 63   SINE NOMINE: A Golden Treasury of Mediaeval Music

Quen quer que ten en desden (Cantiga 153)
Ex ejus tumba / V. Catervatim
Estampie
Rosa delectabilis / [Regali ex progenie] /
        Regalis exoritur
Peperit virgo
My heartly service
Alma redemptoris mater, Marian antiphon,
        Advent and Christmas
Sire cuens, j'ai vielé
Conditor alme siderum, Hymn for Advent
        Vespers
Corps feminin

Je ne vis oncques la pareille
Saltarello
Io son un pellegrin
Titurel fragment: Sus lâgen sie unlange
Ad regnum epulentum
Gesegnet sey die frucht
Nu bitt wir den heiligen geist
Petruslied: Unsar trohtin hat farsalt
Ich bins erfreut
Der notter schwanctz
Symphonia virginum: O dulcissime amator
Cormacus scripsit

Release date: 1996   **Cassette:** CSAR 63

CD–SAR 64   RICHARD BURNETT: A Golden Treasury of Historic Pianos

Sonata 35 in Ab, Hob XVI/43; Moderato (Haydn)
Nocturne No. 1 in Eb (Field)
Three Monferrinas, from Op.49 (Clementi)
Sonata in A minor, D.537: Allegretto quasi
        andantino (Schubert)
Romanza from "La Forza del Destino" (Verdi)
Sonata 60 in C, Hob XV1/50: Adagio (Haydn)
Berceuse (Gottschalk)
Nocturne No. 11 in Eb (Field)

Fair Aurora (Arne)
Sonata in A, Hob XVI/12: Andante (Haydn)
Sonata for flute and piano, No.4 in Eb: Rondo vivace (Weber)
Piano quartet in G minor: Rondo (Mozart)
Sonata No. 1 in F minor, Op. 120: Andante un poco Adagio
        (Brahms)
Song: An die Hoffnung (To Hope), Op.32 (Beethoven)
Songs Without Words, Op.62 no. 6 in A & op.67 no. 4 in C
        (Mendelssohn)

Release date: Feb. 1996   **Cassette:** CSAR 64
Compilation of previously available Amon Ra recordings.

CD SAR 0J   VARIOUS ARTISTS: A Golden Treasury of Renaissance Music

England:
  En vray amour (Henry VIII)
  In Nomine à 5 'Crye' (Tye)
  Adieu my hertes lust (Cornyshe)
  Watkins Ale (Anon)
  In Nomine à 4, no. 2 (Byrd)
  Consort pieces (Anon)
  Le Souvenir (Morton)
Italy:
  Occhi del pianto mio (Luzzaschi)
  Toccata (Piccinini)
  Amor dormiglione (Strozzi)
  Anello (Anon)
  Ch'io non t'ami cor mio (Luzzaschi)
  Mercantia (Anon)
  Libertà: Non ci lusinghi più (Strozzi)
Germany:
  In Feuers Hitz (Liederbuch)
  Es ist ein ros entsprungen (arr. Praetorius)

France:
  Bransles de Champagne (pub. Attaignant)
  L'amour de moi (Anon)
  Baisez moi (Willaert) / J'ay le rebours (Certon)
  Pavane et Galliarde d'Angleterre (Gervaise)
  Dont Vient Cela (Sermisy)
  Tuba Gallicalis (Anon)
Low Countries:
  Missa pro defunctis (Kyrie) (de la Rue)
  Je veuil chanter de cuer joyeux (Dufay)
  Nato canunt omnia (Brumel)
  Den haghel ende die calde snee (Obrecht)
  Preter rerum seriem (Josquin)
Spain:
  Fantasia que contrahaze la harpa en la manera (de Luduvico
        Mudarra)
  Todos los biennes del mundo (Encina) / Dindirin, Dindirin
        (Anon)

Release date: spring 1997   **Cassette:** CSAR 65
Compilation of previously available Amon Ra recordings. 1, 3, 6, 18, 20 & 21 by Musica Antiqua of London; 2 & 5

---

by Fretwork; 4, 7, 11, 13, 15, 16, 17, 22, 26 & 29 by The York Waits; 8, 10, 12 & 14 by Musica Secreta; 9 by Paula Chateauneuf; 23, 25 & 27 by New London Chamber Choir; 24 by Frances Kelly; 28 by Nigel North.

CD–SAR 66   VARIOUS ARTISTS: A Golden Treasury of Georgian Music

Sonata op. 5 No. 2 in C min/maj for harpsichord,
       two violins & cello (Avison):
 con giubilo
 con tenerezza
Tom Bowling (Dibdin)
Harpsichord Sonata No. 2 in E min (Arne):
 andante
 adagio
 allegrissimo
Bawdy ballads (from "Pills to Purge
       Melancholy"):
 Sometimes I Am A Tapster New
 There Was a Lass of Islington
 Come Jug, My Honey, Let's To Bed
Trio sonata No.2 in G (Arne):
 largo
 con spirito
 largo

 allegro
Begone Dull Care
Trio Sonata (op.2/3) (Handel):
 adagio
 allegro
 adagio
 allegro
Nancy Dawson
Rule Britannia (Arne)
Sonata op. 9/No. I in A for violin, cello, basso continuo (Abel):
 moderato
 vivace
The Miller of the Dee (Arne setting)
The Lass of Richmond Hill (Hook)
Harpsichord Concerto op.10/No. 4 in C min (Stanley):
 vivace
 andante affetuoso
 presto

Release date: Spring 1998
Compilation of previously available Amon Ra recordings. 1, 3, 5, 7, 10 & 13 by London Baroque; 2 by John Potter with The Broadside Band; 4 by Richard Wistreich & Lucie Skeaping with The City Waites; 6, 8, 9, 11 & 12 by Lucie Skeaping & John Potter with The Broadside Band

CD–SAR 67   RICHARD BURNETT: The Romantic Piano

Songs Without Words – Venetian Gondola
       Song in A minor (Mendelssohn)
Songs Without Words – Venetian Gondola
       Song in A major (Mendelssohn)
Andante Spianato (Chopin)
Kinderscenen (Schumann)
Nocturne No.1 in Eb (Field)
Nocturne No. 6 in F (Field)
Nocturne No. 4 in A (Field)
Songs Without Words – Op.67/2 Spring Song
       (Mendelssohn)
Songs Without Words – Op.53/4 (Mendelssohn)

Sonata in A minor , D.537 (Allegretto quasi andantino)
       (Schubert)
Nocturne in E min (Chopin)
Nocturne in C# min (Chopin)
Songs Without Words – Op.67/4 (Mendelssohn)
Songs Without Words – Venetian Gondola Song in F#m
       (Mendelssohn)
Waltz in A flat (Chopin)
Nocturne No. 3 in A flat (Field)
Nocturne No. 12 in G (Field)
Bear Dance (duet) (Field)

Release date: spring 1998
Compilation of previously available Amon Ra recordings. 1 & 2 played on Broadwood pianoforte, London 1823; 3, 5, 8, 9, 10, 11, 12, 13, 15 & 18 played on Graf fortepiano, Vienna 1826; 5 played on Fritz fortepiano, Vienna c.1815; 6, 7 & 16 played on Rosenberger fortepiano, Vienna c.1800; 14 played on Collard & Collard, London c.1840; 17 played on Clementi cabinet piano, London c.1825.

CD–SAR 68   VARIOUS ARTISTS: A Golden Treasury of Baroque Music

Sinfonia from 'Su le Sponde del Tebro' (A.
  Scarlatti)
Concerto in G (Tartini):
 Allegro non molto
 Andante
 Allegro
Harpsichord Sonata Kk 417 in D min (D.
  Scarlatti)
Concerto in F for flute, violin, bassoon and
  continuo: 1st movement (Vivaldi):
 Allegro
Sonata in G minor Op.2a No.3 (Locatelli):
 Largo
 Allegro
 Largo
 Allegro
Sonata V for two bassoons (Boismortier):
 Moderement
 Courante

Musette
Gigue
Cello sonata in D major: First movement (Corrette):
 Allegro moderato
Trio Sonata in G, BWV 1039 (Bach):
 Adagio
 Allegro ma non presto
 Adagio e piano
 Presto
L'hiver (Telemann)
Concerto in E minor 1st movement (Quantz):
 Allegro ma non tanto
Sonata in A minor W. 128: 3rd movement (C.P.E. Bach):
 Vivace
Clarines y Trompetas (Sanz)
Harpsichord sonata in G min (Seixas)
Sonata Op.2 no.5: Larghetto (Handel)
Trio Sonata in G (VII Sonatas) Op. 3 no. 2 (Arne):
 Con spirito

Release date: spring 1998
Compilation of previously available Amon Ra recordings. 1 & 19 by Alan Hacker and Richard Burnett; 2, 3, 4 & 20 by The Cambridge Baroque Camerata with Neil McLaren; 5 by Maggie Cole; 6 by Le Nouveau Quatuor with Andrew Watts; 7, 8 & 9 by Lisa Beznosiuk and Nigel North; 10, 11, 12, 13 & 21 by Frances Eustace and Andrew Watts; 14 by Members of Le Nouveau Quatuor; 15, 16, 17, 18 & 24 by Preston's Pocket; 22 by Barry Mason; 23 by Robert Woolley; 25 by Le Nouveau Quatuor.

CD–SAR 69   VARIOUS ARTISTS: A Golden Treasury of Ancient Instruments

Wind:
 Pipe & tabor: The Carman's Whistle /
  Shawms: Under and Over /
  Rauschpfeifen: Roowe Well
 Shawm (treble) with nakers: La Quinte
  Estampie Real
 Bombarde: An Dro Nevez
 Oboe (baroque) Variations on 'Les Folies
  d'Espagne'
 Crumhorns: Mercantia
 Recorders: En Natus est Emanuel
 Flutes (Renaissance): Crimson Velvet
 Chalumeau: She Moves Through the Fair
 Clarinet (baroque): Sinfonia
 Clarinet (basset): Minuet from Divertimento
  K439b
 Dulzian (curtal) with chamber organ: Sonata 1
  (extract)
 Bassoon (baroque): Sonata in C (allegro)
 English smallpipes with crumhorns: The
  Seven Joys of Mary
 Racket: In Dulci Jubilo
Keyboard:
 Virginals: A Toye
 Spinet: Almand in G
 Clavichord: Prelude in E

Harpsichord: Presto from Sonata No. 7 in A
Regal: Gathering Peascods
Brass:
 Cornett: La Shy Myze
 Busine Tuba: Gallicalis
 Trumpet (slide): Quene Note
 Trumpet (natural): Brando detto il Rucellai
 Sackbut: L'Hom Armé
 Serpent (trio): Foresters, Sound the Cheerful Horn
Strings (bowed):
 Hurdy–gurdy: Il Pastor Fido
 Vielle (mediaeval fiddle): Sire cuens, j'ai vielé
 Rebec: The English Dance
 Viols: Solfaing Song à 5
Strings (plucked):
 Lute: In Nomine
 Vihuela: Fantasia del quarto tono
 Guitar (Renaissance): Pimontoyse
 Cittern: The Lady Nevils Delight, The Whisk, A New Rigaudon
 Gittern: English dance
 Chitaronne: Toccata
 Theorbo: Godere e tacere
 Arch cittern: Mr Lane's Minuet
 Mediaeval harp: L'autrier pastoure seoit
 Gothic harp: Mein Fleiss und Müeh
 Double harp: Partite sopra Fidele

Release date: Feb. 1999
This album has been compiled from the following Saydisc and Amon Ra albums: tracks 15 – 18: Keyboard Collection (CD–SAR 6); tracks 8 –10: Clarinet Collection (CD–SAR 10); tracks 31, 32: Guitar Collection (CD–SAR 18); tracks 2 – 4: Oboe Collection (CD–SAR 18); tracks 33, 37: John Playford's Popular Tunes (CD–SAR 28); tracks 29, 30: In Nomine (CD–SAR 29); track 23: Trumpet Collection (CD–SAR 30); tracks 11, 12: Bassoon

Collection (CD–SAR 35); tracks 38 – 40: Harp Collection (CD–SAR 36); track 35: The Secret Music of Luzzasco Luzzaschi (CD–SAR 58); track 36: Barbara Strozzi – La virtuosissima cantatrice (CD–SAR 61); tracks 27, 34: A Golden Treasury of Mediaeval Music (CD–SAR 63); track 25: Fill Your Glasses (CD–SDL 361); tracks 5, 21, 22, 24: Music From the Time of Richard III (CD–SDL 364); track 28: Christmas Now Is Drawing Near (CD–SDL 371); tracks 1, 7, 20: Music From the Time of the Spanish Armada (CD–SDL 373); track 26: The Music of the Hurdy–Gurdy (CD–SDL 374); track 19: English Country Dances (CD–SDL 393); tracks 6, 13, 14: Old Christmas Returned (CD–SDL 398).

CD–SAR 70 VARIOUS ARTISTS: A Golden Treasury of Flute Music

Sonata for flute & keyboard in C major, BWV 1033 (Bach)
Originaltänze (36) for piano (Erste Walzer), D. 365 (Op. 9) Waltz (Schubert)
Trio Sonata for flute, violin & continuo in D major, RV 84 (Vivaldi)
Trio for flute, cello & piano in G minor, J. 259 (Op. 63) Scherzo (von Weber): Allegro vivace
Trio Sonata for 2 violins & continuo No. 2 in G major (Arne): Allegro
Trio sonata for 2 violins & continuo in G minor, Op.2/5, HWV 390 (Handel): Allegro
Valse de Fleurs for flute, violin & piano, Op 87 (Kohler)
Flute Concerto in G major, L. II–11 Allegro (Benda)
Trio for 2 flutes & cello in C major ("London"), H. 4/1 (Haydn): Allegro moderato
Quartet for flute, violin, viola da gamba (or cello) & continuo No. 2 in G minor (Paris Quartet No. 4), TWV 43:g1 (Telemann): Largo
Sonata for flute & continuo in D major, Op. 14/2 (Corrette)
Le nozze di Figaro (The Marriage of Figaro), opera, K. 492 Voi che sapete (Mozart)
Trio sonata for flute, violin & continuo in G major, H. 586, Wq. 153 (C.P.E. Bach)
Gran Duetto Concertante, for flute (or violin) & guitar in A major, Op. 52 (Giuliani): Menuetto Allegro vivace

Release date: spring 1999
Compilation of previously available Amon Ra recordings. 1 by Lisa Beznosiuk; 2 &14 by Nigel North and Lisa Beznosiuk; 3, 5, 11 & 13 by Nouveau Quartet; 4 by Jennifer Ward Clarke, Stephen Preston and Richard Burnett; 6, 7, 9 & 12 by Preston's Pocket; 8 by Cambridge Baroque Camerata and Neil McLaren; 10 by American Baroque Ensemble.

CD–SAR 1001 RICHARD BURNETT: Richard Burnett's Musical Tour

Sinfonia from 'Su le Sponde del Tebro' (Scarlatti)
Sonata in A, Hob.XV1/12, menuet and trio (Haydn)
Sonata in D , Hob.XV1/50 (Haydn)
Adagio Cantabile (Vanhal)
Der Kuss op. 128 (Beethoven)
Grande Sonata per il clavicembalo con mandolins – allegro con spirito (Hummel)
Monferrinas 11, 12, 14 (Clementi)
Nocturne No 12 in G (John Field)
Nocturnes in E minor and C# minor (Chopin)
Sonata for Piano and Violin Op. 30 No. 2 in C major ("Spring") – Adagio molto espressivo (Beethoven)
Sonata in D for flute and piano (Weber)
Venetian Gondola Song in A minor (Mendelssohn)
Sonatina No 2 in G for oboe and piano (Walmisley)
La Savane (Gottschalk)
Piano Quintet in Eb – Allegro ma non troppo (Schumann)

Release date: Feb. 1994
Issued on CD only. Only available at Finchcocks. Compilation of previously–available Amon Ra recordings.

Matchbox Bluesmaster

The Matchbox Bluesmaster series was compiled by Johnny Parth (of Roots label fame) with sleeve notes by noted blues expert, Paul Oliver, and comprised two catalogue sequences. The MSE 200 series was subtitled "Complete Recordings in Chronological Order" and the MSE 1000 series was described in catalogues as either "The Remaining Titles" or "Mostly New To LP". Those described as "The Remaining Titles" included information on the sleeves as to which other records were required to complete the artists' recordings. The series was rounded off by two double LPs that were released to complement Paul Oliver's book, *Songsters and Saints: Vocal Traditions on Race Records*. The Matchbox Bluesmaster series was only released on LP.

MSE 201   **VARIOUS ARTISTS: Papa Harvey Hull and Long Cleve Reed, Richard "Rabbit" Brown**

Gang of Brown Skin Women (Papa Harvey Hull, acc. Long Cleve Reed & ? Wilson)
France Blues (as above)
Two Little Tommie Blues (as above)
Don't You Leave Me Here (as above)
Mama You Don't Know How (Long Cleve Reed & The Down Home Boys)
Original Stack O'Lee Blues (as above)

James Alley Blues (Richard (Rabbit) Brown)
Never Let the Same Bee Sting You Twice (as above)
I'm Not Jealous (Richard (Rabbit) Brown)
Mystery of The Dunbar's Child (Richard (Rabbit) Brown)
Sinking of the Titanic (Richard (Rabbit) Brown)

Release date: Nov. 1982 (MM89)
Subtitled "Country Blues – The First Generation" and "Complete Recordings".

MSE 202   **WALTER "BUDDY BOY" HAWKINS: Walter "Buddy Boy" Hawkins 1927 – 29**

Shaggy Dog Blues
Number Three Blues
Jailhouse Fire Blues
Snatch It Back Blues
Workin' On the Railroad
Yellow Woman Blues

Raggin' the Blues
Awful Fix Blues
A Rag Blues
How Come Mama Blues
Snatch It and Grab It
Voice Throwin' Blues

Release date: Jan. 1983 (MM89)
Subtitled "Complete Recordings in Chronological Order".

MSE 203   **BO WEAVIL JACKSON (SAM BUTLER): Bo Weavil Jackson (Sam Butler) 1926**

Devil and My Brown Blues
Poor Boy Blues
Jefferson County Blues
Jefferson County Blues (alt. take)
You Can't Keep No Brown
Christians Fight On, Your Time Ain't Long
Heaven Is My View

Pistol Blues
Some Scream High Yellow
You Can't Keep No Brown
When the Saints Come Marching Home
I'm On My Way to the Kingdom Land
Why Do You Moan?

Release date: Jan. 1983 (MM89)
Subtitled "Complete Recordings in Chronological Order". Side 1 credited to Butler, side 2 credited to Jackson.

MSE 204   **VARIOUS ARTISTS: Ragtime Blues Guitar 1928 – 30**

One Way Gal (William Moore)
Ragtime Crazy (William Moore)
Midnight Blues (William Moore)
Ragtime Millionaire (William Moore)
Tillie Lee (William Moore)
Barbershop Rag (William Moore)
Old Country Rock (William Moore)
Raggin' the Blues (William Moore)

Brownie Blues (Tarter & Gay)
Unknown Blues (Tarter & Gay)
Jamestown Exposition (Bayless Rose)
Black Dog Blues (Bayless Rose)
Original Blues (Bayless Rose)
Frisco Blues (Bayless Rose)
Dupree Blues (Willie Walker acc. Sam Brooks)
South Carolina Rag (Willie Walker acc. Sam Brooks)
South Carolina Rag (diff.) (Willie Walker acc. Sam Brook

Release date: Nov. 1982 (MM89)
"Complete Recordings of William Moore, Tarter & Gay, Balyless Rose, Willie Walker in Chronological Order".

MSE 205   PEG LEG HOWELL: Peg Leg Howell (1928 – 29)

Please Ma'am
Rock and Gravel Blues
Low Down Rounder Blues
Fairy Blues
Banjo Blues (with Eddie Anthony)
Turkey Buzzard Blues (with Eddie Anthony)
Turtle Dove Blues

Walkin' Blues
Broke and Hungry Blues (prob. acc. Eddie Anthony)
Rolling Mill Blues (prob. acc. Eddie Anthony)
Ball and Chain Blues (with Jim Hill)
Monkey Man Blues (with Jim Hill)
Chittlin' Supper (with Jim Hill)
Away from Home (with Jim Hill)

Release date: Jan. 1983 (MM89)
Subtitled "Complete Recordings in Chronological Order".

MSE 206   TEXAS ALEXANDER: Texas Alexander Vol.1 (1927 – 28)

Range In My Kitchen Blues (acc. Lonnie
        Johnson)
Long Lonesome Day Blues (as above)
Corn–Bread Blues (acc. Lonnie Johnson)
Section Gang Blues (acc. Lonnie Johnson)
Levee Camp Moan Blues (acc. Lonnie Johnson)
Mama, I Heard You Brought It Right Back
        Home (acc. Eddie Hayward)
Farm Hand Blues (acc. Eddie Hayward)
Evil Woman Blues (acc. Eddie Hayward)

Death Bed Blues (acc. Lonnie Johnson)
Yellow Girl Blues (acc. Lonnie Johnson)
West Texas Blues (acc. Lonnie Johnson)
Bantam Rooster Blues (acc. Lonnie Johnson)
Deep Blue Sea Blues (acc. Lonnie Johnson)
No More Women Blues (acc. Lonnie Johnson)
Don't You Wish Your Baby Was Built Up Like Mine? (as above)
Bell Cow Blues (acc. Lonnie Johnson)

Release date: Nov. 1982
Subtitled "Complete Recordings in Chronological Order".

MSE 207   SKIP JAMES: Skip James 1931

Devil Got My Woman
Cypress Grove Blues
Cherry Ball Blues
Illinois Blues
4 O'Clock Blues
Hard–Luck Child
Hard Time Killin' Floor Blues
Yola My Blues Away
Jesus Is a Mighty Good Leader

Be Ready When He Comes
Drunken Spree
I'm So Glad
Special Rider Blues
How Long "Buck"
Little Cow and Calf Is Gonna Die Blues
What Am I to Do Blues
22–20 Blues
If You Haven't Had Any Get On Down the Road

Release date: Jan. or Feb. 1983
Subtitled "Complete Recordings in Chronological Order".

MSE 208   COLEY JONES & THE DALLAS STRING BAND: Coley Jones and the Dallas String Band (1927 – 29)

Army Mule In No Man's Land (Coley Jones)
Traveling Man (Coley Jones)
Dallas Rag (Dallas String Band)
Sweet Mama Blues (Dallas String Band)
So Tired (Dallas String Band)
Hokum Blues (Dallas String Band)
Chasin' Rainbows (Dallas String Band)
I Used to Call Her Baby (Dallas String Band)

I Can't Stand That (Bobbie Cadillac, Coley Jones & poss.
        Alex Moore)
He Throws That Thing (as above)
Drunkard's Special (Coley Jones)
The Elder's He's My Man (Coley Jones)
Listen Everybody (as tracks 1 & 2, side 2)
Easin' In (as above)
Shine (Dallas String Band: Coley Jones, plus three unknown)
Sugar Blues (as above)

Release date: May 1983 (MM89)
Subtitled "Complete Recordings in Chronological Order".

MSE 209 VARIOUS ARTISTS: Great Harp Players (1927 – 30)

John Henry Blues (William Francis & Richard
    Sowell)
Roubin Blues (as above)
Pot Licker Blues (El Watson acc. C. Johnson)
Narrow Gauge Blues (El Watson)
El Watson's Fox Chase (El Watson acc.
    Robert Cooksey)
Bay Rum Blues (as above with unknown acc.)
Sweet Bunch of Daisies (El Watson)
One Sock Blues (El Watson)
Lost Boy Blues (Palmer McAbee)

McAbee's Railroad Piece (Palmer McAbee)
Railroad Blues (Freeman Stowers)
Texas Wild Cat Chase (Freeman Stowers)
Medley of Blues (All Out and Down; Old Time Blues;
    Hog In the Mountain) (Freeman Stowers)
Sunrise On the Farm (Freeman Stowers)
Mean Low Blues (Blues Birdhead & unknown acc.)
Harmonica Blues (Blues Birdhead & unknown acc.)
Mississippi's Swamp Moan (Alfred Lewis)
Friday Moan Blues (Alfred Lewis)

Release date: May 1983 (MM89)
Subtitled "Complete Recordings of Francis & Sowell, El Watson, Palmer McAbee, Freeman Stowers, Blues Birdhead, Alfred Lewis in Chronological Order".

MSE 210 LEROY CARR: Leroy Carr 1928

How Long – How Long Blues
Broken Spoke Blues
Tennessee Blues
Truthful Blues
Mean Old Train Blues
You Got to Reap What You Sow
Low Down Dirty Blues

How Long How Long Blues No. 2
How Long How Long Blues Part 3
Baby Don't You Leave Me No More
Tired of Your Low Down Ways
I'm Going Away and Leave My Baby
Prison Bound Blues
You Don't Mean Me No Good

Release date: Sept. 1983
Subtitled "Complete Recordings in Chronological Order". With accompaniment from Scrapper Blackwell.

MSE 211 TOMMIE BRADLEY – JAMES COLE: Tommie Bradley – James Cole Groups 1930 – 32

Mama Keep Your Yes Ma'am Clean (A)
Everybody Got Somebody (A)
Where You Been So Long? (B)
Adam and Eve (C)
Runnin' Wild (D)
Sweet LIzzie (D)
Pack Up Her Trunk Blues (E)
When You're Down and Out (C)

Please Don't Act That Way (C)
I Love My Mary (F)
Four Day Blues (B)
Undertaker Blues (G)
Mistreated the Only Friend You Had (H)
Nobody's Business If I Do (I)
Window Pane Blues (J)

Release date: Sept. 1983
Subtitled "Complete Recordings in Chronological Order". A = Walter Cole with, probably James Cole and Sam Soward; B = Tommie Bradley with James Cole, Eddie Dimmitt and Roosevelt Pursley; C = Tommie Bradley with Eddie Dimmitt; D = James Cole's Washboard Four: Cole, Tommie Bradley, Eddie Dimmitt and unknown; E = Tommie Bradley with poss. Walter Cole or Eddie Dimmitt; F = James Cole with Tommie Bradley, Eddie Dimmitt and Roosevelt Pursley; G = Buster Johnson with James Cole, Tommie Bradley, prob. Eddie Dimmitt and unknown; H = James Cole with poss. Sam Soward, probably Eddie Dimmitt, Tommie Bradley or Buster Johnson plus unknown; I = Tommie Bradley with prob. Eddie Dimmitt and unknown; J = Tommie Bradley with James Cole, prob. Eddie Dimmitt and unknown.

MSE 212 CHARLEY LINCOLN: Charley Lincoln (1927 – 30)

Jealous Hearted Blues
Hard Luck Blues
Mojoe Blues
My Wife Drove Me from My Door
Country Breakdown
Chain Gang Trouble
If It Looks Like Jelly, Shakes Like Jelly, It Must
    Be Gelatine

Ugly Papa
Jacksonville Blues (Nellie Florence acc. poss. Charley Lincoln
    or poss. Barbecue Bob)
Midnight Weeping Blues (as above)
Depot Blues
Gamblin' Charley
Doodle Hole Blues
Mama Don't Rush Me

Release date: Sept. 1983
Subtitled "Complete Recordings in Chronological Order".

MSE 213   *VARIOUS ARTISTS: Memphis Harmonica Kings 1929 – 30*

Chickasaw Special (Noah Lewis)
Devil in the Woodpile (Noah Lewis)
Like I Want To Be (Noah Lewis)
Ticket Agent Blues (Noah Lewis' Jug Band)
New Minglewood Blues (Noah Lewis' Jug Band)
Selling the Jelly (Noah Lewis acc. John Estes, Ham Lewis, Mrs. Van Zula Carter Hunt & unknown)
Bad Luck's My Buddy (as above)
I'm Sittin' On Top of the World (Beale Street Rounders)
Talkin' Bout Yo–Yo (Beale Street Rounders)

How Long How Long Blues (Jed Davenport acc. unknown)
Cow Cow Blues (Jed Davenport acc. unknown)
Beale Street Breakdown (Jed Davenport & His Beale Street Jug Band)
You Ought to Move Out of Town (as above)
The Dirty Dozen (Jed Davenport & His Beale Street Jug Band)
Jug Blues (Jed Davenport & His Beale Street Jug Band)
Save Me Some (Jed Davenport & His Beale Street Jug Band)
Piccolo Blues (Jed Davenport & His Beale Street Jug Band)

Release date: Feb. 1984
Subtitled "the Complete Recordings in Chronological Order of Noah Lewis and Jed Davenport". Noah Lewis' Jug Band comprises Noah Lewis, Sleepy John Estes, Yank Rachel and Ham Lewis. Beale Street Rounders comprises Jed Davenport, Henry L. Castle (Too Tight Henry) and unknown acc. The other members of Jed Davenport & His Beale Street Jug Band are unknown.

MSE 214   *TEXAS ALEXANDER: Texas Alexander Vol. 2 (1928 – 29)*

Sittin' On a Log (acc. Lonnie Johnson)
Mama's Bad Luck Child (acc. Lonnie Johnson)
Boe Hog Blues (acc. Lonnie Johnson)
Work Ox Blues (acc. Lonnie Johnson and Eddie Lang)
The Risin' Sun (as above)
Penitentiary Moan Blues (as above)
Blue Devil Blues (as above)
Tell Me Woman Blues (acc. King Oliver, Clarence Williams and Eddie Lang)
'Frisco Train Blues (as above)

St. Louis Fair Blues (acc. Eddie Lang)
I Am Calling Blues (acc. Eddie Lang)
Double Crossing Blues (acc. Little Hat Jones)
Ninety–Eight Degree Blues (acc. Little Hat Jones)
Someday, Baby, Your Troubles Is Gonna Be Like Mine (as above)
Water Bound Blues (acc. Little Hat Jones)
Awful Moaning Blues – Part 1 (acc. Little Hat Jones)
Awful Moaning Blues – Part 2 (acc. Little Hat Jones)

Release date: Feb. 1984
Subtitled "Complete Recordings in Chronological Order".

MSE 215   *RAMBLIN' THOMAS: Ramblin' Thomas 1928 – 32*

So Lonesome
Hard to Rule Woman Blues
Lock and Key Blues
Sawmill Moan
No Baby Blues
Ramblin' Mind Blues
No Job Blues
Back Gnawing Blues

Jig Head Blues
Hard Dallas Blues
Ramblin' Man
Poor Boy Blues
Good Time Blues
New Way of Living Blues
Ground Hog Blues
Shake It Gal

Release date: Feb. 1984
Subtitled "Complete Recordings in Chronological Order" – except, that is, for two tracks from a 1932 session, which remained undiscovered. All tracks credited to Willard "Ramblin'" Thomas except the last two tracks on side 2, which are credited to Rambling Thomas.

MSE 216   *VARIOUS ARTISTS: Country Girls 1926 – 29*

Kitchen Blues (Lillian Miller acc. Hersal Thomas)
Harbor Blues (Lillian Miller acc. George W. Thomas and Charlie Hill)
You Just Can't Keep a Good Woman Down (as above)
Butcher Shop Blues (as above)
Dead Drunk Blues (as above)
Doggone My Good Luck Soul (Hattie Hudson acc. Willie Tyson)
Black Hand Blues (as above)
No Easy Rider Blues (Gertrude Perkins acc. Willie Tyson, Octave Gaspard and unknown acc.)
Gold Daddy Blues (as above)

Twelve Pound Daddy (Pearl Dickson acc. Pet & Can)
Little Rock Blues (Pearl Dickson acc. Pet & Can)
He's Coming Soon (Laura Henton acc. unknown)
Heavenly Sunshine (Laura Henton acc. unknown)
Lord, You've Sure Been Good To Me (Laura Henton acc Bennie Moten, Eddie Durham and Joe Page)
I Can Tell the World About This (as above)
Plenty Good Room In My Father's Kingdom (as above)
Lord, I Just Can't Keep from Crying Sometimes (as above)
Carbolic Acid Blues (Bobbie Cadillac acc. unknown)

Release date: April 1984 (MM89)
Complete Recordings in Chronological Order. Pet & Can was Mahlon & Richard Harney.

MSE 217   *RUFUS & BEN QUILLIAN: Rufus & Ben Quillian 1929 – 31*

Sweet Miss Stella Blues (Blue Harmony Boys)
Jerking the Load (Blue Harmony Boys)
Take It Out Too Deep (Blue Harmony Boys)
Ragged but Right (Blue Harmony Boys)
All In Down and Out (Blue Harmony Boys)
Good Felling Blues (Blue Harmony Boys)
Keep It Clean (Rufus & Ben Quillian acc. James McCrary)
Good Right On (as above)

Working It Slow (poss. acc. Perry Bechtel)
I Got Everything (poss. acc. Perry Bechtel)
Satisfaction Blues (poss. acc. Perry Bechtel)
It's Dirty But Good (poss. acc. Perry Bechtel)
Holy Roll (with James McCrary)
Workin' It Fast (with James McCrary)
Shove It Up In There (as above prob. acc. Rufus Quillian)
Loose Me from This Woman (as above)

Release date: April 1984
Subtitled "Complete Recordings in Chronological Order". The Blue Harmony Boys recordings are by Rufus Quillian, Brother Jackson and poss. James McCrary.

MSE 218   *DE FORD BAILEY & BERT BILBRO: Harmonica Showcase*

Pan American Blues
Dixie Flyer Blues
Up Country Blues
Evening Prayer Blues
Muscle Shoals Blues
Old Hen Cackle
The Alcoholic Blues
Fox Chase

John Henry
Ice Water Blues
Davidson County Blues
O. & N.W. Blues
Mohana Blues
Yes, Indeed I Do
We're Gonna Have a Good Time Tonight
Chester Blues

Release date: Oct. 1985 (MM89)
Subtitled "De Ford Bailey & Bert Bilbro (1927 – 31)" and "Complete Recordings in Chronological Order". All tracks side 1 and first three tracks side 2, De Ford Bailey, last five tracks side 2, Bert Bilbro.

MSE 219   *VARIOUS ARTISTS: Atlanta Blues 1927 – 30*

My Mamma Was a Sailor (A)
Ninety–Nine Year Blues (A)
I'm Gonna Tell God How You Doin' (A)
Slippin' and Slidin' Up the Golden Street (A)
Can't Put the Bridle on That Mule This Morning (B)
Richmond Blues (B)
Crow Jane Blues (B)

Ninety–Nine Year Blues (A)
Slippin' and Slidin' Up the Golden Street (A)
Can't Put the Bridle on That Mule This Morning (B)
Richmond Blues (B)
Furniture Man (C)
Don't Think I'm Santa Claus (C)
Sow Good Seeds (C)
Mother Called Her Child to Her Dying Bed (C)

Release date: Feb. 1986 (MM89)
Subtitled "Complete Recordings in Chronological Order of Julius Daniels – Lil McClintock". Julius Daniels tracks on side 2 are alternate takes. A = Julius Daniels prob. acc. Bubba Lee Torrence; B = Julius Daniels prob. acc. Wilbert Andrews; C = Lil McClintock.

MSE 220   **TEXAS ALEXANDER: Texas Alexander Vol. 3 (1929 – 30)**

Gold Tooth Blues (acc. Little Hat Jones)
Johnny Behrens Blues (acc. Little Hat Jones)
Rolling Mill Blues (acc. Carl Davis)
Broken Yo Yo (acc. Carl Davis)
Texas Special (acc. Carl Davis)
When You Get to Thinking (acc. Carl Davis)
Thirty Day Blues (acc. Carl Davis)
Peaceful Blues (acc. Carl Davis)

Days Is Lonesome
Seen Better Days
Last Stage Blues
Stealing to Her Man
She's So Fair
Rolling and Stumbling Blues
Frost Texas Tornado Blues
Texas Troublesome Blues

Release date: Aug. 1986 (MM89)
Subtitled "Complete Recordings in Chronological Order". Alexander is credited on all tracks as Alger "Texas" Alexander. All side 2 tracks acc. Mississippi Sheiks. The Mississippi Sheiks are probably Bo Carter (Chatman), Sam Chatman, possibly with Walter Vincson.

MSE 221   **PEG LEG HOWELL: Peg Leg Howell Vol. 1 (1926 – 27)**

Coal Man Blues
Tishamingo Blues
New Prison Blues
Fo' Day Blues
New Jelly Roll Blues ("Peg Leg" Howell & His Gang)
Beaver Slide Blues (as above)
Papa Stobb Blues (as above)

Sadie Lee Blues
Too Tight Blues ("Peg Leg" Howell & His Gang)
Moanin' and Groanin' Blues ("Peg Leg" Howell & His Gang)
Hobo Blues ("Peg Leg" Howell & His Gang)
Peg Leg Stomp ("Peg Leg" Howell & His Gang)
Doin' Wrong
Skin Game Blues

Release date: Aug. 1986 (MM89)
Subtitled "Complete Recordings in Chronological Order". Howell credited on all tracks as "Peg Leg" Howell. "Peg Leg" Howell & His Gang comprises Howell, Henry Williams and Eddie Anthony.

MSE 222   **VARIOUS ARTISTS: Sanctified Jug Bands (1928 – 30)**

The Master Came and Called Me (Elder Richard Bryant)
Saul, a Wicked Man (Elder Richard Bryant)
Come Over Here (Elder Richard Bryant's Sanctified Singers)
How Much I Owe for Love Divine (as above)
Lord, Lord, He Sure Is Good to Me (as above)
Watch, Ye, Therefore, You Know Not the Day (as above)
A Lie Was Told, But God Know'd It (Elder Richard Bryant, acc. unknown)
A Wild Man In Town (as above)
He Shut the Lion's Mouth (as above)

A Lie Was Told (Elder Richard Bryant, acc. unknown)
A Wild Man In Town (as above)
He Shut the Lion's Mouth (as above)
Everybody Was There (as above)
He's Got the Whole World In His Hands (Brother Williams Memphis Sanctified Singers)
I Will Meet You at the Station (as above)
Thou Carest Lord, For Me (Holy Ghost Sanctified Singers)
Jesus Throwed Up a Highway for Me (as above)
Sinner, I'd Make a Change (as above)
When I Get Inside the Gate (as above)

Release date: Mar./April 1987

MSE 223   **ST LOUIS BESSIE: (Bessie Mae Smith) (1927 – 30)**

Cryin' for Daddy Blues
High Water Blues
Creepin' Eel Blues
Ghost Creepin' Blues
Boa Constrictor Blues
Dead Sea Blues
Sneakin' Lizard Blues
My Daddy's Coffin Blues
Mean Bloodhound Blues
Death Valley Moan

Sweet Black Woman
Good Feelin' Blues
St. Louis Daddy
Farewell Baby Blues
Sugar Mama Blues – Part 1
Sugar Mama Blues – Part 2
He Treats Me Like A Dog
Meat Cutter Blues

Release date: Mar./April 1987

MSE 224   TEXAS ALEXANDER: Texas Alexander Vol. 4

Blues In My Mind
Mistreatin' Woman
Polo Blues
Normangee Blues
Worried Blues
Prairie Dog Hole Blues
Justice Blues
Katy Crossing Blues

Lonesome Blues
Lonesome Valley Blues
One Morning Blues
Deceitful Blues
Easy Rider Blues
Good Feelin' Blues
Bottom's Blues
Crossroads

Release date: Mar./April 1987
Subtitled "Complete Recordings in Chronological Order".

MSE 1001   BLIND LEMON JEFFERSON: Blind Lemon Jefferson 1926 – 29

Got the Blues
Long Lonesome Blues
Match Box Blues
Hot Dogs (as Blind Lemon Jefferson & His Feet)
He Arose from the Dead (as Deacon L. J. Bates)
Struck Sorrow Blues
Gone Dead On You Blues
One Dime Blues
Change My Luck Blues

Lemon's Cannonball Theme
Lockstep Blues
Hangman's Blues
Disgusted Blues
Empty House Blues
Saturday Night Spender's Blues
The Cheaters Spell

Release date: April 1984 (MM89)
Subtitled "The Remaining Titles", this completes the issue of all recorded work, along with Collector's Classics CC–22, and Roots RL–301 (second pressing), 306 & 331.

MSE 1002   FRANK STOKES: Frank Stokes 1927 – 29

Half Cup Of Tea
Ain't Goin' to Do Like I Used to Do
Hunting Blues
Rockin' On the Hill Blues
Fillin' In The Blues – Part 1
Fillin' In The Blues – Part 2
South Memphis Blues
Bunker Hill Blues
Right Now Blues
Shiney Town Blues

Downtown Blues
Bedtime Blues
What's the Matter Blues
It Won't Be Long Now
I Got Mine
'Tain't Nobody's Business If I Do – Part1
'Tain't Nobody's Business If I Do – Part2
Take Me Back
How Long
Frank Stoke's Dream

Release date: Nov. 1984 (MM89)
Subtitled "The Remaining Titles".

MSE 1003   BLIND BLAKE: Blind Blake 1926 – 29

Skeedle Loo Doo Blues
You Gonna Quit Blues
Wabash Rag
Doggin' Me Mama Blues
C. C. Pill Blues
Hot Potatoes
Southbound Rag
That Lonesome Rave
Terrible Murder Blues

Leavin' Gal Blues
Rumblin' and Ramblin' Boa Constrictor Blues
Detroit Bound Blues
Ramblin' Mama Blues
New Style of Loving
Back Door Slam Blues
Cold Hearted Mama Blues
Guitar Chimes
Blind Arthur's Breakdown

Release date: May 1985 (MM89)
Subtitled "The Remaining Titles".

MSE 1004   *BIG BILL BROONZY: Big Bill Broonzy 1927 – 32*

House Rent Stomp
Tadpole Blues
Papa's Gettin' Hot
Police Station Blues
They Can't Do That
Mr. Conductor Blues
No Good Buddy
Meanest Kind of Blues

I Got the Blues for My Baby
Ain't Goin' There No More
That's the Way She Likes It
Too Too Train Blues
Shelby County Blues
Mistreatin' Mama Blues
Me and O Blues
Rukus Juice Blues

Release date: Sept. 1985 (MM89)
Subtitled "Mostly New to LP".

MSE 1005   *MISSISSIPPI SHEIKS: Mississippi Sheiks 1930 (Vol. 1)*

Driving That Thing
Alberta Blues
Winter Time Blues
The Sheik Waltz
The Jazz Fiddler
Stop and Listen Blues
Lonely One In This Town
We Are Both Feeling Good Right Now
Grinding Old Fool

Jake Leg Blues
West Jackson Blues
Baby Keeps Stealin' Lovin' On Me
River Bottom Blues
Loose Like That
Sitting On Top of The World no. 2
Times Done Got Hard
Still I'm Traveling On
Church Bell Blues

Release date: Sept. 1985 (MM89)
Subtitled "Mostly New to LP".

MSE 1006   *LONNIE JOHNSON: Lonnie Johnson Vol. 1 1926–28*

When I Was Lovin' Changed My Mind Blues
    (with James Johnson & De Loise
    Searcy)
Sun to Sun Blues (with James Johnson)
Bed Of Sand (with James Johnson)
Lonesome Jail Blues (with James Johnson)
No Good Blues (with James 'Steady Roll'
    Johnson & De Loise Searcy)
Newport Blues (as above)
Love Story Blues
Woman Changed My Life (with James Johnson)
Lonnie's Got the Blues (with James Johnson)

You Drove a Good Man Away (with James Johnson)
Ball and Chain Blues (with James Johnson)
To Do This, You Got To Know How
Superstitious Blues (with Joe Brown & De Loise Searcy)
Cotton Patch Blues (with Joe Brown & De Loise Searcy)
Blackbird Blues (with Raymond Boyd & De Loise Searcy)
Unkind Mama (with Raymond Boyd & De Loise Searcy)
Back–Water Blues (with John Erby)
Crowing Rooster Blues

Release date: Feb. 1986 (MM89)
Subtitled "Mostly New to LP".

MSE 1007   *PAPA CHARLIE JACKSON: Papa Charlie Jackson 1924 – 29*

Salt Lake City Blues
Mama Don't Allow It (And She Ain't Gonna
    Have It Here)
I'm Tired of Fooling Around with You
The Judge Cliff Davis Blues
Four Eleven Forty Four
Bad Luck Woman Blues
Gay Cattin'
Look Out Papa Don't Tear Your Pants
Long Gone Lost John

I'm Looking for a Woman Who Knows How to Treat Me Right
Lexington Kentucky Blues
Good Doing Papa Blues
Corn Liquor Blues
Hot Papa Blues No. 2
Tailor Made Lover
Take Me Back Blues No. 2
'Tain't What You Do But How You Do It

Release date: April 1987 (MM89)
This was the first time on LP for 14 of the tracks.

MSE 1008   MEMPHIS JUG BAND: Memphis Jug Band (1927 – 34)

I Packed My Suitcase
Kansas City Blues
Evergreen Money Blues
Coal Oil Blues
Peaches In the Springtime
Jug Band Waltz
Feed Your Friend With a Long–Handled Spoon
I Whipped My Woman with a Single–Tree
Stonewall Blues

He's In the Jailhouse Now (as Will Shade & the Memphis
       Sheiks)
Move That Thing (as Carolina Peanut Boys)
You Got Me Rollin' (as Carolina Peanut Boys)
My Love Is Cold
Jazzbo Stomp
Tear It Down, Bed Slats and All
Fishin' In the Dark
Rukas Juice and Chittlin'
Jug Band Quartette

Release date: Aug. 1986 (MM89)
Subtitled "The Remaining Titles", this completed the issue of all recorded work, along with Collector's Classics CC–2, Roots RL–322 & 337 and Yazoo 1067 (double LP). 1 & 2 = Will Shade, Ben Ramsey, Will Weldon, Vol Stevens & Jennie Clayton; 3 = Will Shade, Will Weldon, Vol Stevens & Charles Polk; 4 & 5 = Will Shade, Ben Ramsey, Will Weldon, Vol Stevens & Charlie Polk; 6 = Will Shade, Ben Ramsey, Charlie Burse, Vol Stevens & Jab Jones; 7 = Will Shade, Ben Ramsey, Charlie Burse, Milton Robie & Jab Jones; 8 = Will Shade, Ben Ramsey, Charlie Burse, Charlie 'Bozo' Nickerson & Jab Jones; 9 = Will Shade, Ben Ramsey, Charlie Burse & Hambone Lewis; 10 = Will Shade, Vol Stevens, Charlie Burse, Jab Jones & Charlie 'Bozo' Nickerson; 11 & 12 = Will Shade, Charlie Burse, Will Weldon (possibly), Ben Ramsey, Charlie Nickerson and unknown jug player; 13 to18 = Will Shade, Charlie Pierce, Jab Jones, Charlie Burse & Robert Burse.

MSE 1009   BARBECUE BOB: Barbecue Bob (Robert Hicks)1927 – 30

When the Saints Go Marching In
Jesus' Blood Can Make Me Whole
Easy Rider Don't You Deny My Name
It Won't Be Long Now – Part 1 (as Barbecue
       Bob and Laughing Charlie)
It Won't Be Long Now – Part 2 (as above)
Goin' Up the Country
Ease It to Me Blues
She's Gone Blues

Cold Wave Blues
Good Time Rounder
Red Hot Mama Papa's Going to Cool You Off
Trouble Done Bore Me Down
Unnamed Title
She Moves It Just Right
Yo Yo Blues No. 2
Darktown Gamblin' – Part 1 (The Crap Game) (as Robert &
       Charlie Hicks)

Release date: April 1987 (MM89)
Subtitled "The Remaining Titles".

**MSE 1010   BOBBIE LEECAN & ROBERT COOKSEY: Bobbie Leecan and Robert Cooksey
       (1926 – 27)**

Black Cat Bone Blues
Dirty Guitar Blues
Dollar Blues (as Martin and Robert [Alfred Martin
       & Robert Cooksey])
Maxwell and Peoria Blues (as Martin and Robert)
South Street Blues (as Martin and Robert)
Hock My Shoes (as Martin and Robert)
Ain't She Sweet
Don't You Let Your Head Hang Down

Royal Palm Special
Blue Harmonica
Macon Georgia Cut Out (as Blind Bobbie Baker)
Nobody Knows You When You're Down and Out (as above)
Memphis Shake (as Dixie Jazzers Washboard Band)
My Old Daddy's Got a Brand New Way To Love (as above)
Kansas City Shuffle (as Dixie Jazzers Washboard Band)
Black Cat Bones (as Dixie Jazzers Washboard Band)

Release date: April 1987 (MM89)
Subtitled "The Remaining Titles". Dixie Jazzers Washboard Band included Tom Morris, Robert Cooksey, Bobby Leecan, Mike Jackson & Eddie Edinburgh.

MSE 1011   ROOSEVELT SYKES: Roosevelt Sykes 1929 – 34

Black River Blues (Roosevelt Sykes)
Bury That Thing (Roosevelt Sykes)
I Love You More And More (Willie Kelly)
Cotton Seed Blues (Easy Papa Johnson)
Drinkin' Woman Blues (Easy Papa Johnson)
In Here With Your Heavy Stuff (Isabel Sykes)
Don't Rush Yourself (Isabel Sykes)
Low Down Rounders Blues (C. McFadden)
Last Journey Blues (Charlie McFadden)

Hold It Where You Got It (Charlie McFadden)
Lonesome Ghost Blues (Charlie McFadden)
Try My Whiskey Blues (Clarence Harris)
Lonesome Clock Blues (Clarence Harris)
Mr. Carl's Blues (Carl Rafferty) (Johnnie Strauss)
Hard Working Woman (Johnnie Strauss)
St. Louis Johnnie Blues (Johnnie Strauss)
Radio Broadcasting Blues (Johnnie Strauss)
Old Market Street Blues (Johnnie Strauss)

Release date: Feb. 1988 (MM89)
Subtitled "Mostly New to LP".

MSE 1012 MISSISSIPPI SHEIKS: Mississippi Sheiks Volume 2 1930 – 34

Sheiks Special
Dear Little Girl
Please Don't Wake It Up
She's a Bad Girl
Tell Me What the Cats Fight About
Kind Treatment
Lazy Lazy River
Too Long
Bed Spring Poker

When You're Sick with the Blues
She's Crazy About Her Lovin'
Tell Me to Do Right
Kitty Cat Blues
Show Me What You Got
Hitting The Numbers
It's Done Got Wet
Ahe's Got Something Crazy
You'll Work Down to Me Someday

Release date: Feb. 1988 (MM89)
Subtitled "Mostly New to LP".

MSE 1013 LONNIE JOHNSON: Lonnie Johnson Volume Two 1927 – 32

Kansas City Blues – part 1
Kansas City Blues – part 2
Carless Love
I Want a Little Some o' That What You Got
You Done Lost Your Good Thing Now – pt. 1
You Done Lost Your Good Thing Now – pt. 2
Death Valley Is Just Half Way to My Home
I Got The Best Jelly Roll In Town – part 2
Don't Drive Me From Your Door

Low Down St. Louis Blues
Beautiful But Dumb
From a Wash Woman On Up
Not The Chump I Use to Be
Best Jockey In Town
Sleepy Water Blues
Cat You Been Messin' Around
Men, Get Wise To Yourself.
Sam, You're Just a Rat

Release date: June 1988 (MM89)

MSE 1014 THE FAMOUS HOKUM BOYS: The Famous Hokum Boys 1930 – 1931

Somebody's Been Using That Thing
Black Cat Rag
Nancy Jane
That's the Way She Likes It
You Can't Get Enough of That Stuff
Come On Mama
Ain't Going There No More
You Do It

That Stuff I Got
Pie Eating Strut
Killing Floor Blues (Kansas City Kitty)
What's That I Smell (Georgia Tom and Jane Lucas)
When Can I Get It (Kansas City Kitty and Georgia Tom)
That Thing's A Mess (Kansas City Kitty and Georgia Tom)
Kansas City Kitty
Root Man Blues (Kansas City Kitty)
Close Made Papa (Kansas City Kitty)

Release date: 1988 (MM89)
Side 1 tracks and first two tracks on side 2 credited to "The Famous Hokum Boys".

MSEX 2001/2002 VARIOUS ARTISTS: Songsters and Saints Vol. 1 Vocal Traditions On Race Records

Side 1– Dances and Travelling Shows
Turkey Buzzard Blues (Peg Leg Howell and Eddie Anthony)
Gonna Tip Out Tonight (Pink Anderson and Simmie Dooley)
Beans ("Beans" Hambone – El Morrow)
Under the Chicken Tree (Earl McDonald's Original Louisville Jug Band)
Mysterious Coon (Alec Johnson, Bo Chatman, Charlie McCoy, Joe McCoy and unk.)
The Coon Crap Game ("Big Boy" George Owens)
He's In the Jailhouse Now (Memphis Sheiks)
Elder Green Blues (Charley Patton acc. H. Sims)
Way Down In Arkensas (Hambone Willie Newbern)

Side 3 – Baptist and Sanctified Preachers
The Hand of the Lord Was Upon Me (and I Went Out in the Spirit) (Rev. Jim Beal)
After the Ball Is Over (Rev. A. W. Nix)
As the Eagle Stirreth In Her Nest (Rev. Isiah Shelton)
Silk Worms and Boll Weavils (Rev. J. M. Milton)
Old Time Baptism – Part 2 (Rev. R. M. Massey)
Baptism By Water, and Baptism By the Holy Ghost (Rev. J. E. Burch)
The Solemn Warning (Rev. E. S. (Shy) Moore)
Prove All Things (Elder Curry acc. Elder Charles Beck and Ann Williams)
God's Mercy To Colonel Lindbergh (Rev. Leora Ross with the Church of the Living God Jubilee Singers)

Side 2 – Comment, Parodies & Ballad Heroes
Furniture Man (Lil McClintock)
Can't Put the Bridle on That Mule This Morning
      (Julius Daniels acc. prob. Wilbert
      Andrews)
The Panic Is On (Hezekiah Jenkins acc. L.
      McLain)
I Heard the Voice of a Pork Chop (Bogus Ben
      Covington)
G. Burns Is Gonna Rise Again (Johnson–
      Nelson–Porkchop)
Good Old Turnip Greens (Bo Chatman acc.
      prob. Charlie McCoy and Walter Vincson)
John Henry Blues (Two Poor Boys)
Railroad Bill (Will Bennett)
Clair and Pearley Blues (Kid Coley acc. Clifford Haynes)

Side 4 – Gospel Soloists and Evangelists
You Have Lost Jesus (Missionary Josephine Mills and Sister
      Elizabeth Cooper)
When I Take My Vacation In Heaven (Mother McCollum)
Down On Me (Eddie Head and His Family)
I Am Born to Preach the Gospel (Washington Phillips)
Telephone to Glory (Blind Roosevelt Graves and Brother
      acc. Uaroy Graves, "Baby Jay" James & Will Ezell)
Death Is Only a Dream (The Guitar Evangelist)
Your Enemy Cannot Harm You (Blind Willie Davis)
Pure Religion (Blind Nesbit)
When That Great Ship Went Down (William and Versey Smith)

Release date: Nov. 1984 (MM89)
2–LP. Special issue to complement Paul Oliver's book, "Songsters & Saints". "Beans" Hambone is James Albert. Earl McDonald's Original Louisville Jug Band comprises McDonald, Lucien Smith, Benny Calvin and Cal Smith. Memphis Sheiks comprises Will Shade, Vol Stevens, Charlie Burse, Jab Jones and Charlie Nickerson. Two Poor Boys are Joe Evans and Arthur McClain. Side 3 tracks are accompanied by congregation unless other credits are given. The Guitar Evangelist is Edward W. Clayborn.

MSEX 2003/2004 **VARIOUS ARTISTS: Songsters and Saints Vol. 2 Vocal Traditions On Race Records**

Side 1 – Medicine Show Songsters
I'm Alabama Bound (Papa Charlie Jackson)
Long Gone Lost John (Papa Charlie Jackson)
Money Never Runs Out (Cannon's Jug
      Stompers)
Can You Blame the Coloured Man (Banjo Joe)
Bye, Bye, Policeman (Jim Jackson)
My Monday Woman Blues (Jim Jackson)
Old Dog Blue (Jim Jackson)
Mr. Crump Don't Like It (Beale Street Sheiks)
Chicken You Can Roost Behind the Moon (Beale
      Street Sheiks)

Side 3 – The Straining Preachers
The Downfall of Nebuchadnezzar (Rev. J. C. Burnett)
The Gambler's Doom (Rev. J. C. Burnett)
Yonder Comes My Lord with a Bible In His Hand (Rev. J. M.
      Gates)
God's Wrath in the St. Louis Cyclone (Rev. J. M. Gates acc.
      Deacon Leon Davis, Sisters Jordan and Norman)
The Eagle Stirs Her Nest (Rev. J. M. Gates)
The Half Ain't Never Been Told (Rev. F. W. McGee, unk. acc.)
Jonah in the Belly of the Whale (as above)
Come and See (Rev. D. C Rice acc. congregation, ? Hunter
      and Louis Hooper)
We Got the Same Kind of Power Over Here (Rev. D. C. Rice
      acc. Sisters Black and Rice)

Side 2 – Songsters East and West
A Chicken Can Waltz the Gravy Around–1
      (Stovepipe No. 1 and David Crockett)
A Woman Gets Tired of the Same Man All the
      Time (as above)
Old Country Stomp–1 (Ragtime Texas)
Bob McKinney (Ragtime Texas)
Arkansas (Ragtime Texas)
Traveling Coon (Luke Jordan)
Cocaine Blues (Luke Jordan)
He's In the Jailhouse Now–1 (Blind Blake
      acc. Gus Cannon)
West Coast Blues (Blind Blake acc. Gus Cannon)

Side 4 – Saints of Church and Street
It's All Right Now (Arizona Dranes)
Just Look (Arizona Dranes acc. unknown)
I Wish My Mother Was On That Train (Blind Jo Taggart acc.
      Emma Taggart)
There's a Hand Writing on the Wall (Blind Jo Taggart acc.
      Joshua White)
If I Had My Way I'd Tear that Building Down (Blind Willie
      Johnson)
The Rain Don't Fall On Me (as above acc. Angeline Johnson)
The Latter Rain Is Fall (Elders McIntorsh and Edwards acc.
      Sisters Bessie Johnson and Melinda Taylor)
He Got Better Things for You (Memphis Sanctified Singers)

Release date: May 1985 (MM89)
2–LP. Special issue to complement Paul Oliver's book, "Songsters & Saints". Banjo Joe is Gus Cannon. Beale Street Sheiks are Frank Stokes and Dan Sane. Stovepipe No. 1 is Sam Jones. Ragtime Texas is Henry Thomas. Side three tracks have accompaniment from the congregation unless other credits are given. Memphis Sanctified Singers are Bessie Johnson, Melinda Taylor, Sally Sumier and Will Shade.

Education packs

Saydisc produced several education packs for use in UK schools. The *Listen To This!* packs included A4–sized books by Music Education Consultant, Christine Richards, whilst *Percussion Around the World* included a large wallchart and was a joint production between Saydisc and PCET Wallcharts. All were available on either CD or cassette and the plastic blister packs were manufactured so as to hold either format. The first two volumes of *Listen To This!* were priced at £19 each, or £35 if buying both. *Religions of the World* was also written by Christine Richards and was another joint production between Saydisc and PCET. All tracks are still in use in schools, these resources now being available online in various educational digital libraries.

CD–KS 1001   VARIOUS: Listen to This! (Key Stage 1)

Song of Papa Kiko (from CD–SDL 403)
Redonna Sorte Waltz (from CD–SDL 359)
Windy Old Weather (from CD–SDL 405)
Bunyoro Madina (from CD–SDL 389)
Clin D'Oeil (from CD–SDL 353)
South Wind (from CD–SDL 394)
Pavane et Galliarde d'Angleterre (from
        CD–SAR 51)
Ansam (from CD–SDL 387)
Kerry Polka (from CD–SDL 348)
Karamajong Children's Song (from
        CD–SDL 389)
The Races (from CD–SDL 325)
Three O'Clock in the Morning (from
        CD–SDL 355)
Rain Forest Dream (from CD–SDL 384)
Rejoice and Be Merry (from CD–SDL 366)
Camel Herders' Song (from CD–SDL 376)
As I Set Off To Turkey (from CD–SDL 402)
Drum Dance (from CD–SDL 403)

Tuba Gallicalis (from CD–SDL 364)
Festival of the Flowers (from CD–SDL 388)
Newcastle (from CD–SDL 393)
Bowl Voices (extract) / Lullaby (from CD–SDL 326)
Coulter's Candy (from CD–SDL 391)
War Drums (from CD–SDL 389)
Scottische (from CD–SDL 374)
Drops of Brandy (from CD–SDL 360)
I'm Off to Charlestown (as above)
Moss Roses (as above)
Music for Kataragama (from CD–SDL 376)
Ronell's Reel (from CD–SDL 343)
Snochti Vecher U Vas Byah (from CD–SDL 396)
Dosto, Mome Dosto (as above)
Staines Morris (from CD–SDL 373)
Pepper is Black (as above)
Sha! Shtil! (from CD–SDL 395)
Avrix Mi Galanica (as above)
Auntie Monica (from CD–SDL 338)
Robert Burns is Born Here (as above)

Release date: January 1995
Cassette: CKS 1001
With book.

CD–KS 1002   VARIOUS: Listen to This! (Key Stage 2)

Kyng Harry VIII Pavyn (from CD–SAR 51)
The Flower Fair (from CD–SDL 325)
What Shall We Do with a Drunken Sailor?
        (from CD–SDL 405)
Lilliburlero (from CD–SAR 28)
Edongo Dance (from CD–SDL 389)
Post Horn Gallop (from CD–SAR 30)
Sailor's Hornpipe (from CD–SDL 359)
Sailor's Hornpipe (diff. version) (as above)
Mire of Eamaki (from CD–SDL 403)
Fourpence a Day (from CD–SDL 402)
Jute Mill Song (from CD–SDL 391)
Kotal Ghurhlo (from CD–SDL 401)
Niel Gow's Lament for the Death of His
        Second Wife (from CD–SDL 348)
Cerga (from CD–SDL 387)
Music from Compline (from CD–SDL 349)
L'Autrier Pastour Seoit (from CD–SAR 36)

Fireside Song (from CD–SDL 376)
The Triumph (from CD–SDL 360)
Arise and Hail This Joyful Day (as above)
Bre Nikola, Nikola (from CD–SDL 396)
Kielder Jock's Dance (from CD–SDL 343)
Happy Reunion (from CD–SDL 368)
Cushion Dance (from CD–SDL 373)
Una Matica de Ruda (from CD–SDL 395)
Ding Dong Merrily on High (from CD–SDL 366)
Change Ringing (from CD–SDL 327)
Down in Yon Forest (as above)
Song with a Harp (from CD–SDL 389)
Sailing (from CD–SDL 380)
Aitutaki Drum Dance (from CD–SDL 403)
Eclats de Rire (from CD–SDL 353)
Birdsong (from CD–SDL 325)
The Night–Peece or The Shaking of the Tree (from
        CD–SDL 393)

Release date: January 1995
Cassette: CKS 1002
With book.

CD–KS 1003   VARIOUS: Listen to This! (Key Stage 3)

Amanecer Andino (from CD–SDL 388)
Chassidic Melody 24 (from CD–SDL 395)
Disguised as a Silverer of Mirrors (from
        CD–SDL 367)
Aki No Shirabe (as above)
Rasti Bore (from CD–SDL 396)
Zebaidir Song (from CD–SDL 389)
Bird Dance (from CD–SDL 403)
Melody Bolero (from CD–SDL 353)
Alleluya Nativitas (extract) (from CD–SAR 59)
Munda Maria (as above)
Shepherds' Music (from CD–SDL 401)
Sama'l Thaqil (from CD–SDL 387)
L'Hom Armé (from CD–SDL 364)
Windsong 3 (from CD–SDL 394)
Alborada (from CD–SAR 22)

Turkish Traditional Tune (as above)
An Dro Nevas (as above)
La Quinta Estampie Real (as above)
Etenraku (as above)
Bergamasca (from CD–SDL 409)
Meditating On the Past (from CD–SDL 368)
The Drunken Sailor (from CD–SDL 348)
Dances from the Time of Queen Elizabeth I (from CD-SDL 373)
Shenpadei Folksong (from CD–SDL 325)
Hoko War Dance (from CD–SDL 389)
African Sanctus (from Silva Classics LP, SILKD 6003,
        African Sanctus)
Prince Rupert's March / Prins Robbert Masco (from
        CD–SAR 28)
Mouth Music (from CD–SDL 411)

Release date: 1996   **Cassette:** CKS 1003

CD–KS 1004   VARIOUS: Percussion Around the World

Vientos Del Sur
Amanecer Andino
Llorando Se Fue
Ubiquity
Euphoria
Asi El Acero
Ansam
Alwan Mizan
The Lilting Banshee
Busoga Fishermen
Teso Fishermen
Bunyoro Madinda

War Drums
Ritual Burial Dance
Jameko
Bowl Voices
Lullaby
The Shepherds' Music
Rag Megh
Demon Dance
Papalotl
Temazcal
Pacific Samba

Cassette: CKS 1004
With wallchart and teacher's notes. For Key Stages 2 and 3.

CD–KS 1005   VARIOUS: Religions of the World

The bell at Sarnath
Buddhism in China: Dao Ti jindeng (Cleaning
        the Golden Lantern)
Tantric Buddhism: Tantra ritual at Gyuto, Tibet
Invocation
Zen Buddhism: Drum Call
Church bells 1 – Anglican church bells
Church bells 2 – Sunday morning bell
Church bells 3 – Coptic Church bell
Plainsong: Veni Creator Spiritus
Benedictus from 'Mass for Four Voices' (Byrd)
18th century hymn style: Lo, He Comes with
        Clouds Descending
Christianity in the Pacific: Voqa Tu Mai
Gospel music: Oh, Happy Day
Greek Orthodox Church: Alleluia
Greek Orthodox Church: Ekphonese – 'We
        Have Seen the True Light'
Russian Orthodox Church: From my Youth
Russian Orthodox Church: Our Father

Russian Orthodox Church: Ne Imany – 'Prayer to the Mother
        of God'
Russian Orthodox Church: Holy God
Hindu Call to Prayer
Arti
Vaishnava Jana
Adhan
Peshrev
Allah Ya Daim
Men's Wedding Song
Hamd (Allah Hoo)
Jain Puja
Shofar Signals
Kol Nidre
Shalom Aleichem
Hashem, hashem
Adon Olam
Shinto Congregational Chant
Adi Granth Recitation
Avo sikh satguru ke piario

With book and wallchart.

Contract pressings

Saydisc organised manufacture for various individuals and organisations with, generally, the marketing of the records being undertaken by those individuals and organisations. There was one deviation from this rule, however, with CP 115 being put on general release. The Jass label was a specialist Dutch label, run by Dick Baaker, for whom (probably) six 7" LPs, playing at 33⅓, were manufactured by Saydisc and marketed by Jass. Although not Saydisc releases, the Jass pressings were assigned places in the SD catalogue sequence, though only two numbers can be confirmed.

Many of these contract pressings were very short runs and are consequently very difficult to find, hence a few more blanks as to track listing in this section. In these cases, either Saydisc does not have file copies, or the file copies are white label copies with no track or artist details. Any information on these releases would be most welcome.

CP 101   UNKNOWN

Gef Lucena has the following to say about this record: "I have a test pressing marked CP101 – it was of some amateur folk group but I don't recall who (not a well–known local group)."

CP 102   UNKNOWN

CP 103   MIKE COOPER JAZZ BAND: Blue Turning Grey Over You

Bugle Boy March	Louisianiay
Take My Hand Precious Lord	China Boy
Wabash Blues	Blue Turning Grey
Rosetta	Indiana
My Blue Heaven	Papa Dip

Release date: 1971
Recorded at the Troubadour in 1971, shortly before the club was closed. Folk fans beware – as the title should suggest, this is not Mike Cooper the blues artists but Mike Cooper the Bristolian trombonist.

CP 104   CARL AMES: The Unforgettable Carl Ames

Release date: 1973
Private recordings of concert harp player, Carl Ames, sponsored and marketed by his brother posthumously. Gef Lucena says, "I seem to remember that this was mis-spelled Unforgetable on the original sleeve!" (Email dated 14th August 2010).

CP 105   CHOIR & INSTRUMENTALISTS OF QUEEN ELIZABETH'S HOSPITAL, BRISTOL: Queen Elizabeth's Hospital, Bristol

Processional: Ein' fest Burg (Bach)	Rejoice in the Lamb (Britten)
Placare Christe Servulis (Dupré)	The Old Hundredth Psalm Tune (Vaughan Williams)
Gagliarda for Brass (Frescobaldi)	
March and Canzona (Purcell)	
Beatus Vir (Monteverdi)	

Release date: 1971
Marketed by the school.

CP 106   UNKNOWN

CP 107   HENBURY SCHOOL: Henbury School Concert

Jerusalem	Gloria from Mass in G No. 12
Jubilate	Something Like a Star
Rosamunde Overture	The Easter Story:
Go Down Jonah	In Lowly Pomp
March from Little Suite No. 2	To Save Us All
Surrey with the Fringe On Top	The Battle Done
	Glad News

Release date: 1972

Subtitled "Colston Hall 1972". White label test pressings in plain sleeve with Saydisc sticker known to exist. Graham Crew, Ralph Rogers & Lorna Aldridge conduct. Includes individual pieces by the School Orchestra, Lower School Choir and the Upper School Choir as well as combined pieces. Organist, Brian Bussell.

CP 108   ECCLESFIELD HANDBELL RINGERS: Ecclesfield Handbell Ringers

Plantation Melodies

Classical Extracts

Russian Parade

Skaters' Waltz (Waldteufel)

Minuet (Boccherini)

Serenade

Song Medley

Minuet and Trio (Mozart)

Overture – Caliph of Baghdad (Boildieu)

Release date: 1974

CP 109   LINDSAY PECK WITH THE FRIARY FOLK GROUP, CLEVEDON: Reality from Dream

Down

Destiny

Careless World

Vagabonds Cry

Arthur Guitar

Floating

Whistling Man

Lovesick Pinks

Forever Farewell

Do You Want to Sing

One Hit Wonder

And It's No Good

Who Can We Blame

Born Traveller

What's Life

Night Child

Free to Dream

Release date: 1975

In a wrap–around card sleeve in PVC outer sleeve. Copies also exist in plain, white sleeve. Recorded in mono with a Saydisc pressing credit on the sleeve.

CP 110   MECHANICAL MUSIC: Concert Choice

Release date: 1976

Reproducing Piano. Recorded for The West Cornwall Museum of Mechanical Music and marketed by the museum.

CP 111   VARIOUS ARTISTS: Barbershop Bonanza

There Goes My Heart (Par Four)

Sweet May (Par Four)

Tree In the Meadow (Par Four)

Bring Back Those Good Old Days (Par Four)

Over the Rainbow (Charnwoods)

It's a Small World (Charnwoods)

Heart of My Heart (Charnwoods)

Edelweiss (Charnwoods)

When You Wish Upon a Star (Shades)

When My Sugar Walks Down the Street (Shades)

Blue Skies (Shades)

If (Shades)

Sitting In a Corner (Prestones)

Back In the Days Gone Me (Prestones)

Back In Dixie (Red Rose Chorus)

I Wanna Girl (Red Rose Chorus)

Battle Hymn of the Republic (Red Rose Chorus)

Release date: 1979

Record sponsored by Carling Black Label. Gef Lucena has the following to say about the recording of this album:

> This was recorded at an entertainment complex at Charnock Richard Services near Preston and the barbershop organizers had managed to get sponsorship from Carling (which was strange in itself as the venue, being part of a motorway service area, was not allowed to sell alcohol) who had paid us in advance to do the recording and produce 1000 LPs. It was, however, a night to remember (or one to forget). The venue was quite popular and attracted large audiences for whatever was put on on a Saturday. We were supposed to be doing a live recording of the various barbershop choruses and quartets performing to this large audience. Unfortunately, the resident compere/DJ had announced the previous Saturday that there was a private booking for the night in question and therefore the auditorium/cum restaurant was closed to the general public. However enough people turned up to get the cash registers tinging constantly and make enough noise to make recording impossible. Not being easily defeated, we managed to find an unused converted barn that was used as a conference room and eventually someone to open it up for us. Good acoustics, quiet and an appropriate size to set up our gear and ferry performers in after their 'stage' performances. Quiet

did I say? That was until the crickets (or cockroaches or some other beasties) behind the old wood-panelling started chirping – very loudly. Not being easily defeated, I said to David Wilkins, our engineer, that we should carry on and we would filter them out later. It should not be difficult, I said, as they appeared to chirp at a fairly precise pitch and could be notched out without affecting the music too much. Not being well versed in the habits of crickets I hadn't allowed for the fact that they get increasingly excited as the evening progresses and with excitement comes a gradual increase in pitch. However, not being easily defeated, I confirmed that we were not going to give up now and that we would sort it somehow. And sort it we did at the editing stage by tracking the steadily rising pitch of the crickets and applying a suitable notch filter. I don't think there is any audible residual cricket noise and the music was not noticeably affected – and we kept our money from Carling. Only recently we started receiving requests for this privately circulated album as someone had chosen a track as a castaway on Desert Island Discs! (Email dated 14th August 2010).

CP 112   VARIOUS ARTISTS: The Rest of British Barbershop – Caister '78

Shine On Harvest Moon (Soundswell)
They Go Wild Over Me / Ma She's Making
    Eyes at Me (Fourth Amendment)
When I'm Walking with My Sweetness Down By
    the Sugar Cane (Harmony Heritage)
Alexander's Ragtime Band (Tynetones)
Back in Dixie Again (C. Siders)
Nightime in Dixiland / Rock–a–Bye Your Baby
    (River Bouys)
My Home Town (First Edition)
Mason–Dixie Line (Mellowtones)
On the Mississippi (Par Four)

Easter Parade (Chesham Buckaneers)
South Rampart Street Parade (Berkshire Barbershoppers)
Strolling Down Harmony Lane (Hove Harmonizers)
If I Had My Way (Charmwoods)
There's a Tree In the Meadow (Nottingham Gateway Chorus)
For Me and My Gal (Harmony Revival)
Goodbye My Lady Love (Harbour Masters)
Dixieland Medley (Saffron Sound)
Piano Roll Blues (Westering)

Release date: 1979
Saydisc recording marketed by the barbershop choirs and quartets. Back of sleeve blank. Side 1 subtitled "Quartets" and side 2 subtitled "Choruses". This was a compilation of out-takes from SDL 295.

CP 113   VARIOUS ARTISTS: With Cheerful Voice

Onward Christian Soldiers
The Lord's My Shepherd
Sweet Is the Work, My God, My King
O Worship the King
The Old Rugged Cross
O Come All Ye Faithful
Away In a Manger
Abide with Me

Praise My Soul the King of Heaven
Praise to the Holiest In the Height
Holy, Holy, Holy, Lord God Almighty
O Love That Will Not Let Me Go
Love Divine All Loves Excelling
Guide Me O Thou Great Redeemer
Angel Voices Ever Singing
All People that On Earth Do Dwell

Release date: 1979
Church congregations & choral societies. Recorded and marketed by BBC Radio Stoke–on–Trent.

CP 114   FUMBLE: Rumble with Fumble

Lucille
Your Mama Don't Dance
Runaround Sue
Mean Woman Blues
Book of Love
Poetry In Motion
That's All Right, Mama

Baby I Don't Care
Get Up
All Shook Up
Corrina Corrina
Say Mama
Ebony Eyes
Nutrocker
Jailhouse Rock
Let It Rock

Release date: 1979
Recorded live and marketed by Fumble, the rock and roll revival band from Weston–super–Mare. Subtitled "The Official Bootleg".

CP 115   PAUL WILSON & BEN VAN WEEDE: The One Eyed Fiddler

Jacob or Enrico / Haul Away the Hawser
Johnny Sands
A Reele
The Ragged Beggarman
The Blue–Eyed Stranger or The Poor But
      Honest Soldier
The Turnpike Gate
The Labouring Man
Hunt the Squirrel
The Rakish Young Fellow
Joan's Ale
The Breast Knot
The Butcher and the Parson
The Favourite Quickstep
The Tippy / A Jig
Long A–Growing
Dribbles of Brandy
Bampton Fair
The One Eyed Fiddler / The Cliff (Hornpipes)
The Southern English Labourer
Miss Richards' Hornpipe

Release date: Nov. 1980 (MM89)
CD: CD–SDL 115
This title was put on general release even though CP prefixes usually denoted private editions marketed by the artist. Paul Wilson, vocals, fiddle, Appalachian dulcimer, banjo, guitar, accordion; Ben van Weede, fiddle, viola, whistles. Folk songs and music from Southern England, including some collected by Thomas Hardy. Note that the recent CD issue was assigned an "SDL" prefix (CD–SDL 115).

CP 116   NATURE: Countryside Calling

Bells of St. Mary's Church, Selbourne,
      Hampshire
Woodland
Garden
Heath
Farm and Downland
The Sea at Totland Bay, Isle of Wight
Seashore
Estuary
Marsh
River

Release date: 1981
Subtitled, "Sounds of Hampshire and the Isle of Wight recorded by Yoland Kemp Robinson". Track names taken from the labels: the sleeve credits track 1 as "Church Bells", track 5 as "Farmland" and track 6 as "The Sea". The LP includes poetry readings by Norman Goodland and Barry Lowe and music from Bob Mills and Dave Williams.

CP 117   VALE OF ARROW CHOIR: Vale of Arrow Choir

Glorious Is Thy Name (Mozart)
The Blue Bird (Stanford)
Harvest Song (Brahms)
All Through the Night
Ave Maria (Elgar)
Come, Let Us Alla-Maying Go (Handel)
Pslam – Belmont
Cytgan Yr Haleliwia (Beethoven)
How Lovely Are Thy Dwellings (Brahms)
Go Lovely Rose
Poet and Peasant Overture (Suppe)
Ave Verum Corpus (Mozart)
Psalm – Orlington

Release date: 1981
Cassette: CPC 117
Marketed by the Choir.

CP 118   RHYMNEY VALLEY FESTIVAL SCHOOLS ORCHESTRA: Rhymney Valley Festival Schools Orchestra

Eine Kleine Nachtmusik (Mozart):
  1st Movement (Allegro)
Festival Suite for String Orchestra (Burtch):
  Promenade and Gallop
Violin Concerto in D minor (Mendelssohn):
  1st Movement (Allegro)
Chanson de Matin (Elgar arr. W. H. Read)
Chorale for Strings (Stoker)
Symphony No. 1 (Boyce):
  Allegro
  Andante docle
  Vivace
Upstairs Downstairs (Waltz theme from the TV series)
Simple Symphony (Britten)
Pizzicato–Polka (J. & J. Strauss)
Brandenburg Concerto No. 3 in G major (Bach):
  1st Movement

Release date: 1980
Marketed by the organisers.

CP 119   VARIOUS ARTISTS: In Every Corner Sing

O Praise Ye the Lord
Bright the Vision That Delighted
As Pants the Hart
Come, Ye Thankful People Come
When I Survey the Wondrous Cross
There Is a Green Hill
Hark the Herald Angels Sing
Alleluya! Sing to Jesus
Soldiers of Christ Arise

Ye Holy Angels Bright
Immortal Invisible
Morning Has Broken
Lead Us Heavenly Father
All Things Bright and Beautiful
Jesu Lover of My Soul
As with Gladness
Amazing Grace
Lead Kindly Light
And Did Those Feet

Release date: 1980
Cassette: CP–C 119
Church congregations & choral societies. Recorded and marketed by BBC Radio Stoke–on–Trent.

CP–C 120   REDNOCK SCHOOL BAND: Rednock School Band (cassette)

Release date: 1981
Recorded by Saydisc in Dursley and marketed by the School.

CP–C 121   COTSWOLD MALE VOICE CHOIR: Cotswold Male Voice Choir (cassette)

Release date: 1981
Marketed by the Choir.

CP 122   LYDBROOK SILVER BAND: Lydbrook Silver Band

The Mill On the Cliff
Edelweiss
NIbelungen March
Cavatina
Cuckoo Waltz
Sailing

The Queen's Own (March)
Forge Hill
Tabarinage (Buffoonery)
Don't Cry for Me Argentina
Gershwin for Brass

Release date: 1981
Musical Director Lyndon Baglin

CP 123   GREATER MANCHESTER RADIO CHORALE: Manchester Carols

O Come All Ye Faithful
The Twelve Days of Christmas
Away In a Manger
Good King Wenceslas
Balulalow / This Little Babe
Pilgrim Caravan

Once in Royal David's City
Ding Dong Merrily On High
God Rest Ye Merry Gentlemen
The Holly and the Ivy
Have Yourself a Merry Little Christmas
While Shepherds Watched Their Flocks
Hark the Herald Angels Sing

Release date: 1981
Cassette: CP–C 123 (see below)
Recorded and marketed by BBC Radio Manchester. Saydisc master list includes cassette catalogue number, though the pressing card does not mention a cassette issue.

CP–C 124   UNKNOWN ARTIST: Music At Christmas (cassette)

Release date: 1981
This was by a children's choir, but the Saydisc master list does not have a record of the choir's name.

CP–C 125   BIRCHWOOD JUNIOR CHOIR: Title unknown (cassette)

Release date: 1981
Marketed by the School.

CP–C 126   BBC RADIO BRISTOL SINGERS: Title unknown (cassette)

Release date: 1982
Recorded by BBC Radio Bristol and marketed by them and the choir.

CP–C 127   FOREST GREEN ROVERS: Forest Green Rovers (cassette)

Release date: 1982
Recorded by Radio Gloucester and marketed by themselves and the football team.

CP 128   GNOSALL HANDBELL RINGERS: The Sound of Bells Vol 2

Radetsky March (J. Strauss)
Arrival of the Queen of Sheba (Handel)
Cornet Carillon (Binge)
Welcome America (medley)
Gaite Parisienne (Offenbach)

Jingle Bells
Carol Medley
King Cotton (Sousa)
Roses from the South (J. Strauss)
The Great Waldo Pepper March
Estudiantina Waltz (Waldteufel)
I Got Rhythm

Release date: 1982
Cassette: CP–C 128
Marketed by the group.

CP 129   KENNET AND AVON HANDBELL RINGERS: Kennet and Avon Handbell Ringers

Skipton Rig
Scarborough Fair
Minuet
Home Sweet Home
Getting Upstairs
The Worshipful Master
Minuet
Bobby Shafto
Military March
Theme and Variations for Handbells

The Sound of Silence
Minuet
Side By Side
Gavotte and Musette
The Londonderry Air
Away In a Manger
Unto Us a Child Is Born
We Three Kings
O Come O Come Emmanuel

Release date: 1983
Cassette: CPC 129

CP 130   MASSED POLICE CHOIRS: 100 Years of Caring

Release date: 1984
Cassette: CP–C 130
Marketed by the NSPCC.

CP 131   VALE OF ARROW CHOIR: Songs for All Seasons

Laudete Dominum
All In the April Evening
Daffodils
As Torrents in Summer
Linden Lea
Holy City
Tyrolean Cradle Song
Close Thine Eyes

A Boy Was Born In Bethlehem
O Leave Your Sheep
Polish Carol
Sweet As the Song the Virgin Sang
In Excelsis Gloria
It Came Upon the Midnight Clear
Now In Bethlehem
The Three Kings
Silent Night, Holy Night

Release date: 1984
Cassette: CP–C 131
Marketed by the Choir. Although a private release, the label design is Saydisc.

CP 132   **BELLES AND BEAUS HANDBELL RINGERS: Ring In England**

Allemande (Vivaldi)
Chorale and Alleluia (Bach)
Toccata (Paradies)
Ebb Tide
Greensleeves
Mood Indigo
Great Day
A German Music Box
Peal of Eight

Radetsky March (J. Strauss)
Gipsy Baron March (J. Strauss II)
Black and White Rag
12th Street Rag
Skaters' Waltz (Waldteufel)
Rainbow Connection
Malaguena

Release date: 1984
Marketed by the group.

CP 133   *UNKNOWN*

CP 134   *UNKNOWN*

CP 135   *UNKNOWN*

CP 136   **TONGWYNLAIS TEMPERANCE BAND: Crazy Music**

Castell Coch
Troublemaker
Our Boys Will Shine Tonight
Playa Del Rey
Sky Train
Strangers In the Night
Trombola
One Voice

Hijack
Barney's Tune
Clochemerle
Crazy Music In the Air
I Write the Songs
Bacharach for Brass

Release date: 1988
Marketed by the band.

JASS 601   **HENRY RED ALLEN ORCHESTRA / J. C. HIGGINBOTHAM SIX HICKS (7" LP)**

Possibly assigned to 180 in the SD sequence, in which case the catalogue number would be 33SD 180.

JASS 602   **JELLY–ROLL MORTON & HIS RED HOT PEPPERS / UNKNOWN (7" LP)**

Pretty Lil
Sing a Little Song Each Day – Jelly–Roll Morton
That'll Never Do – King Oliver

Oil Well
Gambling Jack
Futuristic Blues

The catalogue number 33SD 203 from the main SD sequence was assigned to this contract pressing. The runoff includes the Saydisc matrix numbers. No artist credits on labels.

JASS 603   **Prob. KING OLIVER & HIS ORCHESTRA / UNKNOWN (7" LP)**

White label test pressing known to exist. Runoff includes only Jass matrix number. Probably includes *When You're Smiling (the Whole World Smiles With You)* by King Oliver and His Orchestra.

JASS 604   **Prob. DUKE ELLINGTON / JOE TURNER & HIS MEMPHIS MEN (7" LP)**

Doin' the New Lowdown
That Rhythm Man
Saturday Night Function

I Must Have That Man
Freeze and Melt
Mississippi Moan

The catalogue number 33SD 204 from the main SD sequence was assigned to this contract pressing. The runoff includes the Saydisc matrix numbers. No artist credits on labels. Various 1929 recordings including Duke Ellington.

JASS 605   **UNKNOWN (7" LP)**

Unknown if this was manufactured by Saydisc as no pressing card can be found

JASS 606   PIRON'S NEW ORLEANS ORCHESTRA (7" LP)

New Orleans Wiggle	West Indies Blues
Mama's Gone, Goodbye	Red Man Blues
Do–doodle–oom	Do Just As I Say

Release date: May 1971

White label test pressing known to exist. Runoff includes Jass matrix number only. Label is a lighter shade of green than other records in the series. No artist credits on labels.

JASS 607   Prob. MOUND CITY B. B. / EDDIE CONDON (7" LP)

Georgia On My Mind	Your Rascal, You
I Can't Believe That You're In Love With Me	The Eel
The Darktown Strutters Ball	Home Cooking

Release date: May 1972

Runoff includes Jass matrix number only. No artist credits on labels. The Saydisc pressing card credits "M.C.B.B/Condon". Reviewed in the February 1973 issue of *Storyville*. Very unlikely that an SD number was assigned to this as all contemporaneous SD catalogue numbers are accounted for.

JASS 608   BENNIE MOTEN'S KANSAS CITY ORCHESRTA / JIMMIE LUNCEFORD   & HIS CHICKASAW SYNCOPATORS (7" LP)

Thick Lip Stomp – 1	Muscle Shoal Blues
Harmony Blues – 1	In Dat Mornin'
White Lightnin' Blues	Sweet Rhythm

White label test pressing known to exist. Runoff includes Jass matrix number only. No artist credits on labels. The Saydisc pressing card credits "Moten/Lunceford" and the full artist credit listed above is sourced from http://www.bixeibenhamburg.com/stamps/111/111_shelf_list_2.html. Very unlikely that an SD number was assigned to this as all contemporaneous SD catalogue numbers are accounted for. This may not even have been manufactured by Saydisc as no pressing card exists.

BUP 1   VARIOUS ARTISTS: Evening Post Carol Concert 1983

Hark the Herald Angels Sing (A)	God Rest Ye Merry Gentlemen (A)
Carol Based on 'Greensleeves' (B)	Torches (E)
Saint Nicholas' Day In the Morning (B)	Infant Holy (E)
The First Nowell (A)	Ding Dong Merrily On High (E)
"On Christmas Trees" – extracts from 'The	O Little Town of Bethlehem (A)
Christmas Tree' by C. Day Lewis;	The Grasmere Carol (B)
'The Cultivation of Christmas	The Christmas Bells (B)
Trees' by T.S. Eliot (C)	The Repentance of Scrooge – an extract from 'A Christmas
Innocent Little Lamb (D)	Carol' by Charles Dickens (C)
See Amid the Winter's Snow (D)	O Come All Ye Faithful (A)
Gloucestershire Wassail (D)	
Once In Royal David's City (A)	

Release date: 1984

Marketed by BBC Radio Bristol and Bristol Evening Post. Recorded by Radio Bristol. A = not specifically credited; B = Combined Ladies' Choirs conducted by Abigail Dodds, MBE, accompanist Hazel Wickham; C = readers from the Bristol Old Vic Theatre School (Lisa Hollander and Paul Matthews); D = The Avon and Somerset Police Choir conducted by Sheila Rice, accompanist Lewis Wood; E = singers from the County of Avon A–Level Music Centre conducted by Philip Pratt. Accompaniment by The City of Bristol Band conducted by Alwyn Lloyd; Organist, Colin Hunt; Musical Director and Conductor, John Marsh.

LYN 3248   RIBENA: Sounds of the Sea (7" flexidisc)

No track credits listed on sleeve or record

Release date:

Recorded for Ribena and narrated by Michael Aspel. Two–sided 33⅓ rpm flexidisc in booklet sleeve. Sound effects from the BBC, Edwin Mickleburgh's collection, Ian Strange, Dr. Paul Spong and the Saydisc Electronic Workshop (David Wilkins manipulating white noise from an untuned radio set). The sea shanties are sung by Eric Ilott, the Bristol Shanty Man. Recording produced by David Wilkins, Gef Lucena and Edwin Mickleburgh.

Bornand collection of mechanical music

This series of records of recordings from the Bornand collection of mechanical music in New York was imported from the US and distributed by Saydisc in the UK. The October 1968 Saydisc *Historic and Specialist Records* catalogue priced the 7" EP at 13/8 (approx. 68p), which was the same price as Saydisc's own 7" EPs, though the LPs were priced at 45/– (£2.25), whilst Saydisc's own LPs were priced at 40/– (£2.00). By June 1969, the EP had gone up slightly to 14/– (70p) whilst the LPs were now 46/– (£2.30). AB 3, AB 5, RCB 4, RCB 6 and RCB 7, along with cassette versions, were relisted in MM89 (and some in MM84) as still available via Saydisc as from Nov. 1980. None of these releases were manufactured by Saydisc.

AB 1   UNKNOWN
It is likely that this record was not imported and distributed by Saydisc as there seems to be no mention of it in contemporary catalogues.

AB 2   *MECHANICAL MUSIC: Christmas Music Box (7" EP)*

Silent Night	Auld Lang Syne
Adeste Fideles	Monastery Bells
O Sanctissimo	Hark the Herald Angels Sing
Chimes of Trinity	O Tannenbaum
Jingle Bells	The First Noel

Release date: October 1968?
This was an EP of extracts from AB 3, below. The track listing above is as taken from the October 1968 catalogue and may not represent the correct ordering of tracks.

AB 3   *MECHANICAL MUSIC: Christmas Music Box*

Silent Night	Come All Ye Children
O – Sanctissima	The First Noel
Ave Maria	Auld Lang Syne
Adeste Fideles	O Tannenbaum
The Rosary	Cloister Bells
Hark the Herald Angels Sing	Song of the Bells
Monastery Bells	Unknown
Chimes of Trinity	Unknown
Jingle Bells	Unknown

Release date: October 1968? / Nov. 1980 (MM84)
Cassette: AB–C 3 (Nov. 1980: MM84)
The October 1968 catalogue says the following: "18 Christmas songs and carols from the Bornand collection." 18 tracks altogether, though not all are known. The track listing above is taken from the October 1968 catalogue (augmented by the 1980 *British Heritage And Traditions* catalogue) and may not represent the correct ordering of tracks.

RCB 4   *MECHANICAL MUSIC: Music Box Waltz Melodies*

Invitation to the Dance	Carnival of Venice
Artists' Life Waltz	On a Sunday Afternoon
Merry Widow	In the Good Old Summertime
Treasure Waltz	Edelweiss Glide
Faust Waltz	When the Leaves Begin to Turn
Little Fisher Maiden	After the Ball
Skater's Waltz	Southern Roses
Estudiantina	Wine Women and Song
Chimes of Normandy	Mikado Waltz
Tales of Vienna Woods	Loin du Bel
Waves of the Blue Danube	Angot Waltz
Espana Waltz	Romeo and Juliet Waltz
Blue Danube Waltz	Lagunes Waltz

Release date: October 1968? / Nov. 1980 (MM89)
Cassette: AB–C 3 (Nov. 1980: MM89)

The October 1968 catalogue says the following: "From the Bornand collection, New York, this record contains 26 old favourites from six rare antique music boxes." The track listing above is as taken from the October 1968 catalogue (augmented by the 1980 *British Heritage And Traditions* catalogue) and may not represent the correct ordering of tracks.

AB 5   MECHANICAL MUSIC: Golden Music Box Favourites

Home Sweet Home	Last Rose of Summer
Love's Old Sweet Song	Old Folks at Home
In the Gloaming	Annie Laurie
My Wild Irish Rose	Lorelei
Listen to the Mocking Bird	My Old Kentucky Home
Hearts and Flowers	Silver Threads Among the Gold
Robin Adair	Sanata Lucia
Narcissus	Glow Worm
Juanita	The Harp that Once Through Tara's Halls
Believe Me If All Those Endearing Young Charms	Sweetest Story Ever Told
	Rocked In the Cradle of the Deep
Blue Bells os Scotland	Ben Bolt
In the Shade of the Old Apple Tree	Comin' Thru the Rye
Old Oaken Bucket	

Release date: October 1968? / Nov. 1980 (MM84)
Cassette: AB–C 5 (Nov. 1980: MM84)
The October 1968 catalogue says the following: "6 rare old musical boxes play the final L.P. selection from the Bornand collection of New York." The track listing above is as taken from the October 1968 catalogue (augmented by the 1980 *British Heritage And Traditions* catalogue) and may not represent the correct ordering of tracks.

RCB 6   MECHANICAL MUSIC: Regina Sings Opera

Drinking Song from Traviata (Verdi)	William Tell Overture (Rossini)
La Traviata di Madride from Traviata (Verdi)	Toreador's Song from Carmen (Bizet)
Chorus of Matadors from Traviata (Verdi)	Tannhauser Overture and Grand March (Wagner)
Grand March from Ernani (Verdi)	Overture and Huntsmen's Chorus from Freischutz (Weber)
Chorus of Gypsies from Il Trovatore (Verdi)	Barcaroll from Oberson (Weber)
Misereri from The Troubadour (Verdi)	Intermezzo from Cavatina Rusticana (Mascagni)
Stabat Mater from Barber of Seville (Rossini)	Soldier's Chorus from Faust (Gounod)
Cujus Animan Barber of Seville (Rossini)	+ unknown music by Meyerbeer and Loraine
Cavatinas 1 & 2 Barber of Seville (Rossini)	

Release date: Nov. 1980 (MM84)
Cassette: RCB–C 6 (Nov. 1980: MM84)
The partial track listing above is as taken from the 1980 *British Heritage And Traditions* catalogue and may not represent the correct ordering of tracks.

RCB 7   MECHANICAL MUSIC: Symphonion Music Box: The "Eroica" Three Disc

Tales of Hoffman	Wine Women and Song
Aida March	Poet and Peasant Overture
Bells of Corneville	Monastery Bells
Stephanie Gavotte	The Mocking Bird
Von Hummel Choral	Estudiantina Waltz
Old Hundred Hymn	Silent Night
Spin Spin	Ave Maria
Symphonion March	Wedding March
La Paloma	Skater's Waltz
Come All Ye Children	Stabat Mater
Prayer from Freischutz	Miserere from Troubadour
Verlassen Verlassen	Cavatina Rusticana

Release date: Nov. 1980 (MM84)
Cassette: RCB–C 7 (Nov. 1980: MM84)
The track listing above is as taken from the 1980 *British Heritage And Traditions* catalogue and may not represent the correct ordering of tracks.

Where to buy the music

Saydisc

World suppliers for Saydisc and Amon Ra CDs (excluding USA / Canada)

Wyastone Estate Limited, Trading as Nimbus Records, Wyastone Leys, Monmouth, NP25 3SR, United Kingdom
Tel: 01600 890 007 (outside UK phone +44 1600 890 007)
Fax: 01600 891 052 (outside UK phone +44 1600 891 052)
Email: sales@wyastone.co.uk
Or order online from www.saydisc.com

CDs are available @ £13.99 each, post free in UK (cheque, Maestro, Mastercard or Visa accepted) or outside UK add £1.50 per CD postage and packing (Maestro, Mastercard or Visa accepted)

US and Canadian distributors

Saydisc's US distributor (which also offers a mail order service) is:
Qualiton Imports Ltd, 24-02 40th Ave, Long Island City, NY 11101
Tel: 718 937 8515   Fax: 718 729 3239
www.qualiton.com   email: qualiton@qualiton.com
Qualiton's Website includes Saydisc/Amon Ra catalogue.

Saydisc's Canadian distributor is:
SRI, 638 The Kingsway, Peterborough, Ont K9J 6Z8
Tel: 705 748 5422   Fax: 705 748 5628
Email: info@sricanada.com

Weekend Beatnik

Weekend Beatnik is the successor to Rogue Records which Ian Anderson ran in the 80s, originally as a home for the various bands he was a member of, along with their associates' side projects (English Country Blues Band, Tiger Moth, solos by Maggie Holland, Rod Stradling, etc.), but evolving into one of the pioneering world music labels, putting out the first UK releases by the likes of Senegal's Baaba Maal, tex-mex accordion wizard Flaco Jimenez, and so on.

After that reached a natural conclusion in the 90s, Anderson launched Weekend Beatnik as a way of rationalising "best ofs" from the artists in the Rogue catalogue and earlier masters that he had access to – all at mid price, decently state-of-the-art remastered, full length (75+ minutes) and with full new notes & memorabilia. It's basically a way of taking care of posterity on the "if you want something done properly, do it yourself" principle!

Currently available from the Village Thing archives, Dave Evans "The Words In Between" plus the best of "Elephantasia" on one CD (WEBE 9039), Ian Anderson's own "Time Is Ripe" compilation (WEBE 9045) and the Village Thing label retrospective "Ghosts From The Basement" (WEBE 9046). In the works, Al Jones' "Jonesville +" with the LP tracks remastered from the original tapes plus five extra solo demos from 1974 (WEBE 9047).

Buy Weekend Beatnik CDs now from http://www.frootsmag.com/shop/beatnik/

Bristol folk

A discographical history of Bristol folk music in the 1960s and 1970s

Bristol Folk Publications ISBN 978-0-9563531-0-8

What they're saying about Bristol folk

"a thoroughly absorbing work of reference – to term it as simply a *book* would be a gross understatement"
English Song and Dance magazine, Clive Pownceby

"a remarkable book"
fRoots

"Remarkably researched – I'm flabbergasted by the fellow's diligence"
Pete Frame

In the late 1960s and early '70s, Bristol became nationally renowned for its powerhouse folk and blues scene, and was second only to London for the number and influence of its recorded artists. It's an era still remembered with enormous nostalgia by those who participated, and is nigh-legendary to those who came later.

Although focused on Bristol, *Bristol Folk* should be of great interest, not just to Bristolians, but to all fans of late 1960s and early 1970s British folk and blues music, not to mention that strange beast now known as 'psych' or 'acid folk', because many Bristol-based musicians became nationally-known and influential exponents of these styles. Bristol, because of the national reputation of its folk scene, became a magnet for the brightest and best: established names such as Al Stewart, Stefan Grossman, the Incredible String Band and John Renbourn were enamoured of Bristol's friendly scene and were frequent visitors to clubs, such as the Troubadour, where they were often given a run for their money by Bristol's own resident musicians, many of whom went on to become national names themselves.

Bristol Folk features painstakingly-researched profiles of all artists known to have recorded in and around Bristol's vibrant folk scene: from Ian Anderson's country blues to the 1920s jug-based jazz of the Pigsty Hill Light Orchestra; from Adge Cutler & the Wurzels' novelty rural folk to the sophisticated images of Shelagh McDonald; from the rustic rock of Stackridge to the finely-crafted psych blues' of Al Jones; from the magical ballads of Bob Stewart to ethereal pop hits by Sally Oldfield; from the inspired, original guitar work of Dave Evans to the 'acid folk' of Keith Christmas, and more. These are discussed in the context of the wider music scene, with mention of the numerous and often vastly-popular groups and artists who didn't get to release records, such as the Deep Blues Band, Canton Trig, the Pink Coffee Blues Band and the Biafra Jug Band.

Amongst those who contributed specially-written pieces – included in addition to their profiles – are Ian Anderson, Andy Leggett, Saydisc's Gef Lucena, Rodney Matthews (yes, the world-famous fantasy artist started out designing LP sleeves and gig posters for Bristol's folk set), Bob Stewart, Steve Tilston, Keith Warmington and the late and lamented Fred Wedlock, all of whose diverse careers either started in Bristol or were shaped by their time on Bristol's folk scene.

The 34 pages of illustrations include photographs – many previously unpublished – plus promotional materials and memorabilia from the artists' private collections and from other archives to which the author had special access. Over 80 record sleeve illustrations are also included, as are cuttings from Bristol's (now extremely rare) early 1970s arts and entertainments magazine, *Preview*, and Plastic Dog's near-legendary *Dogpress* newsletter – one edition of which found itself being waved around at a Parliamentary hearing on obscenity!

The book also looks at the local record companies, Saydisc and Village Thing, both of which released many now highly – collectable folk records, as well as at Bristol's numerous folk clubs – from the Troubadour, which put Bristol firmly on the national folk map between 1966 and 1971, and the Stonehouse, to the now less well-known, but equally-missed clubs, such as Bristol Ballads & Blues, White On Black, Folk Blues Bristol & West and many more.

Over 180 records are listed in the discography section, all bar an elusive few with full details. Values are included for almost all of the records included – and these range from 50p to over £1,000. Some very rare and sought-after records were released by Bristol-based musicians...and for those without a record player, there is a supplementary discography of reissues and a list of artists' websites where many of the CDs listed can be bought.

Available at £18.99 (plus shipping) from www.bristol-folk.co.uk

The Famou/ Chari/ma Di/cography

A 40th anniver/ary celebration of one of the mo/t idio/yncratic main/tream. independent label/ of the 1970/

The Record Press ISBN 978-0-9563531-1-5

With foreword/ by Michael Palin and /tring Driven Thing'/ Chri/ Adam/

In the sleeve notes for the 1973 LP, Charisma Disturbance, Tony Stratton Smith wrote that, "A record label is the sum of its artists". In the case of Charisma, however, it can be more than convincingly argued that the record label was the sum of its owner: this book is a 40th anniversary year celebration of Stratton Smith's vision to sign to Charisma "anything good of its kind" and includes:

> Listings of all known UK LPs and singles, all bar a handful with full track listings
> The original label design and release date for the majority of records
> The first published listings of cassette and 8-track releases
> The original recommended retail price for the majority of LPs and tapes
> An organisational history of Charisma, with contributions from those who were there

The Famous Charisma Label was formed in 1969 by the near-legendary Tony Stratton Smith. Those who knew him have said that he named the label after what he himself had in abundance, charisma, from the Greek χάρισμα – an extraordinary power and appeal of personality with an innate ability to inspire a large following. His vision to sign anything good of its kind led to Charisma becoming home to, amongst others, several uncompromising and ground-breaking progressive rock bands, a maverick classical conductor, a cross-dressing Australian satirist, a cult TV comedy combo, a sports commentator or two, a singing school teacher, a well-known psychoanalyst and even the Poet Laureate. Strat, as he was known to all, then got it completely wrong, as far as the music industry was concerned, by actually caring about his acts. The rest, as they say, is history.

The Famous Charisma Discography features painstakingly-researched discographies of all known UK releases by the company, from the first in 1969 to the last in 1987. Those who think that Charisma just meant Genesis are in for a shock. Genesis were there for pretty much the duration, true, but they shared the label with names both well-known and obscure. Where else are you going to find a book that includes Van der Graaf Generator, Lindisfarne, Monty Python, Audience, Rare Bird, Barry Humphries, Automatic Fine Tuning, Brand X, Trevor Billmuss, Malcolm McLaren, The Ferrets, Clifford T. Ward, Charlie Drake, Sir John Betjeman, Michael Nyman, Prince Far I, Delta 5, Peter O'Sullivan, Gary Shearston, String Driven Thing, Bert Jansch, La La, Robert John Godfrey, Refugee, Patrick Moraz, Hawkwind, Peter Gabriel, Steve Hackett, John Arlott, Pierre Cour, Trimmer and Jenkins, Jackson Heights, The Nice, Capability Brown, Joseph Eger, Gordon Turner, Peter Hammill, Bo Hansson, Spreadeagle, Atacama, Hot Thumbs O'Reilly, Vivian Stanshall, Gregory Isaacs and more?

To add value to an already value-rich compendium of information, the book presents the first-known listings of cassette and 8-track cartridge releases, as well as looking at the little-known Charisma Books and Charisma Films offshoots. To contextualise the listings, the book includes a detailed history that discusses both Strat and the organisational set-up at Charisma, supported by memories from those who worked for the company alongside those of artists that made the label such a delight of eclecticism in an industry where confirmation of taste through providing bland, watered-down product is the norm. Charisma bucked this trend and in its heyday provided an intelligent and varied mix of the sublime and the (mostly deliberately) ridiculous for anyone who was willing to listen.

Available at £14.99 (plus shipping) from www.bristol-folk.co.uk

The Great British Record Labels series

The Great British Record Labels series is based on the now near-legendary VinylAttic discographies. These discographies were available online for around three years in the early part of the new Millennium and received over 35,000 unique hits in that time. Since the lists were removed from the Internet, there have been many and constant pleas from collectors and dealers to make these discographies available once again.

Music historian, Mark Jones, the mastermind behind the original online discographies has, in the intervening years, continued in his discographical research to add a great deal more value to the original listings and is now in the process of producing a series of books based on this research.

The Famous Charisma Discography – a 40th anniversary celebration

The first book in the series was *The Famous Charisma Discography*, produced to celebrate the 40th anniversary of Charisma, possibly the greatest rock–oriented, independent British record label that has ever existed, and this book represents the blueprint for future volumes. The intention is to make each book in the series the definitive work on the particular record label covered.

The Saydisc & Village Thing Discography – anniversary celebration

This, the second book in the *Great British Record Labels* series, had its beginnings in 2001, when the author attempted to compile a definitive Saydisc discography for the (now defunct) original VinylAttic website. The fact that it has taken nearly ten years to get this far must show a certain amount of patience – or perhaps obsession is the word here!

If you have enjoyed this book, then you will almost certainly like some of the discographies that are currently in either the writing or the planning stages...

Virgin. Harvest. Manticore. Island. Immediate. Transacord...

Coming in the next few years, future volumes will cover Virgin, Harvest, Manticore, Island's HELP imprint, Immediate and, thanks to the eclectic tastes of the author, railway fanatics will finally be able to own a book that includes the definitive discography of another of the UK's most idiosyncratic labels, (Argo/ASV) Transacord, home to Peter Handford's wonderful world of railway sounds.

The next two books in the series are already well underway, these being *The Virgin Discography: the 1970s* and *Transacord: Sounds of Steam and other Transports of Delight*.

The Virgin Discography looks closely at Richard Branson's Virgin label, from the label's inception in May 1973 to the last release of the 1970s, so covering the 'hippy' years through to the beginnings of the label's transformation into a more mainstream pop label, taking in punk rock, new wave and reggae along the way.

Transacord: Sounds of Steam and other Transports of Delight looks at Peter Handford's extremely well-loved Transacord label, from it's early beginnings in 1953 through to the well-known Argo years of 1961 to 1980 and finally through it's last incarnation on vinyl on the post-Argo ASV label. To put the railway recordings into context, the potted history of Transacord also briefly looks at Peter Handford's main career as an Oscar-winning film sound engineer.